with best wishes
from …,
Charlton

NISHMAT HA-BAYIT

Contemporary Questions on
Women's Reproductive Health
Addressed by Yoatzot Halacha

מגיד
MAGGID
NISHMAT·נשמת
OUPRESS

The Nicole and Raanan Agus Edition

NISHMAT HA-BAYIT

נשמת הבית

Contemporary Questions on Women's Reproductive Health

Addressed by Yoatzot Halacha

Edited by Rabbi Yehuda-Herzl and Chana Henkin

Maggid Books
Nishmat
OU Press

NISHMAT HA-BAYIT
Contemporary Questions on Women's Reproductive Health
Addressed by Yoatzot Halacha

First English Edition, 2021

Maggid Books
An imprint of Koren Publishers Jerusalem Ltd.

POB 8531, New Milford, CT 06776-8531, USA
& POB 4044, Jerusalem 9104001, Israel
www.maggidbooks.com

OU Press
An imprint of the Orthodox Union
11 Broadway, New York, NY 10004
www.oupress.org

The publication of this book was made possible through
the generous support of *The Jewish Book Trust.*

ISBN 978-1-59264-594-7, *hardcover*
Printed and bound in the United States

In memory of

Mrs. Chaya Kimelman

Dedicated by her family and friends

Chaya Kimelman was born in Melbourne, Australia, and lived there until making aliyah in her 70's. "Big Grandma," as she was known to her grandchildren and their friends, was active in community *ḥesed* programs, such as preparing kosher meals for hospital patients and delivering kosher Meals on Wheels. She also helped school children practice their reading, both in English and Hebrew.

Chaya was a vibrant woman who never hesitated to ask a question or voice an unconventional opinion. She would often challenge her grandchildren by demanding, "Where does it say that in the Torah?" Regarding women's roles within the Orthodox community, she was ahead of her time. She was a regular participant in the first women's Gemara *shiur* in Melbourne, and continued studying in Yerushalayim. Her classmates were university students of varied religious affiliations from overseas, and she eagerly joined them in studying Rambam, Midrash, contemporary halakhah, and *Ḥasidut*. She was a prized "*ḥavruta*," and they cherished the opportunity to hear her comments, insights, and life experiences. Following the example of her grandson who taught the class, her classmates affectionately called her "Grandma."

Big Grandma deeply believed in the vision of Nishmat's Yoatzot Halacha and later the Yoatzot Halacha Fertility Counselors Project. Two of her granddaughters are Yoatzot Halacha and she often enquired with interest about their work helping women and couples face modern halakhic and medical challenges.

Chaya passed away on the 20th of Tevet 5781 at the age of 89, leaving two children and their families, including 89 great-grandchildren, who remember her with love and admiration.

Dedicated in honor of my mother

Bella Suchman

and in honor of my daughter and daughters-in-law,

Naomi, Gila, Emily, and Adinah

For the advancement of Nishmat's mission,
to give Jewish women a voice in halakhic discourse,
so that my daughters, and their daughters,
and all of our daughters
may live in a world where women's voices are heard,
their scholarship valued,
and their robust contributions to Jewish life recognized.

Rose Gerszberg

With profound gratitude
to the three most important women in my life:

To my mother

Shoshana Lunzer, a"h

who instilled within me my moral compass.

To my Ezer Kenegdo

Lauren

who has been my rock since the day we met,
and who continues to model for me
what a life's partner is meant to be.

To my daughter

Shoshana Elizabeth

who continues to challenge my prenotions
and in so doing, expands my appreciation
of equality, justice, and inclusiveness.

David Lunzer

Rabbi Menachem Genack
129 Meadowbrook Road
Englewood, NJ 07631

May 24, 2021
13 Sivan 5781

I was delighted to receive from Nishmat in Jerusalem a draft of the forthcoming English edition of their outstanding book, *Nishmat Habayit*. This collaborative work consists of numerous *teshuvot* on subjects related to pregnancy, birth, pregnancy loss, nursing and contraception written by *yoatzot halacha* and reviewed by Rabbi Yehuda Henkin *zt"l* and Rabbi Yaakov Warhaftig. In addition, the sefer contains five medical appendices by Dr. Deena Zimmerman, herself a *yoetzet halacha* as well as a medical doctor.

Each *teshuvah* presents a summary of the practical *pesak halachah* followed by a more detailed look at the classical and contemporary halachic sources on which the *pesak* is based. The *teshuvot* are admirably clear and erudite, and the work as a whole provides an excellent guide to these complex *halachot*.

We owe a debt of gratitude to Rabbanit Henkin not only for her work on this excellent book, but for her vision in founding the program of *yoatzot halacha*. There is no doubt that women are more comfortable asking questions of other women in this sensitive realm. Speaking from my experience as a rabbi in Englewood, New Jersey, I think I can safely say that the *yoatzot halacha* who have served in our community and consulted with me on occasion, have received more questions in their relatively few years here than I have received over a period of many more years.

The phenomenon of bringing questions to women in these areas is not a new one. Rabbi Rabinovich, in his *haskamah* to the Hebrew edition of *Nishmat Habayit*, points to a Talmudic precedent for women advising other women on these matters. In Brisk, the women would bring questions to the wife of the Brisker Dayan, Rav Simcha Zelig, who would bring them to her husband. This system functioned well until Rav Chaim Soloveitchik was asked to be more active in *pesak* for the community. Rav Chaim agreed to answer questions in the area of *taharat hamishpacha* so the women began bringing their questions to Rav Chaim's wife, who brought them to him. However, Rav Chaim had follow-up questions for each case and wanted to speak to the women directly. Since the women did not want to speak directly to Rav Chaim, the old system of bringing the questions to the Dayan's wife was quickly restored. *Yoatzot* trained in these *halachot* make the process of asking questions and receiving responses a smoother one.

In sum, this *sefer* is an important addition to the halachic literature on these subjects and represents the welcome development of a cadre of women who are equipped to provide guidance in the realm of family purity.

Menachem Genack

Rabbi Menachem Genack

בס"ד

הרב אהרן נפתלי אומן

RABBI KENNETH AUMAN

Study
YOUNG ISRAEL OF FLATBUSH
1012 AVENUE I
BROOKLYN, N.Y. 11230
(718-377-4400)
RABBI.K.AUMAN@GMAIL.COM

Residence
1029 EAST 10TH STREET
BROOKLYN, N.Y.11230-4109
(718-338-9412)

ט"ז סיון תשפ"א

For some ten years now, I have had the privilege of working with the U.S. *Yoatzot Halacha* Fellows Program of Nishmat's Miriam Glaubach Center, training *Yoatzot Halacha*. I continue to be in awe of the work and accomplishments of these *Yoatzot*. I am inspired by the intellectual rigor of the women in the program, and the dedicated work of the *Yoatzot* in the field. The women they have helped and the families they have benefitted, number well in the thousands.

A few years ago, the combination of *Torah* scholarship and dedication to assisting women and their families personified by the *Yoatzot* was made visible to a broader public by the publication of the much-heralded *sefer*, *Nishmat Habayit*. In its pages one can see *Torat Chessed*, the *Torah* of kindness and compassion, at work. Thoroughly researched comprehensive analysis of complicated topics is coupled with deep sensitivity to provide *hora'ah*, instruction, that is both halachically accurate, and of great help to women and their families.

With the publication of the English version, this treasure trove of *psak halacha*, insight, and compassion will now be available to the English-speaking public. This past year has unfortunately seen the passing, among other *Gedolei Yisrael*, of Nishmat's founding *Posek*, Rav Yehuda Henkin ז"ל. It was Rav Henkin's uncompromisingly high standard of *Torah* scholarship together with his keen awareness of the challenges of the modern world that is consistently reflected in this work, and it is certainly a merit for his pure soul.

And ייבדלו לחיים טובים וארובים, we acknowledge the role of the *Rebbe* and Posek of the *Yoatzot*, Rav Yaakov Varhaftig, whose teachings permeate this work. And lastly, the true *nefesh* and *neshama* of Nishmat, Rabbanit Channa Henkin, who has the capacity to dream dreams and turn them into reality, was the moving force behind this publication. May they as well as all who participated in the various aspects of this *sefer* merit the blessings of the *Noten Hatorah* to be able to continue to serve Him with ever increasing contributions of *Torah* knowledge and *Chessed*.

אריה שטרן
הרב הראשי לירושלים

Aryeh Stern
Chief Rabbi Of Jerusalem

בס"ד, תמוז תשע"ז

מכתב ברכה

זה כבר כמה שנים שנודע לנו שמה הטוב של **"מדרשת נשמת"** הפועלת רבות בתחום של טהרת המשפחה, בהוראה, בהדרכה ובמתן תשובות הלכתיות מוסמכות ומיידיות.

יפה ומיוחד הוא החידוש של הכשרת והסמכת יועצות הלכה אליהן פונות כל מי שיש לה שאלה ומעדיפה לפנות בענינים אלה לאשה ולא לאיש. היועצות עצמן מכירות את גבולות הגיזרה ויודעות מה הן יכולות לענות בעצמן ואימתי הן צריכות לשאול את הרבנים שיפסקו הלכה בשאלות שטעונות הכרעה.

כעת נוספה מדרגה חדשה עם ההוצאה לאור של הספר בו מרוכזות השאלות והתשובות, ואני מוכרח לציין כי אכן זהו ספר ערוך בטעם, כתוב בבהירות מקיף מבחינת מגוון הנושאים, וגם מבחינת העומק כשכל תשובה ניתנת בקיצור ויש עמה גם הרחבה מפורטת וברורה.

על כל אלה יבורכו ראשי המדרשה הלוא הם: **הרב יהודה הנקין שליט"א הרב יעקב ורהפטיג שליט"א**, והרבנית **חנה הנקין תליט"א**, הם אשר עומדים מאחורי כל הפעולות ועושים הכל בצורה מעוררת כבוד ומביאים לקידוש שם שמים.

עם זאת נראה לי שהספר המצוין הזה צריך להיות מופנה לרבנים, וליועצות ההלכה ולכל מי שעוסק בלימוד הנושא של טהרת המשפחה, ואין ספק שהספר הזה אכן יביא להם תועלת רבה ויישר כוחם של הכותבות והעורכות, אולם נראה לי וצריך לומר שהספר אינו מתאים לכל אשה בביתה, לגביה נשאר הכלל הרגיל לפיו צריך להדריך את הנשים לפנות לרב או ליועצת ההלכה בשאלה, והם יענו את התשובה המתאימה לשואלת, וכמובן ישמחו להיעזר בספר "נשמת הבית" ובצדק.

לסיום שוב שאו ברכה ממני המברך
אתכם על כל מפעלותיכם,

אריה שטרן
הרב הראשי לירושלים

אריה שטרן
הרב הראשי לירושלים
ARYEH STERN
Chief Rabbi of Jerusalem

ישיבת ברכת משה - מעלה אדומים (ע"ר)

YESHIVAT BIRKAT MOSHE – MAALEH ADUMIM

בס"ד
יום שהוכפל בו כי טוב לסדר "אלה החוקים אשר צוה ה' ...בין איש לאשתו" תשע"ז לפ"ק

מסורת עתיקה היא, שבהלכות טהרה נשים פוסקות הלכה. מסופר בגמרא (נדה י"ג, ב) בשם רבי יהודה הנשיא על מקרה קיצוני מאד: "חרשת היתה בשכונתנו - לא דיה שבודקת לעצמה, אלא שחברותיה היו רואות ומראות לה". עתה זכינו לראות ספר "נשמת הבית" בעריכת הר"ר יהודה ורעייתו הרבנית חנה הנקין, שליט"א, העוסק בכל הלכות טהרה - בנושאי היריון, לידה, הנקה, ואמצעי מניעה, בליווי נספחים רפואיים. המשיבות הן כולן נשים חכמות המשרתות כיועצות הלכה של מדרשת "נשמת" בראשות הרבנית חנה הנקין שליט"א. על כל נושא מובאות דעות הפוסקים ובמקום מחלוקת מוצעות דעות החולקים. בנוסף, יש לרוב הנושאים הסברים על פי המדע הרפואי המתקדם ביותר. עם כל זה, הסגנון הוא קריא ובהיר, וברור שכל תלמיד חכם, כולל דווקא גברים, יכול להרבות דעה מלימוד התשובות בנושאים החיוניים האלה.

יהי רצון שזכות הרבים תעמוד לרב יהודה ולרבנית חנה הנקין שליט"א ויזכו לראות דורות של תלמידי חכמים מצאצאיהם.

הכו"ח לכבוד התורה ולומדיה,

נחום אליעזר רבינוביץ

E-MAIL: office@ybm.org.il MIZPEH NEVO, MAALEH ADUMIM 98410 מצפה נבו, מעלה אדומים

WEB SITE: http://www.ybm.org.il FAX. 02-5353947 .פקס ; TEL. 02-5353655 .טל

ארץ חמדה
מכון גבוה ללימודי היהדות
ירושלים
בע"ה, עיה"ק ירושלים ת"ו

Eretz Hemdah
Institute For Advanced Jewish Studies
Jerusalem

ה' בתמוז תשע"ז
29 ביוני 2017
13017

"וַיַּעְתֵּק מִשָּׁם הָהָרָה מִקֶּדֶם לְבֵית אֵל וַיֵּט אָהֳלֹה בֵּית אֵל מִיָּם וְהָעַי מִקֶּדֶם וַיִּבֶן שָׁם מִזְבֵּחַ לַיקֹוָק וַיִּקְרָא בְּשֵׁם ה'"

וברש"י מובא המדרש:
"ויט אהלה אהלה כתיב מלמד שנטע אוהל שרה תחילה ואח"כ נטע אהלו" (בראשית י"ב ח)

מהתיאור המדויק של מיקוד האוהל מהתיאור שבסמוך נבנה מזבח, אין הכוונה לאוהל פשוט למגורים, אלא בית מדרש כמו בפסוק "איש תם יושב אוהלים" וכיון ששרה גיירה את הנשים ואברהם גייר את האנשים נבנו לצורך זה בתי מדרש, ובית המדרש של הנשים קדם לזה של האנשים.
לפני שנים רבות עיתונאית מסוימת שהייתה כותבת בארץ מאמרים עבור עיתונים בחו"ל, סיפרה לי שרבות מחברותיה היו מקפידות יותר בענייני טהרת המשפחה לו הייתה להם כתובת נשית להיוועץ בה.
הרב והרבנית הנקין מצאו דרך מיוחדת להתמודד עם אתגר זה והקימו במדרשת נשמת מסלול מיוחד לנשים שעסקו כבר שנים בלימוד מעמיק של הגמרא ראשונים ופוסקים, ואח"כ הן לומדות בעיון רב את נושא טהרת משפחה וחיי אישות, לימוד המכשיר אותם כ'יועצות הלכה', שיכולות להשיב לשאלות המופנות אליהם מהארץ ומחו"ל, התשובות מלוות בהתייעצות קבועה עם הרב הנקין שליט"א והרב ורהפטיג שליט"א.
במשך השנים הצטברו מאות שאלות ותשובות. ועתה זוכות היועצות להוציא ספר בשם "נשמת הבית", הצלחתי לעבור ולהתעמק בחלק גדול מן הספר נהניתי, החכמתי וגיליתי שאלות מגוונות מאוד בענייני הריון לידה הנקה, לכל שאלה מוצמדת תשובה, התשובות נכתבו בבהירות והן מובנות לכל נפש. יש בתשובות גם התייחסות לנפש השואלת, התשובות מוכיחות את הצורך בבית המדרש של שרה שקדם לבית מדרשו של אברהם. חלק נוסף בתשובה נקרא "הרחבה", זהו חלק של ברור התשובה מתוך הש"ס ראשונים אחרונים פוסקים עד פוסקי דורנו, העמקה מאוד יפה שיכולה להעשיר גם תלמידי חכמים ורבנים שעוסקים בנושאים אלו.
הספר "נשמת הבית" מצטיין בתוכן, בבהירות הדברים ברהיטות הלשון והנספחים הרפואיים שנלוו לספר שמשלימים והופכים למקשה אחת עם המקורות ההלכתיים, כל זה מבטיח שהוא יהיה חלק מהספריה של רבנים מצד אחד ולומדי תורה ומצד שני משפחות צעירות שמתמודדות בשאלות דומות.

"חילכן לאורייתא"!

משה ארנרייך
הרב משה ארנרייך
ראש כולל 'ארץ חמדה'

רח' ברוריה 2 / פינת ר' חייא 2 Brurya St. corner of Rav Chiya St.
ת.ד. 8178 ירושלים 91080 Jerusalem P.O.B. 8178 עמותה רשומה מס' 580120780
טל. 02-5371485 +972 Tel פקס 02-5379626 +972 Fax www.eretzhemdah.org info@eretzhemdah.org

הרב דוב ליאור

רב העיר

קריית ארבע היא חברון ת"ו

בס"ד, טו תמוז תשע"ז

מכתב ברכה

הובא לפניי החיבור הגדול והמקיף 'נשמת הבית', העוסק בנושאים הלכתיים של היריון, לידה וטהרת המשפחה, על פי הדרכת הרבנים החשובים הר"י הנקין והר"י ורהפטיג העומדים בראש המכון בכל הקשור לפסיקת הלכה בנושאים אלו.

עברתי על חלק מהספר ושמחתי לראות חיבור נפלא המברר כל נושא החל ממקורות התלמוד וספרי ההלכה עד פוסקי דורנו. כל דין מבוסס על יסודות ההלכה האיתנים.

אין ספק שהקמת מוסד העונה לנשים הפונות בשאלות בנושאי טהרת המשפחה ע"י יועצות הלכה הוא מבורך, מפני שהרבה יותר נוח לאישה לדבר עם אישה מלב אל לב, וזה יביא להגברת ההשפעה ולשמירת הטהרה בחוגים רחבים.

יישר כוח להוגי הרעיון הר"י הנקין והרבנית חנה הנקין על תרומתם החשובה בהפעלת המכון. יהי רצון שיזכו להגביר את הטהרה בכל רבדי העם וחפץ ה' בידם יצלח.

בשולי הדברים שתי הערות:

א. לסימן כז - כתבתם שדם על נייר קינוח דינו ככתם, ומכיוון שנייר אינו מקבל טומאה - אין לאסור.

לענ"ד נראה שדם קינוח על נייר אין דינו ככתם ואין חלים עליו הכללים שצריך להיות על דבר שמקבל טומאה ובשיעור גריס, אלא דינו כראייה בלי הרגשה (ולפי הש"ך הראשון בסימן קפג הוא טמא מדרבנן) ומטמא גם על נייר וגם בפחות מגריס, מפני שקינוח נחשב כאילו ראתה מגופה, ראה הלכות נדה לרמב"ן (פרק רביעי אות מה) דכתב: "המקנחת עצמה בעד הבדוק לה וטחתו בירכה או שהניחתו תחת הכר או תחת הכסת ונמצא עליו דם, אם משוך טמאה בכל שהוא... הניחתו בקופסא אפילו היה עגול טמאה בכל שהוא". הנה הקפיד לכתוב כאן "המקנחת" ולא "הבודקת", משמע שזה מבחוץ, ומכיוון שאין במה לתלות טמאה בכל שהוא, אלא אם כן זה לאחר הטלת מי רגליים, שלפי שיטת מרן המחבר תולים שהדם בא מהכליות ולא מהרחם. וכן סובר הר"י אייבשיץ ('תפארת ישראל' קפג ס"ק א) שבקינוח טמאה אפילו בכל שהוא.

זכורני שלפני שנים רבות אמר לי הגרי"ש אלישיב זצ"ל, שמי שמטהר ברואה משהו בקינוח נחשב כמעלים עין מן האיסורים.

ב. לסימן יג - סיוע הבעל בחדר לידה. דומה שכל העניין הגיע בא מאמריקה, ואינו תואם את גדרי הצניעות המקודשים בעם ישראל.

.הבעל צריך ללוות את אשתו עד חדר הלידה ותו לא. בחדר לידה יכולה להיות איתה אימה, חברתה או תומכת לידה, אבל לא הבעל.

אין נכון להעמיד את הבעל בניסיון שלא לגעת ולסייע לאשתו, ויש להסביר זאת ליולדת ולהשקיט את המיית לבה.

החותם לכבוד התורה ולומדיה,

דוב ליאור

PARTICIPANTS

Responders: Yoatzot Halacha Zivit Berliner (Z.B.),
Goldie Katz Samson (G.K.S.), Shira Kfir (S.K.),
Ora Krauss (O.K.), Noa Lau (N.L.), Michal Roness (M.R.),
Rachelle Sprecher Fraenkel (R.S.F.), Chana Henkin (C.H.)*

Editors: Rabbi Yehuda and Chana Henkin

Medical Appendices: Yoetzet Halacha Dr. Deena Zimmerman

Dean, Yoatzot Halacha Institute: Rabbi Yaakov Warhaftig

Coordinator, Yoetzet Halacha Institute: Rabbanit Noa Lau

Coordinator, Makhon L'Meḥkar: Yoetzet Halacha Michal Roness

---

* The responder to each of the questions in this book is indicated by her initials.

Contents

PART III: PREGNANCY LOSS

PART IV: NURSING

PART V: CONTRACEPTION

MEDICAL APPENDICES

Foreword

In previous generations, women's lives were centered primarily around the home and child rearing. Women who were prominent in the public sphere, such as *Devorah Ha-Nevi'ah* were rare and exceptional. Indeed, the *rishonim* questioned how she could serve as a judge, and explained either that she had no official position or that it was a unique case.

However, even in the past, women were relied upon in some fields of halakhah, such as kashering meat and midwifery. Rambam wrote that if a woman is skilled, she may be trusted with *sheḥita* (ritual slaughter), and such is *ikar hadin*:

> Whoever knows the laws of *sheḥita*, and slaughters in the presence of a *ḥakham* until he becomes adept, is considered an expert, *mumḥeh*. Any *mumḥeh* may slaughter *l'khatḥilah* in private. Even women and slaves may initially slaughter, as long as they are *mumḥim* (Laws of *Sheḥita*, 4:4).

A woman is certainly trusted with the laws of *taharat ha-mishpaḥah*, as the Torah states (*Vayikra* 15:28):

> She shall count for herself seven days, and after that she shall become *tehorah*.

In modern times, woman's role in society has been fundamentally transformed. Today, women occupy prominent positions in all public spheres; in science, in medicine, in business and so on.

One of the greatest revolutions has occurred in the sphere of Torah learning. Women have progressed to the point of serious scholarship in all fields of Torah – Tanakh, Talmud and Halakhah.

Like in all other realms of *halakhah*, questions regarding *taharat ha-mishpaḥah were* in the past answered by rabbis. However, unlike other topics, discussing intimate and delicate matters with a man is often uncomfortable for the woman. Therefore, often the husband would be the one consulting with the expert rabbi.

The rabbi, with his learning and erudition, is able to render a halakhic ruling; but he is unable to feel all the woman feels. Often, her needs, sensitivities and personal experience of the laws of *taharat ha-mishpaḥah*, greatly influence the proper and correct ruling rendered.

Therefore, Rabbanit Chana Henkin, the dean of Nishmat – the Jeanie Schottenstein Center for Advanced Torah Study for Women, and her husband Rabbi Yehuda Herzl Henkin *z"tl*, Nishmat's *posek* – together with me; reached the understanding that there was an urgent need to train women who would study in depth the laws of *taharat ha-mishpaḥah* with all their halakhic ramifications, from the source of the law to its application in practical life – well above and beyond the training which traditionally was given to *madrikhot kallot* (kallah teachers).

Our goal was not the training of *poskot* (halakhic decisors), and therefore we decided on the title Yoetzet Halacha – halakhic advisor. Our objective was for the Yoetzet to work in tandem with the local rabbi, in accordance with his rulings.

At the outset, we did not foresee how this initiative would take root and develop. Today, thank God, over a hundred and fifty women have completed our program worldwide, after being trained by us rabbis and by Rabbanit Noa Lau, the program coordinator. All have passed comprehensive oral examination by four expert rabbinic examiners, before receiving Yoetzet Halacha certification.

With God's help we opened a branch in the United States, headed by Rabbi Aharon Naftali (Kenneth) Auman, the dean of Nishmat's Miriam Glaubach Center. Four classes have already completed their studies, and now serve in more than thirty communities in North America and beyond.

To date, the Yoatzot have responded, by telephone or over the internet, to more than three hundred thousand questions from all around the world. In complex matters, they were guided by Rabbi Henkin *zt"l* and myself.

Thank God, we see how this program has blossomed and borne fruit, heightening awareness and enhancing observance and punctiliousness of the halakhot of *taharat ha-mishpaḥah*.

This first volume, *Nishmat Ha-Bayit*, presents a collection of some of the most common questions we have been asked. The responses were written by select Yoatzot who worked diligently to give a comprehensive but clear response, and were checked by Rabbi Henkin and by myself. I am confident that this book will join the ranks of authoritative books on the Laws of *taharat ha-mishpaḥah*, adding its unique contribution in fortifying *taharat ha-bayit* of the Jewish People, and *kiddush shem Shamay'im*, sanctifying God's Name.

Yaakov Warhaftig
Dean, Nishmat's *Keren Ariel Yoatzot Halacha* Institute
in memory of Emil (Ariel) Hess

Preface

The Torah directs a woman who has given birth to bring both an *olah,* burnt offering, and a *ḥatat,* sin offering, to the *Mikdash*. According to R. Yitzḥak Abarbanel, the *olah* represents the mother's gratitude for having merited to join together with Hashem in the creation of a new human life and for delivering it safely, as well as her joy at having safely undergone the pain and danger of childbirth. But what sin or fault of hers requires a *ḥatat*?

In her study sheets on Vayikra, Nechama Leibowitz wrote as follows:

> The woman has merited to feel inside herself, in her very flesh, the greatness of the Creator. She saw, felt, lived the growing of life within her – and at the same time this led her to deeply feel her own smallness and insignificance; her being but ashes and dust, her own impurity. For this reason she is commanded to bring a Sin Offering.

In other words, paradoxically, the same uplifting experience which raises her to the greatest heights of human potential, serves at the same time as a reminder of her own insignificance. We have similar feelings upon the "birth" of our *sefer*. On the one hand, from the depths of our hearts, we can fulfill the joyous duty of expressing our gratitude: We were privileged to learn in Nishmat's *Keren Ariel* program for training Yoatzot Halacha, to taste the sweetness of halakhic study, and thanks to our revered teachers – Rabbi Yaakov Warhaftig and Rabbi Yehuda Herzl Henkin *zt"l* – we have had the opportunity to delve deeply into *Hilkhot Niddah*. This halakhic training gave us the practical ability to help thousands of women, with their doubts and questions regarding *taharat ha-mishpaḥah* and women's health. Following upon our initial training as

Yoatzot, as we researched the *teshuvot* contained in this book, we merited to continue to explore the topics from their primary sources as well as discussing them with our rabbis – *shimush talmidei ḥakhamim.*

Just as a woman who gave birth, brings her *ḥatat* as an expression of her sense of smallness – so too we found that as we immersed ourselves in the study of Torah, and encountered the vastness, the breadth, depth and complexity of *halakhah,* that we were continuously, and acutely, made aware of our own insignificance.

Our hearts abound with thanksgiving to all those who accompanied us in this great undertaking: to Rabbanit Chana Henkin, for editing the *teshuvot* meticulously and for her monumental efforts which sustain Nishmat and the Yoatzot Halacha undertaking. To our Teacher and Rabbi, Rabbi Yaakov Warhaftig who guided us throughout our study and writing, being ever patient and welcoming – "*Gadol hu shimusho af yoter mi-limudo,*" the experience of apprenticing with him is even greater than that of learning from him. To Rabbi Yehuda Herzl Henkin *zt"l,* who for years accompanied the Yoatzot Halacha and the authorship of the *teshuvot,* and who was always available to answer any question that arose. Rabbi Henkin is sorely missed, and the immense void he leaves in the Torah world is continuously felt by his students. May we merit spreading his teachings faithfully, so that many more women can continue benefiting from his wisdom and *piskei halakhah.* We are forever grateful to both rabbis for having enabled us to come close to true *talmidei ḥakhamim.*

The *teshuvot* in this volume were written by Yoatzot Halacha and reviewed by Rabbi Warhaftig – and then passed on to the editors, Rabbi and Rabbanit Henkin. Beyond their lucid style, which is clearly reflected throughout the book, the Rav and Rabbanit added linguistic precision, halakhic coherence, and a close and accurate reading of the words of the *poskim.* Further thanks are due to Rabbanit Noa Lau, who read through all the *teshuvot,* clarifying the phraseology and making important comments. Thanks to their efforts, we are confident that this book can achieve its goals, and that it will be accessible and clear to the reader.

We also would like to thank Yoetzet Halacha Rabbanit Dr. Deena Zimmerman, for clarifying the medical aspects of the different questions we were asked; as well as Rabbi David Sperling, with whom we frequently consulted with while studying in the Bet Midrash.

With deep, heartfelt sorrow, we remember and commemorate Rabbi Eitam Henkin *Hy"d,* who participated in editing some of the responses.

We thank Rabbi Elli Fischer for his assistance with the translation, and Yoetzet Halacha Rabbanit Ilana Elzufon for her invaluable glosses and input.

We consulted with medical specialists and other professionals in preparing the *teshuvot*: Dr. Elhanan Baron and Yoatzot Halacha Drs. Eliraz Weinberg and Gila Gold read through the medical appendices and Dr. Avishai Malkiel, Michal Schonbrun and Einat Lev helped clarify various related issues. We owe a debt of gratitude to our colleagues, Yoatzot Halacha Rabbaniot Hindy Feder, Atara Eis, Shira Menitentag, Laurie Novick, Rotem Glasser, Dr. Tirza Kelman and Dr. Ayelet Kaminetzky for their assistance.

Our thanks also to Matthew Miller and the staff of Maggid Books, Reuven Ziegler, Caryn Meltz, and Ruth Pepperman, for their professional guidance.

We express a special sense of gratitude to our families, for their encouragement and support, enabling us to devote a great deal of time to Torah study, and to answering the many thousands of women whom we have had the privilege of helping, and strengthening their observance of the laws of *taharat ha-mishpaḥah*.

We thank Hashem for having merited participating in the Yoatzot Halacha initiatives, and having had the privilege of taking part in authorship of this book. In the name of my fellow Yoatzot Halacha, I conclude with the prayer that this sefer help raise the level of halakhic observance, and that, G-d forbid, no mishap be caused by it.

Michal Roness
Coordinator, Makhon L'Meḥkar
Nishmat

Introduction

Nishmat's *Keren Ariel* Program for training Yoatzot Halacha, in memory of Ariel Emil Hess *zt"l*, was born of my own experience as a Rabbi's wife. When I was young, for a period of years, I devoted most of my energies outside our home to instructing women in *taharat ha-mishpaḥah*. Time and again I encountered women who would not ask a question of a rabbi. Some would act overly leniently, going beyond what is halakhically permitted, while others would be unnecessarily stringent, disrupting their family life. Additionally, I encountered numerous women suffering severe distress because of medical conditions which intersected with halakhic issues.

I approached my husband, Rabbi Yehuda Herzl Henkin *zt"l*, and Rabbi Yaakov Warhaftig who both concurred wholeheartedly with training God-fearing, learned women, to serve as a female halakhic address for women seeking guidance in *taharat ha-mishpaḥah*. To the in-depth study of *halakhah*, we added supplementary studies in women's health on topics intersecting with the laws of *taharat ha-mishpaḥah*, in order to develop a comprehensive toolkit for practical assistance. The program opened in Elul 5757 (September 1997), and since then, over 150 Yoatzot Halacha have completed their studies. Most of them serve in Israel, and some 30 in conjunction with community rabbis outside Israel. Since the inception, Rabbi Warhaftig and Rabbi Henkin *zt"l* served as the address for Yoatzot for questions requiring *psikah*. We chose the name Yoatzot Halacha to convey a posture of humility before the world of *psikah*.

We did not anticipate the overwhelming response of women to the new resource. We have received hundreds of thousands of questions, from Israel and from throughout the Jewish world. The questions reached us via Nishmat's Golda

Koschitzky Hotline and Nishmat's Yoatzot internet site, or were addressed directly to Yoatzot Halacha in their communities. Many of the questions had medical or emotional facets.

This book was born following seventeen years of Yoatzot Halacha work in the field. It is not intended to be a *sefer pesak*, but rather to foster awareness of the halakhic challenges experienced by observant women, and to organize the *halakhah* for the benefit of those who are learning, with the aim of strengthening proper observance of *halakhah* and alleviating the grief which clouds the lives of many couples. Out of the thousands of anonymous questions in our database, we collected for this volume questions dealing with pregnancy, childbirth, and contraception. Their unique value lies in their addressing issues which women are facing today.

This book has two parts: the *teshuvot*, and the medical appendices. In the brief answer, we summarize the response of the Yoetzet Halacha. In personal conversations, by phone, or even in written internet responses – Yoatzot respond empathetically, patiently explaining halakhic concepts and their application in detail, in accordance with the woman's knowledge of *halakhah* and the extent of information she wishes to receive. Often, if need be, the Yoetzet will offer emotional support or personal guidance. We have followed the brief answer with an extensive halakhic analysis. In the second part of the book we have added clinical information which *morei hora'ah* may find beneficial.

The Yoatzot Halacha, and the thousands of women whom they assist, owe a debt of immense gratitude to Rabbi Yehuda Herzl Henkin *zt"l* and Rabbi Yaakov Warhaftig, the two *poskim* who threw open the gates of halakhic learning before women. I wish to thank personally Rabbi Warhaftig and Rabbanit Noa Lau for their partnership in paving the path of the Yoatzot Halacha, and for their wise instruction; and Rabbanit Michal Roness who steered this book from vision to reality. This *sefer* would not be if not for her devotion and determination; and her wisdom and kindness turned every discussion to an edifying experience. I also wish to salute the Yoatzot Halacha who tirelessly strive, with fear of God and love of Man, to raise the standard of purity in Israel and make halakhic life pleasant for Jewish women. May God bless them all.

Work on these *teshuvot* began while my son and daughter-in-law, Rabbi Eitam and Naama Henkin, הַנֶּאֱהָבִים וְהַנְּעִימִם בְּחַיֵּיהֶם וּבְמוֹתָם לֹא נִפְרָדוּ, may God avenge their murder, were still with us. My husband *zt"l* was a *posek* whose influence ran far and wide, and our world would be a different place but for his profound support of women's studying Torah. This volume is a reflection both of his insistence that the methodology of *halakhah* is timeless, and of his refusal to lower the bar for women. His passing has left our family bereft, and the Jewish world with a void that will not easily be filled. May the enhancement of Torah and *taharah* by this book offer some consolation to a grieving wife and mother, as it is written (Tehillim 94:19): "*Tanḥumekha yesha'ashe'u nafshi.*"

Signed with a prayer for God's blessing upon all households of Israel,
Chana Henkin
Jerusalem, Tammuz 5782

Part I

Pregnancy

Siman 1

Panty Liners during the Seven Neki'im When Trying to Conceive

Question

I am 36 years old and trying to conceive. Each month, several days into the seven *neki'im*, red *ketamim* (stains), larger than the size of a *gris*, appear on the white panty liner I use, forcing me to start counting from the beginning. I cannot manage to become *tehorah* before ovulation, and my period (which is otherwise regular) begins just a few days after immersing. Is there any way to resolve this problem?

Answer

Lekhatḥilah, a woman is expected to wear white underwear during the seven *neki'im*. If she sees a red *ketem* that is larger than the size of a *gris* on the underwear, she must start the count over. Many women regularly wear panty liners throughout the month, to absorb natural discharges, and most *poskim* permit this practice even during the seven *neki'im*.

According to many opinions, a panty liner is not susceptible to *tum'ah*. Therefore, unless a woman had a *hargashah* (sensation) that would render her *niddah*, even a large red *ketem* found on the liner would not bring about *niddah* status. However, if such a *ketem* is found on the panty liner during the seven *neki'im*, the woman must perform a *bedikah* (internal self-examination) immediately, and her status is determined by what appears on the *bedikah* cloth, regardless of its size.

This rule applies under normal circumstances. However, in the case of a woman who suffers from *ketamim*[1] and has a hard time becoming *tehorah*, a different rule applies. Under such circumstances, the woman may use a panty liner, either white or dark, during the seven *neki'im* and not examine herself immediately even if she saw a *ketem*. Additionally, she may skip the *bedikot* on days that she sees *ketamim*. However, she may not omit the *bedikot* on the first and seventh day of the *neki'im*.[2]

Based on your description, in your specific situation, you may conduct yourself as a woman who suffers from *ketamim* and ignore the stains that you see on the panty liner. Nevertheless, you must perform a *hefsek taharah*, one *bedikah* on the first of the *neki'im*, and one on the seventh. If they are blood-free, you may immerse.

Halakhic Expansion

The Gemara (*Shabbat* 13b) distinguishes between "days of menstruation" (*yemei niddut*) and "days of whiteness" (*yemei libun*). Rashi (*ad loc.*) explains that "days of whiteness" are the seven *neki'im*, during which "[a woman] must wear white clothing, for examination." It seems that the core meaning of "whiteness" and "white clothing" is laundered and clean; accordingly, *Tur* and *Shulḥan Arukh*[3] rule that during the seven *neki'im*, a woman must wear a clean undergarment that has been checked for stains. However, several *Rishonim*[4] write that a woman must wear white undergarments and use white bedsheets during the seven *neki'im*.[5]

---

1. There are many different possible reasons for irregular menstrual bleeding. It is recommended that a woman who suffers from repeated staining consult her gynecologist to ascertain the cause of the bleeding and the best solution. See Medical Appendix I: The Female Reproductive System, and Medical Appendix V: Contraception.
2. See also below, *Siman* 14: *Mokh Daḥuk* and *Bedikot* following Birth.
3. *Tur* and *Shulḥan Arukh, Yoreh De'ah* 196:3. This is also the ruling of *Arukh Ha-Shulḥan, Yoreh De'ah*, 196:22.
4. *Roke'aḥ, Hilkhot Niddah siman* 317: "She wears clothes, a white robe and a white sheet on her bed; this is 'days of whiteness.'" The formulation of *Roke'aḥ* is cited in *Mordekhai* as well, and Rema rules accordingly in *Yoreh De'ah* 196:3.
5. There is room to comment that since nowadays women sleep in form-fitting undergarments it is not necessary to be meticulous about this. R. Warhaftig and R. Henkin rule that there is no need for white sheets, even *lekhatḥilah*. In contrast, R. Shlomo Levi writes that there is room to be lenient only in times of need (*Sha'arei Orah*, p. 142). See *Taharah Ke-Halakhah*, p 296, n. 78, which rules stringently on this matter based on *Shi'urei Shevet Ha-Levi* (196:3:3, p. 281) and *Igrot Moshe* (*Yoreh De'ah* 4:17, part 27). R. Moshe Feinstein is concerned that women will not distinguish between form-fitting and loose undergarments. R. Wosner notes that technically there is no need for a white sheet, but nevertheless rules that one should be meticulous about this *lekhatḥilah*, as it is a "proper Jewish custom." However, *bedi'avad* or in extenuating circumstances, it is not compulsory. R. Ovadiah Yosef (*Taharat Ha-Bayit*, 2:13:4,

Torat Ha-Shelamim[6] cites two reasons for the need to wear white. First, it is important for the garment to be clean, in order to be certain that there are no prior stains from the days of menstruation, which would produce uncertainty about the woman's present status. Second, it is important that the garment not be colored, so as to establish with certainty that the woman is currently without stains, during the seven *neki'im*. It is only according to the second reason that it is necessary for the garment to be truly white. Nevertheless, all *poskim* agree that under extenuating circumstances, or *bedi'avad*,[7] the seven *neki'im* are valid even without wearing white.

In recent years, it has become common for women to wear a panty liner regularly, throughout the month, to absorb bodily discharges. This practice raises the question of whether one may wear a panty liner during the seven *neki'im*. On one hand, according to many opinions, the liner is not susceptible to *tum'ah*,[8] but on the other hand, it is white, and stains are visible on it. Additionally, wearing a panty liner does not fit with the aforementioned custom of wearing white garments.[9]

Most contemporary *poskim*[10] permit wearing a panty liner during the seven *neki'im*. This raises the question of how to relate to finding a *ketem*, unaccompanied by a *hargashah*, on a liner during the seven *neki'im*. According to most opinions, a *ketem* found on a panty liner at a time when the woman is *tehorah*

---

p. 293) notes that there are different customs vis-à-vis white clothes and sheets, and that everyone should practice according to the custom of their community.

6. *Yoreh De'ah* 196:6–8.
7. For example, if the woman is traveling and does not have a change of clothes. This is the ruling of Rema, based on *Agur* (*siman* 1371) and *Hagahot Sha'arei Dura*.
8. See below, *Siman* 44: Staining on a Panty Liner or Synthetic Clothing, in Halakhic Expansion.
9. If it is white, because of the material from which it is manufactured, which is not cloth; if it is colored, because it is not white.
10. Since this is a recent phenomenon, only contemporary *poskim* address it, and this is the ruling of R. Warhaftig and R. Henkin. R. Wosner (*Shi'urei Shevet Ha-Levi* 196:3:1, p. 281) writes: "During the seven *neki'im*, she may go with a pad made to absorb sweat, and there is no need to be concerned that a drop of blood will be absorbed in it." R. Shlomo Zalman Auerbach writes as follows in response to a question from R. David Dudkevitz as to whether it is permissible to wear a panty liner during the seven *neki'im*: "During the seven *neki'im* they are certainly good, as they are white. However, white sheets are also necessary in case they move around, and with respect to colored ones, we said that they are not susceptible to *tum'ah*" (R. Auerbach's responsum is cited in R. Shlomo Levi's article in *Tzohar*, issue 20 [5765], pp. 21-23). On the basis of this responsum, R. Elyashiv Knohl (*Ish Ve-Isha*, p. 101 and p. 144, n. 21) writes that even a woman who has no particular problems may wear a panty liner during the seven *neki'im*, as long as the liner is of the sort that a bloodstain would be visible on it. R. Zechariah Ben-Shlomo (*Orot Ha-Taharah*, pp. 278–79) writes that one may use a panty liner during the seven *neki'im lekhatḥilah*, and they are even preferable to white underwear, since they remain white and do not darken over time.

does not render her *niddah,* since the liner is made from materials that are not susceptible to *tum'ah.* The same applies during the seven *neki'im,* except that during the *neki'im,* a woman must wear white to ascertain that she has indeed stopped bleeding. Therefore, if she found a red *ketem* larger than *ke-gris* (the size of a *gris*) on a panty liner during the seven *neki'im,* even though the *ketem* does not render her *niddah,* she must perform a *bedikah* immediately to ensure that she maintains her halakhic presumption of cleanness.[11]

Nevertheless, *Ḥakhamim* were lenient in the case of a woman who has a difficult time becoming *tehorah* and who suffers from *ketamim,*[12] permitting her to wear colored garments to save her from *ketamim.*[13] *Aḥaronim*[14] note that this leniency

11. This is the ruling of R. Warhaftig and R. Henkin. This ruling is a compromise between the view that a stain on a panty liner during the seven *neki'im* is akin to a stain on white underwear, and the view that is lenient regarding panty liners during the seven *neki'im* as when the woman is *tehorah.* R. Aharon Naftali (Kenneth) Auman, Dean of Nishmat's Miriam Glaubach Center, does not require a *bedikah* under these circumstances.

    In contrast, according to R. Shlomo Levi, a red stain larger than a *gris* on a panty liner always renders the woman *teme'ah,* and there is no need for a *bedikah.* This is in light of his stringent ruling vis-à-vis panty liners, as they are manufactured as a *kli* and are form-fitting (*Sha'arei Orah,* pp. 89–90). R. Levi disagrees with R. Knohl's understanding of R. Auerbach's responsum, as cited in the previous footnote. According to R. Levi (*Tzohar,* issue 20, pp. 21-23), R. Auerbach indeed permitted wearing a panty liner over white underwear during the seven *neki'im,* but if a stain is found on it, it renders her *teme'ah.* This is the meaning of his distinction between white underwear and colored underwear, over the latter of which one should not wear a panty liner during the seven *neki'im.*

    R. Levi's interpretation of R. Auerbach's words is difficult, in my opinion, and this requires further study. R. Zechariah Ben-Shlomo cites another view. He recommends wearing a panty liner during the seven *neki'im,* adding: "It has already been clarified above that a stain found on a disposable hygienic item is *tahor,* as it is considered something that is not susceptible to *tum'ah*" (*Orot Ha-Taharah,* pp. 278–79).
12. It is not always simple to define who is a "woman who has a hard time becoming *tehorah.*" A *posek* must take into account medical, psychological, and marital information about the woman and her husband, together with halakhic information, and decide when she can be so defined, thus warranting leniency. Simpler situations include, for example, a woman who has not managed to become *tehorah* more than six weeks after childbirth or a woman whose count of seven *neki'im* is negated by *ketamim* that render her *teme'ah* or by *bedikot* that do not emerge clean.
13. Rema, *Yoreh De'ah* 190:10, based on *Niddah* 61b and *Mishneh Torah, Hilkhot Issurei Biah* 9:7.
14. R. Wosner (*Shi'urei Shevet Ha-Levi* 190:9, p. 171) permits this only in the case of a woman who is unable to become *tehorah,* only during the middle days of the seven *neki'im* and after asking a halakhic question, and only as a temporary measure (*hora'at sha'ah*). R. Mordechai Eliyahu (*Darkhei Taharah,* p. 22), cites all the views and rules that a woman with many *ketamim* should ask a halakhic question as to what to do, and to be lenient with regard to colored garments. This is also the ruling of R. Yekutiel Farkash (*Taharah Ke-Halakhah,* p. 297). R. Ovadiah Yosef (*Taharat Ha-Bayit,* 2:13:4, pp. 293–96) addresses this topic. He writes that according to the

applies during the seven *neki'im* as well. Contemporary *poskim*[15] write that instead of wearing colored garments, it is possible, and perhaps preferable, to use a panty liner, which is not susceptible to *tum'ah*. In such a situation, the woman need not perform a *bedikah* immediately upon seeing a *ketem* on the liner; on the contrary, she relies on the laws of *ketamim* and performs only the essential *bedikot*, on the first and seventh days, so that she can become *tehorah*.

N.L.

---

aforementioned ruling of *Shulḥan Arukh* that clean, bloodstain-free garments are sufficient, it is obvious that colored garments may be worn even during the seven *neki'im*. He cites a list of *poskim* who are stringent and require specifically white garments during the seven *neki'im*, even when the woman suffers from *ketamim*, but disagrees with them, claiming that from the moment the woman performed a *hefsek taharah*, she is defined as having a presumption of *taharah* (*ḥezkat taharah*), and therefore no distinction should be made between the seven *neki'im* and when she is *tehorah*. He also addresses the view among *poskim* that colored garments may not be worn specifically during the first three of the seven *neki'im*; R. Ovadiah rejects this view, too (relying on the responsa *Me'il Tzedakah siman* 62 and *Berit Ya'akov, Yoreh De'ah siman* 58), and ultimately permits wearing colored garments even *lekhatḥilah* for a woman who is likely to find *ketamim*. It should be noted that R. Shlomo Levi (*Sha'arei Orah*, p. 142) rules stringently on this matter, writing that only a woman with a *petza* (sore, cut, or abrasion) may temporarily wear a colored garment during the seven *neki'im*. However, a woman who suffers from *ketamim* (such as a nursing mother or a woman taking pills) should not wear a colored garment.

15. R. Yekutiel Farkash (*Taharah Ke-Halakhah*, p. 80) writes that, if possible, in such situations, wearing a pad that is not susceptible to *tum'ah* may be preferable to a colored garment, and "this is more *mehudar*." On p. 80, n. 15*, he writes: "However, with regard to the seven *neki'im*, I have found nobody who discusses [a woman wearing a pad if *ketamim* make it difficult for her to become *tehorah*]. At first glance, it would seem to be clearly permitted – for nowhere do we find that she is specifically obligated to wear a garment that is susceptible to *tum'ah* during the seven *neki'im*. They insisted only that the garment be white, clean, and checked for stains, etc. On the other hand, according to this, all *ketamim* found during the seven *neki'im* would be deemed *tahor*. I asked many of the greatest *poskim* and my teachers, under whom I apprenticed, and no one told me anything clear on this matter – even though, at first glance, it seems quite correct to all of them." As stated, R. Knohl (*Ish Ve-Isha*, p. 101) permits wearing a panty liner even *lekhatḥilah* during the seven *neki'im*, noting that, "These liners can assist the *posek* in cases of uncertainty...." R. Shlomo Levi (*Sha'arei Orah*, p. 89) rules stringently about a *ketem* on a panty liner, but if there is another reason to be lenient, for example, if the woman has an IUD and finds stains on the liner, he rules leniently and deems her *tehorah*, even during the seven *neki'im*, based also on the possibility that it may perhaps be blood from a *petza* (sore, cut, or abrasion) (*Tzohar*, issue 20, p. 23). R. Zechariah Ben-Shlomo (*Orot Ha-Taharah*, p. 312) writes that a *ketem* found during the seven *neki'im* on something not susceptible to *tum'ah* does not cause *tum'ah*, because *Ḥakhamim* made no decree about this. Therefore, it is permissible and worthwhile to place a panty liner *lekhatḥilah* to absorb the *ketamim*. According to him: "The seven *neki'im* must be clean of *tamei* blood that causes *tum'ah*, but it is not necessary for them to be free of blood that *halakhah* deems *tahor*, not because of its appearance, but because of the rules of *ketamim*."

Siman 2

Onot Perishah at the Beginning of Pregnancy

Question

My period is two days late, and I have just gotten positive results from a home pregnancy test. May I ignore the *onat perishah* that falls tonight, given the positive results? My husband is leaving tomorrow for a month of military reserve duty, and I am concerned about becoming *niddah* from the *bedikah*.

Answer

A pregnant woman is halakhically presumed to be *mesuleket damim* (amenorrheic) only once "her fetus is discernible," that is, when three months have passed since she last immersed. Many *poskim* maintain that even nowadays, even if pregnancy has been confirmed by an accurate test, a woman must observe the *onot perishah* (periods of spousal separation) until her cycle is uprooted. This should generally be followed in practice. An established cycle (*veset kavu'a*) is uprooted when the expected date of menstruation passes three times without bleeding, and a non-established cycle (*veset she-eino kavu'a*) is uprooted after one time. In practice, most women today do not have established cycles, and will only need to observe *onot perishah* for the first month.

However, in your situation, where you are facing an extended separation, we can be lenient in accordance with the view of the *poskim* who rely on pregnancy tests to establish *siluk damim* (amenorrhea), and do not require a *bedikah* during the *onot perishah* under such conditions.

Halakhic Expansion

A woman acquires the halakhic status of pregnancy with respect to *siluk damim* once her fetus is discernible.[1] The Gemara establishes that the fetus becomes discernible after three months.[2] This is brought by the *Aḥaronim* as well.[3] Therefore, she must observe *onot perishah* until she is halakhically presumed to be pregnant.[4] The *poskim* disagree about the reason for this. Is it because, in those days, it took three months to confirm the pregnancy?[5] In that case, nowadays, when pregnancy can be confirmed by means of a test, and in light of improved pregnancy tests, a woman is already considered *mesuleket damim* from the beginning of the pregnancy and would not need to observe *onot perishah*. Or is the reason that only after three months does the weight of the fetus prevent the discharge of blood? In that case, a woman is liable to experience bleeding even if she is known to be pregnant.[6]

According to *Shevut Yaakov*,[7] a woman is considered *mesuleket damim* from the moment she knows she is pregnant. Likewise, *Igrot Moshe* states in several places that one may rely on a doctor's examination, even before three months of pregnancy have elapsed, since nature has changed and "immediately upon becoming pregnant, her bleeding ceases";[8] and even if a woman only senses clearly that she is pregnant, one may be lenient.

In contrast, *Sidrei Taharah*[9] states that a woman is considered *mesuleket damim* only once three months have elapsed, since until then she is liable to experience bleeding, as her head and limbs do not yet feel heavy to her.[10] *Responsa Shevet*

---

1. *Niddah* 7b.
2. Ibid. 8b.
3. *Responsa Avodat Ha-Gershuni siman* 21; *Responsa Shevut Yaakov* 1:71; *Ḥokhmat Adam*, principle 108, section 3; *Shi'urei Shevet Ha-Levi* 194:2:2.
4. *Yoreh De'ah* 184:7. The standard for determining that the fetus is discernible is three months; see *Yoreh De'ah* 189:33.
5. This is implied by the story of Tamar: "About three months later…" (Bereishit 38:24), cited in *Niddah* 8b.
6. As will be discussed, from a medical perspective, a woman may experience bleeding during the first three months, and sometimes later, even during a healthy pregnancy.
7. *Shevut Yaakov* 1:71. *Shevut Yaakov* is addressing miscarriage and the age of pregnancy; however, the discussion is also relevant for our question of discerning pregnancy and amenorrhea. Even in the times of the Gemara, some women became amenorrheic at the beginning of pregnancy, but they did not know for certain why their menses were delayed. The Gemara therefore determined that a woman is considered *mesuleket damim* only once her fetus is discernible.
8. *Igrot Moshe, Yoreh De'ah* 3:52 et al.
9. *Sidrei Taharah, Yoreh De'ah* 194:7.
10. *Responsa Mishneh Halakhot* in 7:137 and 10:129 states similarly, see also 10:137. Therefore, she must still observe her *veset*, even if her pregnancy has been confirmed. R. Akiva Eger (1:128)

Ha-Levi[11] likewise states that even today, when it is possible to know for certain, by means of a medical test, that a woman is pregnant, she is nevertheless not considered *mesuleket damim* until three months have elapsed, because it is the passage of time, not the confirmation of pregnancy, that causes *siluk damim*. In another responsum,[12] R. Wosner sharply criticized those who rule leniently before three months have elapsed, stating that they cause the masses to stumble. This, in his opinion, is the straightforward meaning of the Gemara, and this is the explanation of Ramban, Rashba, and Ritva: that three full months must elapse before a woman is presumed to be *mesuleket damim*. Many contemporary *poskim* rule accordingly as well.[13] In their view, only once three months have elapsed are the two necessary conditions fulfilled: the monthly cycle has stopped, and her 'limbs feel heavy to her'. Only then does she acquire the halakhic presumption of *mesuleket damim* who does not observe *vesatot*.[14]

R. Ovadiah Yosef also ruled this way in *Taharat Ha-Bayit*,[15] and he noted that R. Moshe Feinstein, in a pamphlet, retracted his earlier, lenient ruling ("*hadar hu le-kol hasidav*").[16] However, R. Yehuda Henkin notes that the editor of *Responsa Igrot Moshe* claimed emphatically that R. Feinstein explained that he did not change his opinion that one may rely on a pregnancy test in order to create the presumption that a woman is *mesuleket damim*. He did, however,

---

writes that even if she has not experienced bleeding since the beginning of her pregnancy, she is still not considered *mesuleket damim*: "In my opinion, *siluk damim* is only once her fetus is discernible, even though we see that women today are amenorrheic immediately upon conception, and that nature has changed."

11. *Responsa Shevet Ha-Levi* 4:99, section 8.
12. Ibid. 3:114.
13. As explained in *Bet Yosef* at the end of *siman* 189 and in *Responsa Ḥatam Sofer, Yoreh De'ah* 2:169. This is also the ruling in *Taharat Ha-Bayit* 1:2:7 p. 80; *Shi'urei Shevet Ha-Levi* 184:7:1; *Badei Ha-Shulḥan* 184:7 and in the elucidations, s.v. "*mi-shehukar ubarah*." See also *Responsa Mishneh Halakhot* 5:149.
14. See also *Responsa Mishneh Halakhot* 7:137, which states that a woman who menstruates once every three or four months who became pregnant, and her fetus is discernible, need no longer observe *vesatot*, even though three of her cycles have not passed, the reason being that she is *mesuleket damim* because her head and limbs feel heavy to her.
15. *Taharat Ha-Bayit*, 1:2:7, pp. 82–84. See also *Igrot Moshe, Yoreh De'ah* 3:52 regarding the comparison between a pregnant and a nursing woman, that in both cases "nature has changed" in our times. R. Ovadiah Yosef cites numerous *poskim* who incline toward leniency, but ultimately he decides in favor of stringency.
16. Similarly, *Responsa Va-Ya'an Yosef, Yoreh De'ah siman* 119, rules that until three months have elapsed, she is like any woman and observes her original *veset*, whether this results in leniency or stringency.

write according to the stringent view in an English-language piece for *ba'alei teshuvah*, so that they would not be confused.[17]

To summarize: According to most *poskim*, one should not rely on a pregnancy test to presume a woman as *mesuleket damim* before three months of her pregnancy have elapsed. However, under extenuating circumstances, as in the case before us, one may be lenient in accordance with *Igrot Moshe* and not require a *bedikah*.[18]

When circumstances are not extenuating, a woman without a *veset kavua* should observe the *veset ha-ḥodesh*, *veset ha-haflagah*, and *onah beinonit* one time,[19] after which they are uprooted.[20] Since nowadays most women are amenorrheic from the beginning of pregnancy, and since most women do not have a *veset kavu'a*, even though they do not have the presumption of being *mesulakot damim* until three months into the pregnancy, in practice, the *onot perishah* apply only during the first month.[21]

---

17. *Igrot Moshe, Yoreh De'ah* 4:17. R. Warhaftig notes that he was present when R. Moshe Tendler, the son-in-law of R. Moshe Feinstein, reported that before his death, R. Feinstein said to him that he is glad that he never retracted what he wrote in his books. According to R. Warhaftig, there is no need to think that "nature changed." Rather, knowledge changed: Earlier generations attributed amenorrhea to the weight of the fetus, but we now know that the cause is hormonal, that pregnancy hormones prevent the shedding of the endometrium and menstrual bleeding. Even according to the Gemara and *Rishonim* that a woman is considered pregnant with respect to *siluk damim* only once three months have elapsed, if a new type of *siluk damim* is created (using birth control pills, for example), we may rely on this knowledge, and there is no need to observe the previous *veset*. Here, too, there is something new: the positive result of the pregnancy test, which proves that the woman is certainly pregnant – so the woman knows that she is *mesuleket damim* (and can be called, to the same degree, either "pregnant" or "*mesuleket damim* based on a pregnancy test"). The test is performed only because menstruation was delayed, which already raises the prospect that she is pregnant and *mesuleket damim*. Even according to those who are stringent and require her to perform *bedikot* during *onot perishah*, if she has no *veset kavu'a*, the *veset ha-ḥodesh*, the *veset ha-haflagah*, as well as the first occurrence of the *onah beinonit*, have already passed; this is why she performed a pregnancy test. Observing the *onah beinonit* in subsequent months, in accordance with the view of R. Mordechai Eliyahu, seems to be overly stringent, and most *poskim* disagree with him. (See R. Y. Warhaftig, "The *Onah Beinonit* Nowadays," *Teḥumin* 24 [5764], pp. 235–42.)
18. To this *heter* we should add the view that one who leaves on a journey should have relations with his wife, even at a time she anticipates her menses. See *Shulḥan Arukh* and Rema, *Yoreh De'ah* 184:10.
19. *Yoreh De'ah* 189:1 and *Shakh ad loc.* 1.
20. *Yoreh De'ah* 189:15; *Shi'urei Shevet Ha-Levi* 189:33:2.
21. *Darkhei Taharah* p. 84 states that one should continue to observe the *onah beinonit* on day 60 and day 90, but R. Warhaftig maintains that this is overly stringent and that one need not practice accordingly. *Sha'arei Orah* (p. 232) rules that one may be lenient after a single *onah* where she did not experience bleeding.

In contrast, a woman with a *veset kavu'a* for the date of the Hebrew month must observe her *veset* until the end of the third month of her pregnancy.[22] A woman with a *veset kavu'a* for an interval observes her *veset* once. After this, if her menses have stopped, there is no longer a point from which she can calculate further intervals.

Some women do experience bleeding during pregnancy. Sometimes, this bleeding appears once a month even over the course of several months of pregnancy. A woman who experiences bleeding after she has established a presumption of being *mesuleket damim* must separate from her husband as with a *veset she-eino kavu'a*,[23] but she is not required to observe the *onah beinonit*.[24]

In the case of any bleeding during pregnancy, an examination by a gynecologist is recommended. In the case of bleeding and pain in the pelvic or abdominal area, one should be examined by a doctor immediately in order to rule out the possibility of an ectopic pregnancy, which can be life-threatening.

S.K.

---

22. *Shi'urei Shevet Ha-Levi* 189:33:2. Even if the date of her *veset kavua* has passed three times without bleeding, the *veset* should still be observed in the future as a matter of stringency, since it has not been uprooted. That is, she will need to observe her *veset kavu'a* again at the end of the period of *siluk damim*. See below, *Siman* 19: *Onot Perishah* and Establishing a *Veset* Postpartum.
23. However, she does not establish a *veset*. *Yoreh De'ah* 189:33, in accordance with the opinion of Ra'avad cited in *Torat Ha-Bayit, bayit* 7, *sha'ar* 3, p. 12a.
24. *Shi'urei Shevet Ha-Levi* 189:33:5; *Badei Ha-Shulḥan* 189:33, elucidations, s.v. "*le-re'iyah she-tir'eh.*" After the completion of the period of pregnancy and nursing, she goes back to observing the *veset kavu'a* she had established before becoming pregnant.

Siman 3

Blood in Urine during Pregnancy

Question

I am pregnant, and today, after urinating, I found blood on the toilet seat and in the water. I felt a burning sensation while urinating, so although I have not yet been examined by a doctor, I think I have a urinary tract infection. Am I now *niddah*?

Answer

A woman who sees blood on the toilet seat or in the lavatory water is not *niddah* according to Sephardi custom. According to Ashkenazi custom, in a case of a confirmed urinary tract infection – for example, one diagnosed by a doctor or by laboratory tests – she is not *niddah*. Even without a diagnosed infection, only if the blood was found within 15 seconds of urinating would the woman be rendered *niddah*, according to Ashkenazi custom. Blood that is discovered on the toilet seat or in the water after a break of this duration does not render you *niddah*.

In any instance of bleeding during pregnancy, it is advisable to consult your physician. In the case of a urinary tract infection, it is important to begin antibiotics promptly in order to prevent early contractions and premature birth, which can result from the infection.

Halakhic Expansion

Finding Blood on the Toilet Seat or in the Water

When a woman sees blood while urinating, there is concern that it may be uterine blood that became mixed with the urine.[1] Ḥazal disagree about the circumstances in which we must presume this possibility: whether or not she becomes *niddah* if she urinated while standing, and whether the urine trickles or streams from her body.[2] The *Rishonim*[3] disagree about R. Yosei's position that the woman remains *tehorah* whether she urinates while sitting or standing. *Shulḥan Arukh*[4] rules in accordance with Rambam and Rashi that in all cases, we may consider the source of the blood to be urinary and not uterine, so the woman remains *tehorah*. Rema, on the other hand, rules in accordance with the position of Rabbeinu Ḥananel[5] that the woman is *tehorah* only if she urinated in a stream, while sitting, and the blood is found inside the chamber pot and not on its inside walls; in all other cases, she is *niddah*, subject to the leniencies of *ketamim*.[6] Rema deems the woman *tehorah* only if she finds blood inside the chamber pot because then it is evident that this blood came from the urinary

1. *Niddah* 57b discusses the concern that the urine backed up into the uterus and brought out blood. According to current anatomical knowledge, we would need to say that Ḥazal are describing blood from different sources that became mixed together.
2. *Niddah* 14b; 57b; 59b.
3. Ibid. 58b. The Gemara states explicitly that the law accords with R. Yosei. According to Rashi (*Niddah* 59b, s.v. "*mezaneket*") and Rambam (*Mishneh Torah, Hilkhot Issurei Biah* 5:17), R. Yosei deems the woman *tehorah* in all possible situations: whether she is standing or sitting, and whether the urine streams out or trickles out. In their view, one cannot speak of a woman's standing and urinating in a steady stream. According to Rabbeinu Ḥananel (cited in *Tosafot* to *Niddah* 14b, s.v. "*ve-Rabi Yosei metaher*"), R. Yosei does not deem her unequivocally *tehorah*. She is deemed *tehorah* vis-à-vis the *tum'ah* of *niddah* and for the purpose of *taharot*, but R. Yosei concedes to R. Meir that she and her husband are prohibited to each other on account of the *ketem*. However, she is *tehorah* if she urinates in a stream while sitting, and the blood is found inside the chamber pot. According to Rosh (*Niddah* 9:1), R. Yosei maintains that when she was seated, she is deemed *tehorah* under all circumstances, but if she stood, she is *tehorah* only if she urinated in a steady stream into the chamber pot. However, if she stands and urinates in a trickle onto the rim of the chamber pot, she is *teme'ah*, for since there is a constriction, the urine backs up into the uterus and brings blood. Rosh's view is cited thus in Rema, *Yoreh De'ah* 191.
4. *Yoreh De'ah* 191:1.
5. Rabbeinu Ḥananel, cited in *Tosafot* to *Niddah* 14b, s.v. "*ve-Rabi Yosei metaher*."
6. Nowadays we do not have the expertise to distinguish between a trickle and a stream, so one should be lenient only in cases where there are other reasons to permit, for example, when the blood was found on the toilet or in the water, which are not susceptible to *tum'ah*. See *Responsa R. Akiva Eger* 1:62, and, following him, *Badei Ha-Shulḥan* 191:19.

tract and not the uterus. However, even when she finds a *ketem* larger than a *gris* on the toilet seat, which is fixed to the ground, or on the walls of the toilet, the woman can be deemed *tehorah*, as in a case of a *ketem* found on something that is not susceptible to *tum'ah*,[7] and in accordance with R. Neḥemiah's view that anything not susceptible to *tum'ah* is not susceptible to *ketamim* [that render a woman *niddah*].[8] Therefore, if a woman sees a *ketem* on the toilet, so long as there is no concern that she may have experienced a *hargashah* when the blood emerged (regarding the concern for a *hargashah* while urinating, see below), she is *tehorah*, because the toilet is not susceptible to *tum'ah*,[9] and the *halakhah* has been decided accordingly.[10] When the blood was found in the water, there is a need to determine whether toilet water and urine are susceptible to *tum'ah*, or whether the blood found in the water has the status of blood found on a surface that is not susceptible to *tum'ah*.

In *Nidrei Zerizin*,[11] R. Shlomo Kluger writes that since fluids in general are not susceptible to *tum'ah mi-de'Orayta*, and their *tum'ah* is a rabbinic statute, therefore it stands to reason that Ḥazal did not decree *tum'ah* upon stains found on surfaces that are susceptible to *tum'ah* only *mi-deRabanan*, because they do not legislate a decree upon another decree.[12]

Sometimes there is an additional reason for leniency, namely, that the toilet has not been examined. When the woman sees blood in the water but did not check that the water was clean prior to sitting down, it is possible that the blood was there earlier (if others used this bathroom). Finding blood in a toilet that many people use is like finding blood on an unexamined cloth: the woman is *tehorah* because of a double uncertainty (*sfek sfeika*).[13]

---

7. The chamber pot mentioned by the *Rishonim* is a receptacle that is susceptible to *tum'ah*. See below, n. 9.
8. *Niddah* 59b. This is the ruling in *Shulḥan Arukh, Yoreh De'ah* 190:10.
9. *Darkhei Moshe* 190:4 mentions *Hagahot Maimoniyot* on the *Hilkhot Issurei Biah* 9:7:5, in the name of *Sefer Ha-Mitzvot*. The Gemara mentions the finding of blood inside a "*sefel*," which seems to be a sort of chamber pot, an earthenware receptacle that is not attached to the ground and is therefore susceptible to *tum'ah*. The "*bet ha-kisei*" mentioned in early sources, as well as the modern toilet, are attached to the ground and therefore are not susceptible to *tum'ah*.
10. Rema, *Yoreh De'ah* 190:10.
11. *Nidrei Zerizin* (*Kuntres Shirei Shirim* 22); *Minḥat Yitzḥak* 9:93 rules that this reasoning can be combined with other factors for leniency in this case.
12. In contrast, *Noda Bi-Yehudah* 2:109 rules that, so as not to draw distinctions (*lo plug*), even something that is susceptible to *tum'ah* only at the rabbinic level can become *tamei* from a *ketem*. See *Minḥat Yitzḥak* 9:93, which addresses this topic at length.
13. It is uncertain whether it came from her, and even if it came from her, it is uncertain whether it originated in the uterus. Rema, *Yoreh De'ah* 191:1; *Ḥavat Da'at* 191:4; *Ḥut Ha-Shani* 191:2–3.

Thus far we have related to blood found in a toilet as though it is a *ketem* without an accompanying *hargashah*. Yet there is reason to be concerned that the blood seen in the toilet was accompanied by a *hargashah* which the woman did not notice because it was masked by the sensation of urinating. The Gemara mentions three situations where we must be concerned that a woman had a *hargashah* but did not notice it: while performing a *bedikah*, while engaged in marital relations, and while urinating.[14] According to Sephardi custom,[15] there is no concern that a *hargashah* accompanied urination. In contrast, Ashkenazi custom is to be concerned that she may have experienced a *hargashah* while urinating.[16] Therefore, as in a case when blood was found while wiping, if time elapsed between urinating and finding the blood, we can assume that this blood was not accompanied by a *hargashah*, and it therefore has the status of a *ketem*. As long as she did not find the blood within 15 seconds of completing urination, it can be assumed that the blood did not appear together with the urine, so there is no concern that the bleeding was accompanied by a *hargashah*.[17]

Urinary Tract Infections

In the case of a urinary tract infection, it is possible that the infection is the source of the blood. One symptom of such an infection is the presence of blood in the urine.[18] Other symptoms include a burning sensation during urination, an urgent, persistent need to urinate, urine that smells foul or has a different appearance, backaches, and fever.

Shi'urei Shevet Ha-Levi (191:8, p. 220) is lenient in a case where the place was not examined only if the *ketem* is up to the size of a *gris*.

14. *Niddah* 57b.
15. *Yoreh De'ah* 191.
16. *Ḥavat Da'at* 190:1, elucidations, s.v. "*ve-im matz'ah*." However, there were some who were not concerned; see *Ḥazon Ish* 90:5, s.v. "*ve-hineh*." For an expanded discussion of the concern that there may have been a *hargashah* during urination, see below, *Siman* 27: Blood on Toilet Paper.
17. Note 14 of R. Moshe Feinstein's comments on R. Shimon Eider's *Halachos of Niddah*, in *Igrot Moshe, Yoreh De'ah* 4:17:13; *Ḥavat Da'at* 190:1, at the end; *Shi'urei Shevet Ha-Levi* 190, p. 170. For an expanded discussion of the 15-second waiting period, see below, *Siman* 27: Blood on Toilet Paper.
18. This phenomenon is called hematuria. The blood is filtered in the kidneys, where waste matter and excess fluids are removed. The waste passes through the ureters to the urinary bladder, and from there, the urine is expelled from the body through the urethra. Red blood cells can leak into the urine at any stage of this process. The most common cause of hematuria is a urinary tract infection, but it can also be caused by bladder or kidney stones, blockages in the urinary tract, and even certain medications, like certain types of antibiotics and blood thinners like aspirin.

The *poskim* have written that if a woman feels pain while urinating, we can assume that the blood stems from a urinary tract infection, and there is no concern that it is uterine blood.[19] This rule is derived from the *halakhah* that if a woman knows that she has a *petza* (wound or lesion) that can bleed, she may attribute a *ketem* to the *petza*.[20]

Sometimes, and especially during pregnancy, a urinary tract infection is not accompanied by any symptoms other than bleeding. Nowadays, doctors generally perform frequent urine tests during pregnancy, out of concern that a urinary tract infection will cause a kidney infection. Likewise, an infection during pregnancy can put both mother and fetus at risk or can cause early contractions and premature birth. *Shi'urei Shevet Ha-Levi*[21] rules that it is not necessary for the woman to feel pain to attribute the blood to an infection; rather, we may rely on a laboratory test to establish the existence of a urinary tract infection that can cause bleeding. Nowadays it is possible to ascertain immediately whether there are signs of infection in the urine (for example, a high count of white blood cells or nitrites in the urine). Therefore, the blood in the urine can be attributed to infection on the basis of a positive result from a test strip or dipstick that provides immediate results.[22]

Even in the absence of a urine test, if a woman has additional symptoms that indicate a urinary tract infection, she may attribute the blood to the infection. This is in accordance with Rema's statement that if a woman has a *veset kavu'a*, and she feels pain and sees blood in her urine when it is not the time of her *veset*, she is *tehorah*.[23] Likewise, a woman who is *mesuleket damim* (amenorrheic), whether because of medications or because she is pregnant or nursing, may attribute the blood in her urine to the infection, as she is not expecting menstrual bleeding.[24]

M.R.

---

19. *Responsa Ran siman* 49, s.v. "*va-ani omer*"; Rema, *Yoreh De'ah* 191:1.
20. *Yoreh De'ah* 187:5. Regarding a wound that the woman knows bleeds, see below, *Siman* 21: Attributing Blood to a *Petza* during the Seven *Neki'im*.
21. *Shi'urei Shevet Ha-Levi* 191:15, pp. 220–21.
22. This is the view of R. Warhaftig.
23. *Yoreh De'ah* 191:1. Rema adds that regarding a woman who has a *veset* and does not have pain, she is, required to check the source of the blood. For this examination, called "*bedikat* ha-Maharil," the woman places a *mokh*, in place while urinating, and she can thus clarify whether the blood issues from the urinary tract or is vaginal. Rema does not rely on *bedikat* ha-Maharil for a woman without a *veset* who sees blood in her urine, as he is concerned that she will not distinguish between blood in the urine and uterine blood. See also Rema *Yoreh De'ah* 187:5.
24. *Shi'urei Shevet Ha-Levi* 191:15, p. 220.

Siman 4

Spotting and Bleeding during Pregnancy

Question

I am in my eleventh week of pregnancy, and I found light bleeding on a white undergarment. Am I *niddah* because of the bleeding?

Answer

From a medical perspective, light bleeding in early pregnancy is not a cause for concern.[1] Nevertheless, for any bleeding early in pregnancy, a woman should be examined by her physician. If the bleeding is accompanied by pain, she should be examined immediately in order to rule out the possibility of an ectopic pregnancy.[2]

From a halakhic perspective, once the pregnancy is discernible[3] you are considered *mesuleket damim* (amenorrheic), and you need not observe your *veset*. However, if bleeding occurs, its status is determined according to the usual halakhic principles.

Light bleeding (whose volume does not reach that of regular menstruation) that was not accompanied by a halakhically significant *hargashah* that would render one *niddah*, is considered a *ketem* and is assessed according to the rules of *ketamim*.

1. About 25% of women experience bleeding at the beginning of pregnancy. In most cases, the bleeding is uterine. See Medical Appendix II: Pregnancy.
2. On ectopic pregnancy, see Medical Appendix II.
3. See *Siman* 2: *Onot Perishah* at the Beginning of Pregnancy

Since the undergarment is white, if the *ketem* is larger than a *gris* (a circle with a diameter of 19 mm / ¾ of an inch), the *ketem* renders one *niddah*.

If you are uncertain whether the *ketem* is a *niddah* color, it is worthwhile to show it to a halakhic authority. If you are deemed *niddah* after evaluating the *ketem* according to these principles, you have the status of a *niddah* with regard to *harḥakot*, counting seven *neki'im*, and immersing in a *mikveh*.

As a general rule, since spotting is common during pregnancy, we recommend wearing colored underwear, so as to avoid problems and uncertainties due to *ketamim*. It is also permissible to use a panty liner, which is considered a surface that is not susceptible to *tum'ah*, so that *ketamim* that appear on it will not render you *niddah*.

Halakhic Expansion

Uterine blood makes a woman *niddah mi-de'Orayta* only when it is accompanied by a *hargashah*.[4] Such blood makes her *niddah* in any quantity and regardless of the surface on which it is found. Blood that is not accompanied by a *hargashah* is called, in rabbinic terminology, "*ketem*." It does not make her *niddah mi-de'Orayta*, but *Ḥakhamim* ordained that a *ketem* renders a woman *niddah* under certain conditions.[5] For a *ketem* to render a woman *niddah*, it must meet all of the following conditions listed below. When one of them is missing, the woman remains *tehorah*.

Conditions for a *Ketem* to Render One *Niddah*:

1. The color of the *ketem* – The *ketem* is red, reddish brown, or black.[6]
2. It cannot be attributed to something else – There is no other source to which the *ketem* can be attributed (a lesion, hemorrhoids, a yeast infection, etc.).[7]
3. The size of the *ketem* – The *ketem* must be larger than a *gris* – will be discussed at greater length below.
4. The surface on which the *ketem* appears – this will be discussed at greater length below.

---

4. For the definition of a *hargashah* that makes a woman *niddah*, see below, *Siman* 25: The Law of *Hargashah* (Sensation of Menses).
5. *Tur* and *Shulḥan Arukh, Yoreh De'ah* 183:1 and 190:1.
6. For an expanded discussion of the color of a *ketem*, see below, *Siman* 54: Colors on *Bedikah* Cloths. Although that *siman* discusses colors found on an *bedikah* cloth, the same principles apply to the colors of external *ketamim*.
7. For an expanded discussion of this topic, see, for example, *Simanim* 17, 21, 45, 52, and 56.

The Size of the *Ketem*

Regarding the size of a *ketem* that renders a woman *niddah,* the requisite measurement is a *gris* (the size of a *ful,* or broad bean). This ruling is based on the Mishnah and Gemara[8] that address the attribution of a *ketem* to a pubic louse. Most *Rishonim*[9] rule in accordance with R. Ḥanina ben Antigonus, who attributes any *ketem* to a louse, up to (and including, following R. Ḥisda) the size of a *gris,* even if the woman did not kill a louse. *Shulḥan Arukh* likewise rules[10] that *Ḥakhamim* did not ordain the *tum'ah* of a *ketem* unless it is at least the size of a *gris.*

Most *poskim*[11] agree that the size of a *gris* is a circle with a diameter of 19 mm (¾ of an inch), or any other shape with the same area.

Sefer Yere'im[12] writes to be cautious about the size of *ketamim* and to use one's judgment regarding the size of the *ketamim,* as we do not know the size of a *gris.* According to this view, it would seem that we may only attribute to lice a *ketem* of a size that lice actually leave, which is very small.[13] However, many *poskim*[14] maintain that we have only the enactment of *Ḥakhamim* as they decreed at their time, and they made no decree against *ketamim* smaller than a *gris,* which is measured as written above.

Naturally, *ketamim* are not perfectly circular; they will usually appear elongated, and one must calculate whether the area of the *ketem* is larger than a *gris.* In cases where it is difficult to assess, the shape of the *ketem* can be traced onto transparent paper and then placed over a *gris*-sized circle. If part of the *ketem* is of a permitted

8. *Niddah* 58b.
9. Rambam, *Mishneh Torah, Hilkhot Issurei Biah* 9:23; Rashba, *Torat Ha-Bayit, bayit* 7, *sha'ar* 4; Rosh, *Niddah* 8:6; etc.
10. *Yoreh De'ah* 190:5.
11. See *Responsa Me'il Tzedakahsiman* 27. Most latter-day *poskim* follow this view.
12. *Sefer Yere'im siman* 26 (in the older printing, *siman* 192), also cited in *Pitḥei Teshuvah, Yoreh De'ah* 190:9. However, some explain that a *ma'akholet,* the insect in question, is actually a pubic louse, which is much larger than a head louse. See *Responsa Bnei Banim* 2:32.
13. This view implies that nowadays, when we do not have body lice that leave *ketamim,* it may not be possible to attribute *ketamim* to lice at all. However, no *posek* rules this way in practice.
14. *Responsa Ḥakham Tzvi siman* 67; *Responsa Ḥatam Sofer, Yoreh De'ah* 2:150 and 182; *Responsa Igrot Moshe, Yoreh De'ah* 3:46; etc. *Ḥatam Sofer* explains that the entire decree of *ketamim* was enacted only because of *taharot,* so that there would be no situation where the woman is deemed *tehorah* while the garment is deemed *tamei niddah.* Accordingly, nowadays, when we do not practice *taharot,* in theory there is no longer reason for the decree. Nevertheless, since it is a decree of *Ḥakhamim,* it cannot be annulled, so we rule based on what *Ḥakhamim* decreed in their time and certainly not more stringently. Ḥazal never prohibited a *ketem* smaller than a gris, and there is no reason for us to do so today, even though we don't have pubic lice today.

color, only the part whose color causes *tum'ah* is considered.[15] A group of small *ketamim*, each of which is no larger than a *gris*, do not combine to cause *tum'ah*.[16] However, if they are connected, even by a *ketem* of a permitted color, they combine to render the woman *niddah*.[17]

A *ketem* that appears on the woman's body, in a place where it can be presumed to have come from her uterus,[18] has a similar status. The *Rishonim* disagreed about whether a *ketem* on the body can be attributed to a louse as well.[19] Rambam[20] wrote that a *ketem* of any size found on the body causes *tum'ah*, but most *Rishonim* disagreed[21] and ruled that *Ḥakhamim* did not decree *tum'ah* on a *ketem* smaller than a *gris*, even when found on the body. *Shulḥan Arukh* (*Yoreh De'ah* 190:6) cites both views: the majority view as the unqualified first position, and Rambam's position as "some say" ("*yesh omrim*"). According to the principles of *pesikah*, it seems that *Shulḥan Arukh* rules in accordance with the first, unqualified position. This is also attested to several paragraphs later (190:8), where *Shulḥan Arukh* cites an additional dispute that is predicated on the ruling that there is a minimum requisite size even for a *ketem* found on the body, thus demonstrating that this is how *Shulḥan Arukh* rules in practice.

Shulḥan Arukh, Yoreh De'ah 190:8, addresses whether small, separate *ketamim* whose combined size is larger than a *gris* render a woman *niddah*. The discussion is based on the statement of R. Yirmiyah in the Gemara.[22] In practice, it was determined that small *ketamim* are not combined when found on a garment, but there is a dispute among the *Rishonim* vis-à-vis *ketamim* found on the body.[23] *Shulḥan Arukh* first cites, without qualification, the position that small *ketamim*

---

15. *Me'il Tzedakah siman* 62.
16. *Yoreh De'ah* 190:8.
17. *Me'il Tzedakah siman* 62.
18. Such as on her hands or thighs, as detailed in *Yoreh De'ah* 190:11.
19. The basis for the discussion about a *ketem* found on the body is *Niddah* 57b. However, there is no discussion there about the size of a *ketem* that causes *tum'ah*.
20. Rambam, *Mishneh Torah, Hilkhot Issurei Biah* 9:6; this also seems to be the view of Rosh (*Niddah* 8:2).
21. Ra'avad's glosses on *Mishneh Torah ad loc*; Ramban and Rashba cited by *Magid Mishneh ad loc.*
22. *Niddah* 58a.
23. According to Rambam and Rosh, a *ketem* of any size that is found on the body renders the woman *niddah*, so the question of combining *ketamim* is irrelevant. Rashba (*Torat Ha-Bayit, bayit* 7, *sha'ar* 4) brings both views, and although he is inclined to decide that small *ketamim* are not combined even when found on the body, he ultimately rules in favor of the stringent view that they are combined. Ra'avad (*Ba'alei Ha-Nefesh, Sha'ar Ha-Ketamim siman* 3) and *Tosafot* (*Niddah* 58, s.v. "*ke-shurah*") rule that *ketamim* found on her body are combined to a size of a *gris*, and *Tur* (*Yoreh De'ah* 190:8–9) also rules accordingly.

are not combined, without distinguishing between the body and a garment, and then cites, as "*yesh omrim*," the position that *ketamim* found on the body are combined. According to the principles of *pesikah*, it seems that *Shulḥan Arukh* rules leniently, in accordance with the unqualified view. However, *Baḥ*[24] rules stringently here, as does *Torat Ha-Shelamim*.[25] Contemporary *poskim* also ruled stringently that small *ketamim* found on the body are combined to meet the requisite size of a *gris*.[26]

The Surface on which the *Ketem* Appears

This question breaks down into two different issues: the material from which the surface is made, and the color of the surface on which the *ketem* was found. *Ḥakhamim* did not apply their decree to a *ketem* found on something that is not susceptible to *tum'ah*, nor did they apply it to a *ketem* found on a colored garment.[27]

A surface that is not susceptible to *tum'ah*

Two main sources discuss a surface that is not susceptible to *tum'ah*:

1. In the Mishnah,[28] R. Neḥemiah cites the principle that any surface not susceptible to *tum'ah* is not susceptible to *ketamim*. In the ensuing Gemara, a Tannaitic view disputing the words of R. Neḥemiah also appears. However, the Gemara concludes the discussion: "*Ḥakhamim* ruled like R. Neḥemiah."[29] The vast majority of *Rishonim* ruled accordingly,[30] and this is the accepted halakhic ruling.

   Tosafot[31] explain R. Neḥemiah's reasoning: Since the item on which the *ketem* was found is *tahor*, *Ḥakhamim* did not decree *tum'ah* on the woman.

24. *Baḥ, Yoreh De'ah* 190:12.
25. *Torat Ha-Shelamim, Yoreh De'ah* 190:9.
26. *Taharat Ha-Bayit* 1:8:4, p. 377; *Darkhei Taharah*, p. 20, s.v. "*yesh maḥmirim*"; *Shi'urei Shevet Ha-Levi*, summary of *halakhot* 190:8. R. Wosner notes in paragraph 4 of his summary that if there are two small *ketamim* on the body that seem like separate *ketamim* (for example, they are not in the same area), one may be lenient when necessary. R. Ovadiah Yosef explains in a note why the *Aḥaronim* deviated in this instance from the accepted *kelalei pesikah* regarding a view cited as "*yesh omrim*."
27. *Shulḥan Arukh* and Rema, *Yoreh De'ah* 190:10.
28. *Niddah* 59b.
29. Ibid. 60b.
30. *Bet Yosef, Yoreh De'ah* 190:10 brings Ra'avad (*Ba'alei Ha-Nefesh, Sha'ar Ha-Ketamim*, p. 59) as the sole authority who does not rule accordingly.
31. *Niddah* 58a, s.v. "*Ke-Rabi Neḥemiah de-amar kol davar she-eino mekabel tum'ah*."

Ran writes similarly[32] that the entire basis for the decree on *ketamim* concerns *taharot* and the garment. In other words, the accepted halakhic ruling is that "the place of the uterus is *tamei*," and so any blood that issues from it is *tamei*. Therefore, blood that originated from the woman's uterus imparts *tum'ah* to a garment *mi-de'Orayta*. However, when the bleeding is not accompanied by *hargashah*, it does not render the woman *niddah mi-de'Orayta*. Thus, the woman is only *niddah* due to the garment; *Ḥakhamim* decreed her *niddah* lest one come to treat the garment as *tahor*. However, when the surface on which the blood appears is not susceptible to *tum'ah*, the woman is also not *teme'ah*.[33]

2. At the end of the Gemara's discussion of "a woman who sees a *ketem*,"[34] R. Ashi asserts that Shmuel's statement, "If she examined the ground, sat on it, and found blood, she is *tehorah*...," corroborates the aforementioned view of R. Neḥemiah.

Nowadays, the discussion regarding surfaces that are not susceptible to *tum'ah* arise primarily in the context of questions about *ketamim* found on toilet paper, a panty liner, a synthetic fabric, or a toilet seat.[35]

A colored surface

The source for the leniency regarding a *ketem* found on a colored garment is a *baraita* in *Niddah* 61b, in which *tanna kamma* deems it *tamei* and R. Natan (R. Yonatan) deems it *tahor*. Ramban[36] rules stringently, in accordance with *tanna kamma*, whereas Rosh[37] and Rambam[38] rule leniently, in accordance with R. Yonatan. Rashba[39] adopts an intermediate view: one may be lenient with regard to *ketamim*, but one who practices stringently is commendable ("*ha-maḥmir tavo alav berakhah*").

In the *baraita*, R. Yonatan mentions wearing a colored garment as an enactment ("*takanah*") intended to save the woman from the *tum'ah* of *ketamim*. The Gemara

32. *Ḥiddushei Ha-Ran, Niddah* 57b.
33. *Noda Bi-Yehudah* 1:52.
34. *Niddah* 57b–58b.
35. For an expanded discussion of these topics, see below, *Siman* 27: Blood on Toilet Paper; *Siman* 44: Staining on a Panty Liner or Synthetic Clothing; and *Siman* 3: Blood in Urine during Pregnancy.
36. *Hilkhot Niddah* 4:6.
37. *Niddah* 9:1b.
38. *Mishneh Torah, Hilkhot Issurei Biah* 9:7.
39. *Torat Ha-Bayit Ha-Katzar, bayit* 7, *sha'ar* 4, at the end.

discusses whether a woman is obligated to wear colored garments or is merely permitted to do so. Rambam rules in accordance with R. Yonatan, that wearing colored clothes is a *takanah*. *Bet Yosef* rejects the view of Rambam and defines the wearing of colored garments as a *heter*. Rema, in his glosses, cites Rambam and mentions wearing colored garments as a *takanah*: "The woman should therefore wear colored garments, in order to save her from *ketamim*."[40]

The *Rishonim* and *Aḥaronim* dispute whether the Gemara's leniency for a colored garment applies only to *taharot* or whether it can also permit a woman to her husband.[41] Furthermore, some distinguish between a *ketem* found on a form-fitting undergarment and one found on a loose-fitting garment.[42]

In any case, most *Aḥaronim* rely on the ruling of *Shulḥan Arukh* and Rema and deem a *ketem* on a colored garment to be *tahor*.[43]

According to many *poskim*, any color, even a pale color, is considered "colored." However, some treat very pale colors (cream, pale yellow) as white, and therefore, *lekhatḥilah*, if there is another option, it is better not to use them.[44] A woman can therefore wear an undergarment of any other color, even a pale color, in order to

40. Rema, *Yoreh De'ah* 190:10.

41. *Dagul Me-Revavah* on *Shulḥan Arukh, Yoreh De'ah* 190, s.v. "*al begged tzavu'a*" states: "I am astonished that he cites no one who disagrees." He mentions *Hagahot Maimoniyot, Hilkhot Issurei Biah* 9:6, which states in the name of Rabbenu Simḥah and Ra'avan that the Gemara only stated this ruling with regard to *taharot*. Ramban is also stringent on this matter, and it is difficult to rule leniently against three such weighty authorities. *Birkei Yosef* on Rema's gloss to *Yoreh De'ah* 190:10 quotes R. David Corinaldi, who attacks *Shulḥan Arukh* on this point. However, Ḥida (the author of *Birkei Yosef*) himself disagrees with R. Corinaldi and agrees with the lenient ruling of *Shulḥan Arukh* on colored garments.

42. *Responsa Ḥatam Sofer, Yoreh De'ah siman* 161 rules stringently about a form-fitting garment. But see *Responsa Ayalah Sheluḥah*, which states, concerning the ruling of *Ḥatam Sofer*: "There is no room for this stringency. Rather, all of Israel follows Rema ('*yotze'im be-yad* Rema,' a familiar play on Shemot 14:8) that a woman should wear colored clothing, even form-fitting garments." *Responsa Yagel Yaakov*, in the glosses on *Shulḥan Arukh siman* 190, states that *Ḥatam Sofer* apparently meant that a woman should not wear colored garments during her *yemei libun* to save herself from *ketamim*, and is not discussing being stringent about this at other times, as this is against the straightforward meaning of *Shulḥan Arukh*. See also *Me'il Tzedakah siman* 62, which rules leniently on this matter.

43. An expanded discussion of the two points mentioned above (in nn. 65 and 66) and the rulings of the *Aḥaronim* can be found in: *Taharat Ha-Bayit*, 1:8:6, p. 387; *Shi'urei Shevet Ha-Levi* 190:10:4–8; *Taharah Ke-Halakhah* 3:58 pp. 77–79.

44. *Shi'urei Shevet Ha-Levi* 190:4, p. 170.

monitor her status. Using a panty liner can also be helpful in cases of light bleeding not accompanied by a *hargashah*.[45]

A woman who becomes *niddah* from a *ketem* must count, perform *bedikot,* and immerse like an actual *niddah,*[46] but she need not calculate *onot perishah.*

O.K. and N.L.

45. See below, *Siman* 44: Staining on a Panty Liner or Synthetic Clothing.

46. *Shulḥan Arukh* and Rema, *Yoreh De'ah* 190:1. Counting like an actual *niddah* entails, for Ashkenazic women, waiting five days and then counting seven *neki'im,* and for Mizraḥi women, observing one of several possible traditions. See below, *Siman* 57: Waiting before the Seven *Neki'im* after a Stain.

Siman 5

Blood on an Ultrasound Transducer

Question

I am in my 14th week of pregnancy. After a vaginal ultrasound examination, I saw that there was blood on the transducer. The doctor informed me that the cervix is closed and that the blood apparently came from the outside of the cervix. Am I *niddah*? Can I rely on the doctor, who is not religious?

Answer

You are not *niddah*. In this case, you may rely on the doctor's statement that the blood you saw is not from the uterus, and that the bleeding was apparently from an irritation caused by the transducer.[1]

Halakhic Expansion

A vaginal ultrasound examination is used to scan the pelvic organs, including the uterus, cervix, fallopian tubes, and ovaries. To perform this examination, a transducer shaped like a short rod is inserted into the vagina. Viewing the uterus and cervix by means of ultrasound can provide the information that the cervix is closed and that there is no reason to suspect a uterine source of bleeding.

---

1. The vaginal lining is likely to be drier than usual and more sensitive to the penetration of a foreign body during pregnancy or while taking hormonal contraceptives.

Although *Rishonim* and *Aḥaronim* have discussed, and limited, the trustworthiness of doctors,[2] a doctor is trusted when reporting an obvious finding that can be seen via ultrasound, even if he is not a Torah-observant individual,[3] as he is not interpreting the findings but merely reporting what he sees clearly.

With the insertion of an object into the vagina, there are indeed grounds for concern that the bleeding was accompanied by a *hargashah*,[4] and the doctor did not determine that there is a bleeding wound.[5] Nevertheless, in the present case, we factor in the doctor's testimony that the uterus is closed and not bleeding, the woman's status as *mesuleket damim* (amenorrheic), and the certain knowledge that a foreign object of the type that can cause a minor wound was inserted into the vagina.[6]

Therefore, the blood can be attributed to the possibility that the woman was abraded during the insertion of the transducer into the vagina.

R.S.F.

2. See below, *Siman* 16: Observation of Blood by a Physician during the Postpartum Examination.
3. The trustworthiness of a Jewish doctor who is not God-fearing, or of a non-Jewish doctor, is discussed by the *poskim* in the context of treating a *ro'ah meḥamat tashmish* (a woman who bleeds from intercourse). From the perspective of trusting a single witness, who can be relied upon concerning prohibitions, the doctor's statement would seem to be unacceptable. Nevertheless, cases in which the doctor actually sees, assisted by a device, and merely reports the reality before him, are different. Such cases are defined as "matters that will be disclosed" (i.e., they can be reexamined, even if by means of a device), and in such cases, even a non-Jewish physician is trusted. See *Responsa Maharsham* 1:24 and 2:72 and 101; *Responsa Mishpetei Uziel*, vol. 2, *Yoreh De'ah siman* 26; *Shi'urei Shevet Ha-Levi* 187:8:3. See also *Badei Ha-Shulḥan* 187:8, elucidations, s.v. "*ve-im tir'eh ishah.*"
4. See below, *Siman* 60: Finding Blood on a Diaphragm.
5. See below, *Siman* 21: Attributing Blood to a *Petza* during the Seven *Neki'im*.
6. Personal communication with R. Warhaftig.

Siman 6

Bleeding from Placenta Previa

Question

I am in my 22nd week of pregnancy, and recently went on bed rest because of bleeding. During an ultrasound examination, it was ascertained that the bleeding is due to placenta previa.[1] Am I *niddah*, or can the bleeding be attributed to *dam makkah*?

Answer

Placental bleeding can stem from various causes, and the halakhic ruling will depend on the cause of the bleeding. If the source of the bleeding is from the placenta itself, it is considered *dam makkah* (blood from a wound) and does not cause *tum'ah*. In contrast, if the bleeding is caused by placental abruption from the uterine wall, the blood is considered *niddah* blood.

In some cases of placenta previa, the source of the bleeding is in the placenta itself, resulting from pressure on its blood vessels caused by the abnormal location of the placenta.

---

1. Placenta previa is a placenta that lies just above the cervix and blocks the opening of the uterus. Any contact with a placenta previa is liable to cause bleeding and harm the placenta. Placental abruption is a condition in which the placental membranes separate from the uterine wall, whereas under normal conditions, the placenta is hermetically attached to the uterine wall. Placental abruption can be partial or complete, and it generally causes bleeding. Aside from the halakhic question, even if the woman is not *niddah*, the couple need ascertain whether, from a medical perspective, intercourse is permitted. For further information, see Medical Appendix II: Pregnancy.

Therefore, you need to ascertain medically what is causing your bleeding. If it is ascertained that the bleeding is from the placenta only, it can be attributed to a *makkah* and you are *tehorah*. If there is a possibility that the bleeding is from the uterine walls or the membranes between the uterus and the placenta, then you are *niddah*.

Halakhic Expansion

A pregnant woman is considered *mesuleket damim* (amenorrheic).[2] However, if she nevertheless experiences uterine bleeding[3] during pregnancy, it renders her *niddah*[4] unless it can be attributed to a *makkah* either inside or outside the uterus. As part of its discussion of a *ro'ah meḥamat tashmish* (a woman who bleeds from intercourse), the Gemara[5] cites a *baraita* that notes the possibility of attributing the bleeding to a *makkah*. *Shulḥan Arukh* rules accordingly.[6] Rema[7] however limits the attribution of bleeding to a *makkah* to specific situations. However, in the present case of a pregnant woman who is considered *mesuleket damim* and experiences a blood flow, it is clear that, if a medical examination shows that the bleeding was caused by a wound,[8] she may attribute the bleeding to the lesion.

Contemporary *poskim*[9] discuss the situation in which a woman experiences bleeding due to placenta previa, and they ruled as written above, that if the source of the bleeding is from the placenta only, it can be attributed to a lesion, and the woman is *tehorah*. *Nishmat Avraham* writes that if an ultrasound examination[10] shows placenta previa, then it is almost entirely certain (99% of cases after

---

2. Once three months have passed. For further discussion of this topic, see above, *Siman* 2: *Onot Perishah* at the Beginning of Pregnancy.
3. This refers to bleeding accompanied by a *hargashah* or to a flow of blood, not to blood that is evaluated according to the laws of *ketamim*.
4. It is indeed impossible for a woman to experience menstrual bleeding during pregnancy; nevertheless, the basic *halakhah* is that any uterine blood makes a woman *niddah*, not only menstrual blood.
5. *Niddah* 66a: "If she has a lesion in that place, she attributes to her lesion."
6. *Yoreh De'ah* 187:5. For further discussion of attribution to a uterine lesion, see below, *Siman* 21: Attributing Blood to a *Petza* during the Seven *Neki'im*.
7. Ibid.
8. Sometimes such a *petza* can be detected via ultrasound, but this depends on the expertise of the doctor or technician performing the examination.
9. *Nishmat Avraham, Yoreh De'ah* 187:5:2, relying on rulings the author obtained from R. Y. Neuwirth and R. Y.S. Elyashiv. This is also the ruling of R. Dr. Mordechai Halperin in his article, "The Status of a Woman with Placenta Previa and Placental Abruption," *Haberakhah* 8 (Tevet 5771), pp. 74–77.
10. As stated above in note 8, one should be cautious about relying on an ultrasound examination alone.

three months of pregnancy, and a very high likelihood before that as well) that the bleeding is from the placenta and not the uterine walls, due to an abnormality in the blood vessels stemming from the unusual placement of the placenta. The *Nishmat Avraham* turned to R. Yehoshua Neuwirth and to R. Yosef Shalom Elyashiv, who both ruled that in such a situation, the blood is from a lesion, and the woman is *tehorah*.

R. Dr. Mordechai Halperin[11] writes that one may attribute to a lesion only when there is clearly trauma to the placental tissue as a result of contact with it. This is common in cases of placenta previa because of its exposed location at the opening of the uterus. However, according to R. Halperin, if there was no injury or trauma to the placenta itself, and there is nevertheless uterine bleeding, then one should not be lenient.

In contrast, if the source of the bleeding is placental abruption from the uterus, or partial abruption of the placental membranes, the woman is rendered *teme'ah* like a *niddah*.[12] *Nishmat Avraham* writes that this is the case because the woman is considered to be starting to miscarry, even though it is possible that the bleeding will stop and the pregnancy will continue normally. Alternatively, it is possible to claim, that as long as the fetus has not emerged, the halakhic status of a miscarriage does not apply. According to R. Halperin, the bleeding from placental abruption can be defined as *dam koshi* (blood of labor),[13] which under certain conditions does not make a woman *niddah*. However, since these conditions are rarely met, the bleeding should be considered uterine, which makes a woman *teme'ah mi-de'Orayta*.[14]

---

11. "Placenta Previa and Placental Abruption," cited in note 9. *Nishmat Avraham* does not draw this distinction. He apparently holds that any bleeding that clearly came only from the placenta is considered "blood from a lesion," even if there was no external trauma.
12. *Nishmat Avraham*, loc. cit., relying on R. Y. Neuwirth; R. M. Halperin, above.
13. "*Dam koshi*" is continual prepartum blood flow due to the fetus and not due to the woman. Such blood does not make the woman *teme'ah zavah*. Nowadays it is difficult to define exactly what this blood is.
14. R. Halperin, cited in n. 9. *Dam koshi* is mentioned in Mishnah *Niddah* 4:4–5 and in Gemara *Niddah* 36b and 38b. It is very difficult to distinguish it from bleeding during labor or during miscarriage, which always make a woman *niddah*. Moreover, while *dam koshi* is *tahor*, according to the Mishnah and Gemara, this is the case only during the days of *zivah* and not during the days of *niddah*, it is not possible nowadays, after the *ḥumra* of R. Zeira, to deem a woman *tehorah* by virtue of this definition. In my view, it should still be determined whether, according to medical data and halakhic definitions, this is considered *dam makkah* or not. See also *Orot Ha-Taharah*, p. 185, n. 57, which remains inconclusive about this matter and states that it requires further study.

R. Yaakov Warhaftig[15] does not accept these distinctions. In his view, bleeding that originates from the uterine walls causes *tum'ah*, but bleeding that originates strictly from the placenta or its membranes can be considered blood from a lesion and does not cause *tum'ah*. Nevertheless, in cases of uncertainty, one should be stringent.

N.L.

15. Personal communication with the writer.

Siman 7

Bleeding after Cervical Cerclage

Question

I am in my 22nd week of pregnancy. Since I am already dilating, a cervical cerclage was performed to close the opening. After the suturing, I experienced mild bleeding and also found *ketamim*. May I presume that the bleeding is *dam makkah*, or am I *niddah*?

Answer

Cervical cerclage, stitching the cervix closed, is performed when the cervix dilates in the early stages of pregnancy, putting the pregnancy at risk. This is a surgical procedure that causes cervical bleeding. This blood is *dam makkah* and thus does not render a woman *niddah*. It is worth asking the doctor who performed the procedure how long the bleeding could continue, in order to know until what point you may continue attributing bleeding and stains to this procedure.

Halakhic Expansion

The Gemara in *Niddah*[1] states: "*Ḥakhamim* taught... and if she has a *makkah* (lesion) in that place, she attributes the blood to her lesion ... and a woman is trusted to say, 'I have a lesion in the uterus, from which blood comes.'"[2] This *baraita* discusses bleeding experienced as a result of marital relations (*ro'ah meḥamat tashmish*)

1. 65b-66a.
2. The laws of a *makkah* are addressed at length in *Siman* 50: Insertion of an IUD during the Seven *Neki'im*. Therefore, only the main points will be discussed here.

and asserts that when there is known to be a lesion in that area, one may conclude that this is not *niddah* blood, and attribute the bleeding to the lesion. Even though the Gemara is dealing with bleeding that appears after relations, this *baraita* also serves as the source for discussions of *dam makkah* that appears under other circumstances.

Tur rules accordingly:[3] "If she has a *makkah* in that place, we attribute [the bleeding] to the blood of her lesion." The *Rishonim* and *Aḥaronim* differed regarding the degree of certainty required for attribution to a lesion.[4] According to *Shulḥan Arukh*, following *Tur*, knowledge that a lesion exists is sufficient in order to attribute the bleeding to it.[5]

Rema[6] divides this law into several different situations:

1. A woman who has a *veset kavu'a* may attribute [the bleeding] to her *makkah* when it is not the time of her *veset*, even if she does not know whether this lesion normally bleeds – that is, even if there is no absolute certainty that this type of lesion bleeds.
2. A woman without a *veset kavu'a*, where it is uncertain whether the blood is uterine or vaginal, may attribute the bleeding to her lesion by virtue of a double uncertainty (*sfek sfeika*): perhaps the bleeding is vaginal, and even if it is uterine, perhaps it is from a lesion.
3. A woman without a *veset kavu'a*, even if the blood is uterine, if she knows for certain that this lesion bleeds, she may attribute the bleeding to her lesion. *Shakh*[7] comments on this that it is sufficient to know that this lesion is one that normally bleeds; she need not know that the lesion is bleeding at that very moment.
4. At the time of her *veset*, or during the *onah beinonit*, she cannot attribute bleeding to her lesion.

In the present case, when it is known for certain that there is a lesion resulting from the sutures, and the woman has the status of *mesuleket damim* due to her pregnancy, she may attribute the bleeding to the lesion even according to Rema and *Shakh*, therefore the bleeding does not render her *niddah*.

O.K.

---

3. *Yoreh De'ah* 187:5.
4. See below, *Siman* 50.
5. *Yoreh De'ah* 187:5.
6. Ibid.
7. Ibid., 24.

Siman 8

Mikveh Immersion during Pregnancy

Question

I experienced bleeding during the fifth month of pregnancy, and I am scheduled to immerse in the *mikveh* tonight. I'm concerned about sitting at length in the bath to prepare for immersion, and I'm also worried about infection from the immersion itself. Are there any leniencies in the requirements of preparation and immersion for a pregnant woman?

Answer

A pregnant woman who becomes *niddah* must count seven *neki'im* and then immerse, like any woman who is *niddah*. Preparation includes a thorough *ḥafifah* in order to clean the entire body. There is no obligation to bathe specifically in a bathtub to prepare for immersion; the preparations can be done in the shower as well. During the immersion itself, it is permissible for you to immerse only once, even if your custom is to immerse several times.

Medically, it is recommended that a pregnant woman refrain from spending a long time in very hot water – higher than 39°C (102°F). The water of the *mikveh* should not be heated to that temperature, so from that perspective, there should be no problem.

Mikveh water is generally changed very frequently, sometimes daily. Some *mikva'ot* have an advanced filtration system. The water also contains disinfectants, such as chlorine. Therefore, you need not worry about contracting an infection during immersion. If you wish, you can coordinate with the *balanit* (*mikveh* attendant) to be the first to immerse after the water is changed or after the filtration system has been operating for several hours.

Halakhic Expansion

A pregnant woman must avoid spending time in water heated above 39°C (102°F), especially during the first trimester. Prolonged immersion in such heat – such as in a jacuzzi – may increase risk of miscarriage or fetal damage.[1] In contrast, immersion in a *mikveh* heated to a standard temperature, and even spending time in a warm bath while preparing for immersion in the *mikveh*, do not constitute any risk.

The water in a *mikveh* immersion pool is changed frequently. In Israel, the regulations of the Ministry of Health, the body that oversees *mikva'ot*, require the addition of a disinfectant to the water. In light of this, there is no reason to be concerned about contracting an infection during immersion.

The Law of *Ḥafifah*

Mi-de'Orayta, a woman must inspect her hair and body before immersing to confirm that there is nothing that constitutes a *ḥatzitzah* (barrier, obstruction) between her and the water of the *mikveh*.[2] Ezra Ha-Sofer ordained that she must also wash her hair. *Tosafot* quotes the *maḥzor* of R. Shemariah as stating explicitly in Rashi's name that, according to Ezra's ordinance, the woman must wash her entire body.[3] But the *Ba'alei Ha-Tosafot* themselves, as well as most *Rishonim*, disagree, maintaining that Ezra instituted an obligation to wash the hair only, and this is implied by the words of Rashi himself.[4] Albeit *Shulḥan Arukh* rules that she should wash her body and hair in hot water,[5] and this is customary. However,[6] Ra'avad explains that only washing the hair, not the body, is necessary for the immersion to be valid.[7]

A woman is required to wash in hot water to remove *ḥatzitzot*[8] and loosen knots in her hair.[9] The water need not be very hot; the intent of the Gemara

1. See https://academic.oup.com/aje/article/158/10/931/80747.
2. *Bava Kamma* 82a.
3. *Tosafot* on *Niddah* 66b, s.v. "*im samukh le-ḥafifah tavlah.*"
4. *Tosafot* on *Niddah* 66b, s.v. "*im samukh le-ḥafifah tavlah*"; on *Bava Kamma* 82a, s.v. "*ve-shetehe*"; Rashi on *Bava Kamma ad loc.*, s.v. "*ha-ishah ḥofefet.*"
5. *Yoreh De'ah* 199:1.
6. See *Taharat Ha-Bayit*, 3 *Dinei Tevilah*, 2, p. 237.
7. *Ba'alei Ha-Nefesh*, *Sha'ar Ha-Tevilah*, *Hilkhot Ḥafifah*, p. 82.
8. *Niddah* 66b and Rashi *ad loc.*; *Yoreh De'ah* 199:1–2.
9. *Bet Ha-Beḥirah* on *Niddah* 66b.

is rather that the water not be cold.[10] Additionally, the *ḥafifah* need not be performed specifically in a bathtub. It is indeed customary nowadays to bathe in a bathtub in order to clean the body thoroughly. However, a woman who prefers to shower may do so, even if she is not pregnant, as long as she cleans her entire body well.[11]

Is there an obligation to set aside a specific amount of time for *ḥafifah*? The *Rishonim* disagree as to whether it is preferable to wash at night, right before immersing,[12] or during the day, lest at night she will be in a hurry to return home and not do a thorough *ḥafifah*.[13] Therefore, to comply with both views, it is customary to begin *ḥafifah* during the day, continue with preparations until nightfall, and then immerse.[14] Maharshal writes that if she sets aside an hour for a thorough *ḥafifah*, she may even do it at night, as ordained by the rabbis of Italy due to the modesty of women who wished to conceal their immersion.[15] *Shakh* rules accordingly.[16] *Shi'urei Shevet Ha-Levi* explains that the worthy custom of setting aside an hour applies only to a woman who performs *ḥafifah* at night, when she is in a hurry to get home, although some have this custom during the day as well. However, the hour includes all preparations for immersion, not only the time spent in the bath.[17] *Igrot Moshe* states that a woman whose hair is not long and who showers daily, if she knows that she does not need an hour for preparation, she should set aside the amount of time she needs to perform the preparations carefully and thoroughly.[18]

---

10. See *Shi'urei Shevet Ha-Levi* 199:1:8 and 199:2:2. *Roke'aḥ siman* 312 writes in context of immersing during the Nine Days that even lukewarm water is sufficient. The *Aḥaronim* ruled thus with respect to the rest of the year. See *Taharat Ha-Bayit*, 3: *Dinei Tevilah* 4, p.200; *Darkhei Taharah*, chapter 15, p. 142, based on *Darkhei Teshuvah* 199:13.
11. *Badei Ha-Shulḥan, Hilkhot Tevilah* 199:17 infers from the language of *Shulḥan Arukh*, "and she rinses" ("*ve-tishtof*"), that it refers to pouring water over the body; he did not write "*ve-tirḥatz*" ("and she bathes") which would indicate entering the water. See also *Shi'urei Shevet Ha-Levi* 199:1:8. *Mishmeret Ha-Taharah ad loc.* 2:2 writes that a sickly woman, for whom bathing is harmful, may, instead of washing her body with water, wipe her whole body with a wet washcloth and immerse in the *mikveh* after washing her hair and inspecting her body carefully.
12. Cited in the name of *She'iltot* of R. Aḥai Gaon by *Tosafot* on *Niddah* 68a, s.v. "*kakh amru.*"
13. Rashi on *Niddah* 68a, s.v. "*ve-tame'ah al atzmekha he'akh ishah.*"
14. *Yoreh De'ah* 199:3.
15. *Responsa Maharshal siman* 6.
16. *Shakh* 199:3:6. See also *Responsa Rema siman* 18, in the name of Maharam Padua and Mahari Mintz.
17. *Shi'urei Shevet Ha-Levi* 199:3, s.v. "*Shakh* 6."
18. *Igrot Moshe, Yoreh De'ah* 2:81.

Shulḥan Arukh rules that a *mikveh* should not be filled with warm water because of the "bathhouse decree" – lest people mistakenly immerse in a heated pool that is not a kosher *mikveh.*[19] However, *Responsa Nivḥar Mi-Kessef* cites the testimony of R. Eliezer ben Arḥa that, at the end of his life, the author of *Shulḥan Arukh* retracted his requirement of immersion in cold water.[20] Nevertheless, it is proper that the *mikveh* water not be too hot.[21]

The Number of Immersions

There are various customs regarding the number of times a woman immerses,[22] but, according to basic halakhah, a woman fulfills her obligation with a single immersion. In a case where a woman wishes to limit her time in the hot water, it is sufficient for her to immerse once.[23]

S.K. and Editors

19. *Yoreh De'ah* 201:75.
20. *Responsa Nivḥar Mi-Kessef, Yoreh De'ah siman* 17, cited in *Taharat Ha-Bayit,* 3: *Dinei Tevilah* 1, p.227.
21. See *Taharat Ha-Bayit,* 3: *Dinei Tevilah* 1, pp. 224–29; and also 2:15:1, pp. 524–26; *Shi'urei Shevet Ha-Levi* 199:1:8.
22. *Tosefta Mikva'ot,* at the end of chapter 5, states that it is improper ("*meguneh*") to immerse twice. The reason is cited by *Kessef Mishneh* (*Mishneh Torah, Hilkhot Mikva'ot* 1:9): It looks like she is immersing to cool off. See also *Dagul Me-Revavah, Yoreh De'ah siman* 200. However, many women nowadays have the custom to immerse twice and to recite the *berakhah* between the two immersions, as cited in *Ba'er Heitev, Yoreh De'ah* 200:1 in the name of *Shelah,* in order to reconcile between *Shulḥan Arukh,* which rules that the *berakhah* is recited before immersing, and Rema, who rules that the *berakhah* is recited after immersing. *Sefer Ḥasidim siman* 394 states that women generally immerse three times. *Taharat Ha-Bayit* 2:15:5, pp. 546–47, cites *Ben Ish Ḥai, Shemini, siman* 19, that the custom of the women in Iraq is to immerse three times. It also cites a custom to immerse seven times.
23. She does not require *hatarat nedarim* to change her custom. See *Shi'urei Taharah,* p. 463; *Darkhei Taharah,* chapter 18, p. 173.

Part II

Birth

Siman 9

Cervical Dilation and the Onset of Labor

Question

As part of prenatal care, I underwent an internal examination this week. The nurse said that I am 4 cm dilated, even though contractions have not yet begun. I was discharged, and am waiting to give birth. Am I considered *niddah* due to the dilation, even without contractions?

Answer

In the situation described, you are not yet *niddah*, as long as you have not experienced bleeding. A dilation of 4 cm[1] is considered medically appropriate for the onset of labor, but it is possible to have cervical dilation long before birth.[2]

In such a situation, when the dilation is not dynamic, that is, it is not gradually widening, is not accompanied by contractions, and labor has not yet begun, the woman is not *niddah*. Even if contractions began and then stopped, and it becomes clear in hindsight that labor has not yet begun, the woman is not *niddah*.

1. See below, *Siman* 50: Insertion of an IUD during the Seven *Neki'im*, regarding the principle, "There can be no opening of the uterus without blood." This principle applies only when an object is inserted into or exits the uterus; consequently, cervical dilation resulting from uterine contractions prior to the baby's delivery does not render one *niddah*. It should also be noted that the medical term "dilation" relates to the opening of the external os of the cervix, whereas *halakhah* refers to the opening of the internal os, and there is sometimes a disparity between them.
2. This condition is found primarily among women who have delivered several times.

Halakhic Expansion

The Gemara in *Shabbat*[3] discusses a *yoledet* (a woman in the process of, or immediately after, giving birth) with respect to violating Shabbat to save a life. We are obligated to violate Shabbat on behalf of a *yoledet,* whether or not she makes such a request. A woman is considered a *yoledet* from the point that her uterus is open, and this is indicated in three ways: (1) She is sitting on the birthing stool; (2) blood is trickling down; (3) she can no longer walk on her own and her friends support her.[4] Ramban[5] rules that we violate Shabbat even if only one of these indications applies, because we rule leniently when there is *safek pikuaḥ nefesh,* uncertainty in questions of saving a life. His view is cited by *Tur,* and *Shulḥan Arukh* rules accordingly.[6] However, there is a dispute among *Aḥaronim* as to whether uterine opening during labor with respect to violating Shabbat to save a life is identical with the uterine opening that renders a woman *niddah.*

The author of *Naḥalat Shiv'ah*[7] was asked about a woman who thought she was about to give birth and called a midwife to examine her,[8] but ultimately did not give birth. He ruled that the very act of sitting on the birthing stool is considered the onset of labor and causes her to be *niddah,* even though she did not actually give birth until several weeks later.

Many *Aḥaronim* disputed him:

Ḥavat Da'at[9] writes that defining a woman as ill for the purpose of saving a life on Shabbat does not constitute evidence that she is *niddah,* because the halakhic principle that the uterus opening is always accompanied by bleeding applies only if something actually exited the uterus.[10] Therefore, we rule leniently when it

---

3. *Shabbat* 129a.
4. The *Rishonim* disagree about the chronological order of these indications within the birthing process. Rif writes that the second indication precedes the first, and in practice one should wait until she sits on the birthing stool, which is after bleeding has begun. Rashba wonders why Rif did not rule in accordance with the lenient view (according to the chronological stages that he himself adopted). Indeed, Rambam rules that we violate Shabbat on her behalf from the point where blood begins trickling down. (However, in his commentary on the Mishnah, Rambam reverses the order: first she sits on the birthing stool, then the blood trickles.)
5. *Torat Ha-Adam, Sha'ar Ha-Sakanah, inyan ha-meiḥush,* s.v. "*Shabbat* 129a."
6. *Oraḥ Ḥayim* 330:3.
7. *Responsa Naḥalat Shiv'ah* 2:9, s.v. "*u-matzati remez*"; cited in *Pitḥei Teshuvah, Yoreh De'ah* 194:8.
8. The question mentions that the woman was examined by the midwife, and the author of *Naḥalat Shiv'ah* deems this examination as "sitting on the birthing stool."
9. *Ḥavot Da'at, Yoreh De'ah siman* 194, elucidations 1.
10. He adds that since a woman who gives birth by caesarean section remains *tehorah* from *niddah,* even if she sat on the birthing stool, sitting on the birthing stool alone cannot cause *tum'ah.* It

comes to saving a life, but we do not apply the earliest moment of potential danger to the laws of *tum'ah* and *taharah* as well.

Sidrei Taharah[11] writes that the very fact that she did not give birth proves that there was an error, and the uterus did not open, so she is obviously *tehorah*. He adds that *Kereti U-Feleti*[12] writes that while she is sitting on the birthing stool she must conduct herself as *niddah*, but if it becomes apparent that there was an error, she is *tehorah*.[13]

Shi'urei Shevet Ha-Levi[14] writes that even if there are several centimeters of dilation, the woman should not be deemed *niddah* unless there are frequent contractions, and sometimes, even when there are contractions, she should not be deemed *niddah* unless she is no longer capable of walking.[15]

Therefore, if the woman did not give birth, and so long as there is no bleeding, she should not be deemed *niddah* until the onset of the birth.[16]

Z.B.

---

is worth noting that nowadays, a woman who underwent a caesarean section generally does become *niddah* from postpartum vaginal bleeding.

11. *Yoreh De'ah* 194:25.
12. *Kereti U-Feleti, Tif'eret Yisrael siman* 1, at the end; also cited in *Sidrei Taharah*, loc. cit.
13. See also *Igrot Moshe, Yoreh De'ah* 2:76, s.v. "*be-devar ishah,*" which adduces a practical ramification between these two views with respect to *bedikah*.
14. 194:2:4, s.v. "*le-fetiḥat ha-kever,*" pp. 244–45.
15. R. Mordechai Eliyahu (*Darkhei Taharah*, new [5767] edition, p. 138) rules that dilation of 4 cm is the onset of labor and makes the woman *niddah* due to the opening of the uterus, even if she did not subsequently give birth. However, the other *Aḥaronim* did not specify this measure; see, for example, *Taharah Ke-Halakhah*, p. 175. Note that, in most cases, such dilation indeed leads to birth or to medical intervention that will enable birth, and it seems to me that this is the reason for R. M. Eliyahu's stringent ruling on this question. However, see R. Baruch and Michal Finkelstein's *Be-Sha'ah Tovah*, p. 145, nn. 4 and 6, which states in the name of R. M. Eliyahu that dilation of this size, when it is not dynamic and does not lead to birth, does not render her *niddah*.
16. A distinction should be made here between two situations that can render a woman *niddah*: one is the opening of the uterus ("*petiḥat ha-kever*"), which we addressed in this *siman*. The second is the *tum'ah* of childbirth ("*tum'at leidah*"), which applies only when the baby emerges. For discussion of this question, see below, *Siman* 12: Does the Rupture of Membranes Render a Woman Niddah?

Siman 10

Does Expulsion of the Mucus Plug Render a Woman Niddah?

Question

I am pregnant, and my due date is in a week. I am quite certain that the mucus plug already came out, because I found a transparent, yellowish discharge. Am I at the beginning of labor, and do my husband and I have to separate?

Answer

Loss of the mucus plug is generally a sign of impending labor, but it is not necessarily the onset of labor. Therefore, you are not *niddah*. Since the plug is located at the outer end of the cervix, its falling out is not considered the "opening of the uterus."

Nevertheless, there is concern that the source of the secretion you saw was not from the mucus plug, but from the uterus. Therefore, the laws of *ketamim* apply to what you saw (as long as you did not feel a halakhic *hargashah* that would render you *niddah*). Based on your description, the color of the secretion you saw was not a *niddah* color, so you are still *tehorah* and need not observe the *harḥakot* with your husband.

Consult a doctor to clarify whether you may have relations once the mucus plug has been expelled.

Halakhic Expansion

The mucus plug is a viscous, mucous secretion that seals the cervical opening during pregnancy and protects against infection.[1] It can fall out as a single glob or as discharge. When it is expelled, the mucus plug may appear in any of a range of colors: yellow, red, brown, and even clear. It is one of the signs of impending labor. However, labor can develop during the interval that extends from a few hours to two weeks after the mucus plug falls out. Therefore, it is not a clear sign of the onset of labor.[2]

We will address two aspects of this subject: (1) Does losing the mucus plug indicate the onset of labor? (2) Is losing the mucus plug considered an opening of the uterus given its location at the cervical orifice?

Expulsion of the Mucus Plug as the Onset of Labor

The Gemara discusses the classification of a woman as a *yoledet* for the purpose of violating Shabbat to save a life[3] and lists three indications that labor has begun and which warrant violating Shabbat on her behalf.[4] Expulsion of the mucus plug is not one of these indications, and it therefore does not establish the woman as a *yoledet* with respect to violating Shabbat – and likewise not with respect to the *tum'ah* of childbirth.

The Location of the Mucus Plug

The *poskim* disagree about the halakhic location of the mucus plug. Some view it as part of the uterus and thus are concerned that, if the plug falls out as a glob and not as liquid mucus, there is *petiḥat ha-kever*.[5] In *Shi'urei Shevet Ha-Levi*,[6]

---

1. See Medical Appendix II: Pregnancy.
2. It is important to distinguish between the loss of the mucus plug and fresh or considerable bleeding, which may indicate placental abruption, placenta previa, or another condition. In such a case, get to the nearest delivery room as soon as possible.
3. *Shabbat* 129a; see also *Shulḥan Arukh, Oraḥ Ḥayim siman* 331.
4. See further below, *Siman* 12: Does the Rupture of Membranes Render a Woman Niddah? And above, *Siman* 9: Cervical Dilation and the Onset of Labor.
5. *Niddah* 21a records a disagreement about whether there can be *petiḥat ha-kever* without bleeding, that is, whether the very fact of the cervix dilating causes *tum'ah* even if no blood is found. The view of most *Rishonim* is that *petiḥat ha-kever* cannot happen without bleeding. See Ra'avad's glosses to Rambam and *Ba'alei Ha-Nefesh, Sha'ar Ha-Perishah siman* 1; Ramban, *Hilkhot Niddah* 3:6 and 7:15; Rosh, *Niddah* 3:1; Rashba, *Torat Ha-Bayit He-Arokh, bayit* 7, *sha'ar* 6, p. 26b. This is the ruling of *Shulḥan Arukh* and Rema, *Yoreh De'ah* 194:2. See also below, *Siman* 50: Insertion of an IUD during the Seven *Neki'im*. Likewise, see there regarding the question of the size necessary to cause *tum'ah* when there is *petiḥat ha-kever* without bleeding.
6. *Niddah*, 194:2:4, s.v. "*pekak*."

R. Wosner writes that one should be concerned for *petiḥat ha-kever* when the mucus plug falls out and "ask a *she'elat ḥakham*," though he does not decide which cases render a woman *niddah* and which do not. Others explain that if the mucus plug came out as a clump and not fluid discharge, it is considered *petiḥat ha-kever* and the woman is *niddah* even if she did not experience bleeding.[7] *Sha'arei Orah*[8] writes that if the expulsion of the mucus plug is accompanied by bleeding, the woman becomes *niddah*.

In contrast, R. Yaakov Warhaftig maintains[9] that since we know nowadays that the mucus plug does not enter the internal os of the cervix, it is clear that it does not come from inside the uterus and does not even open the internal os of the cervix. In light of this, the expulsion of the mucus plug has the status of a *makkah* that, is outside the uterus.[10] Additionally, the concern that there is *petiḥat ha-kever* when a solid piece falls out is primarily referring to when the fetus comes out. The mucus plug is an accumulation of viscous secretions, but is not part of the fetus.

Nevertheless, since it is difficult to distinguish between a regular viscous secretion and the mucus plug, its expulsion is also judged like any other bloody secretion that a woman experiences: a bloody secretion that is accompanied by a *hargashah* makes her *teme'ah mi-de'Orayta*,[11] and a secretion that is not accompanied by a *hargashah* is judged according to the laws of *ketamim*.[12]

---

7. A solid piece expelled from the uterus is considered to have opened the external os and the internal os of the cervix – the opening of the uterus (*petiḥat ha-kever*) – even if no blood is seen. See *Nishmat Avraham, Yoreh De'ah* 194:1:2, in the name of R. Yosef Shalom Elyashiv and R. Yehoshua Neuwirth; *Mar'eh Kohen*, p. 14, n. 6, in the name of R. Wosner (which differs from what is recorded in *Shi'urei Shevet Ha-Levi*, loc. cit.). However, *Minḥat Yitzḥak* 10:31:3 states in the name of *Tiferet Tzvi* that there is no opening of the uterus for the discharge of a piece as small as a finger, and the woman is *tehorah*.
8. P. 246. In his statements, he makes no distinction between bleeding that confers *niddah* status and a *ketem*.
9. R. Warhaftig rules further that when a red-colored glob is discharged onto a white garment, or even if the woman saw it being discharged from her body, when it is clear that it is the mucus plug, she is not *niddah*, because the plug is outside the uterus.
10. See also below, *Siman* 21: Attributing Blood to a *Petza* during the Seven *Neki'im*.
11. *Yoreh De'ah siman* 183. The same applies if she witnessed the blood leaving her body (as learned from *Gilyon Maharsha* 183:2), since anything that comes out of the vagina is presumed to have originated in the uterus (*Mishneh Torah, Hilkhot Issurei Biah* 9:1). This is certainly the rule if she finds the blood through an internal *bedikah* (*Pitḥei Teshuvah* 183:1, s.v. "*she-targish*"). See further below, *Siman* 25: The Law of *Hargashah* (Sensation of Menses).
12. *Yoreh De'ah siman* 190. This is also the ruling in *Orot Ha-Taharah* 17:16.

In the case described in our question, there is no problem, because the color described does not forbid her,[13] neither *mi-de'Orayta* as when one experiences bleeding, nor *mi-deRabanan* as a *ketem*. In other situations, the surface on which the discharge appeared and the size of the discharge should be examined, in accordance with the laws of *ketamim*.[14]

In sum, although the expulsion of the mucus plug portends the impending labor,[15] it is not a clear sign of the onset of labor, like intense contractions, and therefore does not cause the *tum'ah* of childbirth. In light of what we have seen, the expulsion of the plug does not indicate that the uterus has opened (*petiḥat ha-kever*), and it therefore should be judged according to the laws of *ketamim*.[16]

S.K. and N.L.

13. See below, *Siman* 54: Colors on *Bedikah* Cloths.
14. See below, *Siman* 44: Staining on a PantyLiner or Synthetic Clothing.
15. Therefore, one should consult a gynecologist concerning having relations and bathing in a bathtub after the mucus plug falls out.
16. Unless there was a halakhic *hargashah,* in which case any red discharge renders the woman a *niddah mi-de'Orayta.*

Siman 11

Does Membrane Stripping Render a Woman Niddah?

Question

I am in my 41st week of pregnancy and today my doctor offered to perform membrane stripping to induce labor. I was also told that marital relations induce labor. Are my husband and I forbidden to one another after the membrane stripping? If the stripping doesn't work, are we permitted to have marital relations?

Answer

You are approaching birth, *b'sha'ah tovah*.

Stripping is a voluntary procedure in which the doctor separates the membranes of the amniotic sac containing the fetus from the uterine walls. This stimulates the release of prostaglandins, which should help induce labor. Before having the procedure, it is worth discussing its pluses and minuses with the doctor. Stripping may render you *niddah* even if labor has not yet begun. So that you do not become *niddah* unnecessarily, you should clarify details of the procedure with your doctor immediately following the stripping. If the doctor reports that the stripping caused the cervix to dilate beyond 2 cm, the procedure will render you *niddah* even if no bleeding is detected. However, because the procedure involves the doctor sweeping her (gloved) finger between the thin membranes of the amniotic sac in your uterus, it can abrade the area. Therefore, if the doctor reports that the procedure caused cervical bleeding, such bleeding does not render you *niddah*. If the doctor did not manage to widen the opening and you also did not experience any bleeding that would render you *niddah* due to the stripping, the procedure has not rendered you *niddah*.

Regarding marital relations, in a normal pregnancy that is not at risk, marital relations are medically safe as long as your water has not broken. If, according to the circumstances described, you are not *niddah*, there is no halakhic restriction upon marital relations.

Halakhic Expansion

During labor, the body secretes chemical compounds called prostaglandins, whose function is to soften the cervix and allow the baby to pass through. "Stripping" is a mechanical method of induction in which the doctor inserts a finger or two into the cervix and manually attempts to separate the membranes of the amniotic sac from the wall of the uterus. This action causes the release of prostaglandins, which lead to the ripening of the cervix. Sixty to seventy percent of the time, the procedure is effective in accelerating the birth.[1] Stripping can be done only if there is already cervical dilation that enables the doctor to insert a finger or two and, with a circular sweeping action, to separate the membranes. This action can be performed in the delivery room or in the doctor's clinic. Contractions will generally begin within 24 to 72 hours after the procedure. The process is usually painful, and may cause mild bleeding.

We need to determine:

> The status of such bleeding.
>
> Is there concern that the uterus opened ("*petiḥat ha-kever*")?
>
> Does *tum'ah* of a *yoledet* apply as a result of this procedure?

Most *poskim* consider the woman *niddah* after stripping. However, we have clarified the procedure with gynecologists, and it emerges that due to circumstances that differ from woman to woman, it is impossible to generalize regarding whether the procedure renders the woman *niddah* or not, and it is necessary to clarify with the physician what precisely was done in the procedure, and to rule accordingly.[2]

According to doctors, the bleeding that often occurs immediately following the procedure is almost certainly caused by the separation of the amniotic

---

1. Finucane, Elaine M, Murphy, Deirdre J. Biesty, "Membrane Sweeping for Induction of Labour." *Cochrane Database Syst Rev*. Feb 27, 2020; https://www.cochranelibrary.com/cdsr/doi/10.1002/14651858.CD000451.pub3/full.
2. *Orot Ha-Taharah* (19:23, p. 132) does not render the woman *niddah* after stripping if she did not experience bleeding after the procedure.

membranes from the uterine wall. To reach the membranes, the doctor pushes her fingers through the internal opening (os) of the cervix. This opening is not the same opening to which the doctor or midwife is referring when she states that the cervix is dilated.

If the doctor determines that the bleeding comes from a *petza* on the cervix and not from the uterus itself, the blood does not render the woman *niddah.*[3] The doctor cannot always ascertain the source of the bleeding, and therefore, in a case of uncertainty, the woman should be deemed *niddah* as a result of the procedure.[4]

The second question is: Is there a concern that the principle "there is no *petiḥat ha-kever* (opening of the uterus), without blood" applies to this procedure?

The insertion of the fingers and the sweeping motion that are part of the stripping procedure are performed inside the internal os of the cervix. The opening of the external cervical os, called cervical dilation, often precedes labor, and women who have had numerous births can ambulate for a long time in this state. It is not considered part of labor, and it therefore does not render the woman *niddah.*[5]

The minimal dilation necessary to perform membrane stripping is enough to allow the insertion of one finger into the internal cervical os. According to doctors, the action of stripping itself may increase dilation during the procedure.

In cases where the internal os is dilated 2 cm (¾ of an inch) or more, even if the woman is not in active labor, the additional widening of the internal cervical os renders the woman *niddah,* even if it was already "open."

According to the opinions that are not concerned for *petiḥat ha-kever* from the outside in,[6] the insertion of a finger does not render the woman *niddah*. However, since we follow the ruling that is concerned for *petiḥat ha-kever* from the outside

3. If it causes dilation beyond 19 mm (¾ of an inch), then even if the bleeding does not render her *teme'ah,* she is still *niddah* due to *petiḥat ha-kever*. See below.
4. If the bleeding does not begin right after the procedure, but only later, there are grounds for concern that it is a sign of impending labor and was caused by hormonal activity, and not because of the *petza,* that occurred during the stripping. According to R. Dr. Mordechai Halperin, the procedure can cause bleeding that stems from the separation of the amniotic sac from the uterus. In other words, this is the blood of the onset of labor, and such bleeding causes *niddah* status. See his article, "The Status of a Woman with Placenta Previa and Placental Abruption," *Haberakhah* 8 (Tevet 5771), pp. 74–77. Nevertheless, the laws of *ketamim* would apply to this delayed bleeding, and subject to them alone would she be rendered *niddah.*
5. See above, *Siman* 9: Cervical Dilation and the Onset of Labor.
6. See *Responsa Tzitz Eliezer* 10:25:11; *Ḥazon Ish, Yoreh De'ah* 83:2; *Taharat Ha-Bayit* 2:11:7, p. 60.

in,[7] the width of the opening resulting from the stripping becomes relevant to the discussion. If the procedure itself is what widens the opening of the uterus to more than the 19 mm (¾ of an inch) mentioned by R. Moshe Feinstein,[8] stripping renders the woman *niddah* due to *petiḥat ha-kever*. If the doctor avers that she managed to insert her finger but did not widen the opening more than the amount that would render the woman *niddah*, and there is also no uterine bleeding, the woman is not *niddah*.

Regarding the *tum'ah* of a *yoledet*, a woman who has undergone stripping (and who is sometimes ambulatory for several days after the procedure) is no different from any other *yoledet*, who becomes forbidden only once she sits on the birthing stool.[9]

Regarding marital relations as a means to induce labor, it seems that *Ḥakhamim* and medical professionals are in full agreement on this point. The Gemara in *Niddah* (31a) cites a *midrash*: "During the last three months, marital relations are beneficial for the woman and beneficial for the fetus, for as a result the fetus will become fair and energetic." Amongst doctors, there are those who are of the opinion that the prostaglandins in semen and the compounds released during the female orgasm can induce labor.[10]

R.S.F.

---

7. *Noda Bi-Yehudah* 2:120 at the end; *Igrot Moshe, Yoreh De'ah* 1:83; *Responsa Har Tzvi, Yoreh De'ah siman* 152.
8. *Igrot Moshe, Yoreh De'ah* 1:89, writes regarding the minimum amount that if the opening is not thicker than the pinkie finger, we are lenient. He estimated this to be ¾ of an inch (19.05mm).
9. See above, *Siman* 9: Cervical Dilation and the Onset of Labor.
10. For medical studies on this topic, see Kavanagh, J., Kelly, A.J., and Thomas, J. "Sexual Intercourse for Cervical Ripening and Induction of Labour." *Cochrane Database Syst Rev.* 2001; (2):CD003093. It is also possible that substantial massage of the nipples causes the release of oxytocin and can accelerate labor when conditions are ripe. See Kavanagh, J., Kelly, A.J., and Thomas, J. "Breast Stimulation for Cervical Ripening and Induction of Labour." *Cochrane Database Syst Rev.* July 20, 2005; (3):CD003392.

Siman 12

Does the Rupture of Membranes Render a Woman Niddah?

Question

I am in my third pregnancy. During my two previous pregnancies, labor began when the water broke, and we considered ourselves forbidden to one another from that point. Does the water breaking really cause *niddah* status?

Answer

If there is nothing that resembles blood mixed in with the water, the rupture of the membranes ("water breaking") does not render you *niddah*, and you may continue behaving as usual, until the stage of labor in which you become *niddah* by the experience of bleeding or significant dilation. May everything happen in the right time!

Halakhic Expansion

The rupture of the membranes of the amniotic sac ("water breaking") and the flow of amniotic fluid vaginally just prior to the expected onset of labor[1] is an

1. In about 10% of pregnancies, the water breaks before the onset of labor. In most of these cases, the baby is born within 24 hours of the water breaking. However, 5% of such cases occur during earlier weeks of pregnancy, sometimes when the fetus is not yet viable. This situation is called PROM (premature rupture of membranes).

indicator of impending labor.[2] At the time of birth, the *yoledet* becomes forbidden to her husband like a *niddah*, due to the *tum'ah* of childbirth, or even earlier, when her uterus opens.[3] Of course, if a woman experiences bleeding of a *niddah* type, anytime before that she is rendered *niddah*.

The Gemara[4] lists several indicators of impending labor that warrant violation of Shabbat on behalf of the *yoledet*.[5] This Gemara is the basis for the discussion of when a woman is defined as a *yoledet* for the purpose of *tum'ah* as well. Since the rupture of membranes is not mentioned among the indications of impending labor,[6] it would seem that it does not render the woman forbidden.

However, there are grounds to discuss whether the discharge of amniotic fluid attests to dilation that would render the woman *niddah* due to *petiḥat ha-kever*. According to R. Elazar Fleckeles (*Responsa Teshuva Me'ahava*), there is no concern for *petiḥat ha-kever* when what comes from the uterus is not a piece [of flesh] or chunk, but a liquid.[7] Therefore, the discharge of amniotic fluid does not render her *niddah*. On the other hand, there are *poskim* who pronounce a *yoledet niddah* after the rupture of membranes for another reason: perhaps there is blood mixed in, not because of *petiḥat ha-kever*.[8] Some render her *niddah* only if the water gushes out.[9]

2. From a medical perspective, after the rupture of membranes, inducing labor within 24 hours should be considered, as the fetus is exposed to infectants.
3. This is because the accepted ruling is that there can be no opening of the uterus (*petiḥat ha-kever*) without bleeding (*Yoreh De'ah siman* 188). See above, *Siman* 9: Cervical Dilation and the Onset of Labor.
4. *Shabbat* 129a; see also *Shulḥan Arukh, Oraḥ Ḥayim* 330:3.
5. For an expanded discussion on when a woman is defined as a *yoledet*, see above, *Siman* 9: Cervical Dilation and the Onset of Labor.
6. *Shemirat Shabbat Ke-Hilkhatah* 1:36:9 (p. 490) addresses the water breaking as an indication that violating Shabbat is permitted for this woman, connecting one of the Gemara's indicators, "blood is trickling down," to the discharge of amniotic fluid. However, in the new, third edition (p. 593), he wrote otherwise: "It is forbidden to do so until the advanced stages of the opening of the uterus, or when blood begins to trickle down, or when the woman can no longer walk," and makes no mention of a discharge of fluid. However, n. 22 (*ad loc.*) discusses the discharge of fluid and rules that we violate Shabbat to bring the woman to the hospital, and we take other measures necessary to prevent infection. "However... in the absence of one of the three known indicators, one should not do things that can be postponed."
7. *Responsa Teshuvah Me-Ahavah* 1:116, following *Ḥavat Da'at*. He proves his view from the existence of *dam tohar* (blood that is *tahor*), which originates in the uterus.
8. *Badei Ha-Shulḥan siman* 194, elucidations, s.v. "*mipnei she-i efshar le-fetiḥat ha-kever be-lo dam.*"
9. *Ḥut Ha-Shani*, p. 332; *Shi'urei Taharah*, p. 678; *Shi'urei Shevet Ha-Levi* 194:2:4, p. 245.

According to R. Ovadiah Yosef, as long as blood is not clearly seen to be mixed with the fluid, there are no grounds for concern.[10] R. Shlomo Zalman Auerbach ruled likewise.[11]

It therefore seems that when the membranes rupture long before the expected time for the onset of labor, and when the rupture is partial and the fluid does not gush out, the couple is not forbidden to have physical contact with one another at this stage of childbirth.

Even when the fluid gushes out and labor is expected soon, according to most *poskim*, this indication alone is not sufficient to render the woman *niddah*.

Some contemporary *poskim*[12] write that a woman is not rendered *niddah* as a result of the discharge of amniotic fluid, but marital relations are forbidden as during an *onat perishah*. That is, the couple may not have marital relations, but other forms of intimacy are permitted; and if labor does not progress, an internal *bedikah* must be performed. In practice, however, a woman should not perform an internal *bedikah* or have marital relations after the rupture of membranes, out of concern for exposing the fetus to infection.

Z.B.

10. *Taharat Ha-Bayit* 2:11:6, pp. 53–54.
11. *Maḥshevet Ha-Taharah*, p. 121. Nevertheless, it is preferable to clarify, if possible, that no blood is mixed with the fluid.
12. *Darkhei Taharah*, 2nd edition, p. 138; *Shi'urei Taharah*, pp. 678–79.

Siman 13

Assistance of the Husband in the Delivery Room

Question

I am expecting to give birth in the coming weeks, God willing. I want to know how my husband can help me during delivery. Is his presence during delivery problematic? Can he physically help me cope with the contractions by massaging me, supporting various physical positions, and the like?

Answer

Your husband can give you physical support during early labor until you experience bleeding or the birth reaches the active stage.[1] At that point, physical contact is prohibited and the status of *niddah* already applies. From that point on, your husband may remain in the delivery room and may actively support and encourage you, as long as he refrains from touching you and from gazing at your private parts.

Some women engage a doula to assist them and to mediate between them and the medical staff. This can be an excellent solution for the part of labor during which contact between spouses is forbidden. However, a doula generally begins developing the relationship with her client during the pregnancy, which can be costly, and likewise it is not a one-size-fits-all solution for every *yoledet*. There is no halakhic requirement to employ a doula.

---

1. See above, *Siman* 9: Cervical Dilation and the Onset of Labor, and *Siman* 12: Does the Rupture of Membranes Render a Woman Niddah? – both of which address the onset of labor.

It is important to note that although childbirth is a natural process, a *yoledet* is considered to be a *ḥola she'yesh bah sakanah,* ill to the point that her life is at risk. The halakhic category of assuaging or settling the mind ("*yishuv ha-da'at*") applies as well. Therefore, if you require support during advanced labor and there is no woman present who can support you as a doula, companion, or midwife would, your husband is obligated to fulfill your requests so that your mind is at ease, even if it means physical contact. This contact is permitted only if you demand it.

Halakhic Expansion

Birth is comprised of three stages. The first stage, known as "labor," is from regular contractions until cervical dilation of 10 cm (full dilation). The second stage lasts from full dilation through delivery of the baby. The third stage is the expulsion of the placenta. Despite medical advances, most women giving birth experience mental stress, pain, and fear. For most women, contractions are an acutely painful experience. Delivering the baby also demands a great deal of physical exertion on the part of the mother; and fear of pain and possible complications can increase stress.

A variety of interventions can help women through the birthing process. First, childbirth preparation can help reduce stress and fear associated with childbirth. Second, sedation and anesthesia, such as an epidural, help relieve pain of childbirth for many (but not all) women. In addition, physical and emotional support for the *yoledet* can also help reduce pain and complications.

The needs of different *yoldot* vary, and depend on how labor develops, whether the *yoledet* receives an epidural, and if there is another support person present (such as a doula), as well as the personality and reactions of the *yoledet* herself.

The *yoledet*'s cooperation is critical for the progression of labor and to keep the birth uncomplicated and healthy. She must facilitate and not hinder, the birthing process, which is why many women need mental and emotional support while giving birth. Some also need physical support: to moisten the *yoledet's* lips or forehead, to apply counterpressure to the lower back during contractions, to help her change positions, to massage her back to alleviate pain, to give her a hand to squeeze while dealing with particularly intense pain, and the like. Some women feel most secure with their husbands present to offer support.[2] Even when an epidural is administered, the *yoledet* still needs support to deliver the baby.

2. For an analysis of the halakhic status of the *yoledet*'s fears, see *Responsa Bnei Banim* 1, *Siman* 33.

In the past, many hospitals did not allow men into the delivery rooms. Nowadays, hospitals generally recognize the need for having someone accompany the woman giving birth, and the husband's presence during delivery has become routine.

R. Yitzḥak Yaakov Weiss prohibited the husband's entry into the delivery room even if he would refrain from watching the emergence of the baby, out of concern that it would lead him to sin.[3] R. Ovadiah Yosef[4] responded that there is no halakhic impediment to the husband staying with his wife and providing encouragement while she gives birth, as long as he is careful not to watch as the baby emerges.

Shulḥan Arukh[5] rules that when a couple are forbidden to each other, the husband may not attend to his wife who is ill if that requires his physical contact; and even if the husband is a doctor, he may not take his wife's "*dofek*" (pulse)[6] while she is *niddah*. Rema comments there that when no one else is available to attend to her, the husband may attend to his sick wife.[7]

Bet Yosef states that even if the ill woman's life is at risk, and even if there is no one else nearby to attend to her, it is possible that Rambam may forbid the husband to attend to her because doing so would be an "accessory to a forbidden sexual union" (*avizarayhu d'arayot*). This is in accordance with his position that the prohibition of "you shall not come near to uncover nakedness" (*Vayikra* 18:6) is *mi-de'Orayta*.[8] In contrast, Ramban would likely permit, as he maintains that touching a *niddah* is forbidden only *mi-deRabanan*.[9] *Shakh*, on the other hand,

3. *Minḥat Yitzḥak* 8:30:2. Subsequently, *Shi'urei Taharah*, chapter 33, p. 682, distinguished between the stage of contractions, when the husband may stay by his wife's side, and the stage of active labor, when, in his view, the intensity of the situation may affect the equanimity needed to observe the *harḥakot*.
4. *Taharat Ha-Bayit*, 2:12:28, p. 166.
5. *Yoreh De'ah* 195:15–17.
6. For the location of the *dofek*, see *Responsa Bnei Banim* 1:37, discussing whether the *dofek* refers to the heartbeat, or that the pulse is taken elsewhere in the body.
7. Rema, *ad loc.* It is important to note that taking someone's *dofek* is not part of treatment, but a diagnostic tool. In *Darkhei Moshe He-Katzar, Yoreh De'ah siman* 195, Rema writes: "I found a gloss in *Mordekhai* on the first chapter of *Shabbat* (*Shiltei Ha-Giborim* 69:5) which states, 'R. Meir wrote that those who are careful not to touch their sick wives while they are *niddot* practice a foolish piety (*ḥasidut shel shtut*) – from R. Tuvia of Vienna.'"
8. *Mishneh Torah, Hilkhot Issurei Biah* 21:1.
9. Ramban's objection to *Sefer Ha-Mitzvot*, negative commandment *siman* 353.

writes that even according to Rambam, the *deOrayta* prohibition applies only to contact that is amorous and sexually passionate.[10]

Rema's permissive ruling applies only when there is no one else who can help the woman. However, when the birth takes place in a hospital, the woman is not alone and can avail herself of the delivery room staff. Therefore, it would seem, even according to Rema's ruling, that the *yoledet* does not require her husband's assistance. However, in reality, the medical staff is not always available for all the needs of a woman giving birth. In most cases, the midwife or physician is with the *yoledet* only intermittently, and it is the woman's companion, not the medical staff, who helps alleviate labor pains by adjusting her position or massaging her.[11]

R. Yehuda Herzl Henkin has written that if the *yoledet* is fearful in her husband's absence, he is obligated to be present.[12] R. Henkin notes that *halakhah* treats a *yoledet*'s mental and emotional needs differently than those of other patients with life-threatening illnesses. Regarding other illnesses, most *Rishonim* permit violating Shabbat only to perform actions necessary for healing, but not to for *yishuv hada'at,* the patient's emotional state. When it comes to a *yoledet,* however, we do violate Shabbat for her *yishuv hada'at.* Thus, if a blind *yoledet* asks for a candle to be lit on Shabbat for her attendants, even when the candle is superfluous for them as well as for her – for example, if it is daytime – it is nonetheless obligatory to light the candle. R. Henkin explains that the difference between a *yoledet* and others with life-threatening illnesses is that a *yoledet* is active in the birthing process. She must remain in control during contractions so she can follow the midwife's or physician's instructions to push or relax. It is therefore necessary for her mind to be settled during childbirth, and any support necessary to relax her is a matter of saving lives.[13]

Additionally, R. Henkin questions the stringency of the husband's prohibition to touch his wife during delivery, since at that time, "The *yoledet* is not at all available

10. *Shakh, Yoreh De'ah* 195:20. *Bet Shemu'el, Even Ha-Ezer* 20:1 disagrees with *Shakh.* According to the formulation in *Mishneh Torah, Hilkhot Issurei Biah* 21:1, the Torah's prohibition applies only when the contact can lead to sexual intercourse.
11. Such support is common when the woman giving birth is not anesthetized, and specifically when she is mobile at the time of birth.
12. *Responsa Bnei Banim* 1:33. R. Feinstein addresses this issue as well and permits the presence of the husband in the delivery room. See *Igrot Moshe, Yoreh De'ah* 2:75.
13. Ibid., s.v. "*U-le'aniyat da'ati barukh she-natan me-ḥokhmato li-re'av.*"

for sexual relations."[14] R. Henkin continues that it is proper for the husband to mention gently to his wife that she is a *niddah*, but if she continues to demand his assistance, he must oblige.

R. Shlomo Daichovsky suggests that the husband wear surgical gloves, making the contact less direct.[15]

Z.B. and Editors

14. *Responsa Bnei Banim* 4:16, at the end.
15. S. Daichovsky, "Sedation of a *Yoledet* and a Pregnant Woman," *Teḥumin* 23, p. 237 (Hebrew).

Siman 14

Mokh Daḥuk and Bedikot following Birth

Question

I gave birth three weeks ago. The delivery was difficult, requiring ten stitches. The bleeding has stopped, and I started counting the seven *neki'im*, but the area is still sensitive, and I am worried about the *bedikot*. What should I do?

Answer

Bleeding that results from delivery lasts about 3–4 weeks on average, and even up to 8 weeks is not considered abnormal. Toward the end of this time, the bleeding lessens. It is also common that it stops and then starts again before finally ending. This can make it difficult to become *tehorah*. Women therefore need patience postpartum until it is possible to go to the *mikveh*.

You had a difficult labor, and the area is apparently still sensitive. Technically, for a woman to become *tehorah*, she must perform a *hefsek taharah* examination, a *mokh daḥuk*, and two *bedikot* daily throughout the seven *neki'im*. Since you are a *yoledet* for whom *bedikot* are difficult, you may forego the *mokh daḥuk* and reduce the number of *bedikot*. In addition to the *hefsek taharah*, you must perform at least one *bedikah* on the first day and one *bedikah* on the seventh, and it is also proper to perform a *bedikah* on one of the middle days. You may moisten the *bedikah* cloth with a bit of water or water-based gel to facilitate the *bedikah*.

These leniencies are valid only in the situation you described. They must be reconsidered before the next time you count seven *neki'im*.

Halakhic Expansion

After birth, especially if there are many stitches resulting from an episiotomy or internal tearing, the vaginal area is very sensitive, and it takes time for it to return to normal. The *hefsek taharah* examination is essential, for without it, one may not begin counting the seven *neki'im.*[1] In contrast, the *mokh daḥuk* examination is classified as a "good custom" ("*minhag tov*"),[2] or as a stringency that should be followed *lekhatḥilah,*[3] so one may forego it after childbirth.[4]

In light of the postpartum sensitivity of the region, it is permissible also to reduce the number of *bedikot* as needed. The minimum required is one *bedikah* on the first day and one *bedikah* on the seventh.[5] If it is possible to perform another *bedikah* without causing bleeding in the region, it should be done on one of the middle days.[6] In case of vaginal dryness, a common postpartum occurrence, one may moisten the *bedikah* cloth with a bit of water to facilitate the *bedikah.*[7]

S.K.

---

1. *Yoreh De'ah* 196:1
2. Ibid., citing Rashba.
3. Rema *ad loc.*
4. Many *poskim* are lenient about foregoing the *mokh daḥuk* when necessary, especially for a *yoledet*. See below, *Siman* 18: *Hefsek Taharah* after Sunset, Postpartum.
5. *Yoreh De'ah* 196:4, citing "*yesh omrim.*"
6. The *bedikah* on one of the middle days is important in case the woman forgets to perform a *bedikah* on the seventh day, creating a situation where more than five days elapsed without a *bedikah*. This is based on *Semag*, cited in *Dagul Me-Revavah, Yoreh De'ah* 196:6 and in *Noda Bi-Yehudah, Yoreh De'ah,* 2:128.
7. See also below, *Siman* 24: Reducing *Bedikot* following a Miscarriage.

Siman 15

Counting Seven Neki'im following a Caesarean Section

Question

I had a baby girl this week, *baruch Hashem*, via planned caesarean section, and there was barely any bleeding. Am I *niddah*? If so, may I already count *neki'im* and go to the *mikveh*?

Answer

After birth, two types of *tum'ah* apply: the *tum'ah* of *niddah* and the *tum'ah* of *yoledet*. A woman who gives birth via caesarean section does not become *teme'ah* with the *tum'ah* of childbirth, but she is *teme'ah* with the *tum'ah* of *niddah* due to the vaginal bleeding that accompanies the surgery. Nowadays, becoming *tehorah* from both types of *tum'ah* is identical, with the exception of one detail: because of the *tum'ah* of childbirth, a woman who gives birth to a daughter may not immerse in the *mikveh* before the 15th night after giving birth, since, according to the Torah, she is *teme'ah* for 14 days regardless of whether she experiences bleeding. A woman who gives birth to a son is *teme'ah* for only seven days, and she may immerse in the *mikveh* starting on the eighth night. Since you gave birth via caesarean section and have not become *teme'ah* with the *tum'ah* of childbirth, you may perform a *hefsek taharah* after four or five days, according to your custom, and begin counting the seven *neki'im* on the following day, even if 14 days will not have elapsed by the time you finish counting.

Halakhic Expansion

The Torah mentions the unique *tum'ah* of a woman who has just given birth. This *tum'ah* is not connected to the experience of bleeding, and it lasts for 14 days if the *yoledet* gave birth to a daughter, and seven days for a son.[1] The Gemara calls a bloodless birth[2] a "dry birth"; a woman is rendered *teme'ah* by childbirth even if it is a "dry birth."[3]

The Gemara records a disagreement about whether there can be *petiḥat ha-kever* without bleeding.[4] The expression "*petiḥat ha-kever*" in the Talmud refers to cervical dilation, and *Ḥakhamim* disagree as to whether cervical dilation causes *tum'ah*, even if there was no bleeding. According to R. Yehudah, *petiḥat ha-kever* without bleeding is impossible, so *petiḥat ha-kever* confers *tum'ah*, even if the woman did not find any blood. Most *Rishonim* rule in accordance with R. Yehudah, as does *Shulḥan Arukh*.[5] Therefore, a woman who has a "dry birth" is *teme'ah* with both the *tum'ah* of childbirth and the *tum'ah* of *niddah*, since there was certainly *petiḥat ha-kever* during the birthing process.[6] However, usually there is no halakhically significant cervical dilation in cases of caesarean section, so if there is no bleeding, the woman is not *teme'ah*, as we will see below.

The Mishnah records a dispute concerning a caesarean birth (which it calls "*yotzei dofen*," literally, "emerges from the wall"). According to *tanna kamma*, the days of *tum'ah* and *taharah*[7] do not apply to a caesarean birth, as it is written, "When a woman conceives and gives birth"[8] – she must give birth from the same place that conception occurs. That is, only vaginal birth renders a woman *teme'ah* with the *tum'ah* of childbirth. Therefore, a woman who gives birth via caesarean section is not *teme'ah* with the *tum'ah* of childbirth. According to R. Shimon, however, a caesarean birth has the same status as a vaginal birth; it renders the mother *teme'ah* with the *tum'ah* of childbirth even though the baby emerged through an incision in the abdomen and not vaginally.

---

1. Vayikra 12:2–5.
2. From a medical perspective, bloodless childbirth is theoretically possible, but in reality the phenomenon is unknown.
3. *Niddah* 42b.
4. Ibid. 21a.
5. *Yoreh De'ah* 188:3.
6. Regarding the process of becoming *tehorah* after a normal birth, see above, *Siman* 14: *Mokh Daḥuk* and *Bedikot* following Birth.
7. *Niddah* 40a.
8. Vayikra 12:2.

Regarding the *tum'ah* of *niddah,* a woman who gave birth via caesarean section is *teme'ah* with the *tum'ah* of *niddah* only if she experiences vaginal bleeding. If the blood drains only through the incision in the abdominal wall, she is not rendered *teme'ah* with the *tum'ah* of *niddah.* In the words of R. Yoḥanan in the name of R. Shimon,[9] "A woman is not *teme'ah* unless a flow is discharged from [the place of] her nakedness, as it says, 'And a man who lies with a woman having her flow, and shall uncover her nakedness, he has exposed her source.'"[10] That is, uterine blood that is not discharged through the vagina, but rather in a different fashion, does not cause *tum'ah.* Therefore, in the case of a caesarean section, if the uterine blood discharges through the surgical incision only, and not through the vagina, it does not render the woman *teme'ah.*

All of the *Rishonim* ruled in accordance with the *tanna kamma* that a caesarean section does not cause *tum'ah* of childbirth, and in accordance with R. Yoḥanan that in the case of a caesarean section, if the blood comes out only through the incision in the abdominal wall, the mother remains *tehorah.*[11] *Shulḥan Arukh* likewise rules that in the case of a caesarean birth, if blood came out only through the incision in the abdominal wall, the *yoledet* is *tehorah* – whether from the *tum'ah* of childbirth, *niddah,* or *zavah.*[12]

Among the *Aḥaronim,* the author of *Naḥalat Shiv'ah* wrote that a woman who sat on the birthing stool must count seven *neki'im,* for *petiḥat ha-kever* without bleeding is impossible.[13] The expression "sat on the birthing stool" ("*yeshivah al ha-mashber*") relates to active labor with strong contractions and significant dilation. In his view, a woman who was in active labor before the caesarean section must count seven *neki'im* even if she did not experience vaginal bleeding.[14] This position has been refuted by many poskim.[15]

The *Nishmat Avraham* writes that nowadays it never happens that a woman undergoes a caesarean section but does not experience even a drop of vaginal

9. *Niddah* 41b.
10. Vayikra 20:18.
11. The *Rishonim* ruled in accordance with the *tanna kamma* in the Mishnah, and in accordance with R. Yoḥanan's statement in the name of R. Shimon in the Gemara.
12. *Yoreh De'ah* 194:14.
13. *Pitḥei Teshuvah, Yoreh De'ah* 194:8; see above, *Siman* 9: Cervical Dilation and the Onset of Labor. See also *Badei Ha-Shulḥan* 194:100 (which rules in accordance with *Naḥalat Shiv'ah*).
14. In the case at hand, in which the woman underwent a planned caesarean section, as long as she was not in active labor beforehand, she did not attain the status of "sitting on the birthstool," and thus there is no need to discuss *petiḥat ha-kever* prior to the birth.
15. See above, *Siman* 9, in the expanded answer.

bleeding in which the blood originates in the uterus, at the site where the placenta was attached to the uterine wall,[16] and is not merely the result of the surgery. Therefore, if the bleeding is mild and not a flow, it is evaluated according to the laws of *ketamim*.[17]

Therefore, a woman who gives birth via caesarean section and does not experience vaginal bleeding that confers *tum'ah*[18] is *tehorah*.[19]

G.K.S.

16. It is therefore not considered *dam makkah*.
17. *Nishmat Avraham, Yoreh De'ah* 194:13, p. 196. For an expanded discussion of placental blood, see above, *Siman* 6: Bleeding from Placenta Previa.
18. It is not considered "*petiḥat ha-kever*" if nothing exits the uterus through the cervix. See *Ḥavat Da'at, Yoreh De'ah siman* 194, elucidations *siman* 1.
19. See *Ḥut Ha-Shani* 183:2:4. Regarding the medical question of whether one may immerse in a *mikveh* or engage in marital relations before the medical examination that is generally held six weeks postpartum, it is advisable to consult with a gynecologist.

Siman 16

Observation of Blood by a Physician during the Postpartum Examination

Question

My six-week postpartum medical examination took place while I was counting my seven *neki'im*. The examination was conducted with a speculum, and the doctor commented that he sees a bit of blood. What should I do?

Answer

The process of becoming *tehorah* after childbirth is likely to be prolonged and require patience. There is often recurrent bleeding after birth, and a *yoledet* should be prepared for the possibility that it will be necessary to begin the count anew. There are certain leniencies that can be practiced, especially regarding the number of *bedikot*, if the process persists.[1]

The examining physician is trusted to say that she saw blood coming from the uterus or in the vagina, and this blood renders the woman *teme'ah*. If you can, ask the doctor where, in her opinion, the blood came from. If the doctor does not find a *petza* that causes the bleeding, her assertion that she saw blood negates the counting of seven *neki'im*. In such a case, a new *hefsek taharah* is required, and the counting starts anew.

---

1. For details, see above, *Siman* 14: *Mokh Daḥuk* and *Bedikot* following Birth.

However, *halakhah* does not require you to ask the doctor what she saw, nor is she obligated to report it to you.

Halakhic Expansion

For a detailed discussion of the postpartum medical examination, see below, Medical Appendix III: Birth.

Usually, a woman does not become *niddah* unless she has external evidence of bleeding – for example, an internal *bedikah* that came out with signs of bleeding. In the present case, the physician saw blood in the vagina or cervix that the woman did not find during the *bedikot* she performed during the seven *neki'im*. *Sifra*,[2] the Mishnah,[3] and the Gemara[4] all assert that blood causes *tum'ah* once it leaves the uterus and enters the vagina (the "*prozdor*" – literally, "antechamber,"), even if it has not yet been detected externally.

Regarding the trustworthiness of the doctor to attest that he saw this blood, the *Rishonim* and *Aḥaronim* disagree about how to understand *Ḥakhamim* querying physicians that is described in *Masekhet Niddah*.[5] It seems that if the doctor looked through a device that would enable anyone to see,[6] he is merely reporting the situation as it is,[7] and so he is trusted.[8]

In contrast, if the doctor does not report what he sees, there is no halakhic requirement to interrogate him about what he saw or examine the devices that were inside the body. This holds true regarding both the days of *taharah* and the seven *neki'im*.[9] If, even though there is no obligation to examine them, the woman sees blood on a device or on gloves that were inside her body, she would

2. *Sifra Metzora, Parashat Zavim* 4.
3. *Mishnah Niddah* 2:5.
4. *Niddah* 21b and Rashi *ad loc.*
5. *Niddah* 22b records the case of a woman who would discharge something like red husks. *Ḥakhamim* asked physicians, who determined that she had a wound. *Ḥakhamim* then constructed an experiment to obtain proof. The discussion among the *poskim* hinges on the function of the experiment versus the trustworthiness of the physicians. If they can be trusted, why was the experiment necessary? See *Responsa Rosh* 2:18 and the discussion in the *Aḥaronim*.
6. *Responsa Maharsham* 1:24 and 2:72 and 101.
7. *Responsa Mishpetei Uziel*, vol. 2, *Yoreh De'ah* 26.
8. See the wide-ranging discussion in *Shi'urei Shevet Ha-Levi* 187:3, p. 78ff; *Taharat Ha-Bayit He-Katzar* 5:32.
9. See *Ḥut Ha-Shani* 183:3:5.

be obligated to ask the doctor to explain the blood on the device and whether he abraded[10] her during the examination.[11]

R.S.F.

10. See below, *Siman* 21: Attributing Blood to a *Petza* during the Seven *Neki'im*; and *Siman* 60: Finding Blood on a Diaphragm.

11. On the other hand, this should be considered from the aspect of the prohibition against "placing a stumbling block before the blind" ("*lifnei iver*," the prohibition against misleading others into transgression): Is a God-fearing doctor obligated to report, at his own initiative, the discharges that he sees within her body? (Perhaps there is an allusion to this in the verse, "Do not stand idly by the blood of your companion.") It seems to me that there is no such obligation because the doctor, when performing an internal examination with a speculum, has neither the lighting conditions inside the body nor the halakhic expertise to distinguish the general reddish color of the body's interior and the hues of the discharge. Thus, the woman can be guided to ask the doctor not to report what he sees to her. In contrast, R. Wosner writes in *Shi'urei Shevet Ha-Levi* (188:4, p. 100) that it is good to perform a *bedikat ḥorim u-sedakim* (an internal self-examination that probes the recesses and folds) after the doctor's examination. It seems that in the case of a routine examination, where there is no concern for *petiḥat ha-kever*, and there may be an opposing concern of irritating the vaginal tissue with the speculum and creating a *petza*, there is no reason to examine or seek out such bleeding.

Siman 17

Attributing Bleeding to Hemorrhoids, Postpartum

Question

Since giving birth, I have been suffering from hemorrhoids,[1] which bleed when I wipe in the washroom. This being the case, can I attribute the blood I find on internal *bedikah* cloths to the hemorrhoids? How can uterine blood be distinguished from hemorrhoidal blood?

Answer

If it is possible that you touched the anal region at the time of the *bedikah*, then there are grounds to be lenient and attribute the bleeding on the *bedikah* cloth to hemorrhoids. You should try to avoid touching the hemorrhoidal region during the *bedikah*.

It is very difficult to distinguish between uterine blood and hemorrhoidal blood, because the latter has no characteristic appearance and can manifest itself in different hues, including some that match the appearance of *niddah* blood.

Halakhic Expansion

Any blood found on a *bedikah* cloth is presumed to have come from the uterus. The Gemara discusses the possibility of permitting blood found on the *bedikah* cloth by assuming that the cloth was dirtied with blood from elsewhere, after the

1. Hemorrhoids are swollen veins in the anal region. As blood vessels with thin walls, they tend to bleed after a bowel movement.

bedikah.[2] The Gemara reaches a permissive conclusion when the shape of the stain on the cloth attests that the source of the blood was not the *bedikah,*[3] or when there are other grounds that indicate that this is not uterine blood.

In *Shulḥan Arukh,* R. Yosef Karo rules[4] that it is possible to permit a bloodstain, even one that appears on a *bedikah* cloth, based on the assumption that it is not uterine, when the assumption is supported by two pieces of evidence: the size and shape of the *ketem,* and the cloth having been placed, prior to its inspection, in a place that has not been checked for blood.

In his *Bet Yosef,*[5] R. Yosef Karo writes that using a cloth for *bedikah* need not preclude attribution of even a *ketem* larger than *ke-gris,* when there is a reasonable basis to presume that the blood on the cloth is not from the woman's body – for example, when other kinds of blood were handled in its proximity. This is on condition that she did not sense the discharge of blood from her body,[6] and that the shape of the bloodstain does not attest that it was created at the time of the *bedikah.*

The possibility of attributing the blood on the cloth to an external source hinges on the likelihood of this being the case and on the principles for attributing to a *makkah.*[7] As an example of high likelihood, *Taz*[8] refers to a condition in which a woman suffers from occasional rectal bleeding and writes that she can attribute blood found during a *bedikah* to this source, if she touched the anus when she performed the *bedikah.* This statement is an interpretation of *Bet Yosef,* but *Taz* then adds that the fact that the bloodstain is elongated does not detract from

2. *Niddah* 58b.
3. For example, when it is circular. See *Niddah* 58b; *Yoreh De'ah* 190:34.
4. *Yoreh De'ah* 190:34.
5. Ibid. 190:34–35: "It seems to me that where there are grounds to suspect that the blood on this cloth may have come from the fact that other kinds of blood were handled near where the cloth is, it can be attributed to that, even if [the blood spot] is significantly larger than the size of a *gris.* For the fact that she wiped with it does not preclude us from attributing it to whatever we can, since she did not sense the discharge of the blood from her body."
6. The statement in *Bet Yosef* is predicated on the assumption that the woman did not sense the discharge of blood from her body. However, this assumption can be challenged, since the ruling concerns an internal self-examination with a *bedikah* cloth, and it is possible that she did experience a *hargashah,* which she attributed to the "sensation of the cloth" ("*hargashat ha-ed*"; *Niddah* 57b). See *Ḥavat Da'at,* elucidations, 190:27, which differentiates between a case where it is uncertain that the blood is uterine, in which case we do not attribute the blood or express concern about *hargashat ha-ed,* and a case where the blood is certainly uterine, where there is concern about *hargashat ha-ed,* i.e., that she misattributed a *hargashah* to the cloth. R. Ovadiah Yosef states similarly; see below, n. 16.
7. See below, *Siman* 21: Attributing Blood to a *Petza* during the Seven *Neki'im.*
8. *Taz, Yoreh De'ah* 190:34:23.

this attribution, for the presumption is that the staining indeed occurred during the *bedikah*, just that the source of the bleeding is anal.[9]

Whereas *Taz* presumes, as a basis for his permissive ruling, that the *bedikah* cloth is liable to come into contact with the anus during a *bedikah* and become stained with blood from there, *Ḥatam Sofer*[10] discusses a case where, for some medical reason,[11] there is blood in the vagina that originated in the rectum, not the uterus; some physiological malfunction internally redirected blood from the rectum into the vagina. It should be noted that this is a very rare medical condition.[12] *Ḥatam Sofer* rules that since the source of the blood remains uncertain, one should not be lenient except in the case of *ketamim*, not if the blood was found on a *bedikah* cloth. However, he allows that a woman may perform an initial examination to clean off any external blood, throw away that *bedikah* cloth without looking at it, and then perform the actual *bedikah*.

R. Ovadiah Yosef quotes R. Yaakov al-Faraji (Maharif)[13] regarding a woman who found a bloodstain on a cloth after marital relations and wanted to attribute it to hemorrhoidal blood. Maharif rules that she may indeed attribute the bleeding to hemorrhoids, in light of the conclusion of the Gemara's discussion of *ro'ah meḥamat tashmish* (a woman who bleeds from intercourse), namely, that when there is a *makkah*, one may attribute to it, and there is no need to compare the blood of the *makkah* to uterine blood. Maharif adds that hemorrhoidal blood has no characteristic appearance and can be found in various hues. This runs counter to the views of other *Aḥaronim*[14] that a woman has the duty to provide some evidence that this blood is anal, not uterine.

It seems, however, that the cloth to which Maharif refers is not a *bekidah* cloth used for an internal self-examination, but a cloth she used to wipe herself off after intercourse. For that reason, R. Yosef Ḥayim of Baghdad[15] writes in *Rav Pe'alim* that a *bedikah* cloth may not be permitted on the basis of Maharif's lenient ruling.

9. See also *Arukh Ha-Shulḥan, Yoreh De'ah* 190:97.
10. *Responsa Ḥatam Sofer, Yoreh De'ah* 185, end.
11. *Ḥatam Sofer* states that this condition is caused by an obstruction in what he calls the "*goldene Ader*" ("golden vein").
12. *Noda Bi-Yehudah* 1:49 and 60 comments that vaginal bleeding due to *goldene Ader* is impossible. In fact, there is a relatively rare condition called a rectovaginal fistula, in which a connection develops between the rectum and the vagina.
13. *Responsa Maharif siman* 86.
14. *Devar Shemu'el, Yoreh De'ah siman* 71.
15. *Responsa Rav Pe'alim,* vol. 3, *Yoreh De'ah siman* 13. In fact, he is also reluctant to rule permissively even in the case where she was merely wiping, and ultimately, he permits only in the case of a *ketem*.

R. Ovadiah Yosef[16] rejects the view of R. Yosef Ḥayim, following his own view that the sensation of the cloth is considered a *hargashah* due to uncertainty. In the present case, where the woman has no actual *hargashah,* one should not be stringent due to *hargashat ha-ed* against the assumption that there is a reasonable possibility that the source of this blood is hemorrhoidal. If the woman claims that it is possible that, during the *bedikah,* the cloth touched the anus and became bloodstained from it, he maintains that the cloth should be rendered permissible.

It should be noted that one may attribute bleeding to hemorrhoids even during the first three of the seven *neki'im.*[17]

Nevertheless, the woman should be encouraged to treat the hemorrhoids, both for medical reason and to avoid a situation about which there is halakhic dispute.

Z.B.

16. *Responsa Yabi'a Omer,* vol. 10, *Yoreh De'ah siman* 58.
17. *Taharah Ke-Halakhah,* p. 93.

Siman 18

Hefsek Taharah after Sunset, Postpartum

Question

I gave birth two months ago. I stopped staining several weeks ago, but have not yet regained my strength, so I didn't begin counting the seven *neki'im* till now. I had planned to do a *hefsek taharah* yesterday but forgot. Today I wanted to do a *hefsek taharah*, but remembered a bit late and performed it five minutes after *sheki'ah* (sunset). Is today's *hefsek taharah* valid?

Answer

Six weeks postpartum, the uterus returns to its natural, pre-pregnancy size and condition. Alongside the joy of a new baby joining your family, a mother, postpartum, must cope with extended sleep deprivation, the challenges of nursing and taking care of a newborn baby, and the ongoing management of the home. If possible, it is highly recommended to get some help at home, so you can conserve your energy. If you still feel unwell two months after giving birth, we recommend you see your physician to confirm that everything is as it should be.

A *hefsek taharah* should be performed just prior to sunset.

In the situation described in the question, we advise, first of all, that you check the exact time of sunset where you live, and that you verify that the clock you consulted was accurate. Sometimes, examining these details reveals that the *bedikah* was, after all, performed on time.

If your *hefsek taharah* was indeed performed late, you must perform a new *hefsek* tomorrow. So that you do not forget again, it's a good idea to put a reminder in place: an alert on your cell phone, a post-it note in a prominent place, an entry in your daily planner, etc. It is also advisable to do a preliminary *hefsek* during the day, when it is convenient for you (even in the morning), which, *bedi'avad* can serve as a *hefsek taharah* if you forget or are late again.

Halakhic Expansion

The *hefsek taharah* changes a woman's status from *teme'ah* to *be-ḥezkat taharah* (presumed to be *tehorah*). In the Mishnah and Gemara,[1] *Ḥakhamim* disagree about when a *niddah mi-de'Orayta* may perform a *hefsek taharah*. From here we learn the *halakhah* as well regarding a *zavah*, who must perform a *hefsek taharah* before counting the seven *neki'im*.[2] Most *Rishonim*[3] rule in accordance with Ḥazal's position in the Mishnah, that a *hefsek taharah* may be performed in the morning as well, except when a woman experienced bleeding for only one day. In the latter case, she must perform the *hefsek taharah* specifically during *bein ha-shemashot* (dusk or twilight), near the end of the day.[4]

Tur cites Rosh[5] as saying that this *bedikah* must be "*bein ha-shemashot* of the day that she stops [bleeding]." *Bet Yosef* there explains that his intention is not that the *bedikah* must be performed during *bein ha-shemashot* itself, which is a *safek yom* (i.e., it is uncertain whether it is considered daytime), but as close as possible to *bein ha-shemashot*, and not before *minḥah ketanah* (2.5 proportional hours before *sheki'ah*).

1. *Niddah* 68a-b.
2. According to the Mishnah on *Niddah* 31b and the ensuing Gemara on 33b, so that the seven *neki'im* are complete days, the *hefsek taharah* must take place on the day before she begins counting; the day of the *hefsek taharah* is not counted as the first of the *neki'im* – contra the practice of the *benot Kutim* (Samaritan women). Throughout the *halakhot* of *niddah*, days are calculated from *sheki'ah* to *sheki'ah*, not from *tzeit ha-kokhavim* (the emergence of the stars, i.e., nightfall). The night is defined as *sheki'ah* to *zeriḥah* (sunrise).
3. Rashba, *Torat Ha-Bayit, bayit* 7, *sha'ar* 5; Ramban, *Hilkhot Niddah* 2:1; etc.
4. Regarding a woman who experienced bleeding for only one day, there is concern that her "well" is still open, so a stringency was added whereby her *hefsek taharah* is valid only if it was performed just before *bein ha-shemashot*. The *Rishonim* added that there is also an obligation to insert a *mokh daḥuk* in such a situation, and *Shulḥan Arukh* rules accordingly (*Yoreh De'ah* 196:2). According to Rema, the *hefsek taharah* is valid *bedi'avad* even without a *mokh daḥuk*, as long as it was performed just before *bein ha-shemashot*.
5. *Tur, Yoreh De'ah* 196:1 (3).

Based on this, *Shulḥan Arukh*[6] rules that the *hefsek taharah* should be performed just prior to *bein ha-shemashot*.[7] *Torat Ha-Shelamim*[8] explains further that if the *hefsek taharah* was performed at a time that might be night, or that is certainly night, it is not valid, because the seven *neki'im* must be complete, 24-hour days. It thus emerges that if the *bedikah* was performed after *sheki'ah,* during *bein ha-shemashot,* it is ineffective as a *hefsek taharah* on the outgoing day.

Rema[9] adds that this ruling is *lekhatḥilah;* however, *bedi'avad,* even if she performed the *hefsek taharah* in the morning, it is valid,[10] so long as it is not the first or only day that she experiences bleeding. Therefore, if there is concern that the woman may forget to perform the *hefsek taharah* on time, she should be encouraged to perform a *bedikah* in the morning, just in case; so that if she again forgets to perform a *hefsek taharah* at the proper time, the *bedikah* she performed in the morning can serve, *bedi'avad,* as her *hefsek taharah,* and she will not lose another day.

However, *Aḥaronim* debated the status of a slight lateness in the time of the *bedikah,* i.e., when it was performed a few minutes following *sheki'ah,* during *bein ha-shemashot,* when there is uncertainty as to whether it is daytime or nighttime.

Some *poskim* adopt the approach that there are no grounds to be lenient in any case of lateness, as stated above. This is the ruling of R. Feivel Cohen[11] and R. Shmuel Wosner.[12] R. Meir Brandsdorfer[13] is even more stringent, ruling that even if a woman is unsure whether she performed the *bedikah* before or after *sheki'ah,* she may not begin counting the *neki'im* the next day. Rather, she must wait another day.[14]

---

6. *Yoreh De'ah* 196:1–2.
7. In *Sha'arei Orah,* p. 133, R. Shlomo Levi explains why *Shulḥan Arukh* rules thus, even though no such view appears in the Mishnah.
8. 196:2.
9. *Ad loc.*
10. This accords with the view of *tanna kamma* and *Ḥakhamim* in the Mishnah in *Niddah* 31b, and as cited by the *Rishonim.*
11. *Badei Ha-Shulḥan* 196:6:13, emphasizes that every step of the *bedikah* must be completed before *sheki'ah,* because at the moment the sun sets, there is a state of *safek laylah,* and the *hefsek taharah* examination must be performed specifically during the day. Nevertheless, he adds that if she forgot, or if she could not perform the *hefsek taharah* due to circumstances beyond her control, she should ask a *she'eilat ḥakham.*
12. *Responsa Shevet Ha-Levi* 10:144.
13. *Responsa Kenei Bosem* 1:99.
14. This stringency was not accepted by most *poskim.*

On the other hand, other *poskim* tend to rule leniently in extenuating circumstances. R. Ḥanokh Henokh Pack[15] wrote that there are grounds to be lenient *bedi'avad*, because there are three *sefekot* (uncertainties): (1) perhaps she stopped bleeding before *bein ha-shemashot*; (2) perhaps *bein ha-shemashot* is actually daytime; (3) perhaps the woman is not *zavah*, but *niddah*. R. Ovadiah Yosef[16] questions the validity of some of the *sefekot* raised by R. Pack, but he offers three *sefekot* of his own: (1) perhaps she did not bleed at all during *bein ha-shemashot*; (2) even if she saw a drop of blood after *sheki'ah* and lost it, perhaps *bein ha-shemashot* is actually daytime; (3) perhaps *bein ha-shemashot* should be calculated according to the view of Rabbeinu Tam and not according to the view of the *Ge'onim*. After an extensive discussion of the laws of *sefekot*, R. Ovadiah decides that one may be lenient *bedi'avad*, under extenuating circumstances, or where there is great need according to the evaluation of a halakhic authority, up to 13.5 minutes after sunset (which is the time of uncertainty, whether it is daytime or nighttime).[17]

R. Moshe Feinstein[18] addresses at length the calculations of the relevant times, ruling that in a community that rules in accordance with Rabbeinu Tam's position, one may, *bedi'avad*, render a *hefsek taharah* acceptable up to nine minutes after sunset.[19] However, in a later responsum,[20] he emphasizes that this leniency is available only to those who practice in accordance with Rabbeinu Tam's position, not to those who follow the position of the *Ge'onim*.

---

15. *Zikhron Yosef siman* 58.
16. *Taharat Ha-Bayit* 2:13:1, p. 265ff.
17. In *Taharat Ha-Bayit He-Katzar* 13:5, R. David Yosef restricts his father's ruling and writes that under extenuating circumstances one may be lenient "about 5 or 10 minutes after sunset."
18. *Igrot Moshe, Oraḥ Ḥayim* 4:62.
19. This calculation was made based on the latitude of New York City. Rabbeinu Tam's position was accepted as *halakhah* by *Shulḥan Arukh*, Rema, and *Mishnah Berurah*, apparently because of its compatibility with the time of sunset in certain locations outside of Eretz Yisrael. Against their view is that of the Vilna Gaon, who rules in accordance with the *Ge'onim*. The most common practice today is that *bein ha-shemashot* lasts 13.5 minutes, in accordance with the view of the *Ge'onim* (and 18 minutes according to Rambam). Nevertheless, a minority of the Jewish community in Eretz Yisrael and abroad observe a 72-minute period between *sheki'ah* and *tzeit ha-kokhavim*, in accordance with Rabbeinu Tam. This dispute has both lenient and stringent implications, and a full discussion of it lies beyond the purview of this responsum.
20. *Igrot Moshe, Yoreh De'ah* 4:17:26. R. Yekutiel Farkash (*Taharah Ke-Halakhah* 16:32, p. 288) rules, in light of this responsum, that there are no grounds to be lenient and rely on the view of Rabbeinu Tam in a place where people do not practice in accordance with this view. In his opinion, a *hefsek taharah* after sunset is not effective, even *bedi'avad*.

In light of this, in extenuating circumstances, when a delay of one day might be very significant for the couple (for example, one of them will leave on a trip before the woman can become *tehorah*, or they are trying to conceive), we may be lenient and accept the *hefsek taharah* performed a few minutes late.[21]

N.L.

21. It should be emphasized that the decision as to what constitutes a "singular circumstance" that warrants leniency must be made by a halakhic authority.

Siman 19

Onot Perishah and Establishing a Veset, Postpartum

Question

A week ago, I immersed for the first time since giving birth. Do I need to be concerned about the *onot perishah*? And how am I supposed to calculate them?

Answer

According to *Ḥakhamim,* for 24 months after giving birth, a woman is considered a *meineket* (nursing mother) and is presumed to be *mesuleket damim.* Nowadays, however, most women's menstrual cycle returns before 24 months are up. Therefore, a *yoledet* need not observe the *onot perishah* until after the return of her menstrual cycle, subsequent to becoming *tehorah* from *tum'at yoledet.* After her first period, she must observe two *onot perishah*: the *onah beinonit* (thirty days) and the *onat ha-ḥodesh* (the Hebrew day of the month). After her second period, she observes the *onat ha-haflagah* as well (the interval between the onset of the last two periods). The woman observes these *onot* out of concern for a *veset she-eino kavu'a,* and she cannot establish a new *veset* within 24 months of birth. In contrast, a woman who had a *veset kavu'a* before she became pregnant must observe it even within 24 months, once her menstrual cycle returns.

If the cycle does not return within 24 months, then immediately after the 24 months she must observe the *veset kavu'a* that she had before becoming pregnant. If the *veset kavu'a* is established by means of a fixed interval, she must begin observing it only once her menstrual cycle returns, postpartum.

Therefore, you need not observe any *onot perishah* at present, until your menstrual cycle returns.

Halakhic Expansion

We learn in a Mishnah[1] that four classes of women are considered *mesulakot damim* (amenorrheic), one of which is a *meineket* (nursing mother). According to R. Meir, as long as a *yoledet* continues nursing, she is considered *mesuleket damim,* because the blood "spoils and becomes milk,"[2] but if she weans the child, even within 24 months, her status reverts to that of other women. According to R. Yehudah, R. Yosi, and R. Shimon, however, any recent *yoledet* is deemed *mesuleket damim* for 24 months, whether or not she actually nurses, because her limbs become "dislocated" during childbirth.

Shulḥan Arukh[3] rules in accordance with *Ḥakhamim* that a woman's body does not return to normal for 24 months after childbirth. Therefore, even if the child died or was weaned, there is no presumption that the *veset* that had been established before the pregnancy will return for 24 months after childbirth.[4]

However, most women nowadays begin menstruating again within 24 months after childbirth, even if they continue nursing.[5] According to many *poskim,*[6] nature has changed, and women nowadays are no longer presumed to be *mesulakot damim*

1. *Niddah* 7a.
2. Ibid. 9a.
3. *Yoreh De'ah* 184:7; 189:34.
4. See *Pitḥei Teshuvah* 184:13 regarding the dispute between *Shakh* (*siman* 18) and *Kereti U-Feleti* as to whether a leap month (Adar II) counts toward the 24 months that a *meineket* need not be concerned that her *veset* will return.
5. This may be linked to the extent to which the baby's food is supplemented. Women who only nurse and do not supplement the baby's nutrition are likely not to ovulate for several months. Women who do not breastfeed, or women who took pills to stop lactation, are likely to ovulate 2–4 weeks after childbirth. See "The World Health Organization multinational study of breastfeeding and lactational amenorrhea. IV. Postpartum bleeding and lochia in breast-feeding women. World Health Organization Task Force on Methods for the Natural Regulation of Fertility." *Fertil. Steril.*, September 1999; 72(3): 441–47.
6. *Leḥem Ve-Simlah siman* 189, *simlah* 54; *Igrot Moshe, Yoreh De'ah* 4:14 (184:7), 3:52:1, and 4:17; *Responsa Shevet Ha-Levi* 4:101; *Responsa Mishneh Halakhot* 5:139.

for 24 months;[7] as R. Moshe Feinstein wrote[8] regarding present times, when a woman does not nurse, she will almost always begin menstruating again [within 24 months], and even many nursing mothers experience bleeding and menstruate. Therefore, women who experience bleeding,[9] even within 24 months, are no longer presumed to be *mesulakot damim*, and their status reverts to the norm.[10]

Given the changes in today's reality, there is a question as to whether a nursing mother who experienced bleeding must observe the *onah beinonit* as well. This is the subject of a dispute between *Sidrei Taharah*[11] and *Shulḥan Arukh Ha-Rav*.[12] *Darkhei Taharah* rules like *Sidrei Taharah* that a nursing woman who

7. In contradistinction to the view that "nature has changed," some hold that the earlier return of menses after childbirth is linked to improved health and nutrition of mothers nowadays. This is the view of the author of *Kuntres Pardes Rimonim* (cited in *Responsa Bnei Banim* 1:31): "Nowadays, in any case, even among nursing mothers, menstruation regularly begins within six months of birth. The improved health and nutrition of our generation have lessened the physical difficulties of pregnancy, childbirth, and nursing. A nursing mother, like a mother who is not nursing, must, therefore, observe all of the laws of *niddah*." To this, R. Henkin commented to me, as is the gist of what he wrote there (ibid): "Women who nurse exclusively for the first six months, and whose bodies therefore produce an abundance of milk, and who only add other foods to supplement the nursing after six months, yet continue nursing as the baby wishes – most such women do not begin menstruating again until after a year or two, like in the times of the Gemara. Times have not changed, and these matters are not linked to nutrition, but to hormones in the woman's body. This is well known." The aforementioned dispute was stated with respect to nursing as a form of contraception, not in context of establishing *vesatot*.
8. *Igrot Moshe, Yoreh De'ah* 3:52:1.
9. This applies even when this bleeding occurs on days that would technically render it *dam tohar* (from day 8 to day 40 after the birth of a male, and from day 15 to day 80 after the birth of a female), as implied by the laconic statement of Rema, *Yoreh De'ah* 194:1 (at the end): "Its status is that of all other blood in every respect."
10. *Darkhei Taharah*, chapter 7, p. 84; *Taharat Ha-Bayit*,1:2:8, p. 85. *Badei Ha-Shulḥan* 189:33, elucidations, s.v. "*ḥosheshet le-re'iyah she-tir'eh*," cites *Ḥatam Sofer* (*siman* 143) as stating that she must be concerned for bleeding even during the *yemei tohar*, i.e., 40 days for a male and 80 days for a female. Likewise, *Ḥazon Ish* 87:2 writes that we do not differentiate *yemei tohar* from other days; in other words, *dam tohar* is considered like all other blood in every respect. See Zimmerman, D. R. "Lactational amenorrhea and *mesuleket damim* – a medical and halachic review." *B'Or Hatorah* 2002; 13E:173–82.
11. 189:36, s.v. "*ve-od*." *Pitḥei Teshuvah* 189:31 also cites the view that they need not observe the *onah beinonit*. A woman with a *veset kavu'a* who experiences bleeding at an irregular time must anticipate her regular bleeding but need not observe the *onah beinonit*, since the observance of the *onah beinonit* is for women without a *veset kavu'a*. Certainly, then, *mesulakot damim*, such as pregnant or nursing women, need not observe the *onah beinonit*, which is the average cycle of most women.
12. *Yoreh De'ah* 189:114 rules stringently (in the name of Maharam Padua *siman* 25) that such a woman must observe the *onah beinonit*.

experiences bleeding within 24 months of childbirth must observe the *onat ha-ḥodesh* and the *onat ha-haflagah,* but need not observe the *onah beinonit* – like a pregnant woman.[13] R. Yaakov Warhaftig agrees with this position.[14] However, R. Mordechai Eliyahu notes that some are stringent and observe the *onah beinonit* as well, and that one should show concern for their view. Likewise, *Igrot Moshe,*[15] *Shi'urei Shevet Ha-Levi,*[16] and *Taharah Ke-Halakhah*[17] ruled that a *meineket* should observe the *onah beinonit* if she experiences bleeding.[18]

Thus far, we have addressed the subject of observing *onot perishah.*

The *Rishonim* disagree about a *meineket* establishing a *veset* within 24 months of childbirth. According to Ramban,[19] if a woman experiences bleeding within 24 months of childbirth, it is evident that she is not *mesuleket damim,* and she therefore establishes a *veset* even while she is still nursing. This is also the ruling of *Shakh,*[20] following *Baḥ,* and *Mishneh Halakhot* cites it as the prevailing view.[21]

According to Rashba,[22] the presumption that pregnant and nursing are *mesulakot damim* is absolute, even if they experience bleeding on three occasions at fixed times.[23] Therefore, the bleeding is deemed irregular, and it does not establish a *veset.*[24]

---

13. *Darkhei Taharah,* chapter 7, p. 84. See the halakhic expansion of *Siman* 2: *Onot Perishah* at the Beginning of Pregnancy. This is also the ruling of *Ḥelkat Yaakov, Yoreh De'ah siman* 96.
14. See R. Y. Warhaftig, "*Onah Beinonit,*" *Teḥumin* 24, p. 235.
15. *Yoreh De'ah* 3:52:1.
16. 189:35:5, in accordance with Maharam Padua (*siman* 25).
17. *Taharah Ke-Halakhah,* chapter 24, *siman* 100. The author writes further that even those who maintain that the *onah beinonit* entails the couple separating on both the 30th and 31st days would agree that, in the case of a *mesuleket damim,* observing the 30th day suffices.
18. *Badei Ha-Shulḥan* (189:33, *bi'urim,* s.v. "*ḥosheshet le-re'iyah she-tir'eh*") cites the stringent view of Maharam Padua, namely, that a pregnant or nursing woman who experiences bleeding must observe the *onah beinonit,* but then challenges it: "If she need not observe a *veset kavu'a* that she herself established, why should she be concerned about the *onah beinonit,* which is the average *veset* of regular women?" The discussion ends without resolution, *Taharat Ha-Bayit* 1:2:8 states that it is proper to be stringent about the *onah beinonit,* though one who is lenient has authorities upon whom to rely.
19. Commentary on *Niddah* 11b, s.v. "*mi-de'amrinan.*"
20. *Yoreh De'ah* 189:73.
21. 5:139.
22. *Torat Ha-Bayit, bayit* 7, *sha'ar* 3, p. 12a.
23. At the end of his statements, Rashba writes that one should be concerned for the view of Ra'avad, namely, that bleeding while nursing should be treated as a *veset she-eino kavu'a.*
24. *Responsa Mishneh Halakhot* (5:139) explains the reasoning of Rashba and *Shulḥan Arukh*: although they do not rule in accordance with the Gemara regarding *siluk damim,* with respect to establishing a *veset* while nursing, the status has not changed, due

According to Ra'avad,[25] *mesulakot damim* cannot establish a *veset kavu'a* while pregnant or nursing; rather, they regard bleeding they experience under these conditions as they would a *veset she-eino kavu'a*. This is the ruling of *Shulḥan Arukh*[26] and *Taharah Ke-Halakhah*.[27] *Darkhei Taharah*[28] writes, expanding on this view: "A woman who establishes a *veset* while nursing must observe, within these 24 months, only the *veset* she established. However, the status of this *veset* is not that of a full-fledged *veset*, so when her nursing period ends, she is required to observe the *veset* she established before becoming pregnant, if she had one."[29] This is also the ruling of *Shi'urei Shevet Ha-Levi*[30] and *Badei Ha-Shulḥan*.[31]

When must the woman revert to observing the *veset kavu'a* she established prior to her pregnancy? According to Rashba,[32] she reverts as soon as the 24 months are over, even if she has not yet experienced bleeding. This is also the ruling of *Shulḥan Arukh*.[33] In contrast, Ra'avad and Ramban[34] – and *Shakh* following them[35] – maintain that a woman is considered *mesuleket damim* within 24 months only if she has not experienced bleeding. She reverts to observing the previously established *veset* once she has first experienced bleeding even within the 24 months.

According to R. Mordekhai Eliyahu,[36] after the period of nursing – that is, after 24 months – she reverts to observing the *veset kavu'a* she had established prior to her pregnancy; if she experiences bleeding on the expected day, she is considered to have a *veset kavu'a*, and if she does not, she is considered to have a *veset she-eino kavu'a*. Thus, if, before pregnancy, she had a *veset* on a particular date of the Hebrew month, and after 24 months she reverts to experiencing bleeding on that date, she is deemed to have a *veset kavu'a*. In contrast, she need not observe a *veset ha-guf* until she begins having the expected physical sensation once again.

---

to the weakness caused by childbirth and the dislocation of the mother's limbs – and certainly nowadays, since weakness has descended upon the world.

25. *Ba'alei Ha-Nefesh, Sha'ar Tikun Ha-Vesatot*, p. 55.
26. *Yoreh De'ah* 189:33.
27. Chapter 11, *siman* 10.
28. Chapter 7, p. 85.
29. Cited in *Pitḥei Teshuvah, Yoreh De'ah* 184:14.
30. 189:34:3.
31. 189:33, *bi'urim*, s.v. "*ḥosheshet le-re'iyah she-tir'eh*."
32. *Torat Ha-Bayit, bayit* 7, *sha'ar* 3, p. 13a.
33. *Yoreh De'ah* 189:34.
34. *Hilkhot Niddah* 6:7.
35. *Yoreh De'ah* 189:75.
36. *Darkhei Taharah*, chapter 7, p. 85.

If the *veset ha-guf* returns just once, it has the status of a *veset kavu'a* and is only uprooted if the sensation is absent three times.[37]

A woman who had a *veset she-eino kavu'a* prior to pregnancy need not observe the old dates after 24 months.[38] In contrast, R. Moshe Feinstein[39] maintains that she must observe a *veset kavu'a* as soon as she begins menstruating again, even within 24 months.

In sum, nowadays, most women begin menstruating again within the 24 months of nursing – a period during which *Ḥakhamim* presume her to be *mesuleket damim*. Therefore, a woman who menstruates, even within these 24 months, must observe a *veset she-eino kavu'a*.

S.K.

37. *Yoreh De'ah* 189:34.
38. *Noda Bi-Yehudah*, cited in *Pitḥei Teshuvah* 189:32. This is also the ruling of *Darkhei Taharah*, chapter 7, p. 85.
39. *Igrot Moshe, Yoreh De'ah* 3:52:1.

Siman 20

Bedikot with Uterine Prolapse

Question

Since my most recent delivery, I have been suffering from severe uterine prolapse, and the doctor inserted a pessary. In principle, I can remove it myself, but it is both uncomfortable and complicated to do so. In addition, I am concerned about bleeding because of the uterine prolapse. How am I supposed to perform a *hefsek taharah* or *bedikot* during the seven *neki'im*?

Answer

If you can easily remove the pessary, you must do so while performing *bedikot*, or at least for the *hefsek taharah* and for one *bedikah* during the seven *neki'im*. However, if it is difficult for you to remove it, or if it can only be removed by a physician, you may be lenient and perform the *bedikot* with the pessary in your body, since it is internal.

While performing the *bedikot*, you must try to reach as deep as possible inside without causing yourself pain or harm.

If there is bleeding, or if *ketamim* appear, a medical examination would be necessary, to ascertain whether or not the blood originates in a *petza* (sore, cut, or abrasion) caused by the uterine prolapse. If the bleeding is caused by the prolapse, the blood is deemed to be that of a *petza*. In such a situation, you are required to obtain a clean *bedikah* cloth at the *hefsek taharah*. However, you may perform several *bedikot* (gently, and with breaks of several minutes between each *bedikah*, so as not to exacerbate the *petza* until you obtain one clean *bedikah*.) Additionally, you should try to obtain one clean *bedikah* on the first day and one on the seventh of the *neki'im*. If this is difficult, at least one *bedikah* on the first or seventh day is required to be clean. If this, too, is impossible, at least one clean *bedikah* must be obtained during the seven *neki'im*.

As for all other *bedikot*, if they are not clean, the blood can be attributed to the *petza*. You may also reduce the number of *bedikot* (once daily, once every two days, or only on the first and seventh day, depending on your medical situation).

If the bleeding is not linked to the uterine prolapse, there are no grounds for leniency regarding *bedikot* that are not clean. However, you are permitted to reduce the number of *bedikot* like any woman who is having difficulty becoming *tehorah*.

If the bleeding is caused by the uterine prolapse, it is deemed *dam petza*, and it does not invalidate your count. In such a situation, you are required to obtain a clean *bedikah* cloth at the *hefsek taharah*. Because of your condition, you may perform repeated *bedikot* until you obtain one clean *bedikah*.

Halakhic Expansion

Uterine prolapse is a medical condition in which the uterus "slips" out of its normal position within the pelvic cavity and descends into the vagina. Factors that increase risk of this condition are those that weaken the muscles and ligaments that support the uterus, for example: a history of difficult childbirths, prior gynecological surgeries, obesity, prolonged constipation, chronic coughing, genetic factors, etc. The severity of uterine prolapse can vary; in the worst cases, the cervix and/or the uterus protrude out of the vagina.

Symptoms vary from woman to woman, depending on the severity of the prolapse. Typically, a prolapsed uterus does not constitute a medical problem, but it can adversely affect a woman's quality of life, for example, by making it difficult to walk, causing urine leakage, pain during marital relations and irregular bleeding.

The current common first-line treatment is to change habits by improving one's diet, increasing physical activity, and stopping smoking (if applicable). In addition, physical therapy to improve the pelvic floor muscles has proven effective in many cases. If these steps are ineffective, surgery is a possibility, as is the insertion of a device that provides vaginal support and "lifts" the uterus back into place. This treatment will generally be provided temporarily or for women who cannot undergo surgery. For post-menopausal women, after prior options have been exhausted, the remaining option is a hysterectomy.

Removing the Pessary for *Bedikot*

Use of a vaginal ring to support the uterus against prolapse has been known for several centuries, and a number of *poskim* addressed the question of performing a *hefsek taharah* and *bedikot* with a pessary in place. *Zikhron Yosef*[1] permitted leaving the vaginal device in place during *bedikot*, "for just as the ring does not prevent her husband from engaging in intercourse with her, so it does not prevent the insertion of the *mokh* there." However, *Sidrei Taharah*[2] rejects this view and requires the removal of the device, at least for the *hefsek taharah*. Other *poskim* require the removal of the device even for the *bedikah* of the first of the seven *neki'im*.[3] *Arukh Ha-Shulḥan*[4] conditions the ruling on the woman's ability to remove the device on her own. If she can remove it, then she must; and if she cannot (because it is dangerous, or because it is placed where only a doctor can remove it), she must perform a thorough *hefsek taharah* with a *mokh daḥuk* throughout *bein ha-shemashot*, plus one thorough *bedikah* during the seven *neki'im*, and on the other days she may suffice with gentler *bedikot*; and the pessary does not impede her count. The *Nishmat Avraham*[5] states that this was the ruling of R. Shlomo Zalman Auerbach and R. Yehoshua Neuwirth as well, based on *Ḥeshev Ha-Efod*.[6] However, in his view, since it is usually easy to remove the pessary, it should be removed *lekhatḥilah*. In the present case, the pessary can be removed, but not easily. It therefore seems that one may be lenient when necessary.

Vaginal Bleeding Due to Uterine Prolapse

Tur and *Shulḥan Arukh* address uterine prolapse.[7] Their source is a ruling of R. Shimshon of Coucy, who, based on the Talmud's statement[8] about a woman who delivers a piece of blood-filled tissue, deemed *tehorah* a woman "whose uterus became dislocated, and something akin to pieces of tissue were falling into the vagina ... since it is not normal for a woman to bleed thus."[9]

---

1. *Yoreh De'ah* 10.
2. Ibid. 196:23.
3. *Responsa Binyan Tzion* 1:71.
4. *Yoreh De'ah* 196:29.
5. Ibid. 196:4.
6. *Responsa Ḥeshev Ha-Efod* 2:118 addresses the question of *ḥatzitzah*, but the *poskim* apply the relevant laws to the question of *bekikot* during the seven *neki'im*. Regarding the question of whether a pessary constitutes a *ḥatzitzah*, see below, *Siman* 49: *Mikveh* Immersion with a Contraceptive Ring.
7. *Yoreh De'ah* 188:3.
8. *Niddah* 21b.
9. As recorded by Rosh, cited in *Bet Yosef, Yoreh De'ah* 188:3.

Rema adds:[10] "Even if she experienced bleeding, as long as the pieces are in the vagina, she is *tehorah,* for we attribute the blood to these pieces, since she knows for certain that her uterus is dislocated and that this is due to a *makkah.* This is implied by *Tur,* Rabbeinu Yeruḥam, and Rosh."

In contrast, *Baḥ*[11] rules that the woman is *tehorah* only if she did not experience any bleeding when the pieces of tissue fell from the uterus, and only later found blood in the vagina, because it is not the way of a woman to see [menstrual blood] in this fashion. *Shakh* follows this ruling as well.[12] In practice, *Baḥ* rejected the ruling of R. Shimshon of Coucy (relying instead on Rashi and *Tosafot*). *Taz,*[13] on the other hand, adopts the view of Rema, though not for the Rema's stated reason, namely, that the bleeding can be attributed to a *makkah,* but because this is not the way of a woman to see menstrual blood. A practical ramification of *Taz*'s rationale is that even if the piece of tissue contains menstrual blood, the woman is *tehorah,* because only blood that issues from the uterus while it is in place renders one *teme'ah.*

Pitḥei Teshuvah[14] cites many *poskim* who dealt with this topic and comments that, due to its complexity, only the leading *gedolim* of the generation may decide it. However, in many cases, the vaginal bleeding is caused by irritation of the vaginal lining and/or uterus due to the prolapsed uterus. This type of bleeding does not render a woman *niddah.* Therefore, the matter can be resolved in favor of leniency. So writes *Arukh Ha-Shulḥan,*[15] who cites the views of the *Rishonim* and *Aḥaronim* on the subject and then notes:[16] "On the contrary, one of the great sages said that it stands to reason that *vorfall* [= uterine prolapse] is treated more leniently than the view of R. Shimshon according to the interpretation of the earlier authorities, for in this case she did not experience bleeding at all before the uterus lapsed into the vagina, and when the uterus lapsed, there was tissue but no blood. The blood began to flow from within the vagina, which is not a place of *tum'ah* at all [*Pardes Rimonim* on *Taz* §5]."

10. *Yoreh De'ah* 188:3.
11. Ibid. 188:3.
12. Ibid. 188:9.
13. Ibid. 188:5.
14. Ibid. 188:7.
15. Ibid. 188:23ff.
16. Ibid. 188:58.

Vaginal Bleeding Caused by Shedding of Uterine Lining

If the bleeding is from within the uterine cavity itself, most *poskim* rule stringently and deem the woman *teme'ah*, in accordance with the view of *Shakh*.[17]

Noda Bi-Yehudah addressed this matter in two of his responsa. In the first,[18] he discusses a young woman of child-bearing age who had a prolapsed uterus. He vehemently disagrees with the *poskim* who permit, based on R. Shimshon of Coucy, cases of bleeding from a prolapsed uterus. He claims that R. Shimshon of Coucy only ruled permissively when pieces of tissue came out of the uterus and not in cases of bleeding, which would be considered *niddah* blood in every respect, not the blood of a *makkah*. *Noda Bi-Yehudah* further claimed that even if the uterus lapsed, when menstrual blood flows from it, it is *k'darkah,* blood which flows in the "way" women see blood, despite the dislocation of the uterus. Even granting that there is a *makkah,* this is a wound regarding which it is not known whether this *makkah* bleeds. Therefore, we must be stringent in this situation.

In contrast, in the later responsum,[19] he discusses the case of a 60-year-old post-menopausal woman suffering from uterine prolapse. There he rules that in the case of a post-menopausal woman, one may attribute the bleeding even to a *makkah* that is not known to bleed, and especially if the woman experiences pain. She is therefore *tehorah*. Nevertheless, he conditions this ruling on her not having experienced a *hargashah*. Moreover, due to the severity of the matter, he wrote that his ruling should only be implemented in practice if another leading sage concurs with it.

Noda Bi-Yehudah[20] and many other *poskim* discuss *Me'il Tzedakah*'s alternate interpretation[21] of R. Shimshon of Coucy's ruling. According to him, R. Shimshon's words, "pieces (*ḥatikhot*) of tissue" should be emended to "a piece (*ḥatikhat*) of tissue." That is, he refers to the lapse of the uterus itself, as a single piece. The bleeding that the woman experiences in such a case is not considered bleeding in "the way women bleed" and therefore does not cause *tum'ah*. *Noda Bi-Yehudah* rejects this interpretation, but other *poskim* are inclined to accept it.[22]

---

17. Ibid. 188:8.
18. *Noda Bi-Yehudah* 1:58.
19. Ibid. 2:114.
20. 1:58.
21. *Responsa Me'il Tzedakah siman* 34.
22. See, for example: *Sidrei Taharah* 188:4 (at the end), which is inclined to concur with *Me'il Tzedakah* but was wary of ruling against the view of most *poskim*; *Ḥatam Sofer* cited below.

Ḥatam Sofer[23] also discusses a woman who suffered from uterine prolapse and could not become *tehorah* due to green and white discharges that would turn red after drying. *Ḥatam Sofer* was inclined to accept the interpretation of *Me'il Tzedakah* and rejected the reasoning of *Noda Bi-Yehudah* but was wary of ruling leniently since Rambam did not rule like R. Shimshon of Coucy. He therefore conditioned his ruling on the ruling of an additional sage and found grounds for leniency based on the unique combination of circumstances: there was no *hargashah* (except for the sensation of a wet discharge, which he does not deem to be a *hargashah*); the discharges were initially a halakhically acceptable color but only later turned red; and the woman has the *makkah* of a prolapsed uterus, which, according to some *poskim*, renders the bleeding "not in the way women see blood" and therefore *tahor*. He then gave the woman specific instructions about what procedures to follow during the seven *neki'im* (see below).

Based on these and other *poskim*, R. Yehudah Assad[24] ruled leniently in the case of a 73-year-old woman, and *Arukh Ha-Shulḥan*[25] argued that there is no disagreement between R. Shimshon of Coucy, on one hand, and Rashi and *Tosafot*, on the other, so there are grounds for leniency.

R. Shmuel Wosner wrote likewise:[26] "A woman who suffers from uterine prolapse … and during a *bedikah* she touched there, and blood came out, and the doctor said that there is a bleeding *petza* there, it is obvious that she may attribute. …"

In light of this, and given the ability nowadays to medically determine the most likely cause of the bleeding, it seems that we can make the following distinction: If it is clear that the source of bleeding is outside the uterus, one may be lenient in all cases. If the bleeding is from within the uterine cavity, a post-menopausal woman may be lenient. Regarding a woman who still menstruates, it must be ascertained whether the source of the bleeding is *niddah* blood or from a *makkah*, and a decision should be reached accordingly.

The Required Number of *Bedikot*

If there is bleeding or spotting, one should ascertain, by means of a medical exam, whether the bleeding is that of a *petza* resulting from the uterine prolapse. Bleeding caused by uterine prolapse is considered to be the blood of a *petza*. Therefore, when performing the *hefsek taharah*, a blood-free *bedikah* cloth should be

23. *Responsa Ḥatam Sofer*, vol. 2, *Yoreh De'ah* 145.
24. *Responsa Yehudah Ya'aleh*, *Yoreh De'ah* 1:219, s.v. "*ha-yom paniti*."
25. *Yoreh De'ah* 188:23–64.
26. *Shi'urei Shevet Ha-Levi*, *hosafot*, p. 378.

obtained. (One may make several attempts to obtain a clean *bedikah.*) Likewise, the woman may reduce the number of *bedikot* to once daily, once every two days, or only on the first and seventh day, depending on the situation.[27]

One should try to obtain, at the very least, one clean *bedikah* on the first day and one on the seventh of the *neki'im.* If this is difficult, at least one *bedikah* on the first or seventh day must be clean. If this, too, is impossible, at least one clean *bedikah* must be obtained during the seven *neki'im.* If, after obtaining a clean *hefsek taharah* and *bedikah* on the first day, she finds blood during *bedikot,* she may attribute this blood to a *petza.*

For the present purposes, let us add the words of *Arukh Ha-Shulḥan*:[28] "If a God-fearing *posek,* who is wise in Torah and who understands the medical situation, presumes that this woman has a dysfunction in her uterus, or in the tissue around her uterus and the like, such that she cannot become *tehorah* for her husband, and she has a *veset kavu'a* so that she is *tehorah* when it is not her time to menstruate, then she requires only a clean *hefsek taharah* plus one clean *bedikah* during the seven *neki'im.* She may then immerse to become *tehorah* for her husband. Let her not look at *bedikot* that were not clean or at her *ketamim*...."

If the bleeding is not linked to the uterine prolapse, there are no grounds for leniency regarding *bedikot* that are not clean. However, she may reduce the number of *bedikot* as with any woman who is having difficulty becoming *tehorah.*

N.L.

---

27. This matter was discussed extensively above, *Siman* 14: *Mokh Daḥuk* and *Bedikot* following Birth, based on *Shulḥan Arukh, Yoreh De'ah* 196:4 and 6; *Noda Bi-Yehudah, Yoreh De'ah* 2:129; *Shi'urei Shevet Ha-Levi,* loc. cit.; *Darkhei Taharah,* p. 134; *Sha'arei Orah,* p. 137. *Igrot Moshe* ruled that if there is a painful *petza,* the woman may suffice with a single *bedikah* during the seven *neki'im* (*Igrot Moshe, Yoreh De'ah* 2:69; see also 3:56:3). *Responsa Har Tzvi* (*Yoreh De'ah* 146) cites *Responsa Maharash Engel* (3:83) that a *bedikah* on the first or seventh suffices. See immediately below, *Siman* 21: Attributing Blood to a *Petza* during the Seven *Neki'im.*
28. *Yoreh De'ah* 188:8. This is also the ruling of *Shi'urei Shevet Ha-Levi, hosafot,* p. 378.

Siman 21

Attributing Blood to a Petza during the Seven Neki'im

Question

I am 32 years old and gave birth a year ago. I breastfeed, and four months ago I resumed getting my period once again. Since giving birth, it has been difficult for me to perform *bedikot* during the seven *neki'im*. The *hefsek taharah* and initial *bedikot* come out clean, but after a few days, I find blood on the *bedikah* cloth, and it is another few days before I can manage to do another *hefsek taharah*.

I do not find any discharge on my underwear, and the *bedikot* are not painful. I consulted a doctor who explained that the bleeding is apparently due to vaginal dryness and does not require medical treatment. I have been *niddah* for a month and a half because of this situation, and in the meantime, I got my period again, before I could even go to the *mikveh*. What can be done?

Answer

Natural excretions are discharged into the vagina to lubricate the region, so under normal circumstances, *bedikot* do not cause a *petza* (sore, cut, abrasion or wound). However, due to hormonal changes during nursing, such as lowered estrogen levels, the vaginal area may become drier and more irritable. In the absence of lubricants, repeated internal *bedikot* can abrade the area and cause bleeding on a *bedikah* cloth. Spreading a lubricant on the area can help prevent this. If an over-the-counter lubricant does not improve the situation, we recommend that you see a doctor to look into the possibility of a prescription ointment.

Given your physician's diagnosis of vaginal dryness that is likely to result in bleeding, we may presume that the blood you saw originates in a *petza*. You may therefore count seven *neki'im* and attribute the blood that you find during those days to the *petza*. There is no need to start the count over each time.

Since you experience bleeding after several days of *bedikot*, it seems that the *bedikot* are what cause the bleeding. So as not to exacerbate your situation, after performing a *hefsek taharah*, you may perform a single *bedikah* on the first day and a single *bedikah* on the seventh. It is also worthwhile to moisten or put a water-based gel on the *bedikah* cloth before performing the *bedikah*.

Even when attributing to a *makkah*, you should try, at the very least, to obtain one fully clean *bedikah* on the first and one on the seventh of the *neki'im*. If your situation makes this impossible, at least one *bedikah* on the first or seventh days must be clean. If even this is impossible, at least one *bedikah* at some point during the seven days must be clean. If, after obtaining a clean *hefsek taharah* and *bedikah* on the first day, you find blood during *bedikot*, you may attribute this blood to a wound.

There are, however, no grounds for leniency vis-à-vis the *hefsek taharah*. If that *bedikah* does not come out clean, you may wish to seek assistance in performing it from a nurse-practitioner specializing in *taharah* examinations or from your physician.

Halakhic Expansion

When a doctor observes bleeding tissue in the vagina,[1] the woman is deemed to have a known *makkah* that can bleed.[2] The Gemara says of this, "If she has a wound in that place, she attributes to her wound."[3]

The *Rishonim* disagree about when to permit the attribution of blood to a wound to release a woman from *niddah* status. According to Rashba, one may be lenient

1. On the possibility of attributing to a *makkah* based on the blood's location on the *bedikah* cloth or on pain experienced during the *bedikah*, see below, *Siman* 45: Suspected Wound and Stain Location on the *Bedikah* Cloth. The *poskim* cite a dispute about the degree of credibility and knowledge of physicians. *Ḥatam Sofer* writes that a physician's opinion is presumed to be based only on general knowledge, so one may not reach a permissive ruling based on a doctor's statement. However, most contemporary *poskim* disagree. See *Pitḥei Teshuvah, Yoreh De'ah* 187:38; *Taharat Ha-Bayit* 1:5:8, p. 243; *Shi'urei Shevet Ha-Levi* 187:8. See also above, *Siman* 16: Observation of Blood by a Physician during the Postpartum Examination.
2. The permissibility of attributing to *makkah* is discussed in Gemara with regard to a woman who bleeds as a result of intercourse (*Niddah* 66a). The *Rishonim* rule in accordance with R. Yehuda Ha-Nasi in that passage.
3. *Niddah* 66a.

and attribute the blood to a *makkah* even if it is not known for certain that the *makkah* bleeds.[4] On the other hand, according to *Sefer Ha-Terumah*, while it need not be absolutely certain that the blood observed at this moment came from the wound, but it must be known for certain that the wound is of the type that bleeds.[5]

Shulḥan Arukh[6] writes that if there is a *makkah* in that location [i.e., the vaginal area], one may attribute bleeding to the *makkah*, but does not discuss the degree of likelihood that a wound exists that would warrant attribution to it. Rema distinguishes between three situations. A woman with a *veset kavu'a* may attribute bleeding to a wound if she observes blood at a time when she is not anticipating her *veset*, even if she does not know that the *makkah* bleeds. A woman with a *veset she-eino kavu'a*, who is uncertain whether the blood comes from the uterus or the sides [of the vagina] may also attribute the bleeding to her wound by virtue of a double uncertainty (*sfek sfeika*): perhaps the bleeding is vaginal, and even if it is uterine, perhaps it is from a *makkah*. However, if it is certain that the blood is uterine, one must know for certain that the wound bleeds in order to attribute the bleeding to it.

In the question at hand, we may rely on the doctor's diagnosis that the vaginal tissue may sometimes bleed from contact, and therefore, we may attribute the blood observed to a *makkah*. The bleeding caused by dryness does not cause *tum'ah* because its source is known to be non-uterine. However, the woman must obtain clean *bedikot* in order to establish a presumption of *taharah*, and her bleeding makes that difficult.

However, as distinct from *teliyah be-makkah*, attributing bleeding to a wound when the woman is *tehorah* in order to prevent *niddah* status – attributing bleeding to a *makkah* during the seven *neki'im* is more complicated. Rema writes that one may not attribute *ketamim* during the first three of the seven *neki'im* except to a wound that is known to bleed.[7] *Shakh*[8] is more stringent, stating that even when the *makkah* is known to bleed, one may not attribute to it during those first three days. In practice, those who follow *Shulḥan Arukh* may attribute bleeding to a *petza* throughout the seven *neki'im*, and those who follow Rema may attribute only when the *makkah* is known to bleed. Note that the special status of the

---

4. *Torat Ha-Bayit, bayit 7, sha'ar 4*, p. 23.
5. *Bet Yosef, Yoreh De'ah* 92.
6. *Yoreh De'ah* 187:5.
7. Ibid. 196:10.
8. Ibid. 196:13.

first three days applies only to a woman who became *teme'ah* from menstruation.[9] However, if she overturned her counting and was required to begin counting anew, she may attribute the bleeding to a wound on any of the seven days. In the question at hand, had the woman turned to us earlier, during her previous *yemei libun* and before she began menstruating again, we could have attributed her bleeding to a *petza* and enabled her to continue counting *neki'im*. However, since she has begun menstruating a second time,[10] she should now be taught how a woman with a vaginal abrasion performs a *hefsek taharah* and subsequent *bedikot* during the seven *neki'im*.

The *hefsek taharah* comes to remove a woman from the *ḥazakah* of her established *niddah* status. Therefore, attribution of blood in the *hefsek taharah* to an abrasion would render it ineffective, because ultimately a *bedikah* with no blood on it is required to ascertain that the uterine bleeding has stopped. Therefore, many *Aḥaronim* wrote that even when a woman has a vaginal *petza*, a completely blood-free *bedikah* is necessary for the *hefsek taharah*. With respect to this *bedikah*, according to these *poskim*, bleeding even if attributed to a wound, cannot override the *ḥazakah* of *niddah*.[11]

However, other *Aḥaronim* wrote that one may be lenient and attribute blood to a *makkah* even for a *hefsek taharah*, under the assumption that it is not the *bedikah* that removes a woman from her established *niddah* status. Rather, it is normal for a woman to bleed for several days and then stop, and if there has elapsed sufficient time in which most women would have stopped bleeding, we may attribute further bleeding to an abrasion.[12] Thus, R. Ovadiah Yosef ruled that one may attribute to a wound even for a *hefsek taharah*.[13]

R. Mordechai Eliyahu[14] ruled that when a woman is certain that the blood she observed originated in an abrasion – for instance, when the blood always appears

9. In this case, there is a presumption that "her uterus is open"; see *Dagul Me-Revavah* 196:10, s.v. "*yesh omrim*."
10. It is worth considering whether, had she not become *niddah* anew, there would be grounds to be *metaher* her retroactively, or whether, due to the principle of *shavyah a-nafshah* (that when a person considers something forbidden, it becomes forbidden to them), she has already accepted the prohibition on herself. This question applies in general when a woman mistakenly thinks something is prohibited. See below, *Siman* 59: A Spot on a Tampon.
11. *Responsa Ḥatam Sofer, Yoreh De'ah* 177; *Ḥavat Da'at* 196:3; *Ezrat Yehudah, Yoreh De'ah* 29; *Sidrei Taharah* 196:23 at the end.
12. *Responsa Zikhron Yosef, Yoreh De'ah siman* 10.
13. *Taharat Ha-Bayit* 1:5:10, pp. 252–53.
14. *Darkhei Taharah*, 2nd edition (2007), pp. 34–35.

on one side of the *bedikah* cloth – she may attribute it even for a *hefsek taharah*. However, he adds that to do so she must repeat the *bedikah* three times – in the evening, the morning, and the next evening – and the blood must continue to appear on that side, in order to establish a presumption of *taharah*.[15]

A similar problem arises with respect to *bedikot* during the seven *neki'im*. When a woman has a *petza*, she should not be instructed to perform all of the *bedikot* that would be performed *lekhatḥilah* during the seven *neki'im* lest she further aggravate her wound. Rather, in addition to the *hefsek taharah*, she should perform one *bedikah* on the first day and one on the seventh day, and no more. If she observes blood during these *bedikot*, she may attribute it to an abrasion. However, the question remains whether such a *bedikah* fulfills the obligation to perform a *bedikah*. This is a matter of dispute among *Aḥaronim*, similar to the dispute about the *hefsek taharah*.

According to *Ḥavat Da'at*,[16] she must obtain a clean *bedikah* at least on the first day, in addition to the *hefsek taharah*. On the other hand, *Ḥatam Sofer* disagrees,[17] writing that one may attribute bleeding to a *petza* throughout the seven *neki'im*. This is because, in contrast to *Ḥatam Sofer*'s explanation of the purpose of the *hefsek taharah*,[18] the purpose of *bedikot* is not to remove a woman from the presumption of being *niddah*, but to confirm her *taharah*.

R. Shmuel Wosner cites this dispute and rules stringently, in accordance with *Ḥavat Da'at*, and requiring that a blood-free *bedikah* be obtained on the first of the seven *neki'im*, in addition to the *hefsek taharah*. Only when this is impossible may we rely on *Ḥatam Sofer*.

R. Tzvi Pesaḥ Frank[19] is yet more stringent: he requires three clean *bedikot*: the *hefsek taharah*, a *bedikah* on the first day, and a *bedikah* on the seventh day.[20]

In practice, the application of this *halakhah* depends on the woman's situation.

Sometimes, a repeat *bedikah*, after blood was found on the previous *bedikah*, can enable a woman to obtain a clean *bedikah* after attributing the blood on the first *bedikah* to a wound. In such a situation, she should try very hard to ensure that

15. Based on the *Aḥaronim* cited in *Pitḥei Teshuvah* 187:24.
16. 196:3.
17. *Yoreh De'ah* 177.
18. Ibid. 177.
19. *Responsa Har Tzvi, Yoreh De'ah siman* 146.
20. *Responsa Maharash Engel* 3:83, cited in *Responsa Har Tzvi*, states that a *bedikah* on the first or the seventh day suffices. Both are not required.

the three *bedikot* mentioned by *Responsa Har Tzvi* are blood-free, obviating the need to discuss attribution to a wound for these *bedikot*.

In some situations, the nature of the abrasion is such that it is impossible to obtain a clean *bedikah*, either because of the location and irritability of the wound, or because the *petza* causes the woman pain. Under such circumstances, it is possible to be lenient, either in accordance with R. Wosner's ruling, based on *Ḥavat Da'at*, requiring a *hefsek taharah* and a *bedikah* on the first day; in accordance with *Ḥatam Sofer* that the *hefsek taharah* alone suffices; or in accordance with the *Aḥaronim* – and the ruling of R. Ovadiah Yosef – who maintain that all *bedikot*, including the *hefsek taharah*, can be attributed to a *makkah*.

The length of time during which a woman may attribute bleeding to a *makkah* varies according to the specific case. See below, *Siman* 52: Bleeding from a *Petza* Caused by IUD, where we address this subject.

Z.B.

Part III

Pregnancy Loss

Siman 22

Counting Seven Neki'im following D & C

Question

I underwent a D & C in the tenth week of pregnancy, after the fetus died in utero. The doctor reported that fetal size, based on the ultrasound, was appropriate for a gestational age of six weeks and three days. When may I perform a *hefsek taharah*? When the bleeding stops? A week after the procedure (assuming there is no bleeding)? Only two weeks later?

Answer

When a pregnancy lasts fewer than 40 days following conception, the woman becomes *niddah* upon termination of the pregnancy, but there is no *tum'at leidah*. In that case, one may perform a *hefsek taharah* and begin counting the seven *neki'im* normally, as soon as the bleeding stops.

If the pregnancy terminates more than 40 days following conception, but before it is known whether the fetus was male or female, there is a 14-day wait before immersion in the *mikveh*, but the process of becoming *tehorah* may be performed earlier, as soon as the bleeding stops.

In your case, the dilation and curettage ("D & C") was performed in the tenth week, which is the eighth week according to the halakhic calculation, and more than 40 days by any calculation. Even though there are grounds to assume that the fetus died some time before the procedure, it remains possible that 40 days had passed since conception.

Therefore, you may perform a *hefsek taharah* as soon as the bleeding stops and begin counting seven *neki'im*, but you may only immerse in the *mikveh* 14 days after the D & C. Nevertheless, it's important to know that the bleeding sometimes continues much longer, and you may begin the *taharah* process only once the bleeding stops.

Halakhic Expansion

Niddah 30a records a dispute between R. Yishmael and *Ḥakhamim*. R. Yishmael maintains that the form of a male fetus is completed after 40 days of pregnancy, whereas a female is completely formed only after 80 days. *Ḥakhamim* maintain that the form of both male and female fetuses is completed after 40 days. The *halakhah* accords with Ḥazal, and therefore, whenever a pregnancy is terminated before 40 days,[1] we presume that the form of the fetus was not completed, and the bleeding is considered "mere water,"[2] not a birth. Nevertheless, she becomes *niddah* from the terminated pregnancy and must count seven *neki'im*, like following menstruation.[3] This is the ruling of all *Rishonim*, and it is brought as the *halakhah* in *Shulḥan Arukh*.[4]

In addition, *Bet Yosef* cites a discussion among the *Rishonim*[5] – cited in *Taharat Ha-Bayit*[6] and *Shi'urei Shevet Ha-Levi*[7] as well – that perhaps she does not even have the status of a *niddah* if there was no bleeding, since the fetus is still considered "mere water," and the small size of the fetus does not cause the opening of the uterus. *Shulḥan Arukh* rules that she is *niddah* even if she saw no blood, and all following him rule accordingly. She is all the more so considered *niddah* in the usual case, where there is bleeding.

---

1. The same applies if the loss of pregnancy occurred on the 40th day, according to the Mishnah in *Niddah* 30a.
2. See *Yevamot* 69b. The meaning of the term "mere water" ("*maya be-alma*") is that there is no living body of a fetus yet, but only fluids.
3. This is the ruling in *Yoreh De'ah* 194:2. Rema explains that she is *niddah* because "there can be no opening of the uterus without blood" (as *Shulḥan Arukh* rules in *Yoreh De'ah* 188:3). Likewise, if part of the uterine lining or a fetus is found that is larger than 19 mm (¾ of an inch), the woman is *niddah* because she discharged something of that size, which caused the opening of the uterus. (See further, Medical Appendix IV: Miscarriage.) For more on the question of the opening of the uterus, see below, *Siman* 50: Insertion of an IUD during the Seven *Neki'im*.
4. 194:2.
5. *Yoreh De'ah* 194:2. Rashba maintains that she is not *niddah* if there is no bleeding, but Ra'avad and Ramban disagree.
6. *Taharat Ha-Bayit* 1:11:6 and *Mishmeret Ha-Taharah ad loc.*
7. 194:2:2.

In contrast, a woman who miscarries more than 40 days after conception, once the form of the fetus is complete, has the status of a *yoledet* with regard to *tum'at leidah*. According to the Torah,[8] a woman who gives birth to a son waits seven days before immersing and becoming *tehorah* from *tum'at leidah*, and a woman who gives birth to a daughter waits 14 days. The days of *tum'at leidah* need not be free of blood from childbirth. When the sex of the fetus cannot be determined, *Shulḥan Arukh* rules that the mother waits 14 days, as for a female.[9]

Moreover, after the institution of the stringency of R. Zeira, the Gemara ruled that every *yoledet* is considered a "*yoledet be-zov*"[10] and therefore must count seven *neki'im*, like any woman who experienced bleeding. The seven *neki'im* can be included within the days of *tum'at leidah* if she does not experience bleeding.[11] This law applies after a miscarriage as well.

The counting of 40 days for determining the status of a fetus raises the question of when to count from. There are different ways of calculating the gestational age of a pregnancy. The conventional medical calculation is to count 40 weeks from the first day of the mother's last menses; that is, the pregnancy "begins" about two weeks prior to conception. Though somewhat illogical, this is the medical convention for measuring the advancement of pregnancy, since generally the date of onset of the last menses is the only date about which there is any certainty. Another way of measuring is based on fetal development, as seen in an ultrasound examination. However, this is imprecise, and there is a reasonable margin of error (approx. one week in either direction during the first trimester).

The halakhic calculation counts the age of the fetus from the estimated date of conception. However, since it is generally not possible to know the precise

8. Vayikra 12:2–5.
9. *Yoreh De'ah* 194:3. See above, *Siman* 15: Counting Seven *Neki'im* following a Caesarean Section.
10. *Niddah* 37a; *Bet Yosef, Yoreh De'ah* 194; *Shulḥan Arukh, Yoreh De'ah* 194:1. A "*yoledet be-zov*" is a woman who was a *zavah* prior to giving birth but who had not yet counted seven *neki'im*. Nowadays, we presume that every woman experienced bleeding before the childbirth process began, and therefore all *yoldot* are considered *yoldot be-zov*, since "there can be no opening of the uterus without blood."
11. *Niddah* 37a records a dispute between Abaye and Rava about the view of R. Marinus, as to whether or not days of *tum'at leidah* during which she does not experience bleeding count toward the seven *neki'im*. According to Abaye, they do not, but according to Rava, they do. Rabbeinu Tam rules in accordance with Abaye (*Tosafot* to *Niddah* 37a, s.v. "*Abaye omer*"), for he maintains that this is one of the six cases in which the *halakhah* accords with Abaye (the "lamed" of the acronym יע"ל קג"ם stands for *leidah* according to him). All other *Rishonim* rule in accordance with Rava, as in most cases. (According to them, the "lamed" stands for "*leḥi ha-omed me-elav*," a case in *Eruvin*.) *Shulḥan Arukh* rules accordingly in 194:1.

day that the ovum was fertilized, different methods of calculation have been suggested, the most accepted of which is to count from the night the mother immersed in the *mikveh* after the most recent menses.[12] According to *Responsa Avodat Ha-Gershuni*,[13] a woman counts 40 days from the night she immersed after menses,[14] not from an immersion due to *ketamim*.[15] However, many *Aḥaronim* challenged this, claiming that a woman may still experience bleeding during her first trimester.[16] R. Ovadiah Yosef[17] addresses this issue at length, ruling that there is no presumption that she may have become pregnant prior to her last menses, so the 40 days are counted from the night she immerses. R. Shmuel Wosner[18] rules accordingly, adding that nowadays an ultrasound examination can determine whether or not the pregnancy predates the bleeding; nevertheless, this method cannot establish the precise age of the fetus, because error is common. Another indication is if the woman knows exactly when she was with her husband.[19]

In most cases, assuming that the woman immersed about two weeks after the onset of her most recent menses, 40 days corresponds to approximately 7.5 weeks in the conventional medical calculation. It is therefore clear that, in the present case, the procedure was performed after the 40th day. However, since this was a "silent" miscarriage, i.e., when the fetus was no longer alive, there are grounds to consider whether the loss of the pregnancy is calculated from the time of the D & C

12. This is derived from Rashi's comment on *Niddah* 30a: "'One who miscarries on the fortieth day' – since her immersion"; as well as from Rambam's formulation in *Mishneh Torah, Hilkhot Issurei Biah* 10:2: "If she miscarried 41 days after intercourse." However, Rambam's language can lead to the conclusion that the count starts at the first intercourse after immersion, not from the date of the immersion itself. It is possible that Rashi also meant the first intercourse after immersion, but due to uncertainty, the count begins on the date of immersion. If they know when they had marital relations, one may count from that date. See *Ḥatam Sofer*, cited in n. 16 below.
13. *Siman* 21.
14. This is also the ruling of *Responsa Shevut Yaakov* 1:71; *Ḥokhmat Adam* 115:20; *Responsa Teshuvah Me-Ahavah* 1:70.
15. See *Pitḥei Teshuvah* 194:3 and *Responsa Kenei Bosem* 2:64.
16. Including *Ḥavat Da'at* 194:2; *Sidrei Taharah* 194:7; and *Responsa Ḥatam Sofer, Yoreh De'ah* 169. All of these are cited in brief in *Pitḥei Teshuvah* 194:3. According to *Ḥatam Sofer*, due to the lack of knowledge as to when pregnancy began, one must always suspect that the miscarriage may have been after 40 days and wait 14 days before immersing, unless the couple abstained from intercourse for a long time prior.
17. *Taharat Ha-Bayit* 1:11:6 and *Mishmeret Ha-Taharah ad loc.*
18. *Shi'urei Shevet Ha-Levi* 194:2:2.
19. As implied in *Mishneh Torah, Hilkhot Issurei Biah* 10:2. See also *Gilyon Maharsha* to *Yoreh De'ah* 194:2 and *Taharah Ke-Halakhah* 1:8, n. 22.

procedure or from the time of the fetus's death, based on the information that is available. Very few authorities have addressed this. *Nishmat Avraham*[20] cites the possibility of combining this uncertainty (when precisely the pregnancy ended) with other uncertainties to incline toward leniency, and *Responsa Kenei Bosem*[21] writes that he thinks the 40 days should be calculated according to the age of the fetus at death, rather than at the time of the procedure. However, he writes that this needs further study, because he did not find this question addressed elsewhere. R. Yehuda Henkin also thought likewise. According to R. Yaakov Warhaftig, if it is known for certain that the fetus died before 40 days, one may be lenient when necessary.

In conclusion, in any case of loss of pregnancy, the woman may perform a *hefsek taharah* as soon as the bleeding stops (on condition that four or five days have elapsed since the onset of bleeding, as with any *niddah*) and begin counting the seven *neki'im*. If the termination occurred before the fetus was 40 days old according to the halakhic calculation, the woman may immerse after the seven *neki'im*, as a *niddah* would. If it occurred after 40 days, she must, due to uncertainty, wait two weeks from the date of the end of pregnancy before she may immerse, even if the seven *neki'im* are completed beforehand. It bears repeating that bleeding after the termination of a pregnancy often continues longer than for regular menses. Each woman should conduct herself in accordance with her specific situation.

N.L.

20. 194:2.
21. *Hilkhot Niddah, Kenei Bosem, Yoreh De'ah, Biurei Sh'ua* 194:6.

Siman 23

Onot Perishah following a Miscarriage

Question

Three weeks ago, I miscarried in the ninth week of pregnancy. According to the doctor, I am supposed to get my period within two weeks. Which *onot perishah* should I observe?

Answer

If a pregnancy terminates more than 40 days after the last immersion in the *mikveh* prior to the pregnancy, the woman is considered *mesuleket damim*. Even though the pregnancy did not result in a live birth, halakhically speaking, she is considered a *yoledet* who is not expected to menstruate for the subsequent 24 months. Therefore, during this time period, she need not anticipate her *veset* until she begins menstruating again.

Nowadays, women resume menstruating within 24 months. Therefore, once the bleeding from the miscarriage ends, when you begin menstruating again, your new menses are treated as a *veset she-eino kavu'a* and relations are therefore not permitted during the *onat ha-ḥodesh* and the *onah beinonit*. The *onat ha-haflagah* (the interval between the onset of the two menses) will apply only after you have menstruated for the second time.

If you had a *veset kavu'a* before pregnancy, you anticipate that *veset* only after you begin menstruating again. Your menses will likely be irregular during the months after the miscarriage.

Halakhic Expansion

A *yoledet* is subject to *tum'at leidah* both in the case of a live birth or a stillbirth. Therefore, a miscarriage that takes place once 41 or more days[1] elapsed since the last immersion before the pregnancy confers the status of a *yoledet*.[2] The 41st day, which indicates that the fetus is completely formed,[3] usually corresponds to the middle of the eighth week of pregnancy according to the medical count.[4]

According to *halakhah*, a *yoledet* is presumed to be *mesuleket damim* for 24 months[5] even if she is not actually nursing, because "her organs become dislocated"[6] due to pregnancy, meaning, the hormonal activity of a *yoledet* does not return to routine for 24 months. This also applies to a woman who miscarries;[7] she does not expect to experience bleeding[8] and does not anticipate the *veset* she had before becoming pregnant.[9] However, once she experiences bleeding, she must observe either her earlier *veset kavu'a* or her new *veset* as a *veset she-eino kavu'a*.[10]

Nowadays, most women begin menstruating again within 24 months.[11] Therefore, a woman who miscarried, once the bleeding from the miscarriage stops,[12] must

1. Until day 40, a fetus is considered "mere water" (*Yevamot* 69b).
2. Mishnah, *Niddah* 30a: "One who miscarries on the 40th day need not be concerned that it was a [formed] fetus; on the 41st day – she must observe [the period of *tum'ah*] for a male, a female, and *niddah*." This is the ruling of Rambam, *Mishneh Torah, Hilkhot Issurei Bi'ah* 10:1; Rashba, *Torat Ha-Bayit, bayit* 7, *sha'ar* 6, p. 28b; Ramban, *Hilkhot Niddah* 7:1; *Shulḥan Arukh, Yoreh De'ah* 194:1.
3. Mishnah, *Niddah* 30a, and see Rashi there. See also *Nishmat Avraham, Yoreh De'ah* 194:4, s.v. *betokh* 40 regarding the medical significance of 40 days.
4. Calculating the advancement of the pregnancy from a medical perspective and counting 40 days from a halakhic perspective are discussed in *Siman* 22: Counting Seven *Neki'im* following D & C.
5. *Niddah* 9a, following most of the *Tanna'im* quoted in the *baraita.*
6. Ibid. 9a.
7. See *Ḥavat Da'at, bi'urim*, 189:38. As written in *Shi'urei Shevet Ha-Levi* 189:33:4, this law does not depend on actual nursing. Rather, since the reason for the rule is the dislocation of the organs, there is no difference between a woman who miscarries and a *yoledet*, as Maharsham writes.
8. Regarding the process of becoming *tehorah* after a miscarriage, see above, *Siman* 22: Counting Seven *Neki'im* following D & C.
9. *Yoreh De'ah* 189:34.
10. Ibid. 189:33, following Ra'avad (*Ba'alei Ha-Nefesh, Sha'ar Tikun Ha-Vesatot*) and as cited by Rashba (*Torat Ha-Bayit, bayit* 7, *sha'ar* 3, p. 13a) at the end of his statement. See also above, *Siman* 19: *Onot Perishah* and Establishing a *Veset*, Postpartum.
11. Therefore, even a nursing woman must be concerned about establishing a *veset* (*Igrot Moshe, Yoreh De'ah* 4:14, but above, *Siman* 19, for those who disagree).
12. Bleeding that results from the miscarriage has no significance for the calculation of *vesatot* (*Taharah Ke-Halakhah* 24:5).

observe her next menses as a *veset she-eino kavu'a* – that is, she must observe the *onat ha-ḥodesh* and the *onah beinonit.*[13] After menstruating a second time, she observes the *onat ha-haflagah* as well.[14]

The *poskim* disagree about whether it is possible to establish a *veset* during the 24 months after a miscarriage. *Responsa Mishneh Halakhot* cites *Pitḥei Teshuvah,* which brings the view of *Kereti U-Feleti* and other *poskim,* that if a woman miscarries after three months,[15] she establishes a *veset l'kula,* "for leniency";[16] that is, once she establishes the *veset,* she need not observe the other *onot.* However, she does not establish it *l'ḥumra,* "for stringency," meaning that she does not need three cycles to uproot the *veset.*[17] In contrast, *Igrot Moshe* writes that since nowadays almost all *yoldot* begin menstruating again within 24 months, a *yoledet* can establish a *veset* during this time period.[18] Therefore, once she begins menstruating again, she must observe the *veset kavu'a* that she had established before becoming pregnant, even if she is still nursing. *Darkhei Taharah,* on the other hand, writes that she need not observe her prior *veset kavu'a* until after the 24 months.[19]

If a woman miscarries less than 40 days into pregnancy,[20] she is not considered a *yoledet,* and she observes her *veset* as previously.

S.K.

---

13. See above, *Siman* 19: *Onot Perishah* and Establishing a *Veset,* Postpartum, which cites a dispute regarding the observance of the *onah beinonit* by a *mesuleket damim* nowadays, when most women begin menstruating again within 24 months. *Igrot Moshe, Yoreh De'ah* 3:52:1, *Darkhei Taharah* chapter 7, p. 84, *Shi'urei Shevet Ha-Levi* 189:33:5, and *Taharah Ke-Halakhah* 24:100 rule stringently following *Shulḥan Arukh Ha-Rav* (*Yoreh De'ah* 189:114), based on *Responsa Maharam Padua* 25, that a woman observes the *onah beinonit* even in this situation.
14. *Yoreh De'ah* 189:2.
15. According to this position, the status of *mesuleket damim* applies to a woman who miscarried only after three months. *Mishneh Halakhot* 12:76 leaves this matter without resolution.
16. *Responsa Mishneh Halakhot* 12:76. *Pitḥei Teshuvah* writes in the name of *Sidrei Taharah* that this ruling, that she does not establish a *veset,* was only stated with respect to leniency. That is, her *veset* is uprooted if just one cycle does not follow the established pattern. However, she does establish a *veset* in the sense that she must anticipate the *veset kavu'a* and need not observe the other *onot.*
17. As *Shulḥan Arukh, Yoreh De'ah* 189:33 rules regarding pregnant and nursing women.
18. *Igrot Moshe, Yoreh De'ah* 3:52:1. See also above, *Siman* 19: *Onot Perishah* and Establishing a *Veset,* Postpartum.
19. *Darkhei Taharah,* chapter 7, p. 85.
20. See above, *Siman* 22.

Siman 24

Reducing Bedikot following a Miscarriage

Question

I underwent an induced labor due to fetal demise at week 27 of pregnancy. Two weeks have passed and the bleeding has stopped, so I want to count the seven *neki'im*. May I forego the internal *bedikot* out of concern for infection following a difficult medical procedure? I am quite worried about this.

Answer

A woman must perform a *hefsek taharah* before counting the seven *neki'im,* and *lekhatḥilah* should perform an examination with a *mokh daḥuk* and two *bedikot* on each of the seven *neki'im*. *Bedi'avad,* or if there is great need, it is possible to reduce the number of *bedikot* and forego the *mokh daḥuk*. We advise performing the *bedikot* gently. When necessary, the *bedikot* need not be deep, as long as they are still internal.

In the event of a late-stage abortion of a dead fetus, the woman undergoes a physiological process akin to childbirth but also must cope psychologically with the loss of her pregnancy.[1] On the other hand, two weeks after the abortion, there is generally no longer concern that the *bedikot* might cause vaginal or cervical infection. To become *tehorah,* a *hefsek taharah* must be performed, though you may forego the *mokh daḥuk*. Regarding *bedikot* during the seven *neki'im,* you should, at the very least, perform one on the first and one on the seventh of the

1. For more on the medical and psychological aspects of miscarriage, see Medical Appendix IV: Miscarriage. See also: Kansky, C. et al. "Normal and Abnormal Puerperium." https://emedicine.medscape.com/article/260187-overview.

neki'im. It is recommended to perform at least one additional *bedikah* above the minimum, on the third or fourth day.

If there is vaginal dryness – a common occurrence after a miscarriage or childbirth – you may ease the *bedikah* by moistening the *bedikah* cloth with a bit of water or using a water-based lubricant like KY jelly.[2]

These leniencies are valid only in the situation described and should be revisited before the next time you must count seven *neki'im*.

Halakhic Expansion

The *taharah* process includes three types of *bedikah* (internal self-examination): *hefsek taharah*, *mokh daḥuk*, and the *bedikot* of the seven *neki'im*.

The *hefsek taharah* is essential; without it, the count of the seven *neki'im* cannot begin.[3] It establishes that the bleeding has stopped and transitions the woman from a state of *tum'ah* to a state of "presumed *taharah*" ("*be-ḥezkat taharah*"). Most *poskim* maintain that the *hefsek taharah* has the status of a Torah obligation.[4] Therefore, even in sensitive situations, one may not forego it.[5]

In contrast, the *mokh daḥuk* appears in *Shulḥan Arukh*, following Rashba, as a "good practice,"[6] and Rema notes that it is a *lekhatḥilah* stringency; if a woman did not perform one, *bedi'avad*, she is *tehorah*.[7] Therefore, there are grounds to forego it after childbirth or a miscarriage.[8]

The number of *bedikot* during the seven *neki'im* is discussed extensively in the Mishnah and Gemara. It emerges from the Mishnah[9] that, *lekhatḥilah*, one should

2. For further details, see above, *Siman* 21: Attributing Blood to a *Petza* during the Seven *Neki'im*.
3. *Shulḥan Arukh, Yoreh De'ah* 196:1, based on the Mishnah and Gemara in *Niddah* 68a. The origin of the term "*hefsek taharah*" is the Gemara in *Niddah* 33a, which states that Samaritan men have marital relations with *niddot* because Samaritan women "count the day they stop [bleeding] in the seven [*neki'im*]."
4. See *Taharat Ha-Bayit* 1:13:1, p. 229ff.
5. In especially problematic situations, a woman may wish to request the assistance of an Orthodox gynecologist or *bodeket taharah* with the *hefsek taharah*.
6. *Yoreh De'ah* 196:1.
7. Ibid. 196:1–2.
8. As there is no concern for an "open spring" [*ma'ayan patuah*] after a miscarriage. Many *poskim* are lenient and permit foregoing the *mokh daḥuk* when necessary. See *Pardes Rimonim*, p. 31; *Ḥut Ha-Shani* 196:1:16; *Taharat Ha-Bayit* 2:13:1, p. 261. See also the article by Yoetzet Halacha Michal Roness, "The Parameters of Placement of the *Mokh Daḥuk*," *Teḥumin* 31 (5771). *Sha'arei Orah* (p. 129) and *Ish Ve-Ishah* (p. 100) note this explicitly.
9. *Niddah* 68b.

perform one *bedikah* on each of the seven *neki'im*, but *bedi'avad*, just one *bedikah* on the first day and one on the seventh suffice for the counting of the days, in accordance with the view of R. Eliezer. The Gemara rules that the *halakhah* accords with him, and the *Amora'im* disagree about how far R. Eliezer's leniency extends. R. Ḥanina follows the straightforward understanding of R. Eliezer's view, namely, that the minimum required is one *bedikah* on the first day and one on the seventh. Rav, however, maintains that even a single *bedikah* at the beginning **or** the end of the seven *neki'im* suffices. Most *Rishonim* rule in accordance with Rav, though some ruled stringently, in accordance with R. Ḥanina.[10]

Shulḥan Arukh[11] rules in accordance with the view of several *Rishonim*[12] that *lekhatḥilah* one should perform two *bedikot* daily. *Aḥaronim* wrote that if it is difficult for a woman to perform two daily *bedikot*, for instance, postpartum, then one daily *bedikah* suffices.[13] *Shulḥan Arukh* first brings, without qualification, the view that, in *bedi'avad* circumstances, the number of *bedikot* can be reduced to one (at the beginning, middle, or end of the seven *neki'im*), and then brings that "some say" ("*yesh omrim*") that the minimum is one *bedikah* on the first day and one on the seventh, concluding, "and one should not be lenient."[14]

The general principle regarding *Shulḥan Arukh* is that when one view is brought without qualification ("*stam*") and another is brought as a "*yesh omrim*," the *halakhah* accords with the "*stam*."[15] However, in this case, the author of *Shulḥan Arukh*

---

10. Most *Rishonim* (Ramban, Rashba, Ra'avad, Rambam, and others) ruled in accordance with Rav, as the Gemara goes on to discuss his view, and because "the law accords with Rav on matters of ritual prohibition" (Rosh, *Niddah* 10:5). However, some ruled in accordance with R. Ḥanina (*Semag*, *Sefer Ha-Terumah*, Rabbeinu Simḥah), "since this is not a clear ruling, it is proper to be stringent on this matter" (*Semag*, mitzvah 111). Thus, the ruling in accordance with R. Ḥanina is a stringency, not the letter of the law. For further discussion of the various views, see the article by Yoetzet Halacha Noa Lau, "The *Bedikah* on the First of the Seven *Neki'im*," *Teḥumin* 30 (5770).
11. *Yoreh De'ah* 196:4. *Bet Yosef* brings that this is the ruling of *Semag*, *Sefer Ha-Terumah*, *Mordekhai*, and *Roke'aḥ*, against Ramban, Rashba, Rosh, and *Hagahot Maimoniyot* (in the name of *Tosafot*) who ruled that one *bedikah* per day is sufficient.
12. As mentioned above, this is the ruling of Ramban, Rashba, Rosh, and *Hagahot Maimoniyot* in the name of *Tosafot*. *Tur* rules this way *lekhatḥilah*: "All seven days of counting, she must perform a *bedikah* once daily *lekhatḥilah*, and *Sefer Ha-Mitzvot* [= *Semag*] wrote twice, once in the morning and once in the evening" (*Yoreh De'ah* 196).
13. *Darkhei Taharah*, p. 134; *Taharat Ha-Bayit* 2:13:5, p. 302; *Shi'urei Shevet Ha-Levi* 196:4:3, p. 283; *Taharah Ke-Halakhah* 17:14, p. 310.
14. *Yoreh De'ah* 196:4.
15. See *Birkei Yosef siman* 61, *Shiyurei Berakhah* 2, which explains: "For our master [R. Yosef Karo] himself said so." See the expansive treatment in *Ein Yitzḥak*, *Kelalei Shulḥan Arukh*, pp. 462–92.

decided between the two views, adding, "one should not be lenient." It therefore seems that in his view, if one did not perform a *bedikah* on the first and seventh days, she has not counted seven *neki'im.*[16]

Among *Aḥaronim* we find cases in which the ruling was that *lekhatḥilah* one may suffice with *bedikot* on the first and seventh days, in accordance with "*yesh omrim*,"[17] and also cases of great need in which the ruling was that *lekhatḥilah* one may suffice with a single *bedikah* throughout the seven *neki'im*, in accordance with the "*stam*" position.[18]

In the case presented in the question regarding the sensitivity of the vaginal region following a miscarriage, and considering the woman's emotional state, the number of *bedikot* can be reduced as needed, up to a minimum of one *bedikah* on the first and one on the seventh of the *neki'im* (in addition to the *hefsek taharah*). To the extent possible, it is proper to perform at least one additional *bedikah* above the minimum, on the third or fourth day ("*bedikat emtza*").[19] If possible, it is desirable to perform at least one *bedikah* on each of the middle five days as well.

N.L.

16. However, see *Taharat Ha-Bayit* 2:13:5, pp. 306–7, which cites various *poskim* who maintain that here, too, *Shulḥan Arukh* rules according to the first ("*stam*") view. For example, this is the opinion of *Shi'urei Taharah* (56:3), *Responsa Tiferet Adam* (*Yoreh De'ah* 51:1), and *Responsa Sho'el Ve-Nish'al* (3:332; 7:168). Some of these *poskim* explained that the principle that "'*stam*' versus '*yesh omrim*,' the *halakhah* accords with the '*stam*'" overrides even the decision of *Shulḥan Arukh* himself. Others explain that the concluding words, "one should not be lenient," are part of the view of the "*yesh omrim*" and do not indicate that this is the view of *Shulḥan Arukh*.
17. For instance, the case of a woman who has a *petza*, making *bedikot* difficult; see *Taharat Ha-Bayit* 2:13:5, pp. 303–12; *Taharah Ke-Halakhah* 17:15, p. 311.
18. See *Arukh Ha-Shulḥan, Yoreh De'ah* 196:26, and *Taharat Ha-Bayit* loc. cit. (and in greater detail in the *Teḥumin* article cited above, n. 10). The leniency of performing only one *bedikah* throughout the seven *neki'im* is intended for the most extreme cases; the present situation does not seem to be such a case.
19. The *bedikah* on one of the middle days is important in case the woman forgets to perform a *bedikah* on the seventh day, creating a situation where more than five days will have elapsed without a *bedikah*. This is based on *Semag*, cited in *Dagul Me-Revavah, Yoreh De'ah* 196:6 and in *Noda Bi-Yehudah, Yoreh De'ah*, 2:128 (cited in *Pitḥei Teshuvah, Yoreh De'ah* 196:6), where R. Yeḥezkel Landau (author of both *Dagul Me-Revavah* and *Noda Bi-Yehudah*) explains the importance of the framework of the first and seventh days so that five days do not elapse without a *bedikah*. According to those who maintain that the framework of the first and seventh days is essential, if the woman performed a *bedikat emtza* and then forgot about the seventh day, the *bedikat emtza* can be considered the *bedikah* of the first day, and the seven *neki'im* can proceed from that day. According to those who maintain that the main purpose is so that five days do not elapse without a *bedikah*, in a situation where she forgot the seventh day *bedikah*, one may perform a *bedikah* on the eighth day and then immerse.

Part IV

Nursing

Siman 25

The Law of Hargashah (Sensation of Menses)

Question

I take Micronor, a contraceptive pill for breastfeeding women. Recently, I have been finding a large number of *ketamim*, stains. Sometimes I feel the wetness of my underwear, and sometimes the sensation of discharge seeping out of my body. I wear colored underwear as well as a panty liner. May I treat this bleeding as *ketamim* that do not render me *niddah*?

Answer

The Micronor pill frequently causes substantial bleeding and spotting among some users, as you experienced. Many women suffer from these effects during the first months of use, as the body adjusts to the new hormone, or alternatively, when there is a reduction in the frequency of nursing, such as when solids are introduced. Some women experience significant improvement in the second or third month of use. Taking the pill at the same time every day, with a glass of water, may help keep the bleeding to a minimum. Your situation may stabilize over time, but it is also possible that you will need to stop the Micronor because of the numerous *ketamim* and switch to a different contraceptive that does not cause staining, such as the diaphragm or non-hormonal IUD. The diaphragm does not hinder milk production or cause bleeding, so it is worth considering switching to it.

Many *poskim* maintain that only three *hargashot,* sensations, render a woman *niddah*: *petihat hamakor,* the opening of the uterus, *za'azu'ah ha-guf,* bodily tremors, and *zivat davar laḥ,* the flow of fluid within the vagina. In their opinion, if you do not experience one of these three sensations when the blood is discharged from your body, or alternatively, a physical sensation such as back or abdominal pain that always accompanies your menstrual bleeding, your discharge is assessed according to the laws of *ketamim.*

Therefore, as long as the discharge appears on a panty liner or colored underwear, you are not *niddah.* Wetness on colored underwear, without a *hargashah,* does not render one *niddah.* Nevertheless, although marital relations are technically permitted when there are *ketamim,* we recommend abstaining from them, lest you find blood immediately following intercourse, which would raise the complicated question of *ro'ah meḥamat tashmish* (one who bleeds from intercourse). Refraining from intercourse will also allow you to ascertain whether the spotting will develop into actual menstrual bleeding.

If you continue taking Micronor and despite precautions do become *niddah,* you may find that you are unable, for an extended time, to achieve the clean *bedikot* needed to become *tehorah.* If that happens, you may consider switching to an alternative progesterone only pill or try another contraceptive method that does not cause stains.

If the staining persists, it is recommended that you wipe the outside of the vaginal area with toilet paper before having sexual relations, to confirm that you are clean. However, you should not perform this wipe within 15 seconds of urinating. Even if you find a stain in this manner, it will not render you *niddah.* It is also recommended that you use colored sheets and that you clean yourselves after intercourse using colored towels – and that you do not look at the towels afterward – because when a woman is *tehorah* and it is not the time when she must anticipate the onset of menses, there is no obligation to search for stains.

If the staining continues, it is worth discussing with your health provider the possibility of switching to a different contraceptive method. You can switch to a different type of "mini-pill," but there is likely to be a one- or two-month period of adjustment to the new pill as well. Depending on the age of the baby, you might consider switching to a combined pill (COCP), since after a few months of nursing, a decrease in milk production might not be as significant for the baby.

If the discharge intensifies and becomes comparable in flow to menstruation, you are *niddah.*

Halakhic Expansion

Micronor[1] is a progesterone-only "mini-pill." Progestogen-only pills (POPs) are given to nursing mothers, since, as opposed to combined oral contraceptive pills (COCPs), containing estrogen, progestogens have less of an effect on the quantity of mother's milk.

Unfortunately, according to current medical data, 40 to 70% of women who use POPs experience staining during an adjustment period.[2] Some women will experience improvement in the second or third month of use, but others will continue to experience spotting even beyond, and still others will experience spotting as the frequency of breastfeeding diminishes. On the other hand, some women experience no spotting at all, and POPs can even arrest all bleeding for months at a time.[3]

In the case of frequent spotting, the optimal solution from a halakhic perspective is to switch to a contraceptive method that does not cause spotting, such as a diaphragm or non-hormonal IUD.[4] COCPs can also be considered, though, as mentioned, they can hinder milk production.[5]

If, despite efforts to take precautions,[6] a woman taking Micronor becomes *teme'ah* from a *ketem* on her skin, her husband's skin, or otherwise, the couple is likely to need far-reaching leniencies during the seven *neki'im* in order to render her *tehorah*.[7]

---

1. For a detailed explanation of the different types of contraceptive pills and their effects, see Medical Appendix V: Contraceptives. The active ingredient of Micronor is norethindrone, a synthetic progestogen similar to progesterone; other pills are based on different synthetic progestogens.
2. Side-effects can include spotting, prolonged menstrual bleeding, and frequent menstruation. See Medical Appendix V.
3. Ibid.
4. Ibid. See also below, *Siman* 35: Diaphragm Use, as well as *Responsa Si'aḥ Naḥum siman* 95.
5. This is more significant during the first few months of the infant's life, before milk is supplemented.
6. As long as the woman is spotting without a *hargashah* that would render her *niddah*, she should be instructed not to look for *ketamim*. See *Responsa Maharaḥ Or Zaru'a siman* 112 and *Hagahot Maimoniyot* (*Hilkhot Issurei Biah* 4:16) in the name of Maharam Rothenburg, adding in his name that the *bedikot* before and after sexual intercourse are mentioned only in context of *taharot* (i.e., foods that must be eaten in a state of *taharah*) and are not required for the purpose of marital relations. Maharam even rebuked a woman who would perform a *bedikah* after intercourse; why should she be stringent at her own expense over something that was prohibited by *Ḥakhamim*? After all, "They said that when blood [of a *ketem*] is found, she is a *niddah*, and they said not to perform a *bedikah*!" (*Responsa Maharaḥ Or Zaru'a siman* 112; a similar formulation appears in *Hagahot Maimoniyot*. *Responsa Maharam Lublin siman* 2 rules likewise.
7. Such as sufficing with only one *bedikah* during the entire seven days; see *Shulḥan Arukh, Yoreh De'ah* 196:4, and *Shakh ad loc.* 8.

The Law of *Hargashah*

In *Niddah* 57b, Shmuel derives from a Torah verse that only blood accompanied by *hargashah* renders one *teme'ah mi-de'Orayta*.[8] Bleeding that is not accompanied by *hargashah* is judged according to the laws of *ketamim*, and anything that can be attributed to some other cause, even one that is highly unlikely, is so attributed.[9] There are four views of this matter among the *Rishonim*:

1. According to Rambam, Ramban, Rashba, and many other *Rishonim* (*Sefer Ha-Eshkol, Semak,* Meiri, Maharaḥ Or Zaru'a, *Hagahot Maimoniyot* in the name of Maharam Rothenburg, *Orḥot Ḥayim, Kol Bo,* Tashbetz, Rabbeinu Yeruḥam, Ran, *Terumat Ha-Deshen, Sefer Ha-Ḥinukh,* etc.),[10] if a woman does not sense the discharge of the blood, she is not *teme'ah mi-de'Orayta,* and this blood is judged according to the laws of *ketamim*. This is also the ruling of *Tur* and *Shulḥan Arukh*.[11] However, Rambam adds that uterine blood is presumed to have been accompanied by a *hargashah,* so a woman who finds blood from a *bedikah* inside the vaginal canal, even if she thinks she had no *hargashah,* we can presume with certainty that she had a *hargashah* and is *teme'ah mi-de'Orayta*.[12] It emerges from his words that menstrual blood, even if the woman experienced no sensation, makes her *teme'ah mi-de'Orayta,* because it is known that menstrual blood comes from the uterus, and blood

---

8. Rav Ashi and Rav Yirmiyah disagree about the status of bleeding from the uterus that is not accompanied by *hargashah* – that is, whether *hargashah* is a symptom or a cause and essential condition for *tum'ah mi-de'Orayta*. Most *Rishonim* rule that *hargashah* is the cause of *tum'ah*; see further below. See also: *Shi'urei Shevet Ha-Levi* 190:1:14, p. 159. However, *Responsa Tzemaḥ Tzedek* (Lubavitch) *siman* 95 explained differently, namely, that "blood, not a *ketem*" is a decree of the Torah ("*gezeirat ha-Katuv*").
9. *Niddah* 58b. See also *Sidrei Taharah* 190:67, s.v. "*naḥzor,*" and elsewhere.
10. Rambam, *Mishneh Torah, Hilkhot Isurei Bi'ah* 9:1; Ramban, *Hilkhot Niddah* 4:1 and Novellae on *Niddah* 52b; Rashba, *Torat Ha-Bayit, sha'ar* 4; *Sefer Ha-Eshkol, Hilkhot Niddah siman* 42; *Ḥiddushei Ha-Ran* on *Niddah* chapter 8, s.v. "*tartei shamat minah*"; *Semak siman* 293; *Kol Bo siman* 85; *Orḥot Ḥayim, Hilkhot Niddah* letter 2; *Responsa Tashbetz* 3:58 *par.* 15; *Bet Ha-Beḥirah* on *Niddah* 57b, s.v. "*ketem*"; *Responsa Maharaḥ Or Zaru'a siman* 112; *Hagahot Maimoniyot Hagahot Maimoniyot, Hilkhot Issurei Biah* 4:20; *Terumat Ha-Deshen siman* 246; *Sefer Ha-Ḥinukh siman* 207. See also *Taharat Ha-Bayit* 1:1:3, who provides a list of *Rishonim* and *Aḥaronim*.
11. *Yoreh De'ah siman* 183.
12. *Mishneh Torah, Hilkhot Issurei Biah* 9:1. This is challenged in *Responsa Tzemaḥ Tzedek* (Lubavitch), *Yoreh De'ah* 95:1. Rambam's view can explain why a woman cannot wear colored garments to avoid becoming *niddah mi-de'Orayta* when she menstruates. This is against *Arukh Ha-Shulḥan, Yoreh De'ah* 183:54, which maintains that a woman who experiences blood flow without a *hargashah* is not *teme'ah mi-de'Orayta*.

from the uterus has a *ḥazakah,* halakhic presumption of certainty, that it is accompanied by *hargashah* and is therefore *tamei.*[13]

2. According to Rashi,[14] it is possible that the woman experienced a *hargashah* but did not notice or forgot about it over time, as a woman "knows on her own when blood is discharged from her body."[15] Therefore, a woman who finds a *ketem* is *niddah* out of uncertainty.[16] Ra'avan likewise writes that a woman does not experience menstrual bleeding unaccompanied by *hargashah,* and therefore, if she finds a *ketem* that she cannot attribute to something else, she presumably experienced a *hargashah* and did not notice, or mistook her *hargashah* for a sensation of urination. For this reason, *Ḥakhamim* deem her *teme'ah misafek,* out of uncertainty.[17]

3. Rif,[18] Ra'avad, *Sefer Yere'im, Sefer Ha-Terumah, Semag,* Rosh, and *Sefer Ha-Agur* omit the law of *hargashah.*[19] *Semag* brings the ruling of Shmuel – that if a woman inspected the ground, found it clean, sat down, and then found blood upon it when she arose, she is *tehorah* – according to R. Neḥemiah's view that anything that is not susceptible to *tum'ah* is not susceptible to *ketamim,*[20] whereas Ra'avad writes that any blood that cannot be attributed to something else confers *niddah* status. Rashba writes in the name of Rabbeinu Yonah[21] that as long as she sees blood in the way women see, she is *teme'ah mi-de'Orayta* – without conditioning this on the sensation of *hargashah.* R. Ḥayim Or Zaru'a wrote in the name of his teacher, R. Ovadiah, that "until she senses

13. *Mishneh Torah, Hilkhot Issurei Biah* 5:5. With the exception of blood from a *makkah* and other types of blood that the Torah does not deem *tamei.*
14. *Niddah* 58a s.v. "*mi-deRabanan.*"
15. *Niddah* 3a, s.v. "*merageshet.*"
16. R. Moshe Feinstein (*Igrot Moshe, Yoreh De'ah* 4:17:12) explained that Rashi does not mean that one who is uncertain whether she experienced a *hargashah* is *teme'ah mi-deRabanan,* for we rule stringently in the case of uncertainty regarding Torah-level prohibitions ("*safek deOrayta le-ḥumra*"). Rather, *Ḥakhamim* decreed *tum'ah* even on a woman who knows for certain that she experienced no *hargashah,* lest she experience a mild *hargashah* that escapes her notice. See also *Arukh Ha-Shulḥan, Yoreh De'ah* 183:48.
17. *Sefer Ra'avan, Niddah siman* 321.
18. Rif, *Shavu'ot* 3a (Rif pagination) explains on the word "*bivsarah*" ("in her flesh") only *metamah mibifnim ke-vahutz,* that she becomes *niddah* when the blood is inside just as when it is outside, but does not mention the law of *hargashah.*
19. Ra'avad, *Ba'alei Ha-Nefesh, Sha'ar Ha-ketamim; Sefer Yere'im siman* 192; *Sefer Ha-Terumah siman* 92; *Semag,* negative commandment *siman* 111; Rosh, *Niddah,* chapter 9; *Agur, Hilkhot Niddah siman* 367.
20. See *Tosafot* on *Niddah* 58a, s.v. "*Ke-Rabi Neḥemiah,*" which states that since the *ketem* on the ground is *tahor, Ḥakhamim* did not decree *tum'ah* on the woman.
21. Cited in Rashba's commentary on *Niddah* 57, s.v. "*tartei shamat minah.*"

it in her flesh" ("*ad she-targish bivsarah*") means that she finds blood on her flesh – such as blood found in the vaginal canal – and not necessarily a physical sensation.[22] It seems that all of these authorities maintained that *tum'ah mi-de'Orayta* is not contingent on a bodily *hargashah*.[23]

4. A fourth view is that of Rashi and *Tosafot* as explained by the author of *Sidrei Taharah*,[24] and of *Tosafot Rid*,[25] who hold that *hargashah* is not a decree of the Torah ("*gezeirat ha-Katuv*"), i.e., that a woman who has a sensation is *teme'ah*, but rather evidence that the blood came from the uterus. Therefore, a woman is *teme'ah mi-de'Orayta* even without a *hargashah* if it is evident that the blood came from her uterus.[26]

What is considered a *hargashah* that causes *tum'ah*?

1. The opening of the uterus and bodily tremors

Shmuel did not explain the nature of a *hargashah* that causes *tum'ah*.[27] The *Rishonim* mention two types of *hargashah* that cause *tum'ah*: Rambam mentions *za'azu'ah ha-guf*, bodily tremors,[28] and *Terumat Ha-Deshen* mentions the opening of the uterus.[29] Among *Aḥaronim*, *Noda Bi-Yehudah* maintains that the primary form of *hargashah* is *zivat davar laḥ*, the sensation of fluid flowing.[30]

---

22. *Responsa Maharaḥ Or Zaru'a siman* 112, at the end. *Arukh Ha-Shulḥan, Yoreh De'ah* 183:57 also explains that a *hargashah* is not necessarily a bodily experience, but also knowledge. See below.
23. Contra *Arukh Ha-Shulḥan*, who wrote: "All of our masters, *Rishonim* and *Aḥaronim*, agree that according to the Torah a woman is not *teme'ah* when she discharges blood unless the blood was discharged with a *hargashah*." He apparently means that they did not explicitly dispute the law of *hargashah*, and even if they omitted the law, they do not disagree with it. This assertion is very questionable.
24. 190:93, s.v. "*terem akhaleh*" and in the summary, s.v. "*naḥzor al ha-rishonot*."
25. *Niddah* 57b, s.v. "*amar Shmuel*."
26. This possibility was raised and rejected by Maharam Lublin almost 200 years before the *Sidrei Taharah*. See *Responsa Maharam Lublin siman* 2. Many *Aḥaronim* reject the explanation of *Sidrei Taharah*; see *Taz, Yoreh De'ah* 192:1, citing *Maggid Mishneh*; *Arukh Ha-Shulḥan, Yoreh De'ah* 183:48. See also *Taharat Ha-Bayit* 1:1:3 pp. 8–10.
27. Rashi to *Niddah* 3a, s.v. "*merageshet*," explains likewise, "She knows on her own when menstrual blood flows from within her," and does not mention any specific sensation.
28. *Mishneh Torah, Hilkhot Issurei Biah* 5:17.
29. *Siman* 246, as well as *Responsa Maharaḥ Or Zaru'a siman* 112. See further regarding the sensation of menses ("she feels pain in the pit of her stomach and her lower abdomen") mentioned by Rambam.
30. *Responsa Noda Bi-Yehuda, Yoreh De'ah*, 1:55. Thanks to R. Yosef Zvi Rimon, who pointed out to me that this view is already mentioned in the *Rishonim*, in *New Responsa Maharik siman* 49: "It is necessary that she have sensation when it discharges from the uterus into the vagina." *Ḥavat Da'at* rules accordingly, as will be discussed below.

Pitḥei Teshuvah brings these three types of *hargashah*, and following him, numerous subsequent *Aḥaronim* cite them as the *hargashot* that cause *tum'ah*.[31]

On the other hand, most women attest that alongside menstrual pains, which vary from woman to woman and even from menstrual period to menstrual period,[32] when the blood discharges all they feel is an outflow from the outer opening of the vagina or a flow within the vaginal canal, and they do not identify any sensation of the uterus opening or of bodily tremor.[33] This sensation of a flow of discharge is very common. How is it possible that *poskim* and women are so divided over the existence and description of *hargashah*? This is a crucial question, as most of the leniencies that apply to *ketamim* hinge on the absence of *hargashah*.

There are three explanations for this discrepancy:

a. **Nature has changed ("*nishtanu ha-teva'im*").** Nowadays, most women do not sense the opening of the uterus or bodily tremors.[34] As R. Asher Weiss explains:[35] "Nowadays, all of these *hargashot* are quite uncommon, and we have not heard about our women that they sense the opening of the uterus, bodily tremors, or a discharge from within the uterus."[36]

---

31. See *Arukh Ha-Shulḥan, Yoreh De'ah* 183:57–58; *Ḥut Ha-Shani, Hilkhot Niddah* pp. 29 and 342; and many others.
32. Many women experience lower abdominal or pelvic pain of varying intensity several days before menstruation, which subsides at the onset of menstruation. In some women, the pain continues or even first emerges during the first days of menstruation. See Medical Appendix I: The Female Reproductive System.
33. R. Yaakov Poppers, author of *Shav Yaakov*, already wrote (in correspondence with R. Shmuel Schotten who passed away in 1719): "It is hard for me to understand that *hargashah* mentioned in the Talmud and *poskim*, namely, that she feels her uterus opening. I asked the women, and they cannot solve this for me; only that they sense something wet flowing from themselves" (*Responsa Shav Yaakov* 1:40); and he continues that their description does not cohere with the Gemara's challenge to Shmuel, from a woman who relieves herself (*Niddah* 57b). Similarly, R. Shlomo Yehudah Tabak writes in *Teshurat Shai* 1:497 (published in 1905) that he asked older women who reported that they do not feel the opening of the uterus at all, only the flow of discharge.
34. *Kovetz Teshuvot siman* 84.
35. *Minḥat Asher, Hilkhot Niddah* 1:4.
36. R. Weiss continues that it is cited in the name of Ramban's commentary on *Niddah* that he asked older women, who attested that they have no *hargashot* nowadays. However, R. Waldenberg already demonstrated (*Responsa Tzitz Eliezer* 6:21) that these are not the words of Ramban. Rather, R. Tzvi Hirsch Shapira made a "gross error" in *Darkhei Teshuvah* (183:6) by misattributing the words of *Teshurat Shai* to Ramban. Others have also followed *Darkhei Teshuvah* in misattributing these words to Ramban.

b. **The terminology has changed.**[37] According to *Tzitz Eliezer,*[38] the menstrual *hargashot* listed by Rambam ("she hiccups, or sneezes, or she feels discomfort in her stomach and her lower abdomen, or she shivers, or her head or limbs ache, or the like")[39] have the status of *hargashot* that cause *tum'ah mi-de'Orayta*[40] and are included in the term "bodily tremors." Apparently Rambam holds that the term "*za'azu'ah ha-guf*" does not refer to bodily tremors,[41] but to hormonal changes or fluctuations that are sometimes accompanied by abdominal pain, back pain, "or the like." Maharam Schick wrote similarly that *tum'ah mi-de'Orayta* is caused by "other bodily occurrences that are common at the time of menstruation," including an aching head or limbs, all of which are called *hargashah,* and a woman knows with certainty from these *hargashot* that blood is flowing in her flesh.[42] This explanation, that the terminology has changed, can also resolve the difficulty intimated by the author of *Sha'arei Orah*[43] with respect to the opening of the uterus: "It is known today that the uterus does not open at all when menstrual blood flows from it." The depiction of the uterus opening is based on an assumption regarding a woman's physiology, as if a woman's body has a sort of valve that opens to let blood out of the uterus. *Tosafot* write accordingly,[44]

37. R. Yehuda Herzl Henkin notes that the advantage of this approach, which interprets the *hargashot* mentioned by *poskim* in terms that fit the contemporary reality, is that it minimizes the need to dictate to women what they feel.

38. 6:21. Compare *Ḥut Ha-Shani, Hilkhot Niddah* 183:1:4, that if one regularly experiences bleeding accompanied by these *hargashot,* then there is concern that it constitutes *veset ha-guf,* and she must perform a *bedikah.*

39. These are learned from *Mishnah Niddah* 9:8; see *Mishneh Torah, Hilkhot Metamei Mishkav U'Moshav* 3:6.

40. *Arukh Ha-Shulḥan* (*Yoreh De'ah* 183:59) rejects the possibility that the menstrual *hargashot* mentioned by Rambam (sneezing, abdominal pain, etc.) are deemed *hargashot* to cause *tum'ah mi-de'Orayta,* as it does not stand to reason that the sensation of urination and the like would mask *hargashot* felt elsewhere in the body. This is questionable, though, because bodily tremors also cannot mask the sensation of bleeding, as they do not occur in the same place in the body, yet all agree that bodily tremors are considered *hargashot.* The explanation must be that urination and the like can mask only some *hargashot,* but not all.

41. Similarly, *Tzitz Eliezer* 6:21:2 explains similarly, contrary to the explanation of many others that "*za'azu'ah*" refers to an actual shaking of the whole body. See, for example: *Responsa Tzemaḥ Tzedek* (Lubavitch), *Yoreh De'ah siman* 142; *Arukh Ha-Shulḥan, Yoreh De'ah* 183:58–59, 190:9, and 191:3. However, in *Mishneh Torah, Hilkhot Issurei Biah* 5:17, Rambam mentions a woman who urinates, "and even if her body experienced a *hargashah* and trembled." This refers to an actual tremor.

42. *Responsa Maharam Schick, Yoreh De'ah siman* 184: "Granted that many women do not sense the opening of the uterus, but they feel other bodily occurrences ... and we must interpret the language of our Sages such that she feels when the blood comes to her flesh."

43. P. 70.

44. *Niddah* 4a, s.v. "*ve-ha ishah mekhusah hi.*"

and *Pardes Rimonim* explains:[45] "*Midrash Rabbah* on Vayikra 14 explains that the uterus is always filled with blood. This is the meaning of what the Talmud and *poskim* state everywhere regarding her menses, 'the uterus is opened.' For the uterus is always filled with blood, but when she is not menstruating, it is sealed, and when her menses arrive, the uterus opens, and the blood exits."

c. **Sensations have weakened.** *Hargashot* occur exactly as described by the *poskim*, but today's women cannot identify them.[46] Alternatively, women are mistaken; they have *hargashot*, but they do not know to identify the *hargashah*. *Arukh Ha-Shulḥan* says this about the women who reported to R. Shmuel Schotten that some of them do not sense the opening of the uterus but only sense the flow of blood: "The mouths of these women utter nonsense, and they do not know what they are saying."[47] R. Moshe Feinstein supports this view of *Arukh Ha-Shulḥan*,[48] and *Pardes Rimonim* follows this line of reasoning as well.[49]

According to the "nature has changed" approach, we may rely on a woman who reports that she did not sense the opening of the uterus or a bodily tremor in order to permit a *ketem* that was not accompanied by a *hargashah*. According to the "sensations have weakened" approach, we must be concerned that she may have sensed the opening of the uterus but did not identify it. According to the "terminology has changed" approach, we would need to investigate whether she had any sensation at all typical of menstruation. If she did, we would say that these are the *hargashot* that used to be called "the opening of the uterus" or "bodily tremor," and the *ketem* is *tamei mi-de'Orayta*.

R. Yosef Shalom Elyashiv wrote[50] that since women nowadays do not have *hargashot* at all, a *hargashah* is not required for a *ketem* to be rendered *tamei mi-de'Orayta*. He proved this from the fact that a one-day-old baby can become

45. *Pitḥei Niddah, ḥakirah* 5. He adds that blood from a *makkah* can be discharged from the uterus without it opening. This may be why the main concern of *Ḥakhamim* was for the onset of menses, when, in their view, the uterus opened, until it closed again at the end of menstruation.

46. See, for example, *Responsa Teshurat Shai* 1:457: "It seems to me that due to the weakening of the senses and of concentration"; *Ḥut Shani, Kitzur Hilkhot Niddah*, p. 29; *Responsa Shevet Ha-Levi* 10:142; *Shi'urei Shevet Ha-Levi siman* 190, at the beginning and the end.

47. *Arukh Ha-Shulḥan, Yoreh De'ah* 183:61. His depiction of the internal organs of the female reproductive system is derived from the aforementioned *Tosafot*.

48. *Igrot Moshe, Yoreh De'ah* 4:17: "We see that they know exactly when they became *niddot*." However, many women attest that this is not their experience.

49. P. 26: "One can say that women are not proficient in sensing the opening of the uterus."

50. *Kovetz Teshuvot* 1:84. He further wrote that the leniency of *ketamim* applies only if she found blood on a garment, as opposed to a sanitary napkin, because one may attribute it to something from the environment.

teme'ah niddah, and *hargashah* cannot apply to a baby. However, this is questionable, because babies cannot experience *hargashah* at all, whereas women can experience *hargashah* even if they, in fact, do not.[51]

2. The flow of "something wet"

As mentioned, the sensation of a flow is the most common sensation among women, yet many *Aḥaronim* do not deem it a *hargashah* that renders one *niddah*.

The first to mention this was R. Shmuel Schotten (Maharsheshakh), who turned to R. Yaakov Poppers (author of *Responsa Shav Yaakov*) to render *tehorah* a woman who suffered from pubic lice. She would regularly feel the leakage of a "white discharge" and would perform a *bedikah* because of the *hargashah*, and find drops of blood within the discharge.[52] R. Schotten asked women to describe their *hargashot*, and some described "a strong sensation of something falling from the opening of the uterus," whereas other felt only "that something wet flowed from them." Therefore, if not for the fact that he could attribute the small drops of blood to the pubic lice, he would deem the woman *niddah* because of the drops of blood accompanied by *hargashah*. *Shav Yaakov* rejected R. Schotten's argument and permitted her on the grounds that *zivat davar lakh*, the flow of something wet, is not considered *hargashah*, since, in contrast to a *hargashah* of the opening of the uterus, *zivat davar lakh* does not attest uncontestably to bleeding. He proves this from the fact that Rambam renders *tehorah* a woman who finds blood in her urine, even though she certainly sensed a flow. Even a woman who urinates while standing[53] and finds blood in her urine is *tehorah* if she is certain that she did not feel the opening of her uterus; and we attribute the sensation of a flow to urination.[54] The author of *Sidrei Taharah* writes at length to prove this view.[55]

In contrast, *Noda BiYehudah*[56] writes that the flow of discharge is precisely the *hargashah* to which Shmuel referred in his explication of the verse: "in her flesh

51. My husband, R. Yehuda Herzl Henkin, commented thus to me on this statement of R. Elyashiv.
52. *Responsa Shav Yaakov* 1:39.
53. As to the opinion of R. Meir in the Gemara, he maintains that since a woman normally urinates while sitting, if she urinates standing because she cannot hold back the stream until she can sit, there was apparently a great deal of pressure, and that pressure caused the urine to back up into the uterus and bring out blood. In contrast, a woman who manages to sit before urinating did not experience particular pressure, and so we do not claim that "the urine backed up into the uterus and brought out blood."
54. *Responsa Shav Yaakov* 1:39, s.v. "*ve-od kasheh alai me'od ke-da'at R. Yosei.*"
55. *Siman* 190, at the beginning.
56. *Yoreh De'ah* 1:55.

(*bivsarah*) – until she senses it in her flesh." *Hakhamim* derived an additional law from "*bivsarah*": that she becomes *niddah* by finding blood "inside" just as by finding blood "outside" ("*mitam'ah bifnim ke-vahutz*"), i.e., that she becomes *niddah* only from the "teeth" (beside the cervix)[57] and outward (the vagina). Consequently, the flesh on which she must sense the bleeding is outside the cervix, namely, the vaginal wall. Thus, one cannot explain that Shmuel required her to sense the opening of the uterus, and that is why the verse stipulates "flesh," not the "uterus" ("*makor*"). The author of *Hayei Adam*,[58] a student of the author of *Noda Bi-Yehudah*, adds that Ramban and Rashba wrote that a woman becomes *niddah* only by means of a *hargashah* at the time that the blood goes out on her flesh. *Levush* copies this language as well – and they do not mention the sensation of the uterus opening. We learn from all of them that it is necessary to have "whatever *hargashah* there is."

Havat Da'at,[59] on the other hand, states that one is *teme'ah* only when she senses a flow from the uterus to the vagina, not in the vagina only.[60] *Pardes Rimonim*[61] explains that the author of *Havat Da'at* had a question: According to *Noda Bi-Yehudah*, where does the *tum'ah* originate? If she had no *hargashah* of the blood leaving the uterus, the blood is *tahor*, so why would *tum'ah* apply to *tahor* blood in the vagina?[62]

Hatam Sofer[63] rejects the position of *Noda Bi-Yehudah* as a "new invention" that is not based on the words of the earlier authorities. It is enough that a *hargashah* of the opening of the uterus causes *tum'ah mi-de'Orayta*, and there is no need

57. These are the folds of tissue on the sides of the vaginal canal near the uterus; see Rashi and Meiri on *Niddah* 41b, and against *Responsa Maharam Schick, Yoreh De'ah siman* 184, which states that the "teeth" refers to the cervix itself.

58. *Binat Adam, Sha'ar Ha-Nashim siman* 7. He goes on to say that between one menses and the next, and certainly during pregnancy, a woman who regularly senses the flow of a "white" [=colorless] discharge, and cannot perform *bedikot* due to the frequency of the discharge, is *tehorah* as long as she only senses the flow of fluid.

59. 190:1.

60. In the glosses of R. Barukh Frankel (author of *Barukh Ta'am*) on *Noda Bi-Yehudah, Yoreh De'ah* 1:55, s.v. p. 4 line 1, he writes that it is known and straightforward that there is no sensation of something wet flowing within the body; the flow is only sensed "where air can penetrate." This displaces the view of *Havat Da'at* as well.

61. *Pithei Niddah, hakirah* 5, p. 24b.

62. *Responsa Maharam Schick* (*Yoreh De'ah siman* 184) dismissed the question of *Havat Da'at*, answering that according to *Noda Bi-Yehudah*, the status of blood that comes from the uterus is indeterminate; it is not considered *tahor* until it passes through the entire vaginal canal without her sensing it in her flesh.

63. *Responsa Hatam Sofer, Yoreh De'ah siman* 167.

for new stringencies, and the sensation of *zivat davar lakh* is not considered a *hargashah* that causes *tum'ah mi-de'Orayta*. Likewise, *Arukh Ha-Shulḥan*[64] disproves the evidence mustered by his predecessors who prohibit based on the sensation of *zivat davar lakh*, and so too, *Responsa Shevet Ha-Levi*[65] maintains that the sensation of a flow without the sensation of the uterus opening, bodily tremor, or the like, is not considered a *hargashah*. *Taharat Ha-Bayit* cites a long list of *Aḥaronim* who rely on *Ḥatam Sofer*.[66]

How could *Ḥatam Sofer* disregard the most common *hargashah* among women? Because the sensation of a flow is not mentioned in the Gemara or among the *Rishonim*. *Noda Bi-Yehuda* explains Shmuel's statement based on his own reasoning, as described above. In contrast, *Ḥatam Sofer* cites *Shav Yaakov*'s reasoning: *Ḥakhamim* all agree that a woman who sits and urinates and finds blood is *tehorah*,[67] even though she certainly sensed the flow of liquid, as the bladder is right next to the uterus. *Ḥatam Sofer* goes on to add a long list of his own proofs from the Gemara against the reasoning of *Noda Bi-Yehudah* – proofs that, in the words of his great disciple Maharam Schick, "truly have no rebuttal."[68] To wit, according to Shammai, a sleeping woman awakens at the onset of menses because of the pain,[69] and one would have to strain to explain that she awakens because of a flow.[70] Another proof is from a woman who suffers from a prolapsed uterus, and pieces of tissue fall into the vagina, and she experiences bleeding along with the pieces; Rabbeinu Shimshon deems her *tehorah*, as this is not the normal way for a woman to experience bleeding, and this is the ruling in *Tur* and *Shulḥan Arukh*;[71] even if this blood comes into contact with the vaginal walls just before being

64. *Yoreh De'ah* 183:63–66.

65. 5:113.

66. 1:1:4, p.14 in *Mishmeret Ha-Taharah*. The author also lists a number of *Aḥaronim* who follow *Ḥavat Da'at*.

67. *Niddah* 57b, and see n. 64 above.

68. *Responsa Maharam Schick, Yoreh De'ah siman* 184.

69. *Niddah* 3a.

70. That is, even though it is possible to give a forced interpretation and explain Shammai as referring to the majority of cases, meaning, that a woman awakens upon bleeding profusely, but even mild bleeding is considered *hargashah* so as not to introduce fine distinctions ["lo plug"], nevertheless, no *Rishonim* interpret Shammai's view this way. On the contrary, Rambam and *Shav Yaakov* seem to take the opposite view. Therefore, according to *Ḥatam Sofer*, there are no grounds for introducing this novel interpretation. Yet this is still very questionable. What is the pain to which Shammai refers? It is quite common for women to wake up in the morning, without having woken up in the middle of the night, and find that they began to menstruate overnight.

71. *Tur* and *Shulḥan Arukh, Yoreh De'ah siman* 188.

discharged from her body, she is nevertheless *tehorah*. This demonstrates that "*bivsarah*" – where blood causes *tum'ah* – is further in than the *"bayit hahitzon"* (the vagina); this term refers to the *"prozdor,"* which is, according to *Ḥatam Sofer*, the cervix.[72] Additionally, the sensation of *zivat davar laḥ* in the vagina does not conclusively indicate the discharge of blood,[73] as there are many *tahor* discharges in the vagina, such as the vaginal lubrication released when libido increases.[74]

Regarding the flow of discharge out of the external opening of the vagina, R. Moshe Feinstein writes[75] that since nowadays women do not distinguish between blood flow from the uterus and blood flow from the vagina, any sensation of blood flow out of the vagina is considered a *hargashah*. However, according to most opinions, this is not a *hargashah* that prohibits [the woman]. All agree that the sensation of wetness and moisture outside the body is not considered *hargashah*.[76]

3. Other bodily *hargashot*

According to R. Eliezer Waldenberg,[77] bleeding that is accompanied by menstrual sensations, including stomach and back aches, render a woman *teme'ah mi-de'Orayta*, and these are what Rambam meant by "bodily tremors." He further maintains that in *Ḥatam Sofer*'s view, bodily tremors and pain "like the sting of

72. *Responsa Ḥatam Sofer, Yoreh De'ah siman* 167. The identification of the "*prozdor*" of the Mishnah with the cervix and not the vaginal canal accords with Rambam, *Mishneh Torah, Hilkhot Issurei Biah* 5:3, against *Tosafot*.
73. This is similar to R. Poppers's argument in *Shav Yaakov*. However, all of the many women whom I asked could distinguish between the sensation of menstrual bleeding and the sensation of urination. The latter is a voluntary action that can be controlled; the flow of urine can even be stopped by contracting the pelvic muscles. This is not true of menstrual blood, which is discharged involuntarily. Some can distinguish urination from menstruation based on the fact that it comes from elsewhere in the body and is accompanied by relief of pressure on the bladder. It must be that when the Gemara says, "it is a sensation of urination," it does not mean that the two sensations are identical, but that the sensation of urination can mask the sensation of bleeding, just as the other two situations that can weaken or mask the sensation of bleeding, but do not mean that women may confuse the sensation of blood flow with the sensation of insertion of a *bedikah* cloth or of the male organ.
74. *Responsa Ḥatam Sofer, Yoreh De'ah* 167, states: "According to medical knowledge, women experience most such discharges out of desire and sexual arousal." Similarly, *Ḥokhmat Adam* (*Sha'ar Bet Ha-Nashim* 113:2) writes that a pregnant woman who sensed the opening of her uterus but did not find a *tahor* discharge is nevertheless *tehorah*, as we attribute the opening of the uterus to the discharge of white or green liquid, and *Arukh Ha-Shulḥan* writes that it is known that pregnant women have many discharges.
75. *Igrot Moshe, Yoreh De'ah* 4:17:7.
76. See *Shi'urei Shevet Ha-Levi* 190:2, p. 156, as well as *Igrot Moshe* loc. cit.
77. *Tzitz Eliezer* 6:21.

urine"[78] are themselves the *hargashot* of the opening of the uterus and render a woman *teme'ah mi-de'Orayta*. Maharam Schick, too, was uneasy with limiting types of *hargashah* to two, and he writes[79] that Shmuel's explication, "until she senses it in her flesh," refers to the flesh of her entire body, not only to the flesh of the vagina. Therefore, "other bodily manifestations that are common at the time of menstruation" cause *tum'ah mi-de'Orayta,* and this is what Rambam meant when he wrote at the beginning of chapter 9 of the *Hilkhot Issurei Biah* that there is a presumption that menstrual bleeding is accompanied by *hargashah.*[80] Thus, in his view, a woman who finds a *ketem* that is accompanied by physical sensations that clearly indicate the onset of menses, is *teme'ah mi-de'Orayta.*[81] *Arukh Ha-Shulḥan* writes that the requirement that she sense that the uterus has opened does not refer to a specific sensation of one sort or another, but to knowledge, that she must know that the uterus has opened. This, in his opinion, is Rashi's view that the woman "knows on her own when she discharges blood."[82] Thus, according to these *poskim,* a woman becomes *teme'ah mi-de'Orayta* from a *ketem* accompanied by a stomach ache, backache, etc. if that is normal for the onset of her menses.

Hormonal bleeding when menses are not expected: Attributing to an external cause

The law of *teliyah,* attribution, is predicated on the possibility that the *ketem* originates from some external cause (for example, lice), even if the possibility is very remote, because *Ḥakhamim* prohibited *ketamim* only where there is no possibility of attribution whatsoever.[83] Nevertheless, some have questioned

78. The Gemara in *Niddah* 3a mentions that women wake up at night from pain at the onset of menses, and *Ḥatam Sofer* explains that this pain is like the sting of urine. Perhaps he refers to the burning sensation that sometimes accompanies urination. Others explain it as the relief of pressure on the bladder after urination (*Arukh Ha-Shulḥan* 183:60) or the pain of holding in urine (*Yabi'a Omer,* vol. 5, *Yoreh De'ah siman* 15), which, it stands to reason, would wake someone up.
79. *Responsa Maharam Schick* 184:1. It emerges that according to Maharam Schick, blood flow in the vagina does not cause *tum'ah,* but menstrual sensations everywhere else in the body do cause *tum'ah*. See further in *Pardes Rimonim, Pitḥei Niddah,* p. 24a.
80. So is written in *Pardes Rimonim, Pitḥei Niddah, ḥakirah* 5, p. 24.
81. Maharam Schick's position implies that a woman is not prohibited by a sensation of flow in the vagina, but would be prohibited by a sensation in any other location of the body. This requires considerable study.
82. *Arukh Ha-Shulḥan, Yoreh De'ah* 183:57. He brings proof from the language of *Ḥakhamim* in aggadic statements, for example, in *Megillah* 15b: "Perhaps the Omnipresent will sense and perform a miracle for us." The term "sense" ("*yargish*") does not refer to a physical sensation in this context.
83. See *Sidrei Taharah* 190:92 at length.

the ability of halakhic authorities to permit *ketamim* caused by progesterone-based pills, about which we are not only certain that the blood comes from the woman's body, but the hormonal mechanism that causes spotting is also well-known and familiar to us.[84] However, Maharam Lublin writes explicitly[85] that the reason *Ḥakhamim* say that a woman does not become *teme'ah* unless she experiences a *hargashah* is not because it proves beyond all doubt that the blood comes from her body, in that it cannot be attributed to any other cause, but because it is a decree of the Torah ("*gezeirat ha-Katuv*") that only in this way does she become *teme'ah mi-de'Orayta*. For if the *hargashah* is only to prove that the blood comes from her, why would the Torah require a *hargashah* rather than proof? *Hargashah* is one method of proof, but there are likely to be others.

R. Ovadiah Yosef also writes against the position of *Sidrei Taharah* and rules leniently regarding a *ketem* even when it is clear to the *posek* that the blood comes from her body, as long as she had no *hargashah*, since the *tum'ah* of such a *ketem* is rabbinic in origin, and as Maharam Lublin puts it, "they said [it is *tamei*] and they said [it is *tahor*]."[86]

Summary of views regarding sensation of zivat davar laḥ, fluid flowing

Those who deem it *tamei*: According to *Noda Bi-Yehudah*, *Ḥokhmat Adam*, *Sidrei Taharah*, R. Shlomo Kluger,[87] and, among contemporary *poskim*, R. Moshe Feinstein and R. Eliezer Waldenberg – a *ketem* accompanied by the sensation of *zivat davar laḥ* is deemed to be blood accompanied by *hargashah*, and it causes *tum'ah* in any quantity. *Ḥavat Da'at* deems it *tamei* only if she senses a flow from the uterus to the vagina – an uncommon, and perhaps nonexistent, sensation; R. Moshe Feinstein, however, rules that it is *tamei* even if she only sensed a flow from the vagina out of the body, not only within the vaginal canal. Maharam Schick does not deem *zivat davar laḥ* to be a cause of *tum'ah*, but he deems *tamei* any sensation of menses anywhere else in the body, for by this she "knows" that blood came from her uterus.

Those who deem it *tahor*: Maharam Lublin, *Shav Yaakov*, *Ḥatam Sofer*, *Arukh Ha-Shulḥan*, and, among contemporary *poskim*, R. Shmuel Wosner, R. Ovadiah Yosef, and others all judge such cases according to the laws of *ketamim*.

---

84. For example, R. Yaakov Ariel wrote along these lines in his approbation to *Sha'arei Orah*, p. 11.

85. *Responsa Maharam Lublin siman* 2.

86. *Taharat Ha-Bayit* 1:8:6, p. 387.

87. *Mei Niddah*, p. 130, at the end.

In the present case

Since we are speaking of a dispute among *poskim* over the course of several centuries, from the time of Maharam Lublin until today, and given that our case involves not just a single *ketem* but the expectation of prolonged spotting, it is proper to advise the questioner to switch to a different contraceptive method that does not cause *ketamim*, in order to be spared from complex questions.[88] In any event, in the present case it is possible that even one who is concerned about the view of R. Waldenberg and others would admit that the questioner's bleeding should be judged according to the laws of *ketamim*, since she is nursing and is *mesuleket damim*, and the main concerns of the *poskim* is the experiencing of bleeding at the anticipated time, at the onset of menses.[89] Many follow the lenient view even when the woman is not *mesuleket damim*.[90]

C.H.

88. This is how my husband, R. Henkin, rules.

89. In accordance with the statement of R. Akiva in *Niddah* 58b: "blood, not a *ketem*." This also appears in *Binat Adam, Sha'ar Bet Ha-Nashim* 7, at the end; *Tzitz Eliezer* 6:21 states: "Anyhow, our women as well experience one of all these *hargashot* before or at the onset of menses." See also *Responsa Ḥatam Sofer, Yoreh De'ah* 145, at the end, and elsewhere. *Responsa Divrei Ḥayim* (*Yoreh De'ah* 1:37) writes that the sensation of the outflow of blood must be definite, and a woman will certainly identify this *hargashah* if it happened. Therefore, in his view, if a woman is unsure whether she experienced a *hargashah*, it is not considered a *hargashah* that would render her *teme'ah mi-de'Orayta*.

90. This is how R. Warhaftig rules, based on the position of R. Ovadiah Yosef.

Siman 26

Pain and Reduced Libido

Question

I gave birth six months ago. Ever since, I experience great pain during intercourse. The perineal stitches have long since healed and no longer hurt, and I have no idea what is causing the pain. As a result, I have neither the desire nor the strength for marital relations. I am nursing and not getting my period, so I have no breaks during which we must be apart. The pain makes things difficult for me, and, on top of this all, I'm exhausted from the demands of the baby, the household, and my job—to which I returned a month ago. My husband is frustrated by my constant refusal. I don't know what to do.

Answer

You do not have an obligation to endure pain for the sake of marital relations. However, it is important to treat your condition, for your sake and for the sake of a healthy marital relationship.

Recovery from childbirth usually takes up to six weeks, after which marital relations should not be painful. If the pain persists beyond this period, there are many possible causes, so it is advisable to see a gynecologist for diagnosis and treatment. Among other possibilities, the hormonal changes that accompany nursing can reduce libido and cause vaginal dryness, making intercourse painful. Alternatively, the pain may indicate the presence of an infection or sore in the vaginal area, or another condition that requires treatment. Most factors causing pain during intercourse can be treated medically.

Lack of interest in marital relations can stem from additional factors as well, including ongoing lack of sleep, postpartum depression, and use of hormonal contraceptives. To deal with exhaustion, it is worth considering arranging help at home and resolutely sticking to scheduled rest times. If this does not bring about improvement, we recommend consulting your gynecologist for a diagnosis and a treatment plan. You can also try making "quality time" with your husband and go out to eat, take a walk together, or engage in physical contact without marital relations. Such steps may arouse your desire for closeness with him.

Aside from the pain, your question raises the issue of a woman's obligation to engage in marital relations, and the limits of that duty. Marriage is based on mutual obligations that the spouses have toward one another. One of these basic obligations is marital relations. The husband is obligated to have relations with his wife with a specific degree of frequency, as well as when she manifests the desire for intimacy. The wife, too, is obligated to have relations with her husband. The practical scope of this obligation hinges on variables that change from couple to couple, depending on occupation, desire, and physical capability.

To fulfill your mutual duties, it is worthwhile investing in the creation of open lines of communication about your relationship. That way, over time, each spouse learns to be attentive to, and inclusive of, the particular needs of the other spouse. If there is no improvement, professional counseling is recommended.

Even in the absence of pain, you are not obligated to have relations with your husband when your emotional state does not allow it. On the other hand, keep in mind that you are his only partner for intimacy, and even if he is sensitive to your difficulties, it provides no outlet for his needs. Prolonged separation will certainly be difficult for him and may even lead him astray.

It is especially important to coordinate your expectations while you are nursing, when there will be long periods of time during which you will not be *niddah*. In this situation, a woman sometimes needs breaks to recoup her physical or emotional strength.

Halakhic Expansion

A couple's obligation to be physically intimate is derived from the very essence of *kiddushin*. After fulfilling the mitzvah to procreate,[1] the husband may not abstain

1. Rambam, *Mishneh Torah, Hilkhot Ishut* 15:1; see also *Shulḥan Arukh, Even Ha-Ezer* 76:6.

from marital relations without his wife's consent,[2] unless he is ill or incapable,[3] and even then, only for six months.[4] Separation for longer than this is grounds for divorce, and the wife may sue for her *ketubah*. At the same time, just as a husband may not withhold marital relations from his wife in order to torment her,[5] so too she may not refrain from marital relations to spite or torment her husband.[6] A woman who refuses marital intimacy on principle is deemed a rebellious wife (*moredet*), and this is grounds for divorce.[7]

Nevertheless, *halakhah* recognizes that a woman is not always willing to engage in marital intimacy, and so she need not accede to her husband whenever he wants it. As long as she does not refuse him categorically, she is entitled to refuse him whenever it is difficult for her,[8] and certainly when marital relations are painful and cause distress.[9]

Marital relations are supposed to bring pleasure and satisfaction to both spouses. Ḥazal describe the husband's marital duty as "to bring joy to his wife through this mitzvah."[10] The husband is commanded to have relations with his wife with a specific degree of frequency, and he must also be attentive to her expressions of the desire for intimacy.[11] The wife likewise is obligated to have marital relations with her husband at the frequency determined by Ḥazal, and also when he is in distress,[12] that is, when he desires intimacy. The frequency determined by Ḥazal for marital intimacy depends on the husband's profession and occupation, which impact his needs and capabilities.[13]

---

2. If they both accede, it is permissible. See *Igrot Moshe, Even Ha-Ezer* 1:102.
3. *Mishneh Torah, Hilkhot Ishut* 14:7.
4. The six-month period is derived from the marital responsibilities of sailors, who may stay away from home for six months. The question of whether the husband may leave home for such prolonged periods nowadays, when long-distance travel is more comfortable and affordable, requires further study.
5. *Mishneh Torah*, loc. cit.
6. Ibid. 15:18.
7. Ibid. 14:8–9.
8. See *Shem Yosef* on *Mishneh Torah*, loc. cit. 15:18.
9. *Igrot Moshe, Oraḥ Ḥayim* 4:75 states simply that "at a time that it is difficult for her to consent to marital relations, she is exempt" from her obligation to her husband.
10. *Pesaḥim* 72b.
11. *Shulḥan Arukh, Oraḥ Ḥayim* 240:1.
12. *Igrot Moshe, Oraḥ Ḥayim* 4:75, s.v. "*ve-hinei agav*." Note that very few *poskim* addressed such questions.
13. *Shulḥan Arukh*, loc. cit.; *Igrot Moshe*, loc. cit.

R. Moshe Feinstein[14] raised the premise that the mitzvah of *onah,* the husband's obligation to provide for his wife sexually, like his obligation to provide her with food and clothing, is defined by the wife's needs, and Ḥazal determined a fixed frequency because the wife, out of modesty, is likely to conceal those needs. This explanation appears earlier in the writings of Ra'avad.[15]

Even though a husband should not demand to be with his wife when she does not want to,[16] "for she is not a captive at sword-point who must have relations with him at any time,"[17] and she has no obligation to endure pain in order to fulfill the desires of her husband,[18] it is worthwhile for her, too, to recognize that balancing the needs and desires of both spouses requires her to understand that her husband must contend with his urges and drives, that by being responsive to him, she distances him from sinful acts,[19] and that her prolonged refusal can lead him astray.

The couple should be encouraged to communicate openly. This will allow them to deal with the new challenges that emerge alongside their halakhic duties and the overall sensitivity of intimate life. The wife should take her husband's needs into consideration and be aware of her responsibilities toward him, but, by the same token, she must also know that if she has no strength for marital relations, she need not engage in them. She has every right to expect her husband to understand and accept her situation.

M.R.

14. *Igrot Moshe, Even Ha-ezer* 3:28, s.v. *"al kol panim keivan de-ḥazinan."*
15. *Ba'alei Ha-Nefesh, Sha'ar Ha-Kedushah,* p. 117.
16. See *Nedarim* 20b and *Igeret Ha-kodesh* (attributed to Ramban), chapter 6.
17. *Responsa Maharit* 1:5. See also *Mishneh Torah, Hilkhot Ishut* 14:8 and *Divrei Yatziv, Even Ha-Ezer* 55.
18. The Talmud (*Ketubot* 22b and *Tosafot ad loc.,* s.v. *"ve-afilu"*) tells of the wife of Shmuel, who would claim that she is *niddah* to avoid relations with him that night. R. Feinstein (*Igrot Moshe* loc. cit.) wonders why she felt a need to lie to her husband if he has no right to compel her to be with him when it is difficult for her. He answers that she lied because she wanted to take his feelings into consideration, for it would hurt him to know that she felt weak.
19. *Yevamot* 63a, Ra'avad *Ba'alei Ha-Nefesh, Sha'ar Ha-Kedushah,* p.117, s.v. *"ve-harevi-it she-hu mitkaven li-gdor et atzmo."* Maharsha *Ḥidushei Agadot Yevamot* 62b, s.v. *"be-ein homa she-ne-emar nekaiva tesovev gever."* See also *Responsa Ḥatam Sofer, Yoreh De'ah 2, siman* 162. The obligation of the woman stems, amongst other reasons, from the fact that after *Ḥerem DeRabbenu Gershom,* she is the sole partner for her husband and he has no other outlets to fulfill his needs.

Siman 27

Blood on Toilet Paper

Question

I am nursing and have not been getting my period. Yesterday, while wiping in the bathroom, I found blood on the moist wipe, and today I saw blood again, this time on the toilet paper. Am I *niddah*?

Answer

Toilet paper, tissues, and baby wipes are not susceptible to *tum'ah*. Therefore, as long as you did not experience a halakhically significant *hargashah*, then even if you see blood on one of these surfaces, you are, in principle, not *niddah*. However, if you wiped immediately after urinating, then according to Ashkenazi ruling, we must presume that there may have been a discharge of blood accompanied by a *hargashah* during urination, and that the *hargashah* was mistakenly attributed to the sensation of urinating. In such a situation, a woman is deemed *niddah* out of uncertainty. However, if a woman waits about 15 seconds before wiping, this uncertainty does not apply, and the blood is considered a *ketem* found on a surface that is not susceptib*'ah*, and she is not *niddah*. According to Sephardi custom, there is no concern that the sensation of urinating will mask the sensation of bleeding, so a woman who finds blood on toilet paper is always *tehorah*.

Thus, if you follow Sephardi custom, you are not *niddah*. If you follow Ashkenazi custom, you must ascertain whether you waited approximately 15 seconds before wiping. If you did, you are not *niddah*; if you wiped immediately after you finished urinating, you are considered *niddah*, and you must wait five days, including the day you found the *ketem*, perform a *hefsek taharah*, count seven *neki'im*, and immerse in a *mikveh*.

Halakhic Expansion

To clarify the status of a woman who finds blood when wiping after urination, we must address several topics: the concern for a *hargashah* while one is urinating; the status of toilet paper and its susceptibility to *tum'ah*; the status of a *ketem* found on a surface that is not susceptible to *tum'ah*, but which is placed on something that is susceptible to *tum'ah*; and the laws of *ketamim* found in the vaginal area.

Concern for a *Hargashah* While Urinating

Ḥazal identified three activities that can mask the sensation of uterine bleeding: urination, performing an internal *bedikah*, and intercourse.[1] Some maintain that a woman who finds blood when wiping after urination becomes *niddah*, as we presume that the bleeding may have been accompanied by a *hargashah*, while she mistakenly thought that the only sensation she experienced was the flow of urine.[2] In such a case, we cannot rely on the woman's report that she did not sense the discharge of blood, because the "sting" of the urine may have masked the sensation of bleeding. Therefore, the woman would become *niddah* even if the blood was found on paper that is not susceptible to *tum'ah*. Rambam[3] is not concerned about this possibility.[4]

However, even those who presume that urination masks the sensation of bleeding are only concerned in a case where the woman hurriedly wiped herself immediately after urinating. If she waited a bit before wiping, another uncertainty accrues, as the blood she found may not have been discharged while she was urinating; it may have been discharged later, at a time when she would have sensed the discharge. Therefore, if she waited to wipe herself, there is no concern that she may have experienced a *hargashah*, and the blood is judged according to the laws of *ketamim*, which do not cause *tum'ah* when found on a surface, like toilet paper, that is not susceptible to *tum'ah*.

Aḥaronim disagree about the amount of time she must wait in order to negate the presumption that the bleeding was accompanied by a *hargashah*. The relevant amount of time can be derived from the "*shi'ur veset*," the time between completing intercourse and finding blood. This measure of time is mentioned with regard to a woman who finds blood after intercourse, where there is concern for *ro'ah*

---

1. *Niddah* 57b.
2. *Ḥavat Da'at* 190:1, *bi'urim*, s.v. "*ve-im matz'ah*." However, there are those who are not concerned about *hargashah* at the time of urination; see *Ḥazon Ish* 90:5, s.v. "*ve-hineh*."
3. *Mishneh Torah, Hilkhot Isurei Bi'ah* 5:17.
4. *Taharat Ha-Bayit* 1:1:5 p. 24, rules accordingly, so Sephardic women need not be concerned that they experienced a *hargashah* while urinating.

meḥamat tashmish (a woman who bleeds from intercourse). The *shi'ur veset* is mentioned in the Gemara[5] in context of the internal *bedikot* that a woman must perform before and after intercourse.[6] This is how the Gemara describes this amount of time: "It is comparable to an attendant and a witness who are standing by a doorway. When the attendant exits, the witness [immediately] enters." This is a very short span of time, less than the time it takes for a woman to perform a *bedikat ḥorim u-sedakim* (an internal self-examination of the recesses and folds). In practice, only a quick, external wiping can be performed within the *shi'ur veset*.[7] Consequently, *Ḥavat Da'at*[8] deems the woman *niddah* only if she finds blood upon wiping within the *shi'ur veset*.

Shulḥan Arukh[9] determines that the *shi'ur veset* is "the time it takes for her to reach under the pillow, take a cloth, and wipe." Rema rules in accordance with Ra'avad that we are not proficient at judging this measure of time precisely, and therefore we need be concerned about any blood found just after ("*samukh*") the time we suspect the possibility of a *hargashah*.[10]

In *Badei Ha-Shulḥan*,[11] R. Feivel Cohen rules stringently if there is any doubt that the wiping may have taken place right after urinating; however, he adds[12] that if the blood she finds is smaller than a *gris*, and she says that she is certain that she did not experience a *hargashah*, we can combine these with the fact that it is irregular for women to experience menstrual bleeding while urinating, and thus rule leniently.[13]

Some *poskim* give only the general parameters of a *shi'ur veset*, without specifying an amount of time. Thus, *Ḥazon Ish*[14] distinguishes between a woman who wiped immediately after urinating and a woman who finds blood after a while.

---

5. *Niddah* 12a.
6. We do not follow Rambam's opinion, so there is no obligation to perform a *bedikah* before and after intercourse. See *Shulḥan Arukh, Yoreh De'ah* 186:1.
7. In the words of *Shulḥan Arukh, Yoreh De'ah* 190:51: "She wiped herself with the cloth in her hand right when the blood was found. However, if she waited enough time to perform a *bedikah*, that is, to wipe the recesses and folds...."
8. *Ḥavat Da'at* 190:1, *bi'urim*, s.v. "*ve-im matz'ah*."
9. *Yoreh De'ah* 187:1.
10. For more on this subject, see *Siman* 43: Post-Coital Bleeding with Hormonal Contraception.
11. 190:104.
12. 190:104, elucidations, s.v. "*keitzad*."
13. He relies on *Neta Sha'ashu'im, Yoreh De'ah* 21.
14. *Yoreh De'ah* 190:1

In contrast, R. Wosner rules[15] that if the woman wipes and finds blood on the toilet paper within a minute of the completion of urination, it is considered "*samukh*," and she is considered *niddah* due to the uncertainty about whether an unnoticed *hargashah* accompanied the bleeding, which would render her *teme'ah mi-de'Orayta*.[16] However, in light of the aforementioned sources that indicate an amount of time that is shorter than the time it takes to perform a *bedikat ḥorim u-sedakim*, a minute seems to be an excessive amount of time.

Against this, *Pri De'ah*[17] writes in favor of adopting the shortest description of "*samukh*" in the Gemara, which is the time it takes to walk 22 *amot*. This amount is cited in *Shulḥan Arukh*[18] as the definition of the term "*tekhef*" ("immediately") with regard to waiting between hand-washing and breaking bread. *Tosafot* in *Sotah*[19] write that the duration of "immediately" is derived from the practice of laying hands ("*semikhah*") on a sacrifice, which must be performed just before ("*samukh*") it is slaughtered. This measure of time applies even when the *semikhah* is performed 22 *amot* away from where the slaughtering takes place. Based on the calculation of the time it takes to walk a *mil*, we can determine that walking 22 *amot* takes about 15 seconds.[20] A woman who waits this long and then wipes need not presume that she experienced a *hargashah*, and the blood she finds upon wiping has the status of a *ketem*. Since the *Rishonim* and many *Aḥaronim* did not cite the presumption of experiencing a *hargashah* while urinating, those who presume a *hargashah* in such instances may rely on the shorter measurement of *Pri De'ah*. This is the ruling of R. Yaakov Warhaftig.

If the woman cannot say for certain that she waited 15 seconds before wiping following urination, it is possible to ask whether she had reason to leave the bathroom hastily. R. Moshe Feinstein[21] introduces a novel interpretation: that the presumption of *hargashah* is only while the last drops of urine are being discharged, because it is not the way of blood to be discharged along with a

15. *Shi'urei Shevet Ha-Levi* 187:1:11, p. 68; 190:10:3, p. 170.
16. According to *Shi'urei Shevet Ha-Levi* (loc. cit.), when actual blood is found, i.e., when the woman is certain that there is bleeding (and not just a brown stain) that does not originate in a urinary tract infection, *lekhatḥilah* she should be stringent even if she waited longer than a minute.
17. *Siftei Levi* 187:7.
18. *Oraḥ Ḥayim* 166.
19. *Sotah* 39, s.v. "*kol kohen she-lo natal yadav*."
20. A *mil* is 2,000 *amot*, and it takes between 18 and 24 minutes to walk a *mil*. (See *Shulḥan Arukh, Oraḥ Ḥayim* 459:2.) At the faster pace, it takes 11.88 seconds to walk 22 *amot*, and at the slower pace, it takes 15.84 seconds. If she waits longer than this amount of time, it is not considered "*samukh*" or "*tekhef*."
21. *Igrot Moshe, Yoreh De'ah* 4:17:13.

stream of urine. Accordingly, a woman who was pressed to leave the bathroom to deal with a crying baby, a boiling pot on the stove, or the like, and therefore wiped herself hurriedly, while the last drops of urine were still leaving her body, is *teme'ah,* as we presume that a *hargashah* may have accompanied the blood she found when wiping. However, if she waited and did not wipe until she had completely finished urinating – "she sat until all the drops came out, wiped, and found blood without having sensed anything, it has the status of a *ketem*." She need not presume that the blood she found when wiping was accompanied by a *hargashah.*

The Susceptibility of Paper to *Tum'ah*

The assumption underlying our discussion, that today's toilet paper is not susceptible to *tum'ah,* is explicit in the *poskim*. R. Moshe Feinstein says that even according to the view that paper, in principle, can be susceptible to *tum'ah,* our toilet paper is not, since it was not made for enduring use.[22] R. Ovadiah Yosef rules likewise in *Taharat Ha-Bayit*.[23] Paper towelettes and baby wipes have the same status as toilet paper.[24]

Something That Is Not Susceptible to *Tum'ah* Placed on Something Susceptible to *Tum'ah*

Sidrei Taharah[25] raises another concern: Even though the blood is found on toilet paper, which is not susceptible to *tum'ah,* one should be stringent about

22. *Igrot Moshe, Yoreh De'ah* 3:53 and 4:17:14: "For it is not made for enduring use, nor is it suitable for something durable." Many *poskim* have discussed the status of paper. *Noda Bi-Yehudah* 2:105 rules stringently, as does *Ḥokhmat Adam* 113:8. In contrast, *Responsa Ḥatam Sofer* 6:81 is lenient regarding paper, even if it is made from worn-out clothing. However, there is a difference between paper as it was manufactured in the past and the paper we use today, and according to most *poskim,* even if paper is made of material that is susceptible to *tum'ah,* since it is first made into pulp, which completely changes its form, it is no longer susceptible to *tum'ah*. *Divrei Yatziv* (*Yoreh De'ah* 89:5, s.v. "*ve-gam she-haneyar tzavu'a*") distinguishes between white and colored toilet paper; blood on colored toilet paper certainly does not render a woman *niddah* due to a *ketem* (*Yoreh De'ah* 190:10). *Igrot Moshe* (*Yoreh De'ah* 4:17:28) states that it is not necessary to use white toilet paper, even during the seven *neki'im,* and using it leads to uncertainties and stringencies about the colors that appear on the paper.
23. Part 1, 8:10:10. He lists many other *poskim* who are lenient about our paper. For further discussion of items that are not susceptible to *tum'ah,* see below, *Siman* 44: Staining on a Panty Liner or Synthetic Clothing.
24. This is the ruling of R. Henkin and R. Warhaftig, as a towelette is similar to a tissue in that both are used once and then thrown out, and both are made from paper, not cloth.
25. 190:93, s.v. "*mi-zeh yatza*." In general, *Sidrei Taharah* rules that a *hargashah* is not necessary for a woman to become *teme'ah mi-de'Orayta,* and the certainty that the blood is from her body

it, since the paper itself is in the woman's hand, so it should be considered like blood that is found on something that is susceptible to *tum'ah*. However, *Igrot Moshe*,[26] *Badei Ha-Shulḥan*,[27] and *Taharat Ha-Bayit*[28] disagree, writing that blood found on toilet paper has the same status as blood found on anything else that is not susceptible to *tum'ah*.[29]

The Status of *Ketamim* in the Genital Area

Another claim that has been raised is that blood found while wiping should be treated as a *ketem* found on the body, since clearly the blood was first on the woman's body and was transferred to the toilet paper while wiping. Therefore, there is no room to claim that the *ketem* was found on something not susceptible to *tum'ah*, and the woman should be deemed *niddah* if the *ketem* is larger than a *gris*.[30] *Taharat Ha-Bayit*[31] disagrees, writing that the blood is judged according to where it was found; it is like the case where a woman examined the ground, where the blood certainly came from her body, yet she is *tehorah*, in accordance with the law regarding a *ketem* found on something not susceptible to *tum'ah*.[32]

Another reason to be stringent in the case at hand is that there are grounds to say that the leniency of a *ketem* smaller than a *gris* does not apply to blood found when wiping the vaginal area, since the blood certainly came from the body, as no lice are to be found there.[33] Therefore, the woman should be deemed *niddah* even if the *ketem* is smaller than a *gris*.[34] *Igrot Moshe* rejects this view and writes

is sufficient to render her *niddah*. For further discussion of this, see above, *Siman* 25: The Law of *Hargashah*.

26. *Yoreh De'ah* 4:17:15.
27. 190:10, *bi'urim*, s.v. "*davar lo mekabel tum'ah*," citing *Ḥatam Sofer* and R. Yitzhak Zev Soloveitchik, who rule against *Sidrei Taharah*.
28. Part 1, 8:12:12.
29. One who takes the view of *Sidrei Taharah* into account can solve the problem by using colored toilet paper. This is why brides-to-be are often instructed to prefer colored toilet paper. However, since most *poskim* do not accept the view of *Sidrei Taharah*, there is no need to proffer this guidance. The main thing is to ensure that women do not think that they become *niddot* if they use white toilet paper.
30. *Kenei Bosem, Yoreh De'ah* 1:77. A similar argument is found in *Responsa Ḥeshev Ha-Efod* (2:75), and this is the ruling in *Be-Tzel Ha-Ḥokhmah* 6:125.
31. 1:5, p. 25.
32. For an expanded discussion of blood found on the body, see below, *Siman* 41: Extending the Cycle via Hormonal Contraception.
33. See *Niddah* 14a.
34. See *Torat Ha-Shelamim* 183:1. *Taharah Ke-Halakhah* 2:13 rules this way in practice as well.

that the laws of *ketamim* apply even to blood found by wiping, because when she wipes, she touches the entire area, not just the vagina itself.[35]

In general, women who follow Sephardi custom need not be concerned about blood found on toilet paper. For those who follow Ashkenazi custom, some *poskim* recommend that women simply not look at the toilet paper.[36] However, since this instruction stresses some women, and since it is vital for a woman to know what is happening in her body,[37] Ashkenazi women should be instructed to wait approximately 15 seconds before wiping, and as long as the wiping is only external, even if a woman finds blood on the toilet paper, she is not *niddah*.[38]

M.R.

35. *Igrot Moshe, Yoreh De'ah* 4:17:16. *Shi'urei Shevet Ha-Levi* 190:6:6 rules similarly.
36. *Shi'urei Shevet Ha-Levi* 191:20, p. 222; *Sha'arei Orah*, p. 89; *Taharah Ke-Halakhah* 2:16.
37. For various reasons, it is important for a woman to know whether she is spotting or bleeding. From a medical perspective, it is important for identifying irregular discharges that warrant a doctor's examination. It is important halakhically as well, so that she can know when to expect the onset of menses and avoid marital relations when she is likely to experience bleeding.
38. If the woman knows that she is suffering from hemorrhoids, she may attribute the bleeding to the hemorrhoids. For further discussion, see above, *Siman* 17: Attributing Bleeding to Hemorrhoids, Postpartum.

Siman 28

Breastfeeding a Toddler after an Interruption

Question

My husband and I are scheduled to take a week's vacation alone, without children. I'm still breastfeeding our son, who is 26 months old. Although he does not depend on breastfeeding, I want to continue nursing him as long as possible. I heard that there is a halakhic problem with resuming breastfeeding an older baby who has already been weaned. If I don't breastfeed for a week, can I resume once we return?

Answer

Breastfeeding is considered halakhically desirable as it benefits the child's health. Current medical thought concurs: The longer breastfeeding continues, the more beneficial it is for the child's health. Nevertheless, after the age of two, if breastfeeding has been interrupted for 72 hours, it is halakhically forbidden to resume breastfeeding. This is on condition that the interruption was in accordance with the child's wants; however, if the interruption was due to an illness of the child or mother, breastfeeding may resume until the age of 4 or 5.

Therefore, if you stop breastfeeding for a week during your vacation, it is considered against the child's will, because the parents chose to travel, but the child did not choose to be weaned. Therefore, if the child cries and tries to resume nursing after you return, you may resume breastfeeding. However, if the child does not demand it, you may not resume nursing.

Halakhic Expansion

There is consensus nowadays that breastfeeding is the preferred way to feed a baby. Doctors recommend that for their first six months, babies should be fed breast milk exclusively, and afterwards nursing should continue, alongside additional, suitable nutrition, until the child is one year old. Thereafter, it should continue for as long as mutually desired by mother and child.[1]

The Gemara[2] says that "the typical baby is at risk with regard to milk." Given the importance of breastfeeding, Ḥazal allow a mother to express milk on Shabbat under certain conditions.[3] In addition, they prohibited a nursing widow to remarry for two years, lest she prematurely wean and thus endanger the child.[4] Nursing of babies is listed among a wife's duties to her husband.[5] Although it is possible nowadays to feed an infant formula, the benefits of breast milk are still greater than those of any artificial alternative.

Ḥazal indicate 24 months as the normative duration of breastfeeding.[6] If the child stopped nursing before reaching the age of 24 months, it is permissible to resume breastfeeding.[7] After 24 months, *halakhah* permits breastfeeding the child, without interruption, until age 4 for a healthy child, and age of 5 for a child who is weak or who is vulnerable to disease.[8] Rambam[9] writes thus, and so it is codified in *Shulḥan Arukh*.[10] However, if a toddler over the age of 24 months stopped nursing for longer than three days, the mother may not resume breastfeeding if the child weaned himself of his own will, and not because of illness.[11]

1. The World Health Organization (WHO) recommends breastfeeding until two years of age. See the Israel Ministry of Health's guide to nutrition of babies and toddlers, for professionals: https://www.health.gov.il/hozer/bz25_2012.pdf. See also: American Academy of Pediatrics: Section on Breastfeeding. Breastfeeding and the Use of Human Milk. *Pediatrics* 2012:120: e827–e841. Available at: https://pediatrics.aappublications.org/content/129/3/e827.
2. *Yevamot* 114a.
3. *Shulḥan Arukh, Oraḥ Ḥayim* 328:35.
4. *Yevamot* 36b. See also *Shulḥan Arukh, Even Ha-Ezer* 13, regarding one who breastfeeds another's child.
5. *Ketubot* 59b.
6. *Yevamot* 36b and Rashi *ad loc.*, s.v. "*davar aḥer*"; *Ketubot* 60a; *Niddah* 9a. For further discussion of this topic, see D. R. Zimmerman, "Duration of Breastfeeding in Jewish Law," in M. Halperin and C. Safrai, eds., *Jewish Legal Writings by Women*. Jerusalem: Urim, 1999.
7. Rambam, *Hilkhot Ma'akhalot Asurot* 3:5; *Shulḥan Arukh, Yoreh De'ah* 81:7.
8. *Ketubot* 60a and *Tosafot ad loc.*, s.v. "*Rabi Yehoshua omer.*" *Shittah Mekubetzet ad loc.* brings the students of Rabbeinu Yonah, who say in the name of the French rabbis that it is permissible to breastfeed even beyond five years.
9. *Mishneh Torah, Hilkhot Ma'akhalot Assurot* 3:5.
10. *Yoreh De'ah* 81:7.
11. *Yerushalmi Ketubot* 5:6; codified in *Shulḥan Arukh, Yoreh De'ah* 81:7.

Breastfeeding a child over 24 months of age who has been weaned is rabbinically prohibited and considered "nursing something detestable" (*"yonek sheketz"*).[12] The *Aḥaronim* raised the concern that people may infer from the permissibility of mother's milk that the milk of non-kosher animals is kosher: If a child who has been weaned may nurse from a woman even though it is forbidden to eat human flesh, there is concern that people will mistakenly permit the milk of a non-kosher animal.[13]

If the child over the age of 24 months was weaned of his own will, but should preferably continue getting breast milk for health reasons, the mother should express and feed the breast milk in a cup. If the child refuses to be fed in this manner, some write that the mother may resume breastfeeding as long as the child is deemed to have a non-life-threatening illness (*"ḥoleh she-ein bo sakanah"*) with respect to the need for breast milk.[14]

If the child over the age of 24 months became ill, and resuming breastfeeding is desirable to fortify his health, she may breastfeed him while he is ill, but after recovery she must stop breastfeeding, since the resumption of breastfeeding was permitted only because of the illness.[15]

R. Moshe Zev Zorger[16] permits a woman who went abroad for a week without her son, in an attempt to wean him after he reached 24 months of age, to resume breastfeeding, since the child's cries demonstrate that he did not stop breastfeeding "as a healthy child" and is not forbidden for him to nurse from his mother. However, if the toddler who does not cry or demand to nurse, the mother may not resume breastfeeding.

Therefore, in the present case, when the mother returns, if the toddler cries and seeks to nurse, it indicates that he misses nursing and has not been weaned, so the mother may resume breastfeeding him.

M.R.

---

12. *Shulḥan Arukh, Yoreh De'ah* 81:7. See Rashi to *Ketubot* 60a, s.v. *"ke-yonek sheketz,"* where he explains this to mean that the child is nursing something detestable – the milk – and not nursing from a detestable creature. For a discussion about whether the prohibition relates to the milk itself or to the act of breastfeeding, see R. Yehoshua Neuwirth, "Breastfeeding a 3-Year-Old Child for Medical Purposes," *Ateret Shlomo* 4 (5759), pp. 154–59 (Hebrew).
13. *Taz, Yoreh De'ah* 81:9. See also: *Arukh Ha-Shulḥan, Yoreh De'ah* 81:32; R. Yosef ibn Walid, *Shemo Yosef siman* 267, p. 50.
14. *Responsa Yabi'a Omer* 5:11:4 (*Ḥelek Yoreh De'ah*), relying on Rashba, who permits feeding a child rabbinically prohibited foods as long as it is for the sake of the child himself.
15. *Shakh, Yoreh De'ah* 81:22.
16. *Responsa Vayashev Moshe* 1:27.

Siman 29

Passing a Baby between Parents during Niddut

Question

I gave birth to twins a month ago, and we now have five children age 8 and younger. My husband and I are exhausted and irritable due to the pressure and lack of sleep. Since the births, I am having a lot of trouble with the *harḥakot* and with the long separation from my husband right when I most need emotional support. Now that I need my husband's help constantly, it is very difficult for me to observe the stricture on handing the babies or other objects to each other. It's also exhausting to drag the double stroller up the stairs instead of lifting it together. Is there no way to be lenient about these things?

Answer

First of all, a hearty double mazal tov!

The purpose of the prohibition on handing objects from one to another is to prevent contact and physical closeness between the couple when they are prohibited to one another. This poses difficulty for many parents, whether because of the need for emotional support or because of the practical need for physical assistance during this demanding time. We recommend that one spouse put the baby down and the other to pick him up immediately. Sometimes you can pass the baby to one another through a third person. This is the origin of the custom of having a "*kvatter*" at a *brit* – so that the parents do not have to pass the baby directly from one to the other. Still, situations naturally arise, especially during the first weeks after childbirth, and certainly after the birth of twins, in which it is impossible to place the baby on a stable surface to avoid passing directly to one another. Therefore, in difficult and painful circumstances, you may rely on those who permit passing the babies directly to one another, while taking care not to touch.

If there is no one who can help you lift the stroller, you may lift it together. One authority permits this even when help can be sought, as long as it can be done in such a way that you will not touch each other.

Halakhic Expansion

One of the *harḥakot* applying when a woman is *niddah* is the prohibition on handing things to one another.[1] The source of this *halakhah* is the Gemara in *Ketubot*,[2] which forbids a woman from pouring a drink and passing it to her husband. The views of the *Rishonim* on this matter break down into three groups:

1. The prohibition applies only to passing a cup, as it is an expression of affection or intimacy. (Rambam and *Sefer Yere'im*)[3]
2. The prohibition applies to any object, lest they touch one another. (Ramban, Rashba, *Tosafot Ha-Rosh*, Rabbeinu Yeruḥam, *Sefer Ha-Ḥinukh*, and *Tur*)[4]
3. There may be grounds for leniency when it comes to large objects, about which there is no concern of touching or intimacy. (Rashi, *Tosafot*, and *Sefer Ha-Terumah*)[5]

According to Rema, the prohibition includes even throwing objects to one another[6] and passing long objects, about which there would seem to be no concern that they might touch.[7]

Some differentiate between babies and other objects. *Pitḥei Teshuvah*[8] brings a responsum of Tashbetz,[9] who writes that babies are not included in the prohibition

1. *Shulḥan Arukh, Yoreh De'ah* 195:2.
2. *Ketubot* 61a.
3. *Hilkhot Ishut* 21:8, and *Maggid Mishneh ad loc.*; *Sefer Yere'im siman* 26, s.v. "*u-veKetubot*."
4. Ramban on *Ketubot* 61a, s.v. "*ve-yesh mi she-omer*"; Rashba *ad loc.*, s.v. "*u-mezigat ha-kos*"; *Tosafot Ha-Rosh ad loc.*, s.v. "*maḥlefa lei*"; Rabbeinu Yeruḥam, *Toldot Adam Ve-Ḥavah, netiv* 26, part 4, s.v. "*peirush mezigat ha-kos*"; *Sefer Ha-Ḥinukh* mitzvah 207; *Tur, Yoreh De'ah* 195.
5. Rashi cited in *Maḥzor Vitry siman* 499; *Tosafot* on *Ketubot* 61a, s.v. "*maḥlefi deveihu be-yada de-smala*"; *Sefer Ha-Terumah, Hilkhot Niddah siman* 89.
6. *Shulḥan Arukh* and Rema, *Yoreh De'ah* 195:2; *Darkhei Moshe ad loc.* 1.
7. *Bet Yosef ad loc.*; *Shakh ad loc.* 3.
8. *Yoreh De'ah* 195:3, s.v. "*ve-lo yekableno mi-yadah*."
9. *Responsa Tashbetz* 3:58 and 230.

on passing things, because a baby is a "*ḥai she'nosei et atzmo*" (a living being that is mobile):[10] "He goes by himself from his mother's lap to his father's lap." Therefore, parents may pass him to one another.[11]

Does the status of "*ḥai she'nosei et atzmo*" apply only to a baby who can move from one parent to the other on his own, or does it apply to a newborn baby as well?[12] Some say that the permissibility of handing the child to one another hinges on the child's ability to move on his own from one parent to the other. Accordingly, if the child is small or ill and immobile, it is forbidden to hand him from one to another.[13] On the other hand, some accept the permissive ruling of Tashbetz, despite the challenges to his rationale, and permit passing a baby of any age.[14]

Contemporary *poskim*[15] have written that *lekhatḥilah* it is proper to avoid handing a baby from one to the other, since it is hard to avoid contact. Under pressing circumstances, one may be lenient regarding a mobile child, and even regarding a newborn.[16] Of course, one should be careful not to place a child in a dangerous place in an attempt to avoid the prohibition of passing an object.[17]

With regard to lifting a baby carriage together, if the load is not heavy, it indicates that assisting is an act of affection, which is not done out of necessity, and

---

10. This is also the ruling of *Birkei Yosef, Shiyurei Berakhah, Yoreh De'ah* 195:7.
11. *Arukh Ha-Shulḥan, Yoreh De'ah* 195:5 disagrees with Tashbetz and prohibits passing a child, even when the child is mobile; *Responsa Shevet Ha-Levi* 2:92 comments that Tashbetz, accordingly, would permit throwing things to one another. However, according to those who forbid throwing, it would also be forbidden to pass a child who can go from one parent to the other on his own. And in 4:112, he disagrees with Tashbetz's permissive ruling. *Badei Ha-Shulḥan* (195:2:24, *tziyunim* 93) maintains that even Tashbetz would forbid passing a small baby, and perhaps a sleeping baby as well.
12. There is a similar disagreement within the laws of Shabbat: Is an 8-day-old baby considered a "*ḥai she'nosei et atzmo*" with respect to a *brit milah* on Shabbat? See *Magen Avraham* 308:70; *Pri Megadim, Eshel Avraham* 308:71; *Eliyahu Rabbah* 308:84, s.v. "*de-ḥai nosei*."
13. *Darkhei Taharah*, p. 43.
14. See *Birkei Yosef, Shiyurei Berakhah, Yoreh De'ah* 195:7. *Taharat Ha-Bayit* 2:12:7 p. 101 permits passing a child but adds that Ashkenazim should be stringent about this matter.
15. R. Asher Weiss (*Minḥat Asher, Hilkhot Niddah* 6:1, p. 47) writes: "It is proper, as an expression of piety (*mi-midat ḥasidut*) to refrain from such a thing, because it is hard to hand a baby over without any touching whatsoever of her skin or her clothes, which are like her skin…but in pressing circumstances, one who is lenient has upon whom to rely."
16. *Taharat Ha-Bayit* 2:12:7 p. 101. *Ḥut Ha-Shani* 195:2:6 (*Sha'ar Ha-Tziyun* 18) permits a man to pick up a child from his wife's lap, because this does not constitute "passing." Rather, he is picking the child up from where he is. However, a spiritually conscientious person ("*ba'al nefesh*") should be strict with himself.
17. This comment was made by R. Mordechai Willig, quoted in *Seder Taharat Ha-Kodesh*, p. 314.

therefore should be avoided.[18] If the stroller or carriage is heavy or too unwieldy to lift alone, lifting it is a matter of assistance, not affection, and it is permitted with a *shinui* (i.e., performing the act not in the usual fashion).[19]

M.R.

18. See *Igrot Moshe, Yoreh De'ah* 2:75. *Nishmat Avraham, Yoreh De'ah* 195:3, s.v. "*horadah ve-ha'alat agalat yeladim,*" brings in the name of R. Shlomo Zalman Auerbach that it is proper to be stringent about all strollers, even heavy ones.
19. As written in *Teshuvot Ve-hanhagot* 1:502; however, he permits only under pressing circumstances and with an obvious *shinui* and says that it is preferable to ask for help or to avoid a situation in which it would be necessary. See also *Responsa Tzitz Eliezer* 12:58.

Part V

Contraception

Siman 30

Family Planning following Childbirth

Question

I have two daughters under the age of three, and I do not want to become pregnant in the near future. Can I wait? And if so, for how long?

Answer

The mitzvah of procreation (*"piryah u-riviyah"*) is the first mitzvah in the Torah and one of the central objectives of marriage. The mitzvah is defined as fathering a viable son and daughter. Although, as a woman, you are not obligated in the mitzvah of procreation, you nevertheless have a duty to help your husband fulfill it. Therefore, as long as you have not had a son and daughter, you must keep trying to fulfill the mitzvah in full. Even after having a son and daughter, a man is commanded not to neglect procreation completely.

On the other hand, for two years following birth, you have the status of a *meineket* (nursing mother), under the presumption that it takes two years for a woman's body to recover from childbirth. This period is defined as the period of nursing even if you are not actually nursing your baby; it is devoted to caring for the child. Therefore, if you feel that you have not returned to full strength, you may use contraception for two years after childbirth.

Once two years have elapsed, the duty to fulfill the mitzvah of procreation returns. However, even after two years, *halakhah* takes other factors into consideration, such as the woman's health, the child's health, the family's economic capacity, etc.

Therefore, if after this period you feel that it is best for you and best for the family that you wait longer, it is desirable to consult further, to examine the different various aspects of the situation through the lens of *halakhah*.

Halakhic Expansion

The question before us relates to a situation where, after two consecutive births, the mitzvah of procreation still has not been fulfilled, so the husband's obligation is a mitzvah *deOrayta*. This discussion will focus on three issues:

1. The husband's obligation versus the wife's exemption.
2. The effort to fulfill the mitzvah versus the results of the effort.
3. Factors that mitigate toward contraception after birth.

1. The husband's obligation versus the wife's exemption

Although both husband and wife are essential to have a child, their obligations vis-à-vis having children differ.[1] The husband has a mitzvah *deOrayta* of procreation ("*piriyah u-riviyah*"), a mitzvah *deRabanan* of "in the evening (*la-erev*), do not withhold your hand," and a third mitzvah of rabbinic provenance, "He formed it for habitation," *la-shevet,* which, according to some *poskim,* obligates women as well. The mitzvah of *piriyah u-riviyah* requires having a son and daughter; "*la-erev*" requires that one does not completely neglect procreation; and "habitation" requires having one child, or, according to some *Aḥaronim,* two children, even of the same sex.[2] According to Rambam, a woman may voluntarily forego her conjugal rights as long as her husband has fulfilled the obligation of *piriyah u-riviyah*. She may even drink an infertility potion that renders her incapable of having children.[3] *Shulḥan Arukh* rules accordingly.[4] However, if the husband has not fulfilled his obligation of *piriyah u-riviyah,* he is obliged to have marital relations at the prescribed times until he has children.[5] Even when the mitzvah has not yet been fulfilled, the frequency of the obligation to have marital relations is derived from the duties of the mitzvah of *onah* (i.e., his conjugal duties), which in turn derives directly from the man's occupation and stamina and the woman's desire and stamina.[6]

---

1. See *Siman* 31, in the Expanded Answer.
2. See below, *Siman* 31: Contraception after Several Births.
3. *Mishneh Torah, Hilkhot Ishut* 15:1.
4. *Even Ha-Ezer* 5:12. Nowadays, when it is possible to ascertain the days on which a woman can become pregnant, it is proper to have marital relations on those days.
5. *Mishneh Torah, Hilkhot Ishut* 15:1, 4.
6. See R. Yigal Ariel, "Spacing Between Pregnancies", *Tzohar,* 10, 5762.

Although a woman is exempt from the mitzvah of *piriyah u-riviyah* and may even drink an infertility potion,[7] she is obligated to be a partner in her husband's fulfillment of the mitzvah, as part of the duties she accepted upon herself by marrying.[8]

Many *Aḥaronim* address the amount of effort the woman must put into her husband's obligation to have children[9] *Ḥatam Sofer* rejected the view that forbids a woman to drink an infertility potion and firmly established the following:[10]

a. A woman who experiences an evidently hazardous degree of pain during childbirth may drink an infertility potion even if she has no children, because a woman's responsibility for her own health precedes her duty to populate the world.

b. Once she has fulfilled the mitzvah of "*shevet*," a woman may drink an infertility potion even if she does not experience pain, as long as her husband consents, as he is obligated in the mitzvah of "*la-erev*." The permissibility of drinking an infertility potion even without the husband's consent, and even in the absence of suffering, pertained to the era before Rabbeinu Gershom's ban of polygamy, when a man could marry a second wife to fulfill the mitzvah of "*la-erev*."

c. If there is intense pain, she has no obligation to torment herself for the sake of her husband's mitzvah of "*la-erev*," even if her husband does not consent.

These rules apply only to contraceptives such as pills, which work indirectly, like an infertility potion.[11]

2. The effort to fulfill the mitzvah versus the results of the effort

R. Yaakov Ariel[12] addresses the distinction between delaying and neglecting the mitzvah of *piriyah u-riviyah*. The mitzvah of *piriyah u-riviyah* never goes away, but neither is its fulfillment attached to a specific time. Since it can be fulfilled over the course of many years, its fulfillment may be postponed for justified reasons like planting a vineyard or building a house (i.e., for considerations of livelihood), or to study Torah, and it is not considered a dereliction of the mitzvah. Moreover,

7. See below, *Siman* 31: Contraception after a Number of Births.
8. *Responsa Ḥatam Sofer, Even Ha-Ezer siman* 20.
9. See *Otzar Ha-Poskim, Even Ha-Ezer* 5:12:72.
10. *Responsa Ḥatam Sofer, Even Ha-Ezer siman* 20.
11. For further expansion on this topic, see below, *Siman* 32: IUD Use and the Ranking of Contraceptive Options.
12. Response to Article by R. Aviner. *Assia* 4, pp. 184–88 (https://www.medethics.org.il/articles-main/?pdf=9504).

the mitzvah of *piriyah u-riviyah* is unique in that whereas a man is commanded to perform this mitzvah, its complete fulfillment depends on factors out of his control. He can make every effort yet still not manage to fulfill the mitzvah, whether because he has not produced viable offspring or because all of his children are of the same sex. In light of this, R. Ariel concludes, the mitzvah is defined as the effort to fulfill it, and as long as a man postpones it for compelling reasons, he is not considered to be neglecting the mitzvah.

3. Factors that mitigate toward contraception after birth

Halakhah grants a woman the option of spacing births for the sake of her own health and the benefit of the child. Spacing pregnancies for these reasons is not considered neglect of the mitzvah, and sometimes delaying the mitzvah allows for its more optimal fulfillment at the right time.

In *Responsa Bnei Banim*, R. Yehuda Henkin writes in the name of his grandfather, R. Yosef Eliyahu Henkin,[13] that it is permissible to prevent pregnancy for 24 months after giving birth, and if necessary, even longer, so long as it is for the sake of the child and not due to other considerations. During this period, it makes no difference whether the husband has fulfilled the mitzvah of *piriyah u-riviyah*. According to him, spacing pregnancies apart by 24 months does not require consultation with a halakhic authority.

Another consideration for permitting contraception to space births apart is the woman's health. A *yoledet* is defined as *mesuleket damim* for 24 months because "throughout the 24 months, her organs become dislocated, and she does not return to herself until 24 months have elapsed."[14] Ḥazal thus note that pregnancy and childbirth weaken a woman, and she needs time to recoup her strength. This expression describes the general physical state as well as the psychological state of a *yoledet*, which differs from woman to woman and hinges on many variables, including the woman's overall health, the type of birth, characteristics of the child, the amount of help that the woman has, etc.[15] Thus preventing pregnancy for two years after birth is halakhically permissible, to allow the mother to recoup her strength, nurse, and give her baby the best care possible. This is permissible even before the complete fulfillment of *piriyah u-riviyah*.

---

13. *Responsa Bnei Banim* 1:30–31.
14. *Niddah* 9a.
15. Dr. Uri Levi, "On the Duty to Maintain Health Generally, and the Health of a *Yoledet* and her Children Specifically," *Tzohar* 10 (2002), pp. 205–16 (Hebrew). However, R. Yoel and Dr. Chana Catane claim that "her organs become dislocated" relates only to the functioning of the endocrine system. See "Family Planning According to *Halakhah*," *Tzohar* 10 (2002), pp. 217–21.

As we have seen, a woman may postpone pregnancy for two years after giving birth without consulting a halakhic authority. If, after this period, the woman feels that she still needs more time, she should consult with a halakhic authority.

O.K. and Editors

Siman 31

Contraception after Several Births

Question

We have five children, three girls and two boys. My feeling is that right now, and perhaps in general, this family size is right for me in many respects. My husband feels that since I am the one who carries the pregnancy, gives birth, and naturally assumes the lion's share of the child-rearing, the decision should be mine to make, and he will happily accept whatever I decide. May I suffice with the current family size and use contraceptives?

I want to mention that I am 36 years old; I know that I am nearing the end of my fertile years. Nevertheless, I feel that I do not have the strength to have and raise another child.

Answer

Your question comes from a very personal place and yet pertains to God's very first commandment to human beings after their creation. God's words to Adam and Ḥavah, "Be fruitful and multiply (*peru u-revu*) and fill the land" (Bereishit 1:28), is variously interpreted as a blessing or a commandment. Apparently, this is how we are to view the task of building a family and raising children: It is a blessing and a privilege, and it is also an important part of a person's duties in this world.

The mitzvah to have children includes three obligations that vary in scope:

1. **The mitzvah of *piriyah u-riviyah* ("be fruitful and multiply")** is from the Torah and applies only to a man. In practice, one fulfills this obligation by fathering a son and a daughter.
2. **The mitzvah of "in the evening (*la-erev*) do not withhold your hand"** (Kohelet 11:6) is a rabbinic mitzvah requiring that one not completely neglect having children after *piriyah u-riviyah* has been fulfilled. This mitzvah likewise applies to men only. Unlike the obligation of *piriyah u-riviyah*, the parameters of the mitzvah of "*la-erev*" are not defined, implying that it means that one must not completely neglect having children. One authority maintains that this obligation is fulfilled by having an additional son and daughter.
3. **The mitzvah of "habitation"** ("*shevet*") is a rabbinic mitzvah that, according to some opinions, obligates women as well. The mitzvah is derived from the Book of Yeshayahu (45:18), which describes the purpose of the world's creation: "He did not create it a wasteland; He formed it for habitation." Accordingly, a person must take part in populating the world. According to many *Aḥaronim*, the implication is that the mitzvah of "habitation" is fulfilled by having one child, son or daughter, or by having two children, even of the same sex.

There is no "correct" or "optimal" family size. What is good for one woman can be beyond the capacity of another woman, and thus beyond the capacity of the family. Once the mitzvah of *piriyah u-riviyah* has been fulfilled, it is necessary to find the right balance for your family's continued growth – between the lofty value of having more children and building the Jewish people on the one hand, and factors such as health, livelihood, *shalom bayit*, and the patience and the wherewithal to educate and raise your children, including children with special needs. Obviously, you must also clarify which contraceptive methods are halakhically permissible.

Halakhic Expansion

The Mitzvah of *Piriyah u-Riviyah*

The Mishnah in *Yevamot* (65b) records a dispute about the mitzvah of *piriyah u-riviyah*. According to *tanna kamma*, a man is commanded in the mitzvah of *piriyah u-riviyah*, but not a woman, and according to R. Yoḥanan ben Beroka, the obligation applies to both men and women, because the Holy One commanded both Adam and Ḥavah, "Be fruitful and multiply and fill the land." The Gemara offers two rationales for *tanna kamma*'s view, which is accepted as *halakhah*: firstly, the end of the verse, "fill the land and conquer it," is addressed to the man only, because it is the way of man to conquer, but not the way of a woman. Consequently, the beginning of the verse should also be understood as addressing man and not woman. The second rationale is that God's command to Yaakov to procreate is stated in the singular: "God said to him, 'I am the Almighty God; be fruitful and multiply; a nation and an assembly of nations shall descend from you'" (Bereishit 35:11). *Tosafot* therefore explain that the address to Adam and Ḥavah was a blessing, but not a commandment, and the mitzvah applies to the man only.[1]

Another Mishnah in *Yevamot* (61b) records a dispute between Bet Shammai and Bet Hillel regarding the parameters of the mitzvah of *piriyah u-riviyah*: according to Bet Shammai – two males, and according to Bet Hillel – a male and a female.[2]

Rambam, *Tur*, and *Shulḥan Arukh* rule in accordance with *tanna kamma* that the commandment applies only to men, and in accordance with Bet Hillel regarding the parameters of the obligation.[3]

The Mitzvah of "*La-erev*"

The aforementioned Mishnah[4] begins: "A person should not neglect *piriyah u-riviyah* unless he has children." The Gemara infers that a person may neglect *piriyah u-riviyah* after fulfilling his obligation, even though he is still obligated to be married.

Later in the discussion, however, the Gemara brings the position of R. Yehoshua: "R. Yehoshua says: If he had children in his youth, he should have children in his old age, as it is stated: 'In the morning sow your seed, and in the evening (*la-erev*) do not withhold your hand; for you do not know which shall prosper or whether both alike shall be good' (Kohelet 11:6)." And later, the Gemara continues: "Rav Matna said: The *halakhah* is in accordance with R. Yehoshua." According to R. Yehoshua, man is extremely limited in his capacity to plan his life, so he must, for his part, make the maximum effort.

R. Yehoshua's view is brought *l'halakhah* as a rabbinic mitzvah,[5] while there are disagreements among the *Rishonim* about its authority and implications.

---

1. *Tosafot* to *Yevamot* 65b, s.v. "*ve-lo ka'amar.*"
2. The Gemara brings two other views on the parameters of the obligation, but *halakhah* does not follow them.
3. Rambam, *Mishneh Torah, Hilkhot Ishut* 15:2, 4; *Tur* and *Shulḥan Arukh, Even Ha-Ezer* 1:5 (on the parameters of the obligation being a son and daughter) and 1:13 (on it being a man's obligation, not a woman's).
4. *Yevamot* 61b.
5. Rif, *Yevamot* 19 (Rif pages); Rambam, *Mishneh Torah, Hilkhot Ishut* 15:16; *Tur* and *Shulḥan Arukh, Even Ha-Ezer* 1:8.

Rambam writes that "Even if a man has already fulfilled the mitzvah of *piriyah u-riviyah,* he is commanded *mi-divrei Soferim* not to refrain from procreation as long as he is able."[6] This is also the position of *Halakhot Gedolot*: "It is forbidden for a man of Israel to refrain from *piriyah u-riviyah*."[7] However, the rest of the *Rishonim* do not hold thus. Ramban writes,[8] "However, since it is a rabbinic mitzvah akin to proper practice (*minhag derekh eretz*)... it is a mitzvah *lekhatḥilah*... and one who does not wish to engage in it is not considered a sinner."[9] This is also implied by the language of the *baraita*: "If he had disciples in his youth, he should have disciples in his old age, as it says, 'In the morning sow your seed.'" Thus, it is not a true obligation, but rather sound advice. *Tur* and *Shulḥan Arukh* make no mention of any prohibition to refrain from fulfilling the mitzvah of "*la-erev*." Moreover, *Responsa Ḥatam Sofer* states,[10] "If [the husband] yearns for children and wants to fulfill, 'in the evening (*la-erev*) do not withhold your hand,'" implying that it depends on his desires. *Arukh Ha-Shulḥan*[11] cites another ruling of Rambam,[12] that a man should not marry a woman who cannot have children unless he has already fulfilled *piriyah u-riviyah,* implying that the mitzvah of "*la-erev*" is "akin to the beautification of the mitzvah and a proper practice."[13]

R. Yehuda Henkin writes in *Responsa Bnei Banim* that it stands to reason that the rabbinic measure is like the Torah measure, namely, a son and a daughter[14] – in addition to the obligation to have a son and daughter in fulfillment of the mitzvah of *piriyah u-riviyah.*

---

6. *Mishneh Torah, Hilkhot Ishut* 15:16.
7. *Hilkhot Ketubot,* p. 165 (Venice edition).
8. *Milḥamot Hashem, Yevamot* 20a in the Rif pages.
9. Rema (*Even Ha-Ezer* 1:8) writes accordingly that a widower, who is obligated to remarry, may marry a woman who cannot have children if he is concerned about discord between the children of his first marriage and of his [second] wife. *Bet Shmuel* (*ad loc.*) explains that one may neglect "in the evening (*la-erev*) do not withhold your hand" if he is concerned about discord, and it is not a transgression.
10. *Even Ha-Ezer siman* 20, at the end.
11. Ibid. 70:8.
12. *Mishneh Torah, Hilkhot Ishut* 16:7.
13. *Otzar Ha-Poskim, Even Ha-Ezer* 5:12:72 cites *Bet Moshe*: "Further study is required to determine whether a married woman may drink an infertility potion, for even if he has already fulfilled *piriyah u-riviyah,* he is obligated to fulfill '*la-erev*.' Thus, if she drinks an infertility potion, the husband will not fulfill '*la-erev*.'" However, the entry cites neither Ramban nor *Arukh Ha-Shulḥan*.
14. This is based on the principle that "All that *Ḥakhamim* enacted, they patterned on the Torah." *Responsa Bnei Banim,* vol. 4, *Kitzur Ha-Pesakim,* p. 152. Accordingly, the mitzvah of "*la-erev*" also has a requisite quantity.

The Mitzvah of "Habitation" ("*Shevet*")

The Mishnah in *Gittin* (41a) states that a person who is half slave and half free must be emancipated because "He did not create it a waste; He formed it for habitation." *Tosafot* ask why the Mishnah uses this verse – from the Book of Yeshayahu – as a prooftext when it could have used the Torah's explicit commandment to "be fruitful and multiply."[15] They offer several explanations: (1) If the slave had any possible way to fulfill the mitzvah of "*shevet*" there would be no obligation to emancipate him just so he could fulfill *piriyah u-riviyah*. However, his combined inability to fulfill either commandment requires his emancipation. (2) The mitzvah of "*shevet*" is a "great mitzvah" – an especially weighty mitzvah, apparently because it expresses the fulfillment of God's desire for the world to be inhabited.[16] (3) The mitzvah of *piriyah u-riviyah* applies only to a free man. A slave does not have freedom of choice and therefore is not obligated in this mitzvah. However, even a slave is obligated in the mitzvah of "*shevet*" because it is a general mitzvah to populate the world, which applied to all of humanity. Based on this reasoning, women, too, are obligated in the mitzvah of "*shevet*."

According to some views, one fulfills the mitzvah of "*shevet*" with one child (son or daughter), and according to other views, one fulfills the mitzvah by having two children, even of the same sex.[17]

Therefore, in the present case, where the woman already had two sons and more than two daughters, she has no obligation to have more children to fulfill the mitzvah of "*la-erev*."[18]

---

15. *Tosafot* to *Bava Batra* 13a, s.v. "*she-ne'emar*"; *Gittin* 41b, s.v. "*lo tohu bera'ah*."
16. According to *Ḥatam Sofer*, it is because it is in addition to the mitzvah of *piriyah u-riviyah*; see *Responsa Ḥatam Sofer, Even Ha-Ezer siman* 20.
17. Fulfilling the mitzvah by having one child is implied by *Ḥatam Sofer, Even Ha-Ezer siman* 20 and *Ha'amek She'elah, She'ilta* 18:2. However, *Otzar Ha-Poskim, Even Ha-Ezer* 1:5:30 infers from *Nimukei Yosef* on *Yevamot* 20a (Rif pages) that the mitzvah is fulfilled by having two children, even of the same sex.
18. R. Yigal Ariel ("Space Between Pregnancies," *Tzohar* 10 [5762], pp. 223–36 [Hebrew]) wrote the following fine words:

> We should rejoice over this revolution of larger families today. Families that, in the past, grew through the laws of nature, Jewish law, and social norms are now growing at their own initiative and free choice. When a woman feels well and wishes to, any couple can decide to have more children than the Torah obligates them to have.... On the other hand, there are families that have grown beyond what they can handle physically, emotionally, financially, and educationally. They totter on the brink of disaster. The mother is without strength to sustain herself, and so they cannot take care of children or raise them to Torah and fear of God. There is a great desecration of God's name when people mistakenly

Addendum: Contraception by a Woman

The Gemara in *Yevamot* (65b-66a) tells a story about Yehudit, the wife of R. Ḥiya:

> Yehudah and Ḥizkiyah were twins. One of them was fully developed after nine [months of pregnancy] and the other at the beginning of the seventh. Yehudit, the wife of R. Ḥiya, had [severe] birthing pain. She changed her clothes [i.e., she disguised herself], came before R. Ḥiya, and asked: "Is a woman commanded to procreate?" He said to her: "No." She went and drank an infertility potion. Eventually the matter was discovered. He said to her: "If only you had given birth to one more belly for me." As I said, "Yehudah and Ḥizkiyah are [twin] brothers; Pazi and Tavi are [twin] sisters."

Several conclusions emerge from this story:

1. Yehudit's question is about a woman's obligation in the mitzvah of *piriyah u-riviyah*.[19] From R. Ḥiya's answer, she concludes that she may drink an infertility potion. There is no criticism of this conclusion anywhere in halakhic literature.[20]
2. Yehudit's need for contraception was due to pain, not risk.

Rambam, *Tur*, and *Shulḥan Arukh* rule without qualification that a woman may drink an infertility potion.[21]

The *Aḥaronim* disagree about whether we can infer a general permissibility from the actions of Yehudit, or only in cases of painful birth or when her children are

---

think that a halakhic norm obligates this and forces them into this situation, and that it is forbidden to do anything to change the situation.

19. It is clear from the story that Yehudit and her husband had already fulfilled the mitzvah of *piriyah u-riviyah*, so her question is puzzling. *Tosafot* (*Shabbat* 110b, s.v. "*ve-hatanya minayin*") and *Arukh La-Ner* (*Yevamot, ad loc.*) raise this question as well and answer that her question was really about the mitzvah of "*la-erev*," and that this teaches that the mitzvah of "*la-erev*" applies only to one who is obligated in *piriyah u-riviyah*.
20. However, *Responsa Ḥatam Sofer, Even Ha-Ezer siman* 20 states that a woman was permitted to drink an infertility potion without the husband's knowledge only before Rabbeinu Gershom's ban of polygamy, when a man could marry a second wife to fulfill the mitzvah of "*la-erev*." However, subsequent to Rabbeinu Gershom's ban, she should not drink without her husband's consent, unless it is because of the pain of childbirth, as her duties to her husband do not obligate her to cause herself pain.
21. Rambam, *Mishneh Torah, Hilkhot Ishut* 16:12; *Tur* and *Shulḥan Arukh, Even Ha-Ezer* 5:12. However, *Sefer Yere'im* (*siman* 382 in the old printing; *siman* 381 in the new edition) rules permissively only when there is pain, due to the mitzvah of "*la-erev*."

not following the straight path.[22] Either way, many *poskim*[23] do not mention the pain of childbirth as a condition for permitting an infertility potion, and several state explicitly that it is permissible even if there is no such pain.[24] However, it should be noted that the permissibility of drinking an infertility potion when there is no pain was stated only in a case where the mitzvah of *piriyah u-riviyah* has already been fulfilled, as we learn from the story of Yehudit.

Nowadays, the birth control method closest to an infertility potion would seem to be the pill. Both are taken orally and indirectly affect the reproductive organs. Therefore, according to many *poskim*, once *piriyah u-riviyah* has been fulfilled, a woman may prevent further pregnancy by means of the pill even if there is no pain of childbirth, as in the case of an infertility potion.

O.K. and Editors

22. *Yam Shel Shlomo, Yevamot* 6:44. However, *Taz, Even Ha-Ezer* 5:7, s.v. "*ve-ishah muteret*," concludes: "The distinction between the pain of childbirth is not implied at all by the *poskim*."
23. Rambam, *Mishneh Torah, Hilkhot Ishut* 16:12; *Tur* and *Shulḥan Arukh, Even Ha-Ezer siman* 5; *Bi'ur Ha-Gra, Even Ha-Ezer* 5:11.
24. *Ḥelkat Meḥokek, Even Ha-Ezer* 5:6; *Taz, Even Ha-Ezer* 5:7; *Be'er Heitev, Even Ha-Ezer* 5:11.

Siman 32

IUD Use and the Ranking of Contraceptive Options

Question

In recent years, I've been on the pill, but recently I read studies warning of side-effects of hormones. I'm looking to switch to a different method of contraception. Is an IUD permissible? Is there a halakhic difference between the different types of IUD? Finally, does *halakhah* give weight to health considerations when choosing a contraceptive method?

Answer

If you have a *heter* to use contraception, then you may use an IUD.

There are two types of IUD. The first is made primarily of copper. It is inserted into the uterus, where it creates a hostile environment for sperm cells, preventing them from reaching and fertilizing the ovum. There are several kinds of devices of this type. All of them can cause spotting and bleeding. For some women, the copper IUD causes heavier and longer menstrual bleeding, and it can even shorten the cycle, effects that can lessen the number of days that the woman is *tehorah*. These effects are common during the first month of use and are supposed to improve within three months, but some women continue to experience heavier bleeding even after the adjustment period.

The second type is the hormonal IUD, which releases progesterone. The progesterone thickens mucus in the cervix to stop sperm from reaching or fertilizing an egg, and thins the lining of the uterus and partially suppresses ovulation. This device causes irregular bleeding for up to 6 months, including frequent spotting during the first months after insertion. After this period, though, most women experience lighter and less frequent menstrual bleeding, and some women experience no menstrual bleeding at all.

From a halakhic perspective, the copper IUD is preferable to the hormonal IUD, which is likely to lead to weighty halakhic questions as a result of the persistent spotting. Nevertheless, it is important to note that the hormonal IUD is also halakhically permissible. Regardless of which type of IUD you choose, it is recommended that you review the laws of *ketamim* before its insertion, so that you know what to do in case of spotting.

Halakhic Expansion[1]

Like any medication, hormonal contraceptives can have side-effects, leading many women to seek out other methods of contraception. The choice of method should strike a balance between the various medical and halakhic considerations.[2] On one hand, there are considerations relating to contraception: the prohibition against destroying sperm (*hashḥatat zera*),[3] the question of using an absorbent material (*shimush b'mokh*),[4] the requirement of normal relations (*k'derekh kol ha'aretz*),[5] and concerns about aborting the fetus.[6] On the other hand, there are considerations relating to the laws of *niddah*, and especially *ketamim*.[7] Finally, there are medical considerations with halakhic implications: how the various contraceptive methods affect the woman's body and whether they might be hazardous to her health.

The proper balance between these considerations is ambiguous, and medical knowledge changes over time. Therefore, different *poskim* rank contraceptives differently. The recommendation of a specific method should take the woman's medical and personal background, and familial considerations, into account.

1. See Medical Appendix V: Contraception.
2. This responsum does not address the permissibility of contraception. Rather, it ranks the different contraceptive methods from a halakhic perspective. On the permissibility of contraception, see above, *Siman* 31.
3. See below, *Siman* 33: Condom Use when Pregnancy is Contra-Indicated.
4. See below, *Siman* 35: Diaphragm Use.
5. See below, *Siman* 33: Condom Use when Pregnancy is Contra-Indicated, and *Siman* 35: Diaphragm Use.
6. See below, *Siman* 26: Emergency Contraception (The 'Morning After' Pill).
7. For an extended discussion on the laws of *ketamim*, see below, *Siman* 41: Extending the Cycle via Hormonal Contraception.

A General Survey of Contraceptive Methods

The reversible[8] contraceptive methods in use nowadays are: (1) Hormonal methods that combine estrogen with progesterone or contain progesterone only; (2) copper and hormonal IUDs; (3) barrier methods, including the diaphragm, contraceptive sponges, and spermicides (foams, suppositories, and films); (4) fertility awareness method (FAM); (5) condoms. Below, each method will be discussed and ranked, to the extent possible, according to the various opinions among *poskim*.

Hormonal Methods

Hormonal methods of contraception (pills, vaginal rings, patches, injections, and subdermal implants) have a halakhic advantage in that they do not destroy sperm or involve the use of a *mokh*, and their contraceptive effects do not linger after use. They are convenient and easy for women to use, and in the case of methods that combine estrogen and progesterone, it is possible (in consultation with a physician) to combine packets (i.e., skip the placebo pills) or continue using additional patches or rings, in order to calibrate the menstrual cycle so that the woman becomes *niddah* at specific times, and even to significantly extend the interval between menstrual periods.[9] When taking progesterone only, sometimes menstruation is prevented entirely for long periods of time. On the other hand, hormonal methods can expose a woman to hazardous side-effects,[10] cause frequent spotting (especially progesterone-only methods) and suppress the woman's libido.[11]

8. In contrast to irreversible contraceptive methods.
9. During the first months of use, until the body adjusts to the hormone levels, combining packets is liable to result in intermenstrual spotting. See below, *Siman* 41: Extending the Cycle via Hormonal Contraception, n. 1. It might be possible to minimize or prevent this spotting by gradually extending the number of consecutive days that one takes the pill.
10. The estrogen component increases risk of the formation of blood clots, which can reach the lungs (pulmonary embolism), heart (myocardial infarction), or brain (stroke). The linkage between estrogen-containing contraceptives and breast cancer is the subject of disagreement. The prevailing approach in contemporary research is that there is no direct linkage, but many doctors remain wary of administering estrogen-containing treatments to women with a significant family history of breast cancer. About a third of women who use hormonal contraceptives report that it affects their mood. Changes in mood, especially depression, and weight gain are common side-effects of progesterone-based contraceptives (even though weight gain was not proven for long-term use). More recent studies show that there is no connection between progesterone-only methods and breast cancer. See Medical Appendix V: Contraception.
11. Decreased sexual desire is a common side-effect of hormonal contraceptives, but doctors do not always apprise women of this fact.

Intrauterine Devices (IUDs)

There are two types of intrauterine device (IUD): The first is a piece of copper (in the shape of a T or in a different shape); the copper alters conditions within the uterus and generally prevents fertilization of the ovum. The device releases copper ions into the uterine cavity, creating an environment that damages the viability of sperm cells and their ability to fertilize the ovum. Concomitantly, the presence of a foreign body within the uterus changes the composition of the endometrium, such that even if the egg is fertilized, it will be exceedingly difficult for implantation to occur. This type of IUD often causes increased and prolonged menstrual bleeding, intermenstrual bleeding, and a narrowing of the interval between one cycle and the next – all of which can reduce the woman's days of *taharah*. The "Gynefix" IUD is also made from copper, but it has a different shape and is more flexible. One study claims that it causes less bleeding, but this has not yet been scientifically proven.[12]

The second type of IUD contains progesterone (and is presently sold under the brand names "Mirena," "Kyleena" and "Skyla"). It consists of a coil that contains progesterone, which is gradually released and causes the thickening of the cervical mucus, thinning of the endometrium, and other effects that prevent fertilization. As mentioned, this device has a common side-effect of frequent spotting for up to six months following its insertion. Over time, the bleeding often decreases in intensity and frequency, and for some women, there is no bleeding at all. For other women, the staining continues and makes it difficult to become *tehorah*.

Although a physician must insert the device into the uterus, its advantage is that (unlike the pill) the woman does not need to remember to do anything for this method to work. It is therefore highly effective. On the other hand, since the body requires an adjustment period during which staining is common, IUDs are relevant primarily for long-term contraception.

Diaphragm[13]

The diaphragm does not cause staining, does not present a risk to the woman's health, and does not affect sexual desire. Some *poskim* consider the diaphragm

12. Cao X, Zhang W, Gao G, Van Kets H, and Wildemeersch D. "Randomized Comparative Trial in Parous Women of the Frameless GyneFix and the TCu380A Intrauterine Devices: Long-Term Experience in a Chinese Family Planning Clinic." *European Journal of Contraception and Reproductive Health Care* 5(2) [June 2000], pp. 135–40.

13. A diaphragm is a dome-shaped piece of latex or silicone that covers the opening of the cervix, blocking the path of sperm cells and preventing them from entering the uterus. Together with a spermicide, it is possible to impair the function of sperm cells that might overcome this barrier.

to be the most preferable method of birth control, and others deem it forbidden as a form of *mokh*. See below.

Spermicide

Spermicides contain substances that impair the movement and viability of sperm cells. This prevents fertilization of the ovum, thus preventing pregnancy. They are available as foams, creams, suppositories, and films. Their effectiveness is limited, so they are primarily used along with other contraceptives, such as the diaphragm.

Fertility Awareness Method (FAM)

FAM involves no artificial intervention, and it therefore has no medical or halakhic drawbacks, but it limits the number of days during which the couple may have marital relations. Therefore, those who use this method will generally also opt to use a barrier method during the fertile days.

Condom

A condom is a physical barrier that prevents the passage of semen into the vagina. Combined with spermicide, which impairs the function of sperm cells, it is even more effective. The most prevalent type of condom is designed for use by the man. A female condom is a latex tube with thin walls and a flexible ring at either end. The inner end is closed. The ring on the closed end is used to insert the condom deep into the vagina and to hold it in place, and the ring on the open, outer end remains outside the opening of the vagina.

Condoms, whether male or female, are halakhically the most problematic method, first and foremost because the semen does not enter the woman's body, and also, in the case of a male condom, because the man is commanded in the mitzvah of *piriyah u-rivyah*. Therefore, use of the condom is absolutely forbidden except in the most exceptional cases.[14]

Ranking Contraceptive Methods by Halakhic Preferability

According to *Tzitz Eliezer*, hormonal contraceptives are the equivalent of the Gemara's "infertility potion."[15] Therefore, if what the doctors say – namely, that the risks have been mitigated and hormonal contraceptives hardly ever endanger a woman anymore – is true, then the pill should be given the first preference, since it neither destroys sperm nor directly

---

14. See below, *Siman* 33: Condom Use when Pregnancy is Contra-Indicated.
15. See *Shulḥan Arukh, Even Ha-Ezer* 65:12, based on *Yevamot* 65b. See also above, *Siman* 31: Contraception after Several Births.

causes infertility, and the infertility it causes is only temporary.[16] Regarding diaphragms and IUDs, in that same responsum from 5727 (1967), R. Waldenberg writes[17] that the diaphragm is preferable to the IUD, since the IUD works to destroy the husband's sperm and the woman's ovum, and if fertilization occurred, it even destroys the embryo. Therefore, even though blocking the cervix with the diaphragm to prevent the entry of sperm cells is somewhat problematic, it is still preferable to the actively destructive function of the IUD. However, in a later responsum from 5730 (1970),[18] once it was clarified to him that the IUD does not destroy the sperm or the embryo but prevents fertilization and implantation by altering the uterine environment, he changed his mind and preferred the IUD to the diaphragm. His reasoning is that since the IUD is located deep within the uterus, it is not sensed during intercourse and allows unimpeded entry of sperm cells into the uterus. In contrast, the diaphragm blocks the opening of the uterus to the entry of sperm cells. Therefore, in his view, there is concern for destroying sperm, and it is also possible that the diaphragm will be felt during intercourse. His order of preference is therefore: the pill, then the IUD, and then the diaphragm.[19]

According to *Igrot Moshe*, the diaphragm is the equivalent of the "*mokh*" – an absorbent wadding used as a contraceptive – discussed in the Gemara, which may be used only in a case of physical or mental risk,[20] and only by a modest woman who would not tell her friends about it.[21] Despite the problematic nature of the diaphragm due to the *hashḥatat zera* (destruction of sperm) that it causes, where there is risk, it is preferable to the pill[22] and to an IUD since it does not cause staining or impair the woman's health. In contrast, the pill, which is the equivalent of the Gemara's "infertility potion," is a relatively good method from the perspective of the laws of contraception, and it is therefore permitted even in cases of weakness, not only of risk; if the mitzvah of *piriyah u-rivyah* has already been fulfilled, the pill is permitted when there are financial pressures or any other need. Nevertheless, the pill is problematic from a different perspective, as it causes staining and is hazardous to the woman's health.[23] Therefore,

16. *Responsa Tzitz Eliezer* 9:51, chapter 2.
17. Ibid.
18. Ibid. 10:25:10.
19. *Sha'arei Orah, sha'ar* 2, p. 44 ranks contraceptive methods in accordance with *Tzitz Eliezer*.
20. *Igrot Moshe, Even Ha-Ezer* 1:63 (dated 5695), 4:74 (dated 5720), and 3:21 (5725).
21. Ibid. 1:13.
22. At the time R. Feinstein wrote the teshuva, the only form of hormonal contraceptive was the pill. His concerns would apply to other hormonal options available today.
23. *Igrot Moshe, Even Ha-Ezer* 4:72.

he permits the pill only to a woman who performs an "extensive examination" by using a sanitary napkin for an entire month, to confirm that the pill does not cause her to stain. As to health concerns and safety of the pill, R. Feinstein changed his mind. In two early responsa, he completely forbade the pill on the grounds that it endangers the woman's health.[24] Twenty years later, when the dosage of hormones in the pill was reduced, he once again invoked concerns about the woman's health, but in a more restrained fashion and without issuing an unambiguous ruling.[25] As for the IUD, R. Feinstein completely forbade it, for three reasons: It causes bleeding that can render the woman *niddah*, it might be felt during intercourse,[26] and there is a slight concern that it will cause the fetus to abort.[27] Thus, according to R. Feinstein, the ranking of contraceptive methods is as follows: In cases of danger, a woman may use a diaphragm, which presents no risk to her health and no problems of staining. A woman who is weak or suffers greatly may not use a diaphragm but may use the pill, but only after a month-long examination. IUDs are forbidden in all cases. In general, *Igrot Moshe* was very concerned about contraceptives that cause staining, since the blood certainly came from the woman's body.[28]

R. Shlomo Zalman Auerbach ranked the various contraceptive methods as follows:[29] Most preferable is the pill, as there is no concern for destroying sperm. Next is the IUD, since it allows for regular intercourse and has no actively destructive effect; rather, pregnancy is prevented indirectly. According to him, there is no problem of the IUD causing the fetus to abort, as it primarily prevents fertilization,

---

24. Ibid. 2:17 (5722) and 3:24.
25. Ibid. 4:72.
26. Ibid. 3:21. It is difficult to know what R. Feinstein meant when he wrote, "The tube [of the IUD] is occasionally sensed and felt when he penetrates," because the IUD is placed inside the uterus. Perhaps he was referring to the string attached to the IUD that dangles slightly from the uterus into the vagina.
27. *Igrot Moshe, Even Ha-Ezer* 3:21. *Responsa Mishneh Halakhot* 9:287 forbids an IUD completely on the grounds that it is murder, as it prevents pregnancy by aborting the fetus. However, *Igrot Moshe* states that there is only a remote risk of abortion. See below, *Siman* 36: Emergency Contraception (The 'Morning After' Pill), as well as the article by R. Yoel and Dr. Chana Catane, "Concern for Feticide by an IUD and Use of the Pill by Mature Women," *Assia* 65–66, Elul 5759 [Hebrew].
28. R. Shabtai Rappaport shared orally that even in the case of a woman who wears form-fitting underwear, according to R. Feinstein whatever she sees is deemed "wiping" and not a *ketem*. Therefore, anyone who rules stringently with respect to wiping will also be stringent about a *ketem* found on form-fitting underwear.
29. R. Auerbach's letter, dated to 8 Nissan, 5735, is cited in R. Yoel Catane, "Using a Diaphragm to Prevent Pregnancy," *Assia* 77–78, 5766, pp. 124–35 [Hebrew].

and we don't need to concern ourselves with the unlikely possibility that it prevents implantation. Moreover, even if it does prevent implantation, the embryo is still within the first 40 days after fertilization, during which it is considered "mere water."[30] In third place is the diaphragm, and there is disagreement about R. Auerbach's position on the diaphragm. According to R. Dr. Mordechai Halperin, R. Auerbach changed his mind on this subject.[31] Initially he ranked the diaphragm below the IUD but indicated that it is not the same as a *mokh* because it does not fill the entire vaginal cavity. He therefore permitted its use in cases of significant suffering, serious damage to the woman's health, and for the sake of *shalom bayit*. Later, R. Auerbach ranked the diaphragm as the equivalent of the IUD, after he realized that semen is ejaculated into the vaginal canal, and the diaphragm merely blocks its entry into the uterus. R. Yoel Catane, on the other hand, claims[32] that R. Auerbach never changed his mind.

As for R. Shmuel Wosner, in the limited number of situations where he permits contraception, he permits use of an IUD.[33] According to him, an IUD is not akin to using a *mokh* because it is inserted deep within the uterus and does not block the sperm from entering the uterus; it merely prevents fertilization.

In contrast with the above views, R. Yehuda Henkin maintains that it is impossible to determine an unambiguous, fixed ranking of contraceptive methods due to the large number of considerations, some of which vary from woman to woman: *ketamim, shikhvat zera le-vatalah* ("wasting sperm"), regular intercourse, health, limiting the number of days that a woman is *niddah*, and the effectiveness and convenience of the method.[34] Likewise, in his opinion, it is impossible to compare and contrast the views of different *poskim*, as contraceptive methods have changed over time. Just as his grandfather, R. Yosef Eliyahu Henkin,[35] permitted the use of a diaphragm, so does he;[36] in their opinion, the diaphragm is not like a *mokh* because it does not fill the entire vaginal canal and therefore allows for normal intercourse, and it is not similar to *meitil al etzim v'avanim* ("ejaculating on wood and stones").

30. Ibid.
31. Ibid.
32. See below, *Siman* 35: Diaphragm Use.
33. *Responsa Shevet Ha-Levi* 3:179.
34. The writer heard this directly from R. Henkin.
35. *Responsa Bnei Banim* 1:30.
36. He explains that the *mokh* of the Gemara was placed in the vagina after intercourse, so it would absorb the semen. This follows Rashi on *Ketubot* 39a, and both Rashi and Rabbeinu Tam agree that it was placed in the vagina after intercourse. See *Responsa Bnei Banim*, loc. cit.

According to R. Yehuda Henkin, a diaphragm is even preferable to hormonal methods as it does not cause staining or pose a risk to the woman's health, and there is no concern that it will impair the milk supply of a nursing infant.[37] R. Nachum Rabinovitch likewise rules that a diaphragm is preferable to hormonal contraception and forbids the use of the hormonal contraception by a nursing mother.[38]

It should be noted that when beginning to use hormonal methods and even the copper IUD, one must be extremely cautious in order to avoid *ketamim* that would render her *niddah*.

G.K.S. and Editors

37. According to R. Henkin, despite the widespread use of hormonal contraceptives, it is possible that negative effects on the mother, and even on nursing infants, will be discovered in the future. One who values her life will act cautiously.

38. *Responsa Si'aḥ Naḥum simanim* 94–95.

Siman 33

Condom Use When Pregnancy Is Contra-Indicated

Question

I was not fully vaccinated for rubella when I was younger. I am scheduled to get my missing measles mumps and rubella vaccine in the near future, but my doctor insists that in the meantime, we absolutely must avoid pregnancy, for at least the next three months.[1] I thought to use spermicide suppositories, but the doctor was adamant that this is not safe enough in my situation. He recommended using a condom. Considering the circumstances and the danger to such a fetus, may we use a condom?

Answer

Even though a condom is a readily available and easy-to-use method – among the most widespread contraceptive methods today, especially for short-term use – it is the most halakhically problematic of all methods, for two reasons. First, when a condom is used, the semen does not enter the woman's body, so there is *hotza'at zera le-vatalah,* wasting sperm. The second reason is that the man, not the woman, uses the condom, and since the man is commanded in the mitzvah of *piriyah u-riviyah,* it is forbidden for him to prevent pregnancy directly, and it is therefore forbidden for him to use a condom as a contraceptive. Nevertheless, the Sages ascribed great significance to the mitzvah of *onah* (marital sexuality), so in

1. The rubella vaccine is a live vector vaccine, and there is concern that even the weakened virus can cause abnormalities in the pregnancy. It is therefore recommended to wait three months after vaccination before becoming pregnant.

extremely rare and exceptional cases, such as when there is concern of transmitting a life-threatening disease, or it is dangerous for a woman to become pregnant and no other contraceptive is relevant, there are grounds for halakhic consultation about the permissibility of using a condom – after obtaining a credible assessment from a doctor and exhausting all other options. In your situation, there are options that have not been examined, and there is no *heter* to use a condom.

It should be noted that from a medical perspective, a condom is not a particularly effective contraceptive as compared with other methods. Its sole advantage is its short-term convenience, as no medical intervention is needed.

Halakhic Expansion

Using any method of contraception entails, by definition, the neglect or postponement of the mitzvah of *piriyah u-riviyah*. Therefore, even when there is a *heter* to prevent pregnancy, there is a preference for methods used by women over methods used by men, because the man is directly commanded in this mitzvah.[2]

The Gemara[3] addresses the severity of *hotza'at zera le-vatalah,* wasting sperm. Based on this Gemara, and following the *Zohar, Shulḥan Arukh* rules[4] that "this sin is more severe than all of the transgressions in the Torah" and immediately adds: "Therefore, a man should not thresh inside and winnow outside" (withdrawal before ejaculation). That is, even in context of marital relations, it is sinful if the semen does not enter the woman's body.[5]

The prohibition of wasting sperm during marital relations appears in the Gemara (*Yevamot* 34b). Ḥazal reject the view of R. Eliezer, who maintains that on account of the danger to a nursing infant if his mother were to become pregnant, thus drying up her milk supply, his parents may practice withdrawal without ejaculation in

---

2. See *Tosefta Yevamot* 8:4 (the MS Erfurt version, which corresponds to the first printed edition): "A man is not permitted to drink an infertility potion so that he will not sire [a child], but a woman may drink an infertility potion so that she does not give birth." See also *Yevamot* 65b and *Shulḥan Arukh, Even Ha-Ezer* 4:12.
3. *Niddah* 13a-b.
4. *Even Ha-Ezer* 23:1.
5. The *Rishonim* disagree regarding the reason for the prohibition of wasting sperm. Some explain that it is prohibited because it neglects the mitzvah of *piriyah u-reviyah* (*Tosafot* to *Sanhedrin* 59b, s.v. "*ve-ha piriyah u-riviyah*"). Others explain that it is an independent prohibition, because all semen has the potential to create life (Ramban, *Ḥiddushim* to *Niddah* 13a). These two approaches are summarized in *Responsa Seridei Esh* 1:162:27–28.

the course of marital relations for up to two years after childbirth.[6] In contrast, Ḥazal maintain that this manner of intercourse is like the act of Er and Onan.

It emerges from this Gemara that Er and Onan wasted their sperm so that Tamar would not become pregnant, though each of them acted from a different motive. Onan's intent was not to have a son,[7] whereas Er's intent was to keep pregnancy from impairing Tamar's beauty. Both of these motives are sinful and violate the prohibition of wasting sperm in context of marital relations.

It also emerges from the Gemara that Er and Onan were punished for *bi'ah she-lo ke-darkah*[8] with Tamar; this indicates that *bi'ah she-lo ke-darkah* is forbidden.

On its surface, this conclusion contradicts the Gemara in *Nedarim* 20b,[9] which indicates that there are no limitations on a couple in context of marital relations, and the prohibition of wasting sperm is not mentioned at all. The *Rishonim* disagree about how to reconcile these two passages. Rambam[10] rules in accordance with the Gemara in *Nedarim,* though with the qualification that there be no wasting of sperm. However, the formulation, "except that he must not waste seed," which appears at the end of Rambam's words in printed editions, does not appear in manuscripts of *Mishneh Torah.*[11] Likewise, Rambam's commentary on chapter 7 of Mishnah *Sanhedrin,* he does not condition his permissive interpretation on not wasting sperm. It is thus likely that he did not view it as a condition.[12]

Tosafot in *Yevamot*[13] quote Rabbeinu Yitzḥak of Dampierre (Ri Ha-Zaken) as offering two other ways to harmonize the contradictory passages: The first accords with Rambam's view as printed, namely, that *bi'ah she-lo ke-darkah* is permitted as long as it does not result in wasted sperm. The second conditions the permissive

6. Although this is not accepted as *halakhah,* clearly R. Eliezer does not think that wasting sperm is "more severe than all of the transgressions in the Torah" if he maintains that it is permitted for the sake of the baby's health.

7. He did not want a son who would belong to his deceased brother.

8. The *Rishonim* disagree about the exact parameters of *bi'ah she-lo ke-darkah;* a full discussion is beyond the scope of this book.

9. The Gemara in *Nedarim* also contradicts the Gemara in *Yevamot* in that the former considers *bi'ah she-lo ke-darkah* to be legitimate, based on the phrase "*mishkevei ishah*" ("lyings with a woman"; Vayikra 18:22), which is formulated in the plural, thus indicating that *bi'ah she-lo ke-darkah* is considered a form of "lying with a woman." See also *Sanhedrin* 54a and elsewhere in the Gemara and Midrashim. It is therefore technically permitted.

10. *Mishneh Torah, Hilkhot Isurei Bi'ah* 21:30.

11. R. Henkin notes this in *Responsa Bnei Banim,* 4:18, and that it also does not appear in R. Kapaḥ's edition of *Mishneh Torah,* and this is noted in the Frankel edition.

12. See at length in *Responsa Bnei Banim,* 4:18.

13. 34b, s.v. "*ve-lo ke-ma'aseh Er ve-Onan.*"

view on the fulfillment of two criteria: (1) proper intention ("it is not considered an act of Er and Onan unless he intends to waste sperm"); and (2) frequency ("and he is habituated to do so always. However, as a chance occurrence [*b-akrai b-alma*] ... it is permitted").[14]

Tur[15] brings both Rambam as well as the second answer of Ri Ha-Zaken as *halakhah*. *Bet Yosef*[16] notes that Rosh rules in accordance with the second answer of Ri Ha-Zaken, but expresses that he himself has reservations and does not accept this ruling due to the severity of the prohibition of wasting sperm; and in the *Shulḥan Arukh*, he omits this law. On the other hand, Rema[17] brings the words of *Tur* in their entirety. *Aḥaronim*[18] rule in accordance with the lenient position brought by Rema, namely, that a man may have *bi'ah she-lo ke-darkah* with his wife, even if he will ejaculate, "if he does so by chance and not regularly."

R. Yeshayah di Trani (Rid)[19] states that the prohibition of wasting sperm depends on the intent of the person who commits it; the act is only forbidden if the intent is to waste. Unlike Ri Ha-Zaken, Rid does not mention that the act must be infrequent. It emerges from his words that if the intent is not to waste, but, to the contrary, the intent is to fulfill the mitzvah of *onah* in a situation where there is a danger in having regular marital relations,[20] it is always permitted.

---

14. Ri Ha-Zaken connects these two criteria, and it seems from his words that the permissibility of this practice requires that both criteria are met. For an analysis of Ri Ha-Zaken's statement, see the article by R. Yitzchak Roness, "Physical Contact of a Married Couple," *Assia* 97–98 (vol. 25, 1–2), 5775, pp. 134–40. [Hebrew].
15. *Even Ha-Ezer siman* 25.
16. Ibid., *siman* 25, s.v. "*u-mah she-katav be-shem Ri*": "Rosh wrote there that the latter answer is the primary one. But it is difficult to permit him to stumble and waste sperm, even sporadically. One who guards his soul will stay away from this." These words are understood in light of what he wrote, as we have seen, in *Shulḥan Arukh, Even Ha-Ezer* 23:1, regarding the gravity of the prohibition of wasting sperm. Here, he writes further, in *Bedek Ha-Bayit*, that if Ri Ha-Zaken would have seen what *Zohar* says about wasting sperm, he would not have ruled as he did. However, many *Aḥaronim* do not accept this claim. See the aforementioned article by R. Roness.
17. *Even Ha-Ezer* 25:2.
18. See *Ezer Mi-Kodesh, Even Ha-Ezer* 25:2 and *Igrot Moshe, Even Ha-Ezer* 1:63. At the end of his responsum, R. Feinstein lists the *Rishonim* who rule leniently against those who rule stringently, and it is apparent that the majority rule leniently, like Rema.
19. *Tosafot Rid* to *Yevamot* 34b, s.v. "*tanei*."
20. R. Henkin (*Responsa Bnei Banim*, loc. cit.) infers from *Tosafot Rid* that if the intention of the act is to satisfy his lust for *bi'ah she-lo ke-darkah*, it is completely permissible; but if it is because of risk (with respect to intercourse with a *mokh*) it is permitted *mi-de'Orayta* but rabbinically forbidden. However, R. Moshe Feinstein (*Igrot Moshe, Even Ha-Ezer* 1:64) sharply opposes the view of *Tosafot Rid* and demonstrates that the prohibition does not depend on intent. Therefore,

The Status of a Condom

Maharsham[21] permits the use of a "pessary" (a device similar to a diaphragm used in the 19th and early 20th centuries in a case where pregnancy would endanger the woman) because intercourse takes place in the normal way: Ejaculation takes place inside the vaginal canal, but the semen reaches the *mokh* and not the uterus. In contrast, he writes, there is no leniency to use a "pouch that covers the [man's] entire organ" (i.e., a condom), even in a case where pregnancy would endanger life, because the couple could abstain entirely from intercourse and thus avoid the danger.[22]

This opinion, that it is better to abstain from marital relations than to use a condom, is supported in *Responsa Dovev Mesharim*,[23] which cites Maharsham and adds: "The great skill and strength of that eminent prince of Torah to rule permissively (*be-koḥa de-heteira*) is well known; and if he is afraid to decide leniently, then I, too, am afraid to be lenient about this."

However, *Responsa Aḥiezer* disagrees[24] and brings two reasons to permit use of a condom when there is danger and where the couple has already fulfilled the mitzvah of *piriyah u-riviyah*. First, as *Tur* and Rema wrote, the prohibition of *ma'aseh Er v-Onan* applies only where there is intent to waste sperm and when one always does so; it does not apply where there is risk, and occasionally.[25] Second,

---

he concludes, *bi'ah she-lo ke-darkah* is permitted only "*be-derekh ishut*" (the expression seems to mean that the semen is ejaculated inside the wife's body). R. Henkin disagrees and explains why intent is a determining factor in the case of *bi'ah she-lo ke-darkah*, as stated by *Tosafot Rid*.

21. *Responsa Maharsham* 3:268. Most *poskim* permit using a diaphragm, at least in cases of risk. See below, *Siman* 35: Diaphragm Use.
22. This claim appears (and is rejected) in *Igrot Moshe*, cited below. It seems that when dealing with the very short term, there are grounds to abstain from intercourse entirely. However, over time, refraining from marital relations can impair marital life, and a different solution should be sought.
23. 1:20.
24. 3:24.
25. Different explanations have been offered for the word "*be-akrai*." R. Henkin (*Responsa Bnei Banim*, vol. 4, pp. 64–65) says that according to the language of Rabbeinu Yeruḥam (*Toldot Adam Ve-Ḥavah*, *netiv* 23, part 1) one can infer that "*be-akrai*" means once. However, this does not mean once in a lifetime (as *Shelah* explains), but once per menstrual cycle. R. Henkin further proves from the Gemara in *Nedarim*, which records stories about women who asked rabbis about "turning over the table" (i.e., anal penetration), that the question was not about a one-time practice, because women would not have come to rabbis to complain or ask; what had happened in the past would remain in the past. The language of *Tur* and Rema also indicate that "*be-akrai*" means several times, as long as it is not most times. In light of this, R. Henkin rules in *Responsa Bnei Banim* that "*be-akrai*" can mean from the night she immerses until the onset of the next menses. Thus, as long as the act is not permanently established, but only temporary and for a limited amount of time, it remains within the parameters of "*be-akrai*."

since this is a rabbinic prohibition[26] and not *mi-de'Orayta*, it can be overridden by the mitzvah of *onah*.

R. Moshe Feinstein[27] considers whether a condom ("rubber" in his parlance) can be equated with a *mokh*. His conclusion is that they can be equated, and therefore, according to Ri Ha-Zaken and those who follow his ruling[28] – who permit use of a *mokh* in cases of risk and when marital relations would be permanently forbidden, and who hold that this is not considered wasting sperm because it is for the sake of the mitzvah of *onah* – condom use can be permitted in cases of danger and when there is no other choice, because of the mitzvah of *onah*.

However, according to those who maintain that the *heter* of a *mokh* is because it does not impede normal intercourse, use of a condom would not be permitted, because if the semen is not ejaculated into the woman's body, the act is not considered "the normal way of intercourse." *Igrot Moshe* rejects *Aḥiezer*'s view that even intercourse with a condom is considered "the normal way of intercourse," arguing that the semen remains on the man's body even after he withdraws, and it never enters the woman's body. Therefore, only in exceptional cases, where there is significant concern about endangering the woman, and where if intercourse with a condom is not permitted, they will never be able to have marital relations, it is possible to rely on the *heter* that is based on the position of Ri Ha-Zaken. As R. Feinstein writes: "The majority of *poskim*, including Rema, are worthy of relying upon under such drastic circumstances and such mental anguish, where they would never be able to have relations, and to make peace between husband and wife, for the Torah and Ḥazal were lenient about many things." However, he conditioned his *heter* on the concurrence of one of the *Gedolei Hador*.

To summarize, use of a condom as a contraceptive is very problematic, and therefore, in general, its use is forbidden.[29] Only in a few highly exceptional cases is

---

26. The responsum of R. Eliyahu Klatzki (Klatzkin), mentioned in *Aḥiezer* (*Responsa Devar Eliyahu siman* 65), addresses a case in which the husband already fulfilled the mitzvah of *piriyah u-riviyah*, and his intent is to prevent his wife's endangerment. R. Klatzkin therefore views this as a rabbinic prohibition only. *Aḥiezer* concurs in this case, but it is not clear that he would agree in other cases (such as when the couple has not yet fulfilled the mitzvah of *piriyah u-riviyah*).
27. *Igrot Moshe, Even Ha-Ezer* 1:63 (at the end).
28. It seems that this group constitutes the majority of *poskim*.
29. There are various cases in which a condom is required to prevent the spread of a life-threatening disease. For example, if the husband is HIV-positive, or even if he merely suspects he is (for example, if he was pricked by an unsterilized needle), or if the husband has CMV and the wife

it possible to consider condom use when the couple has no other options, and after consultation with an eminent halakhic authority.

Female Condoms

In recent years, the female condom has also emerged as a method of contraception.[30] Unlike the diaphragm, the female condom covers the woman's entire vaginal canal, not just the cervix. Therefore, it is halakhically problematic as a contraceptive.

Nevertheless, in dangerous circumstances, it is preferable to the male condom because the woman performs the act of contraception when she inserts the condom into her body, and because the semen remains in her body after intercourse, until she removes the condom. Therefore, in those rare cases where condom use is permitted, it is preferable to use a female condom.[31]

N.L.

is not immune to it (and especially while she is in the first trimester of pregnancy), the only way to continue normal marital life is regular, long-term use of a male or female condom.

30. http://www.plannedparenthood.org/health-info/birth-control/female-condom.

31. R. Moshe Feinstein did not address this possibility in his responsum because the female condom was not in use during his lifetime. However, his words imply that it should be treated more leniently than the male condom.

Siman 34

Spermicide Use

Question

I had a miscarriage a month ago, followed by a D & C. The doctor said that I cannot become pregnant until after my next period. He recommended using a condom, but I know that is forbidden. How should I prevent pregnancy for the next month?

Answer

After a miscarriage or abortion, physicians often advise postponing pregnancy for at least one menstrual cycle, to allow the body to recover and to verify that the body and the reproductive system have resumed normal functioning.

Selecting a short-term contraceptive is a challenge that demands weighing halakhic factors, the woman's medical status, the degree to which pregnancy must be prevented, and the risks entailed if the contraceptive fails.

The choice of contraceptive methods is limited. Condom use is forbidden except in extreme situations that always require consultation with an eminent halakhic authority. Hormonal methods and IUDs require an adjustment period and are therefore unsuitable for short-term use. This is especially true after a miscarriage, when we certainly do not want to disrupt the recovery of the endocrine system, particularly when a woman hopes to become pregnant again soon. A diaphragm must be fitted and ordered.

Spermicides are sold over the counter, are simple to use, and come in different forms: suppository, foam, cream, and film. Although these contraceptives are known to have a consequential failure rate, this can be reduced somewhat by meticulously following the instructions, especially regarding the length of time that must elapse between insertion of the spermicide and intercourse.

Another method that works in a similar way is a contraceptive sponge. Its effectiveness is similar to that of spermicide suppositories, and it is suitable for short-term use. It, too, requires no prescription and is available in pharmacies. Like a diaphragm, it blocks the entry of sperm into the uterus, and the spermicide in the sponge impairs the motility of sperm cells that manage to pass the sponge and enter the uterus.

Halakhically, use of spermicide is not considered *hashḥatat zera,* since it does not impede normal intercourse and does not prevent sperm from entering the uterus. Therefore, when contraception is permitted, spermicides are permitted. The sponge is less preferable because it is larger than a suppository, and there is a chance it will be felt during intercourse. However, if for any reason it is not possible to obtain a spermicide, one may use a sponge.

It is important to know that the effectiveness of both the condom and spermicides is not particularly high.[1]

Halakhic Expansion

For an extensive discussion of the prohibition of a condom, see above, *Siman* 33: Condom Use.

Spermicides contain a substance that arrests the movement of sperm cells and prevents fertilization of the ovum, thus preventing pregnancy.

According to R. Moshe Feinstein,[2] use of spermicide is not considered wasting sperm[3] since it does not block the entry of sperm into the uterus. Therefore, in his opinion, it is a halakhically preferred method of contraception. However, he concedes that it is not very effective and therefore not recommended for someone who is forbidden to become pregnant. *Minḥat Yitzḥak* also permits use of spermicide, for the same reason.[4]

---

1. According to data from the World Health Organization: https://www.cdc.gov/reproductivehealth/unintendedpregnancy/pdf/contraceptive_methods_508.pdf.
2. *Igrot Moshe, Even Ha-Ezer* 1:65.
3. For further discussion of the prohibition of "wasting sperm," see above, *Siman* 33: Condom Use.
4. 1:115, s.v. "(12) *u-vazeh*."

Divrei Yatziv adds that spermicide allows for normal intercourse, and one who uses spermicides is no different, from this perspective, from an infertile or post-menopausal woman, who may have marital relations despite the inability to become pregnant.[5]

The sponge is a barrier method of contraception, like the diaphragm.[6] As with a diaphragm, marital relations while using a sponge are completely normal, and it is therefore permitted for use under the same conditions that a diaphragm is permitted.[7]

G.K.S.

5. *Responsa Divrei Yatziv, Even Ha-Ezer siman* 31, s.v. "*u-ve'emet me-odi.*" This reason was mentioned earlier by Maharshal (*Yam Shel Shlomo, Yevamot* 1:8) in context of the Gemara's discussion of three women who may use a *mokh*.
6. See below, *Siman* 35: Diaphragm Use.
7. See below, *Siman* 35.

Siman 35

Diaphragm Use

Question

I discussed contraceptives with my doctor and, among the other options, she mentioned the diaphragm. This is the first I have heard of this contraceptive. Is it halakhically approved for use?

Answer[1]

The question of diaphragm use requires a prior discussion of the permissibility of using a contraceptive. Assuming that you are permitted to do so, the diaphragm is one of the contraceptives which is permitted halakhically. Like any other contraceptive you may choose, it is worth educating yourself about the advantages and disadvantages of the diaphragm before making a choice.

Halakhic Expansion

A diaphragm is a dome-shaped piece of latex or silicone that closes off the opening of the uterus and blocks sperm from entering it, thus preventing fertilization.[2] The instructions for using a diaphragm call for the use of a spermicide, which is placed on the diaphragm before its insertion into the vaginal canal. The user folds the diaphragm and inserts it deep inside the canal. This can be done up to an hour before relations, and it must remain in place (where it is not felt) for at least six hours following relations.

1. This *siman* deals only with diaphragm use. Regarding the permissibility of family planning, see above, *Siman* 30: Family Planning Following Childbirth. Together with the diaphragm, one should use a spermicide; see above, *Siman* 34.
2. For an expanded clinical discussion of the diaphragm, see Medical Appendix V: Contraception.

The halakhic discussion of the permissibility of using a diaphragm centers on the Gemara of "*shalosh nashim meshamshot be-mokh,*" three women have marital relations using a *mokh*, in *Yevamot* 12b:

> Rav Bibi taught a *baraita* before Rav Naḥman: Three women engage in intercourse using a *mokh*: A minor, a pregnant woman, and a nursing woman. A minor – lest she become pregnant and die; a pregnant woman – lest her fetus become sandal-like; a nursing woman – lest she wean her child, and he will die.
>
> And who is considered a minor? [A girl] from the age of eleven years and one day to the age of twelve years and one day. [If she was] younger than this or older than this, she has relations normally – these are the words of R. Meir. But *Ḥakhamim* say: Both this one and that one have relations in the normal way, and Heaven will have mercy upon her, for it is said: "The Lord protects the simple" (Tehillim 116:2).

The *baraita* addresses the possibility that, due to health risks, three women (a minor, a pregnant woman, and a nursing woman) may prevent pregnancy, despite the prohibition for the husband to waste sperm. It records a dispute between R. Meir and *Ḥakhamim*. The *Rishonim* disagree about the nature of the dispute between the *Tanna'im*, and their discussion hinges on two main questions.

First, do the *Tanna'im* disagree about what is forbidden versus what is permitted, or about what is obligatory and what is optional? In other words, does R. Meir permit these three women to use a *mokh* but forbid for all other women, whereas *Ḥakhamim* prohibit for all women; or does R. Meir require or encourage these three women to insert a *mokh*, and others may do as they please, whereas, according to *Ḥakhamim*, it is a permitted option for all women, but no one is obligated? Second, what does the expression "engage in relations using a *mokh*" ("*meshameshet be-mokh*") mean: insertion of the *mokh* into the vaginal canal before relations, thus preventing the sperm from entering the uterus, or wiping or sponging the semen after intercourse by inserting a *mokh*? The explanations of Rashi[3] and Rabbeinu Tam[4] with regard to these two questions form the basis

3. Rashi to *Yevamot* 12b, s.v. "*meshameshet be-mokh*"; *Niddah* 3a, s.v. "*meshameshet be-mokh.*"
4. *Tosafot* to Yevamot 12b, s.v. "*shalosh nashim.*"

for the halakhic discussion, but there are many different and opposing interpretations of these explanations as well.[5]

According to most *Rishonim*,[6] it is not permissible to use a *mokh* at the time of intercourse, even when the woman is at risk, because it entails the destroying of the husband's sperm, "and it is like he is spilling his seed on wood and stones."[7] Nevertheless, some *Rishonim* permit all women to use a *mokh* during intercourse – in accordance with *Tosafot Rid*.[8] Also worth noting is the view of Maharshal,[9] who explains, like Rashi, that the *baraita* deals with the insertion of a *mokh* prior to intercourse, yet permits its use to all women because he does not deem this a waste of sperm, since intercourse takes place in the normal way and there is no impairment of the pleasure of either spouse (just as relations with a minor does not constitute a waste of sperm even though it is not possible that it will result in pregnancy).

As a matter of practical *halakhah*, there is a dispute among latter-day *poskim* about the permissibility of inserting a *mokh* prior to intercourse when it is dangerous for the woman to become pregnant.[10] Most *poskim* rule permissively, but both

5. A summary of the views of the *Rishonim* appears in *Encyclopedia Talmudit*, vol. 11, "*Hashḥatat Zera*," section E – "*derekh bi'ah*"; and in R. Yoel Catane, "Using a Diaphragm to Prevent Pregnancy," *Assia* 77–78, 5766, pp. 124–35 [Hebrew]. R. Henkin has a unique understanding of the dispute between Rashi and Rabbeinu Tam. See *Responsa Bnei Banim* 1:30.
6. Rabbeinu Tam, Rosh, Rashi according to the interpretation of R. Henkin, and others.
7. This is the formulation of Rabbeinu Tam in *Tosafot*, loc. cit. Another question that arises here is whether the prohibition on wasting sperm applies only to the man, who is commanded in the mitzvah of *piriyah u-riviyah*, or also to the woman, who is exempt from the mitzvah of *piriyah u-riviyah*. However, even if there is no independent prohibition that applies to the woman, it is still forbidden for her to be an accessory to her husband's transgression, though her prohibition is not as severe.
8. To *Yevamot* 12b, according to R. Henkin's interpretation, loc. cit.
9. *Yam shel Shlomo, Yevamot* 1:8. This interpretation synthesizes Rashi's and Rabbeinu Tam's explanation of the Gemara.
10. Those who forbid rely on the view of *Responsa R. Akiva Eger* (1:71) and *Responsa Ḥatam Sofer* (*Yoreh De'ah* 172), which forbids in all situations. Among those who forbid: *Responsa Binyan Tzion* 137; *Responsa Rav Pe'alim*, vol. 4, *Yoreh De'ah* 17. Opposing them is a long list of *poskim* who permit, including: *Responsa Maharsham* 1:58; *Responsa Ḥemdat Shlomo siman* 46; *Responsa Tzemaḥ Tzedek* (Lubavitch), *Even Ha-Ezer* 1:89; *Responsa Melamed Le-Ho'il* 3:18; *Ḥazon Ish, Ishut siman* 37. Many *poskim* note that if *Ḥatam Sofer* had seen Maharshal's words, he, too, would have ruled permissively. R. Henkin makes this claim, op. cit. p. 94. A partial list of *poskim* who rule permissively and strictly appears in *Encyclopedia Talmudit*, loc. cit., notes 175–78, R. Yoel Catane's article (cited above), and *Responsa Yabi'a Omer, Even Ha-Ezer* 10:24, which cites many *poskim* and likewise rules permissively – not only when there is substantial risk, but even when there is suspected risk.

they and those who rule strictly agree that a diaphragm is not akin to a *mokh* and therefore has a different status.[11]

The first to compare modern contraceptives with the *mokh* used during intercourse is Maharsham.[12] In his responsum he does not discuss the diaphragm but the "*pessarium*" (pessary), a rubber cap of sorts placed over the opening of the cervix, preventing the entry of sperm into the uterus.[13] According to Maharsham, this method is not comparable to a *mokh* because intercourse can take place normally, and it is not as though the semen is "spilled on wood and stones." Rather, it is akin to intercourse with a pregnant woman, which is permitted even though the cervix is closed. On the basis of this and other[14] responsa, many *poskim* permitted diaphragm use nowadays.

Following Maharsham's reasoning, R. Yehuda Henkin[15] explains the difference between using a *mokh* during intercourse, which he forbids, and using a diaphragm: In contrast to a *mokh,* which fills the vaginal canal and therefore does not allow normal intercourse and is like "spilling seed on wood and stones," the diaphragm does not do so, and it is therefore permitted. This was also the ruling of his grandfather, R. Yosef Eliyahu Henkin. Based on this responsum of R. Yehuda Henkin, R. Nachum Rabinovitch[16] rules that a diaphragm is permitted, since it is inserted deep into the vaginal canal and is therefore not like a *mokh.*

Opposing these rulings, R. Yoel Catane contends[17] that there is a significant difference between a pessary and a diaphragm, and that a diaphragm may therefore be permitted only in cases of risk, just as a *mokh* is permitted during intercourse when there is risk. According to R. Catane, a diaphragm covers more of the vagina than a pessary does, it can be felt during intercourse, and its removal immediately after intercourse constitutes an "active shattering

11. R. Eliezer Waldenberg apparently does not distinguish between use of a *mokh* and diaphragm use; see *Responsa Tzitz Eliezer* 9:51:2. Perhaps this is why he is stricter about its use, permitting it only when the woman is at risk and ranking it lower than other forms of contraception.
12. 1:58; R. Yoel Catane, "Introduction to the Question of the Permissibility of a Diaphragm."
13. This contraceptive was in use from the end of the 19th century through the 1940s. It fell out of use after the invention of the diaphragm, which has many advantages over it. See the article by R. Yoel Catane cited above.
14. *Responsa Seridei Esh* 3:15; *Responsa Igrot Moshe, Even Ha-Ezer* 1:13 and 3:21.
15. *Responsa Bnei Banim,* op. cit., p. 94.
16. *Responsa Si'aḥ Naḥum siman* 94. R. Rabinovitch identifies the "pessarium" of *Responsa Maharsham* with a diaphragm.
17. Op. cit.

of sperm," which is forbidden as an act of destroying sperm.[18] R. Shlomo Zalman Auerbach[19] and R. Yosef Shalom Elyashiv rule accordingly, according to R. Catane.

In his comments on R. Catane's article, R. Dr. Mordechai Halperin (the editor of *Assia*, where R. Catane's article appeared) disagrees about how a diaphragm works and about R. Auerbach's position. In another article,[20] he proves that R. Auerbach changed his mind on this subject. Even before the year 5745, he permitted its use in cases of risk, maintaining that it is halakhically preferable to a *mokh* during intercourse, but after 5745, he was even more lenient.

It should be added in conclusion that the primary disagreement among contemporary *poskim* is where to rank the diaphragm among the various contraceptive methods.[21] According to those who rule stringently,[22] its use is permitted only when other contraceptives are not suitable for the woman for health reasons, and then only when there is risk, or the suspected risk, if she were to become pregnant. The lenient authorities view it as being equivalent to other contraceptives (like the pill and IUDs), or even preferable, and the choice is up to the woman. According to R. Dr. Halperin:[23]

> After retracting, R. Shlomo Zalman Auerbach, of blessed memory, broadened his permissive ruling about diaphragm use, once he recognized that ejaculation during intercourse with a diaphragm is on the inner portion of the vaginal floor, the same place as during normal intercourse, and that the only difference is that the diaphragm, which forms a barrier at the upper-inner portion of the vaginal canal, blocks the way to the cervix. R. Auerbach therefore ruled on several occasions that diaphragm use is permissible, and that its ranking on the scale of contraceptives is in second place, after the pill, exactly equivalent to an IUD.

---

18. He further contends that it is not as reliable as other contraceptives. It should be noted that the user instructions for a diaphragm state that it should not be removed for 6–8 hours after intercourse.
19. R. Auerbach's position is appended to R. Catane's article and cited in R. Halperin's article; see below.
20. R. Mordechai Halperin, MD, *Medicine, Nature, and Halacha* (Jerusalem, 2011), chapter 22; also available at: http://98.131.138.124/articles/ASSIA/ASSIA77-78/ASSIA77-78.17.asp.
21. For further discussion of this, see above, *Siman* 32: IUD Use and the Ranking of Contraceptive Options.
22. *Responsa Tzitz Eliezer*, loc. cit.; R. Yoel Katan, op. cit.; R. Shlomo Aviner, *Assia*, vol. 4 (also available at: http://www.daat.ac.il/daat/kitveyet/assia/tihnun-2.htm).
23. Loc. cit.

According to R. Nachum Rabinovitch,[24] the diaphragm is the preferred method of contraception, and other contraceptives may be used only when, for various reasons, a diaphragm cannot. The reason is that the diaphragm, unlike hormone pills and IUDs, does not interfere with the woman's biological processes, does not cause bleeding,[25] and does not pose a health risk to the woman.[26]

It is worth noting that the in recent years, *poskim* have given greater weight to rationales based on the woman's health, as there is increased awareness of the health risks associated with taking hormones, like the pill, and of concerns about complications arising from the insertion of a foreign element into the body, as with an IUD. It is likely that other *poskim* would change their views given these considerations.[27]

In sum, a couple that has been permitted to prevent pregnancy may use a diaphragm. The selection of this contraceptive over others is at the couple's discretion.

N.L.

24. *Responsa Si'aḥ Naḥum siman* 95.
25. R. Moshe Feinstein forbade using the pill because it causes bleeding. In a case of danger, or suspected danger, a diaphragm is permitted. If not for the bleeding, if the couple already fulfilled the mitzvah of *piriyah u-riviyah,* he would permit using the pill even due to weakness or any other need; see above, *Siman* 32: IUD Use and the Ranking of Contraceptive Options. In contrast, R. Yosef Eliyahu Henkin forbade use of the pill but permitted diaphragm use. See *Responsa Bnei Banim* 1:30.
26. For the same reasons, R. Dov Lior also gives preference to the diaphragm over other contraceptives. His view was published from a letter to his grandson dated 3 Ḥeshvan, 5774.
27. However, R. Yoel Catane vehemently opposes this consideration, maintaining that the risks are miniscule. In my opinion, the woman herself should be allowed to weigh the considerations pertaining to this matter, as it directly affects her health.

Siman 36

Emergency Contraception: The "Morning After" Pill

Question

I usually use a diaphragm, but yesterday, after immersing in the *mikveh,* I forgot to do so. I am very worried about getting pregnant right now, because I, thank God, have a four-month-old baby girl and I am still recuperating from childbirth. I heard about the "morning after" pill for cases like this. Can I use it on a one-time basis?

Answer

There are different kinds of "morning after" pills, all of which are hormone-based. They are taken when intercourse took place without contraception, and it is necessary to prevent pregnancy. Use of these pills as directed, depending on the time of the cycle they are taken and the type used, can prevent fertilization and/or implantation.[1] These pills contain a higher concentration of hormones than the regular birth-control pills, so they cause harsher side effects. It should be noted that within five days of having unprotected intercourse, it is possible to insert an IUD instead of using the "morning after" pill.

Lekhatḥilah, use of these pills is not advised. However, *bedi'avad,* if unprotected intercourse took place and you are in a situation where it is permitted and important for you to prevent pregnancy, you may use this pill. It is best to take it as soon as possible after intercourse. Nursing mothers are given progesterone-only pills so as not to impair milk production. It is important to understand that if you are

1. https://www.ncbi.nlm.nih.gov/pmc/articles/PMC6483633/pdf/CD001324.pdf.

still within six months of childbirth and you nurse fully, with no supplements, and menstruation has not resumed – you have less than a 2% chance of getting pregnant.

Halakhic Expansion

Using the "morning after" pill raises two halakhic questions:

1. Given that the "morning after" pill may prevent implantation of the embryo, is it considered an abortion?
2. Is use of the "morning after" pill considered *hashḥatat zera*, a waste of sperm?

The Concern for Abortion/Feticide

The "morning after" pill is designed to be taken soon after intercourse: It is most effective within 24 hours and reasonably effective until 72 hours have elapsed. It can be taken up to five days after intercourse, but as stated, its effectiveness gradually decreases with time, particularly after 72 hours. Depending on when in the menstrual cycle it is taken, it can prevent ovulation, fertilization, or implantation. This time span is always within 40 days after fertilization, when, according to the vast majority of *poskim*, the fetus is considered "mere water."[2] Although *Responsa Mishneh Halakhot*[3] forbids IUD use on the grounds that it is murder, based on the statement of the Gemara in Sanhedrin that a fetus is endowed with a soul from conception,[4] his reasoning was rejected by R. Henkin,[5] who explains that the Gemara did not refer to a human soul, but to the life force that all animals share, and it is permissible to take the life of animals.

It should be noted that even if fertilization occurred, the "morning after" pill does not actively destroy the embryo but rather prevents the implantation of the fertilized ovum, which is not forbidden.

The Concern for Destroying Sperm

Even though the emergency contraceptive pill and IUDs operate in different ways, nevertheless both can prevent fertilization and even implantation by creating "hostile" conditions within the woman's body. However, unlike the IUD, in the case of the "morning after" pill, at the time of intercourse there was the potential for a viable pregnancy, and only afterwards did the woman, knowingly and intentionally, take action with the objective of preventing the fertilization of

---

2. *Yevamot* 69b.
3. 9:328, s.v. "*u-me'atah yesh lomar.*" *Igrot Moshe, Even Ha-Ezer* 3:21 states that this concern is remote.
4. *Sanhedrin* 91b.
5. *Responsa Bnei Banim* 3:38.

the ovum by the sperm; or, if fertilization had already happened, preventing its implantation. Thus, we can ask whether this constitutes *hashḥatat zera*.

There are grounds to be lenient about an action taken by the woman after intercourse, since the woman is not commanded in the mitzvah of *piriyah u-riviyah*, and therefore, according to many opinions, not commanded in the prohibition of *hashḥatat zera*.[6]

In any case, it seems that the pill's mode of operation should not be considered *hashḥatat zera* since it does not directly affect the sperm, only the cervical mucus and endometrium. This understanding, which is true of the IUD as well, caused R. Waldenberg to adjust the halakhic ranking of IUDs in his responsa.[7]

Due to its side-effects, the "morning after" pill is not recommended, except under pressing circumstances. It is far less effective than conventional hormonal contraception. It should be noted that within five days of having unprotected intercourse, it is possible to insert an IUD instead of using the "morning after" pill.[8]

O.K. and Staff

---

6. The question of the preferability of contraceptives put into effect prior to intercourse versus contraceptives that are activated after intercourse hinges on the dispute between Rashi and Rabbeinu Tam regarding the Gemara's discussion of women who use a *mokh*. It reappears in halakhic discussions and rulings about *mokh*, spermicides, and douching after intercourse. An extensive analysis of all the different views can be found in *Tzitz Eliezer* 9:51:2. See also above, *Siman* 35: Diaphragm Use.
7. *Tzitz Eliezer* 10:25:10. In an earlier responsum, R. Waldenberg had ranked the pill as most preferable, followed by the diaphragm and then the IUDs. Based on updated medical information on how the IUD works, on one hand, and concerns that the pill can impair the woman's health, on the other hand, he altered his ranking and deemed IUDs most preferable.
8. See Medical Appendix V: Contraception.

Siman 37

Depo-Provera (Progesterone Injection)

Question

Because of a medical condition, I am not permitted to become pregnant. My situation is somewhat complicated, as recent bloodwork showed that I have a clotting disorder (thrombophilia), which puts me in danger of developing clots in parts of the body such as deep veins in the legs or in the arteries of the heart. For that reason, it is absolutely forbidden for me to take estrogen. My doctor recommended a Depo-Provera injection, as I tend to be forgetful, so a shot once every three months seems to be a better alternative for me than taking a pill every day. Is this injection halakhically permissible?

Answer

The Depo-Provera injection contains the hormone progestin. The injection is given once every three months, and is a method of taking progesterone to prevent pregnancy without having to do anything on a daily basis.[1] Like other progesterone-based contraceptives, the injection typically suppresses ovulation, keeping your ovaries from releasing an egg, and also thickens cervical mucus to

1. Progesterone-only hormonal methods are typically given to nursing mothers because estrogen can impair the mother's milk supply. Additionally, doctors recommend injections for women who occasionally forget to take pills. Progesterone can also be administered in the form of a subdermal implant. For a broader discussion of the subdermal implant, see Medical Appendix V: Contraception. See above, *Siman* 25, regarding the halakhic challenges of progesterone-only contraceptives.

keep sperm from reaching the egg. After the injection, the progesterone is slowly released into the body, thus preventing pregnancy for three months.

The mechanism of contraception is like other progesterone-based contraceptives (the mini-pill, subdermal implant, or a progesterone-releasing IUD). However, the injection is far more problematic than any other progesterone-based option because its side-effects can't be arrested once the injection is received. Progesterone-based contraceptives are known to cause staining in 40–70% of women in the first several months of use.[2] While the injection's contraceptive effect lasts for three months only, the hormone remains in the body beyond that time, and staining might extend for as long as six months.

As long as you don't experience a halakhic sensation and the discharge appears on a panty liner or colored underwear, you are not *niddah*, even if the condition endures. However, if despite precautions you do become *niddah*, you may find that you are unable to achieve the clean *bedikot* needed to become *tehorah*. In such circumstances, a progesterone-only pill can be discontinued, or a progesterone-based IUD removed, in favor of a contraceptive method that does not cause staining. However, once the injection is given, it is not possible to arrest staining while the progesterone remains active within the body for as long as six months. For this reason, the injection is not halakhically-advised.[3]

In light of your forgetfulness, you might want to consider an IUD, or alternately, to set a daily timer on your phone to take the pill at a fixed time. Before going on any progesterone-based contraceptive, we recommend you study well the laws of *ketamim*, so that you do not needlessly become *niddah*.

Halakhic Expansion

For details on the potential risks posed by hormones to women in various risk categories, see Medical Appendix V: Contraception.

With the use of any progesterone-based contraceptive, numerous questions in the laws of *ketamim* are likely to arise, sometimes requiring excessive leniencies about the number of *bedikot*, etc.[4] In the present case, particularly in light of the

2. See Medical Appendix V: Contraception.
3. My husband, R. Henkin, informed me he would prohibit the injection for this reason.
4. In the early years of the pill's commercial production, R. Moshe Feinstein and R. Yosef Eliyahu Henkin forbade its use due to the many questions that arose in consequence (*Igrot Moshe, Even Ha-Ezer* 4:72). Since then, the dosage of hormones in the pill has been decreased, and spotting has lessened. In any case, it is possible to stop using a particular pill immediately if it causes excessive spotting.

woman's medical condition, the preferred option would be the diaphragm, as it does not interfere with the woman's biological processes, does not cause bleeding,[5] and does not pose a health risk to the woman.[6] However, as the woman's forgetfulness weighs in against the diaphragm, the copper and hormonal IUD can be considered, together with advising the woman to carefully review *dinei ketamim.*

C.H.

5. See above, *Siman* 32: IUD Use and the Ranking of Contraceptive Options. R. Yosef Eliyahu Henkin forbade use of the pill but permitted diaphragm use. See *Responsa Bnei Banim* 1:30.
6. For the same reasons, R. Dov Lior also gives preference to the diaphragm over other contraceptives. His view was published in a letter to his grandson dated 3 Ḥeshvan, 5774.

Siman 38

Onot Perishah with Hormonal Contraception

Question

I started taking the pill this week, in accordance with my doctor's instructions. Before starting, I had a *veset she-eino kavu'a*. Do I observe the *onot perishah* of my last *veset* even while taking the pill?

Answer

When taking pills that combine the hormones progesterone and estrogen, a woman does not expect to bleed, and halakhically she is considered *mesuleket damim* (amenorrheic). When finishing a pack of pills, there is withdrawal bleeding. Meaning, your period now depends on you taking the pills, so you and your husband need not separate at the regular times (*onat ha-ḥodesh, onat ha-haflagah,* and *onah beinonit*), but rather when you stop taking the pills. Your times of separation will vary during the first months that you take the pills, until you establish a *veset* based on the pills.[1]

Halakhic Expansion

Hormonal contraceptives can be divided into two groups: progesterone-only contraceptives and combined (progesterone and estrogen) contraceptives. Nowadays, combined contraceptives can be taken as a pill, patch, or vaginal ring. This *Siman*

1. For specific guidance on this, see below, *Siman* 39: Establishing a *Veset* with Hormonal Contraception.

discusses pills, but it applies as well to other combined hormonal contraceptives, like a ring or patch that releases hormones.[2]

The combined pills are taken daily for three weeks and then stopped for a week, during which a "false period" occurs. Similarly, a vaginal ring is inserted once for three weeks, and after its removal, bleeding will commence. The patch, too, is replaced weekly for three weeks. Some women combine packs of pills (or rings or patches) without a break, to postpone bleeding.

Since medical technology changes frequently, it is vital to stay medically and halakhically updated.

Amenorrhea While Taking the Pill

Experience shows that for millions of women who use contraceptive pills, menstruation is deferred.[3] Contemporary *poskim* base the status of a woman who takes pills upon the status of a woman in hiding, whose fear caused amenorrhea. The Mishnah in *Niddah*[4] states: "If she was in hiding and the time of her *veset* arrived but she did not examine [herself], she is *tehorah*, because fear suspends the flow of blood." *Shulḥan Arukh* rules accordingly.[5]

However, in the case of the woman in hiding, the suspension of bleeding is not absolute. Thus, Rema comments that *lekhatḥilah* a woman in hiding should perform a *bedikah* at the expected time of her *veset*,[6] and *Taz* explains that there is concern lest her fear be temporarily alleviated, whereupon she will experience bleeding.[7] Another reason to require a *bedikah lekhatḥilah*, based on Meiri, is that not everyone agrees about the distinction between fear and panic;[8] fear suspends bleeding, but panic actually causes bleeding, as the Sages interpret the verse, "the Queen became very agitated" (Esther 4:4), to mean that she became *niddah*.[9]

Yet unlike fear, which does not completely prevent bleeding, a pregnant or nursing woman is clearly *mesuleket damim*.[10] The pill acts to produce a physiological

2. Progesterone-only pills and injections require a separate discussion.
3. One authority requires the observance of *onot perishah* for the first three months of using the pill. See *Nit'ei Gavriel, Hilkhot Niddah*, vol. 2, chapter 100, section 1, p. 911; *Mar'eh Kohen* 8:1, p. 152. See below, *Siman* 39: Establishing a Veset with Hormonal Contraception.
4. 4:7.
5. *Yoreh De'ah* 184:8.
6. Ibid. *Tur* (*ad loc.*) rules likewise.
7. Ibid. 184:11.
8. *Bet Ha-Beḥirah* to *Niddah* 9a.
9. *Niddah* 71a; *Megillah* 15a.
10. *Bet Yosef, Yoreh De'ah* 184:8; *Shakh ad loc.* 21; *Taz ad loc.* 11.

state like pregnancy. Therefore, it is more accurate to compare a woman on the pill to a pregnant woman rather than a woman in hiding. Even though *Responsa Mishneh Halakhot* is uncertain about this,[11] others ruled accordingly;[12] *Responsa Kinyan Torah* states straightforwardly: "She is physically *mesuleket damim*, with no connection to her mental state, so why should she be any different than a pregnant or nursing woman?"[13]

Do Pills Suspend Bleeding Immediately, or Only after Some Time?

To what extent may we rely on the effectiveness of the pills to prevent menstruation? Five hundred years ago, Radbaz discussed the *onot perishah* of a woman who drank a solution that prevented menstruation.[14] He writes that one may rely on the solution because, among other reasons, many women have used it, and it worked for them.[15] In contrast, in the last generation, R. Yitzḥak Weiss wrote that there is no treatment that can be presumed in advance, to prevent menstruation.[16] Since then, many have written that one may rely on today's hormonal contraceptives, even more than the solution mentioned by Radbaz, to prevent menstruation.[17]

Thus, *Taharat Ha-Bayit*[18] quotes *Be'er Moshe* as follows: "Since these pills have been tried by millions of women, and it is clear that as long as they take these pills, they do not experience any bleeding, she has the status of a woman in hiding, whose bleeding is suspended by fear." *Taharat Ha-Bayit* concludes that since the laws of *perishah* are *deRabanan*, one may rely on the pill, which has proven to prevent menstruation for most women.[19] R. Wosner wrote similarly.[20]

11. 7:123.
12. *Responsa Kinyan Torah* 2:87:3; *Gufei Halakhot al Hilkhot Niddah*, p. 36, in the name of *Be'er Moshe*. Both sources are cited in *Taharat Ha-Bayit* 1:2:18, p. 118.
13. *Responsa Kinyan Torah* 2:87:3.
14. *Responsa Radbaz* 8:136. The responsum gives several reasons for its ruling.
15. According to Radbaz, the woman is required to observe the *onat perishah* of each cycle, until the medication has shown three times that it effectively prevents her bleeding. See below.
16. *Responsa Minḥat Yitzḥak* 1:127. It should be noted that the pills available when he wrote were not as developed as today's hormonal contraceptives.
17. *Taharat Ha-Bayit* 1:2:18, p. 119; *Responsa Minḥat Shlomo*, vol. 2 (2–3), *siman* 75, which deals with a bride who takes the pill, and it stands to reason that the same applies to all women. See also *Mar'eh Kohen*, p. 184.
18. 1:2:18, pp. 216–19.
19. *Nishmat Avraham* (193:1) quotes *Taharat Ha-Bayit* but then writes that some women experience spotting when they first start taking the pill. It seems that in his opinion, because the pill causes bleeding, it is difficult to presume that pills suspend bleeding. See Medical Appendix V: Contraception regarding bleeding while taking hormones.
20. *Shi'urei Shevet Ha-Levi* 184:8:2.

Considering this, may one be lenient about the regular *onot perishah* while on the pill? *Aḥaronim* and contemporary *poskim* disagree. Some rule, like Radbaz in his day, that the woman must observe the regular *onot perishah* until the pill has prevented her menstruation three times, based on the reasoning that we cannot know for certain that the pill will affect her and suspend bleeding until she establishes a *ḥazakah*.[21] Others disagree and maintain that there is no need to observe the *onot perishah* even before a *ḥazakah* is established, as it has been demonstrated by thousands of women that the pill prevents menstruation.[22]

In any event, once it is demonstrated three times that the pills prevent menstruation, even according to the more stringent position, a woman need no longer observe the *onat ha-ḥodesh, onat ha-haflagah,* or *onah beinonit,* as it is then known that bleeding is determined by the pill and not by the date or a specific interval.[23] Furthermore, some *poskim* are more lenient and do not require observing the *onat ha-haflagah, onat ha-ḥodesh* and *onah beinonit* even before the pills establish a *ḥazakah* of preventing menstruation.

S.K.

---

21. *Responsa Radbaz,* loc. cit.; *Minḥat Yitzḥak,* loc. cit.; *Mishneh Halakhot,* loc. cit.; *Tzitz Eliezer* 13:103.
22. *Responsa Minḥat Shlomo,* loc. cit. requires a *bedikah* but not separation. *Shi'urei Shevet Ha-Levi,* loc. cit., maintains that *bedikot* are required *lekhatḥilah* but not separation, until the woman establishes a *ḥazakah* that she does not menstruate while taking pills. *Taharat Ha-Bayit,* loc. cit., does not require separation, but concludes: "One who is stringent is commendable." R. Warhaftig rules likewise.
23. *Darkhei Taharah,* chapter 7 (p. 86) likewise mentions that a woman need not observe any *onat perishah* while she is on the pill. Regarding *perishah* when she stops taking the pill, see below, *Siman* 40.

Siman 39

Establishing a Veset with Hormonal Contraception

Question

I started taking the pill two weeks ago. According to the instructions on the package, I am supposed to get my period two to four days after I stop taking the pill. How should I calculate the times of separation after I finish the package? Is it possible to establish a *veset* based on taking the pill? How do I conduct myself if I do not get my period at the expected time?

Answer

A woman will generally experience withdrawal bleeding two to four days after taking the last pill in a series. In this situation, the regular *onot perishah* (*onat ha-ḥodesh, onat ha-haflagah,* and *onah beinonit*) do not apply to you, and instead you must calculate the *onot perishah* based on when you stopped taking the pills. The times of separation are likely to vary during the first months, until you establish a *veset* based on the pills.

After you finish the first pack, you and your husband should separate based on the time indicated in the instructions on the package, which specify when you can expect withdrawal bleeding. If they indicate a range of days on which the bleeding may begin, you must separate during all those days, and according to R. Yaakov Warhaftig, only on the last day of the range.[1]

---

1. See below, section 3.

Upon completing subsequent packs, you must separate after the number of days that elapsed between stopping the pills and the onset of withdrawal bleeding during the previous cycle. If the bleeding does not commence at the expected time, you must also separate on the last day of the range indicated in the instructions.

If during three consecutive cycles bleeding commences the same number of days after you last took the pill – always during the daytime or nighttime – then you have established a *veset kavu'a* based on pills. From that point on, you must separate only at that time, as long as you are still taking the pill.

If, in the future, the interval between taking the last pill and the onset of bleeding changes, the following month you observe *onot perishah* based on the *veset kavu'a* as well as the additional bleeding. If during three consecutive cycles the onset of bleeding is not consistent with the *veset kavu'a*, the *veset* is uprooted.[2]

You must perform a *bedikah* during your *onot perishah*.

Halakhic Expansion

We will discuss several questions about determining *onot perishah* for a woman on the pill:[3]

1. Defining "*veset ha-glulot*," a *veset* based on pills.
2. Calculating the *onot perishah*.
3. Must one observe the entire range of days indicated on the package instructions?

---

2. If a woman switches to a different type of pill, she must act as she did when she began taking the previous pill.
3. In addition to their use as a contraceptive, the pill is also used to regulate menstruation for women who experience irregular menses or other hormonal problems. When a woman takes the pill, its synthetic hormones preserve the endometrium (the lining of the uterus). After stopping to take the pill, the drop in hormone levels causes bleeding. This *siman* addresses combined hormonal contraceptive pills (which contain estrogen and progesterone), but the same applies to other combined hormonal contraceptives, such as the ring or patch that releases hormones. Regarding progesterone-only pills or IUDs (like the brand Mirena), see Medical Appendix V: Contraception. See also the R. Shlomo Levi's comprehensive article on hormonal contraceptives in volume 3 of *Teḥumin*. Regarding hormonal injections, see above, *Siman* 37, n. 1.

   In recent years, it has become common for women to combine packs of pills one after another, to lengthen the interval between periods. See below, *Siman* 41: Extending the Cycle via Hormonal Contraception.

Defining a *Veset* Based on Pills

The Mishnah in *Niddah* defines exceptional physical sensations that accompany the onset of menses – such as a series of yawns or sneezes – as "*veset ha-guf*."[4] The Gemara includes voluntary actions in this definition, and Rema rules accordingly: "If she ate garlic and [then] experienced [bleeding], ate onion and experienced, ate peppers and experienced, some say that she has established a *veset* to experience [bleeding] by eating anything sharp."[5] Even though a *veset* based on pills is the opposite of a *veset* based on eating sharp foods – at it is precisely the cessation of "eating" the pills that causes the bleeding – it seems to have certain advantages: When a *veset* depends on a certain action, the causal link between the action and the bleeding is not obvious, because most women can eat sharp foods without it causing them to menstruate. In contrast, when it comes to the pill, there is a clear demonstration, based on the experience of millions of women, that there is no bleeding while one is on the pill, and the reappearance of bleeding when one stops taking the pill.[6]

As with any *veset kavu'a,* with a pill-based *veset kavu'a* as well, a woman performs a *bedikah* during the *onat ha-veset,* the *onah* of the expected onset of bleeding, and there is no need for additional *bedikot.*[7] After stopping the pill, the woman still has a *veset kavu'a* for the first onset of bleeding, but afterwards she no longer observes the *veset* based on the pill, and it is uprooted immediately.[8]

Calculating the *Onot Perishah*

As noted, while taking the pill, a woman does not expect to experience bleeding and is even considered *mesuleket damim.*[9] After finishing the package, the

4. *Niddah* 63a.
5. Ibid. 11a; Rema, *Yoreh De'ah* 189:23. It may be specifically sharp foods, not other foods, that cause the onset of menses; see the article by Yoatzot Halacha Dr. Deena Zimmerman and Dr. Tova Ganzel in *Teḥumin* 20, pp. 365–66.
6. *Sha'arei Orah,* p. 236. It therefore stands to reason that even Rambam and Rashba, who maintain that a *veset ha-kefitzot* (a *veset* based on physical activity like skipping or jumping) can be established only in combination with a time element (*Mishneh Torah, Hilkhot Ma'akhalot Asurot* 8:5; *Torat Ha-Bayit, bayit* 7, *sha'ar* 3), would concur that a *veset* based on pills can be established independent of any time element, like the *veset* for eating sharp foods. See also *Tosafot* to *Niddah* 63b, s.v. "*akhlah shum ve-ra'atah.*" This topic is treated extensively in R. Shlomo Levi's article in *Teḥumin,* vol. 3. (According to R. Levi, due to the clarity of demonstration, the *onot perishah* associated with a *veset* based on pills are *deOrayta.*)
7. *Shulḥan Arukh, Yoreh De'ah* 184:9. See below, *Siman* 55: *Bedikot* of *Onot Perishah* when Woman Experiences Spotting.
8. See below, *Siman* 40: Onot Perishah when Stopping Hormonal Contraception.
9. *Responsa Shevet Ha-Levi* 4:99:9. See above, *Siman* 38: *Onot Perishah* with Hormonal Contraception.

woman and her husband must separate on those days that she expects the onset of bleeding. Among contemporary *poskim*, there are differing opinions about which days they must separate:

1. After completing the first packet:

We calculate the time of separation according to the instructions on the packet of pills, as it varies from one drug to another. *Shi'urei Shevet Ha-Levi*[10] states that the couple must separate 24 hours prior to the expected onset of bleeding, whereas *Taharah Ke-Halakhah*[11] states that they separate from the beginning of the day or night of the expected onset of bleeding. Neither of these authorities determined the duration of the separation, but *Darkhei Taharah* writes that they must separate starting 36 hours after the last pill and continuing until 7 days have elapsed.[12] Others rule that the couple separates for the entire range of days listed on the package. According to R. Yaakov Warhaftig, they separate only on the last of the days when the onset of bleeding is expected;[13] see below.

2. On subsequent occasions, prior to establishing a *veset kavu'a*:

The *onat perishah* after the last pill is determined by calculating the number of days between when she stopped taking the pill and when she started bleeding during the previous cycle – akin to any *veset she-eino kavu'a*.[14]

If the woman did not experience bleeding at the same interval as the previous cycle, according to R. Yaakov Warhaftig, they must also separate on the last of the range of days specified on the package, since experience demonstrates that most women, when they stop taking the pill, do not pass the last day indicated

---

10. 189:23:5.
11. Chapter 24, 106:2.
12. *Darkhei Taharah*, p. 105, *siman* 102.
13. Nevertheless, it is recommended to be careful about engaging in intercourse out of concern that she will become a *ro'ah meḥamat tashmish*, as it is quite possible that bleeding will appear.
14. R. Sinai Adler articulates a dissenting view (*Teḥumin*, vol. 4, p. 461, in response to R. Shlomo Levi's aforementioned article in vol. 3 of *Teḥumin*), namely, that someone on the pill has the status of someone in the first three months of pregnancy – and even more stringent, as it cannot be said that the menses of a woman on the pill have ceased, like those of a pregnant woman; therefore, for the second and third months of taking the pill, she must observe the *veset kavu'a* that she had established prior to taking the pill as well as the number of days between when she stopped taking the pill and when she started bleeding during the previous cycle. R. Adler adds that he heard this from R. Yosef Shalom Elyashiv.

on the package without experiencing bleeding.[15] It is not necessary to continue separating if she does not experience bleeding on that day.

3. **After establishing a *veset* based on the pill:**

If a woman has established a *veset* based on the pill – for example, for three straight months, the onset of bleeding occurred two days after she stopped taking the pill – she observes only the *onah* that has been established.[16]

These guidelines apply both to a woman completing a pack of pills and to a woman who combines several packs (or partial packs) consecutively: In all cases, she calculates the *onot* she must observe based on when she stops taking the pill.

As noted, she must perform a *bedikah* at the end of each *onat perishah*.[17]

Must One Observe the Entire Range of Days Indicated on the Package Instructions?

According to *Noda Bi-Yehudah*,[18] if a woman regularly experiences bleeding during a fixed range of days, and the onset of menses is never before or after the days in that range, these days are considered her *veset kavu'a* and constitute what are called "*yemei ha-mevukhah*" ("days of uncertainty").[19] Those who adopt the view of *Noda Bi-Yehudah* that one must observe all of the *yemei ha-mevukhah* would maintain that after the woman stops taking the pill, the couple must separate for the entire range of days during which she is likely to experience bleeding.[20] For

15. The rationale is that she will experience bleeding at some point – in the language of Ramban, "Will she never see [blood] again?" Ramban addresses the case of a woman who has established a *veset* with an interval of less than thirty days and then does not experience bleeding at the expected, established time. According to Ramban, she must observe the *onah beinonit* when it arrives, for "Will she never see [blood] again?" (Ramban on *Niddah* 15a, s.v. "*ve-hu*"). However, *Shulḥan Arukh* rules in accordance with the view of Rashba (*Torat Ha-Bayit, bayit* 7, *sha'ar* 3, 15a) that only a woman who has no *veset kavu'a* must observe the *onah beinonit*. In the present case, however, it seems that Rashba would agree with Ramban's reasoning because of the proven results of the pill.
16. *Sha'arei Orah*, loc. cit.
17. R. Wosner (*Responsa Shevet Ha-Levi* 3:124 and *Shi'urei Shevet Ha-Levi* 189:23:5) states that she and her husband must remain separated until after she performs a *bedikah*, even in the case of a pill-based *veset she-eino kavu'a*. See below, *Siman* 55: *Bedikot* of *Onot Perishah* when Woman Experiences Spotting.
18. *Yoreh De'ah* 1:46.
19. The "*yemei ha-mevokhah*" oscillate from 3 to 7 days according to the *poskim*; see *Sha'arei Orah*, p. 233.
20. See *Darkhei Taharah*, loc. cit. This also seems to be the view of R. Shlomo Levi in *Sha'arei Orah*, p. 236 and in his aforementioned *Teḥumin* article, where he refers to the days after stopping to take the pill when a woman is likely to experience the onset of bleeding as "days of uncertainty" ("*yamim mesupakim*").

example, if the instructions on the package state that bleeding is expected to begin 24 to 72 hours after taking the last pill, the woman and her husband separate throughout those days.

The prevailing custom,[21] based on the view of *Shakh*,[22] is that the *yemei ha-mevukhah* are not observed, and that separation is therefore based only on the onset of bleeding during the previous cycle. However, after the first month of taking the pill, the woman has no *onot perishah* based on the previous month, because taking the pill uproots all previous calculations. Therefore, according to R. Yaakov Warhaftig, she should observe the last day in the range that appears in the instructions on the package. (For example, if it says that bleeding will begin up to four days after last taking the pill, the couple must separate on the fourth day.)[23]

---

21. This is the custom in Jerusalem, as R. Warhaftig heard from R. Dov Ber Eliezrov.
22. *Yoreh De'ah* 189:39.
23. The explanation of R. Warhaftig's view is as follows: The *onot perishah* for a woman on the pill who has not yet established a *veset kavu'a* is derived from a dispute among the *Rishonim* about the *onah beinonit*. The *Rishonim* disagree as to whether someone with a *veset kavu'a* must observe the *onah beinonit*: According to Rashi (as understood by Ramban and Rashba), every woman, whether or not she has a *veset kavu'a*, must observe the *onah beinonit*, which is the thirtieth day, since that is the day when most women experience the onset of bleeding. In contrast, Ramban and Ran maintain that a woman with a *veset kavu'a* longer than thirty days need not observe the *onah beinonit*, because she will begin menstruating at the time of her established *veset*, which is later than the thirtieth day. However, if her *veset* is shorter than thirty days and she did not experience bleeding then, she must observe the thirtieth day, on which most women experience the onset of bleeding, for "Will she never see [blood] again?" Thus, a woman with a *veset kavu'a* of twenty days who did not experience bleeding on that day must observe the thirtieth day. Rashba, however, writes that this is excessive stringency; rather, any woman with a *veset kavu'a*, even if she did not commence bleeding on that day, need not observe the *onah beinonit*. *Shulḥan Arukh, Yoreh De'ah* 189:1 and *Taz* par. 1 (*ad loc.*) seem to rule in accordance with Rashba. It is apparent that this is also the understanding of *Leḥem Ve-Simlah* 189:2. However, *Pri De'ah, Turei Kesef, simanim* 1 and 31 challenges *Taz*'s ruling based on Ramban and Ran's rhetorical question: "Will she never see [blood] again?" Yet we can question the view of Ramban and Ran: If we accept the rationale of "Will she never see [blood] again?" why wouldn't we be concerned as soon as the time of the brief *veset kavu'a* passed (in the example of *Shulḥan Arukh, Yoreh De'ah* 189:1, "from the 20th to the 20th or from the 25th to the 25th"), even before the thirtieth day? Likewise, if the *onah beinonit* passes and she still has not commenced bleeding, she performs a *bedikah*, and if it is *tehorah*, she and her husband are permitted to each other. But what about the concern of, "Will she never see [blood] again?" It must be that we only observe specific dates: for a *veset kavu'a*, a *veset she-eino kavu'a* (lest it become a *veset kavu'a*), and the *onah beinonit* (because most women commence bleeding then). When there is no clear target date, there is no need to be concerned. Based on this, it seems that in the case of the pill, where the experience of millions of women is even clearer than the *onah beinonit* (see R. Warhaftig's article, "The *Onah Beinonit* Nowadays," *Teḥumin*,

R. Yehuda Henkin rules that even if the prevailing custom accords with *Shakh* that one need not observe the *yemei ha-mevukhah,* that applies to regular cases. In the present case, however, where there is a presumption, based on the experiences of millions of women, that she will experience bleeding within 2 to 4 days, we are stringent, and the couple separates for the entire range of dates at the end of the first month. However, from the second month until she establishes a *veset kavu'a,* they separate based on the previous month's calculation, like any woman with a *veset she-eino kavu'a.*

S.K.

---

vol. 24, pp. 235–42 [Hebrew]), it is certain that a woman on the pill will commence bleeding by the end of the fourth day. Therefore, in this case, one must observe the last day indicated on the package even according to Rashba.

Siman 40

Onot Perishah When Stopping Hormonal Contraception

Question

I have been taking the pill for two years, and am planning to stop shortly so that I can become pregnant, God willing. How should I calculate the days of separation after I go off the pill?

Answer

While on the pill, the *onot perishah* are calculated with respect to the pills only, not according to the *veset* you established before you started taking the pill. When stopping the pill, most women experience "withdrawal bleeding."[1] This bleeding is still dependent on the pills and is therefore not factored into establishing a *veset* or calculating *onot perishah*. Only after you get your first spontaneous period do you start observing the *veset ha-ḥodesh* and *onah beinonit,* and after two spontaneous periods, the *veset ha-haflagah* as well.

If you had a *veset kavu'a* before you started taking the pill, you must observe it starting with the first spontaneous period after you go off the pill.

1. A small percentage of women will not experience this bleeding. Lack of withdrawal bleeding is more common with certain formulations. When starting hormonal contraception discuss with your health care provider what to expect with the specific formulation you are using. Your personal pattern will be clear after a few months of use.

Halakhic Expansion

While on the pill, a woman does not expect to experience bleeding and is considered *mesuleket damim*, like a pregnant or nursing woman.[2] Just as a *yoledet* observes her previous *veset* when she resumes menstruating after childbirth,[3] so too, after going off the pill, a woman resumes observing *onot perishah*.

If she had a *veset kavu'a* before she started taking the pill, she has the status of a nursing mother whose menses resumed, whose status is subject to a disagreement between *Shulḥan Arukh* and *Shakh*. *Shulḥan Arukh* rules in accordance with Rashba that when the time of *siluk damim* ends, a woman reverts to observing her *veset kavu'a*.[4] For example, if she had a *veset kavu'a* for the particular day of the month, when that date arrives, she observes that *onat perishah* immediately. In contrast, *Shakh*[5] rules that a woman resumes observing her *veset kavu'a* only after her menses first resume, in accordance with the view of Ramban and Ra'avad. *Taharah Ke-Halakhah*[6] adopts the stringent view of *Shulḥan Arukh*, but others rule leniently, in accordance with *Shakh*.[7]

After 24 months, the prior *veset kavu'a* of a nursing mother, is uprooted only after three times, even if she does not experience bleeding consistent with her prior *veset*.[8] According to contemporary *poskim*, the same applies to women who go off the pill.

---

2. See above, *Siman* 38: *Onot Perishah* with Hormonal Contraception.
3. A nursing mother is presumed to be *mesuleket damim* for 24 months after childbirth, but nowadays most women resume menstruating before that. Thus, with the resumption of menses, she resumes observance of the *onot perishah* even within 24 months. See above, *Siman* 19: *Onot Perishah* and Establishing a *Veset*, Postpartum.
4. *Yoreh De'ah* 189:34, following Rashba's ruling that when the stage of nursing ends, the mother resumes observance of the *onat perishah* for her first *veset*, and even if her menses have not returned.
5. *Yoreh De'ah* 189:75; see *Sha'arei Orah*, p. 236 as well as *Siman* 19 above.
6. Chapter 24, 106:2.
7. *Ḥokhmat Adam* 112:38 states that according to most *poskim*, she need not observe until she resumes menstruating. *Shi'urei Shevet Ha-Levi* 189:34:2 states that there is not much practical difference between these views because most women do not have a *veset kavu'a*. This is also implied by *Arukh Ha-Shulḥan*, *Yoreh De'ah* 189:85. *Sha'arei Orah*, p. 231 states that Ashkenazim may adopt the lenient view of *Shakh*.
8. *Bet Yosef*, *Baḥ*, *Shakh*, and others at the end of *Yoreh De'ah siman* 189. However, *Darkhei Taharah* 7:92, p. 102, states: "If she does not experience bleeding she has the status of a woman with a *veset she-eino kavu'a*." His words need explanation.

A woman who had a *veset she-eino kavu'a* before going on the pill does not observe it when she goes off the pill,[9] as the pill uproots a *veset she-eino kavu'a.*[10] From a medical perspective, there is no certainty that she will get her period exactly a month after her withdrawal bleeding. Therefore, a woman who had a *veset she-eino kavu'a* before going on the pill observes the *onah beinonit* and the *onat ha-ḥodesh* only after she gets her period spontaneously, without the effects of the pill, as this will demonstrate that she is no longer *mesuleket damim*. She observes *veset ha-haflagah* only after she experiences bleeding a second time.[11]

S.K.

9. Like a nursing mother who had a *veset she-eino kavu'a* before pregnancy; see *Pitḥei Teshuvah* 189:32 in the name of *Noda Bi-Yehudah*. See also *Taharah Ke-Halakhah* 24:106:2 (p. 660) and *Sha'arei Orah* p. 236.

10. *Kenei Bosem, Hilkhot Niddah* 189:23, *Bi'urei Shulḥan Arukh* 31. This is the status of a nursing mother according to *Noda Bi-Yehudah*, cited in *Pitḥei Teshuvah* 189:32, and as explained in *Darkhei Taharah*, ch. 7, p. 85.

11. *Yoreh De'ah* 189:34.

Siman 41

Extending the Cycle via Hormonal Contraception

Question

I'm on the pill. A friend suggested to me that I combine packs to keep me from menstruating for three months. I wanted to clarify whether it is halakhically acceptable to avoid my period, and what is the status of *ketamim* that appear during those three months.

Answer

Assuming that you are permitted to use contraception, you may take packets of pills consecutively just as you may use other hormonal contraceptives.

The status of *ketamim* that appear during these three months, or whatever the duration of the cycle from combined packets, is the same as the status of regular *ketamim*. Thus, if the *ketem* is accompanied by a halakhically significant *hargashah,*[1] and is of a color that *halakhah* recognizes as blood, you might be rendered *niddah*. In such a situation, a halakhic authority should be consulted to evaluate the situation.

If the *ketem* is not accompanied by a halakhically significant *hargashah,* it is assessed according to the laws of *ketamim*. For the *ketem* to render you *niddah, all* of the following conditions must be met; if one is *not* met, you remain *tehorah*:

---

1. See above, *Siman* 25: The Law of *Hargashah* (Sensation of Menses).

1. **the color of the *ketem*:** the *ketem* is red, reddish brown, or black;
2. **the size of the *ketem*:** the *ketem* is larger than a *gris*, which is a circle 19 mm (¾ of an inch) in diameter, or any other shape with the equivalent surface area;
3. **the surface on which the *ketem* is found:** the *ketem* is on a surface that is susceptible to *tum'ah*, such as a white undergarment or your body. Toilet paper[2] and panty liners are not susceptible to *tum'ah*, and a *ketem* on a colored garment does not cause *tum'ah*;
4. **attribution of the *ketem*:** there must be nothing to which the *ketem* can be ascribed (e.g., a lesion, hemorrhoids, a fungal infection, etc.).

Throughout the time you are taking the pill, it is recommended that you wear a colored undergarment or panty liner so that you do not become *niddah*. It is also worth noting several other points:

1. If the spotting continues but does not intensify, it is best to refrain from marital relations as long as you are spotting, in order not to become *niddah* during intercourse. Bleeding during intercourse can have far-reaching halakhic implications, so it is best to be cautious. You can ascertain your status vis-à-vis spotting by wiping externally with toilet paper – which would not render you *niddah* even if you find blood on the paper. (Ashkenazi women must wait at least 15 seconds after urination ends before wiping.)
2. If the spotting begins after you complete the first pack of pills, during the second or third, and does not stop, it is worthwhile to consider stopping the pills, having a regular menstrual cycle, and then restarting. It often takes time for the body to adjust to taking pills, and at some stage, the shedding of the endometrium lining can no longer be controlled, and only stopping to take the pills can stop the spotting.
3. While taking the pill, you are considered *mesuleket damim*, and you therefore need not observe *onot perishah*, even if *ketamim* appear on those dates. On this topic, and regarding which *onot* to observe once you stop taking the pill, see above, *Siman* 40: *Onot Perishah* when Stopping Hormonal Contraception.
4. If the spotting intensifies and becomes a substantial blood flow (like menstruation), you are *niddah*. In such a situation, it is best to stop taking the pill for a week and then restart.

---

2. With regard to wiping immediately after using the toilet, see above, *Siman* 27: Blood on Toilet Paper.

Halakhic Expansion

Taking Pills Consecutively

The importance of keeping the Laws of *Taharat Ha-Mishpaḥah* has often been associated with the idea of refreshing marital life and preserving it over time.[3] The cyclical nature of times when spouses are together and times when they are separate generates mutual longing, and the day that the woman immerses becomes somewhat like a marriage each month. This prevents the erosion of marital life stemming from its routinization.[4]

However, there are times in a couple's life when they are permitted to one another for an extended length of time, and this does not pose a halakhic problem – for example, during pregnancy and nursing and after menopause. We learn from here that there is no halakhic barrier to producing – even artificially – prolonged lengths of time when they may be together.

Nowadays it is possible to prolong the intervals between menstrual bleeding by means of hormonal contraceptives. There are several ways to do so, including combining packs of pills consecutively, without interruption. Pharmaceutical companies even manufacture pills to be taken for three months consecutively, like Seasonale and Seasonique, which are used widely throughout the world to avoid the hassle of menses. These methods offer the possibility of preventing a woman from becoming *niddah* for months at a time, but it should be taken into consideration that during the first months of use, before the body adjusts to the hormone levels, intermenstrual spotting is likely. This spotting can generally be mitigated or prevented by gradually lengthening the amount of time that the pill is taken without interruption. See Medical Appendix V: Contraception.

---

3. For example, *Niddah* 31b states: "R. Meir would say: Why did the Torah say [that a woman is *niddah*] for seven days? Because he becomes accustomed to her and repulsed by her. [So] the Torah said that she should be *teme'ah* for seven days, so that she will be as dear to her husband as when she entered the wedding canopy."
4. It should be noted that this does not guarantee a happy marriage. These *halakhot* enable it if the couple uses them as a tool to improve their relationship. Unless both spouses work to improve their relationship, these *halakhot* will have no effect of strengthening their bond. Moreover, sometimes a negative attitude toward the *halakhot* governing the times when a woman is *niddah* can introduce tension and anger into their marital life. It is clear that one should not observe *halakhah* just for its potential benefits; rather, the *halakhah* stands on its own.

The Laws of *Ketamim*

Many details of the laws of *ketamim* were addressed in earlier chapters,[5] so we will not expand on them here.

The Recommendation to Avoid Intercourse if a *Ketem* is Found

The recommendation to avoid intercourse is just that – a recommendation. Every couple may weigh their options based on the concern for a *ketem* and the nature of the *ketamim*. If they engage in relations, we advise using colored sheets, and wiping with colored towels only, and not look at the towels after using them.

N.L.

5. See above, *Siman* 4, for a general introduction and details regarding the size of the *ketem* and the surface on which it is found. See also *Siman* 42, below: When Staining Renders a *Niddah*. See also below, *Siman* 54: Colors on *Bedikah* Cloths. This last *siman* deals with colors on *bedikah* cloths, but the same principles also apply to the colors of external *ketamim*. Regarding the surface on which the *ketem* is found, see also *Siman* 1: Panty Liners during the Seven *Neki'im* when Trying to Conceive; *Siman* 3: Blood in Urine during Pregnancy; *Siman* 17: Attributing Bleeding to Hemorrhoids, Postpartum; *Siman* 27: Blood on Toilet Paper; *Siman* 44: Staining on a PantyLiner or Synthetic Clothing; *Siman* 52: Bleeding from a Lesion caused by an IUD; and *Siman* 56: Minor Monthly Spotting.

Siman 42

When Staining Renders a Woman Niddah

Question

I am nursing and taking the mini-pill (progestogen-only pills). Recently I've been finding numerous bloodstains, and I can no longer differentiate between staining and actual menstruation. I do not feel anything internally during the discharge, but the discharge is red, and sometimes due to the amount of discharge, I have to change the panty liner several times a day. Does the situation I described make me *niddah*?

Answer

As long as you have not experienced a halakhic *hargashah* accompanying the bloody discharge from your body, *halakhah* relates to the discharge according to the laws of *ketamim*. If you find these *ketamim* on a panty liner or a colored undergarment, you are not *niddah,* even if the condition persists.

Nevertheless, it is worthwhile to refrain from marital relations during these days, lest you find blood that renders you *teme'ah* right after intercourse, thus raising the very difficult question of *ro'ah meḥamat tashmish* (bleeding experienced as a result of marital relations). While refraining, you will also be able to ascertain whether this bleeding will develop into actual menstrual bleeding.

If the stains continue to appear for a prolonged period of time, it is worthwhile for you to perform an external wiping with toilet paper before marital relations, to confirm that you are not staining.[1] It is recommended that you wipe yourselves after intercourse using colored towels, and that you do not look at the towels, because when a woman is *tehorah,* and it is not a time when she must anticipate the onset of menses, she need not look for possible *ketamim.*

However, once the discharge accumulates to a quantity of blood that approximates menstruation, you are *teme'ah.*

If the staining continues even after a long time, we recommend you consult a gynecologist about the possibility of switching to a different contraceptive (a different type of progesterone-only pill, a combined hormonal pill, or a different method of contraception).

Halakhic Expansion

Mini-pills are known as "the breastfeeding pill" because they do not contain estrogen, which can affect milk production. One of its common side-effects is intermenstrual spotting.[2]

Shulḥan Arukh rules in accordance with the view of Shmuel[3] that a woman becomes *teme'ah mi-de'Orayta* only if the flow of blood from her body is accompanied by *hargashah.*[4] *Sidrei Taharah* disputes the ruling of *Shulḥan Arukh* and writes that Rashi and *Tosafot* do not accept Shmuel's ruling, so when it is certain that the blood came from her body, she is *teme'ah mi-de'Orayta* even without a *hargashah.*[5] However, most *Aḥaronim* do not rule accordingly, maintaining that only bleeding accompanied by *hargashah* renders one *teme'ah mi-de'Orayta,* by virtue of a decree of the Torah ("*gezeirat ha-Katuv*").[6]

Pitḥei Teshuvah enumerates three types of *hargashah* mentioned by earlier authorities as rendering one *teme'ah* (the opening of the uterus, bodily tremors, and flowing discharge).[7] Many have noted that most or all women nowadays

---

1. Even if blood is found on the toilet paper, the woman is not necessarily *teme'ah.* For detailed guidance, see above, *Siman* 27: Blood on Toilet Paper.
2. See Medical Appendix V: Contraception.
3. *Niddah* 57b.
4. *Yoreh De'ah* 190:1.
5. *Sidrei Taharah* 190:93, s.v. "*naḥzor al ha-rishonot.*" See also above, *Siman* 25: The Law of *Hargashah* (Sensation of Menses).
6. See *Responsa Maharam Lublin siman* 2; see also *Taharat Ha-Bayit* 1:1:3, p. 8, for a list of *poskim* who disagree with *Sidrei Taharah.*
7. *Yoreh De'ah* 183:1.

do not sense the discharge of blood in a manner that would make them *teme'ot*,[8] and according to them, it is doubtful whether most women ever become *teme'ot mi-de'Orayta* nowadays.[9] If one asks: How can we completely uproot *tum'at niddah mi-de'Orayta*? R. Akiva has long since responded to the Sages' claim that according to his view, a man could never become a *zav*: "It is not your responsibility to make sure there are *zavim*."[10] That is, even if the *tum'ah* of a *zav* is written in the Torah, we have no obligation to ensure that it actually appears. The same applies to the *tum'ah* of *niddah*.

However, there are contemporary *poskim* who write that a woman becomes *teme'ah mi-de'Orayta* when she menstruates, even if they disagree about the reasoning:

1. *Tzitz Eliezer* maintains that premenstrual sensations and ailments that accompany the onset of menses are considered *hargashot mi-de'Orayta*, and in fact are precisely the *hargashot* that Rambam identifies.[11] *Igrot Moshe* states that the fact that women "know exactly when they become *niddot*" demonstrates that they experience *hargashah* and are therefore *teme'ot mi-de'Orayta*.[12] That is, the sensations of menstruation render the woman *teme'ah*.[13]

---

8. *Ḥut Ha-Shani*, p. 29, 183:4; *Responsa Shevet Ha-Levi* 10:142; *Minḥat Asher, Hilkhot Niddah* 1:4. However, *Tzitz Eliezer* 6:21 rejects this assertion and explains that the sensations that women nowadays report, like stomach aches, back aches, and other ailments are the *hargashot* of the uterus opening and bodily tremors described in earlier sources, and that only the terminology has changed. See above, *Siman* 25: The Law of *Hargashah* (Sensation of Menses).
9. *Responsa Divrei Ḥayim, Yoreh De'ah* 1:37. This is the ruling of R. Warhaftig in practice. *Responsa Divrei Yatziv* (*Yoreh De'ah siman* 81, s.v. "*u-vehargashat zivat davar laḥ*") alludes to such a possibility: "I asked women, and they told me that nowadays they have no sensation in the uterus and do not even know the location of the uterus. They likewise know nothing of bodily tremors or a stinging sensation in the uterus. It seems that the senses have been weakened completely, as with a person afflicted with a particular disease, may it not befall us, who does not feel the sensation of urination. Accordingly, it would seem, our wives do not have the status of *niddah mi-de'Orayta*." However, it is apparent from other responsa that he rules stringently in practice. *Shirat Ha-Yam* 25:14, p. 327, is likewise lenient.
10. *Mishnah Zavim* 2:2.
11. *Tzitz Eliezer* 6:21.
12. *Igrot Moshe, Yoreh De'ah* 4:17:12, and *Ḥut Ha-Shani, loc cit. Minḥat Asher, Hilkhot Niddah* 1:4, p. 16, writes that since the primary *niddah* blood is menstrual blood, there is a presumption that it was accompanied by a *hargashah* that the woman did not notice, and she is therefore *teme'ah mi-de'Orayta*.
13. R. Yosef Shalom Elyashiv, *Kovetz Teshuvot* 1:84, writes the following *ḥiddush*: If nowadays women do not normally experience bleeding accompanied by *hargashah*, they become *teme'ot mi-de'Orayta* even without *hargashah*. R. Henkin challenges this ruling; see above, *Siman* 25, n. 51.

2. Others write, based on Rashba, that even if we accept that women nowadays do not experience any *hargashah* whatsoever, they still become *teme'ot mi-de'Orayta* at the onset of menses, as it is normal for women to experience bleeding according to the menstrual cycle.[14] That is, the timing is what actually determines that she has become *teme'ah mi-de'Orayta.*

3. Another approach is that a woman becomes *teme'ah mi-de'Orayta* even if she cannot say that she experienced a *hargashah,* because when she experiences bleeding in large quantities, we presume that it was accompanied by *hargashah.*[15] That is, the quantity of blood is what determines that she has become *teme'ah mi-de'Orayta.*

In the present case, where the woman finds numerous, non-periodic *ketamim* without the *hargashot* that accompany menstruation, she is not *teme'ah mi-de'Orayta,* but it is proper to observe the third view cited above, namely, that one who experiences abundant bleeding, as she would normally experience when menstruating, should presume that the bleeding was accompanied by *hargashah.*

Therefore, as long as the woman is uncertain whether the onset of menses has arrived, she maintains her presumption of *taharah,* and the stains are judged according to the laws of *ketamim,* even according to those opinions who maintain that a woman becomes *teme'ah mi-de'Orayta* at the onset of menstruation, even if there is no *hargashah.* If the bleeding intensifies, one should observe the opinion that a woman becomes *niddah* when she experiences bleeding in a quantity similar to menstruation.

M.R.

---

14. R. Mordechai Willig wrote accordingly in *Kovetz Bet Yitzḥak,* vol. 39 (5767) based on his understanding of what Rashba wrote (*Ḥiddushei Ha-Rashba* on *Niddah* 57b, s.v. "*tartei shamat minah*").

15. *Responsa Divrei Yatziv, Yoreh De'ah siman* 85. *Responsa Bet She'arim, Yoreh De'ah siman* 252, s.v. "*omnam be-lav hakhi nami,*" writes that a small amount of blood can be discharged from the uterus without it opening, but a large discharge of blood is always accompanied by the opening of the uterus. See also: *Be-Shevivei Taharah* 2:9, p. 21; *Responsa Nezer Kohen, Yoreh De'ah* 2:7, p. 208.

Siman 43

Post-Coital Bleeding with Hormonal Contraception

Question

I am on a contraceptive pill that causes occasional spotting, but I always wear black underwear, so in practice I haven't found any *ketamim*. Yesterday, when wiping myself with a towel after relations, I found blood on the towel. Am I *teme'ah*?

Answer

From both a medical and halakhic perspective, we highly recommend that you consult a doctor to ascertain whether the blood on the towel is linked to the pill, or whether it might be the result of a cervical or vaginal lesion that causes bleeding during intercourse. If there is a lesion, you may attribute the bleeding to it, and you are not *teme'ah*.

If the examination does not disclose a lesion, it is presumed that the bleeding originated in the uterus, and your halakhic status hinges on the color of the towel and the exact time that the blood was discovered.

1. If you wiped more than 15 seconds after the end of intercourse (that is, from the time of your husband's withdrawal), the blood you found has the status of a *ketem*. If the towel was colored, you remain *tehorah*. On the other hand, if the *ketem* was found on a white towel and is larger than a *gris*, you and your husband are prohibited to each other, and you must wait four or five days per your custom, perform a *hefsek taharah*, and count seven *neki'im*. We therefore

recommend that you always use colored towels and sheets (and when travelling, we suggest you pack sheets and a towel, as the bedsheets and towels in hotels are typically white). Remember that there is no obligation to search for bloodstains after relations, and so it is better that the couple does not look while they are cleaning themselves.

2. If you found blood immediately, within 15 seconds of the end of relations, or alternatively, if your husband found blood on his body or when he wiped himself, you are *niddah* even if the blood is found on a colored garment or on paper.

In addition to the fact that the woman becomes *teme'ah* in such cases, there is a halakhic concern that blood was discharged from the uterus as a result of intercourse, a condition described as *ro'ah meḥamat tashmish*. If a woman were to establish a *ḥazakah* of bleeding as a result of intercourse, relations would be permanently forbidden. Practically speaking, this condition is extremely rare nowadays, as various halakhic and medical solutions can be found.

Nevertheless, to eliminate this concern, a *bedikah* needs to be performed the next time you have relations: The woman is required to examine herself both before and after intercourse, and the husband must examine himself after intercourse. If blood is found the second time as well, you must immediately consult a doctor to ascertain the source of the bleeding, and likewise consult an experienced *posek* for immediate, further guidance.

Halakhic Expansion

The Mishnah mentions various cases where blood is found after intercourse.[1] When a woman finds blood on her cloth within a time period called "*otyom*,"[2]

1. *Niddah* 14a. Rambam (*Hilkhot Isurei Bi'ah* 4:21) maintains that *ro'ah meḥamat tashmish* is an illness that must be cured, whereas Rashba (*Torat Ha-Bayit, Sha'ar Ha-Perishah, bayit* 7, *sha'ar* 2, p. 6a) maintains that it is a *veset* triggered by an action, like jumping or eating garlic or pepper. Among *Aḥaronim*, *Ḥavat Da'at* (*siman* 187, *bi'urim* 3) rules in accordance with Rambam. Therefore, according to him, the laws of *ro'ah meḥamat tashmish* apply even to a *mesuleket damim* (who needs not be concerned for a *veset*), and they can only be disregarded if the woman is cured of her illness. See also *Shi'urei Shevet Ha-Levi* 187:1:4. *Noda Bi-Yehudah* (*Yoreh De'ah* 1:61), on the other hand, adopts the view of Rashba that *re'iyah meḥamat tashmish* is a *veset* akin to a *veset ha-kefitzot*. Therefore, after one experience of *re'iyah meḥamat tashmish*, a woman must show concern for a *veset she-eino kavu'a*, and after three consecutive experiences, it becomes a *veset kavu'a*. Accordingly, if a woman sees *meḥamat tashmish* once, she must perform a *bedikah* prior to the next intercourse. If she does not experience bleeding the next time she has relations, she uproots the *veset she-eino kavu'a* and need not show further concern for it.
2. Rashi on *Niddah* 14a, s.v. "*otyom*," explains this to mean immediately after intercourse. See below.

or if the husband finds blood on his cloth,[3] even after some time,[4] the couple is rendered *tamei*. In the time of the *Bet Mikdash*, they were obligated to bring a sin-offering for having relations while the woman was *niddah*. In contrast, if the woman finds blood on her cloth "after some time," they are deemed *teme'im* out of uncertainty but are exempt from bringing an offering.[5] If the husband regularly finds blood in his urine, the woman is not *teme'ah* as she can attribute the blood to her husband.[6] The same applies if he finds blood in his semen.[7]

The Mishnah explains that "after some time" means the time it takes for the woman to climb off the bed and wipe herself. Later on, the Gemara[8] records a dispute about the amount of time one must remain concerned that the blood was caused by intercourse: According to R. Ḥisda, blood found within the time it takes "for her to reach under the pillow... take a cloth, and examine [herself] with it" makes her *teme'ah* out of uncertainty, while blood found after that – even within the aforementioned time it takes to climb off the bed and wipe herself – does not render her *teme'ah*, not even out of doubt. R. Ashi disagrees and maintains that these two measures of time (the time it takes to take a cloth from under the pillow and the time it takes to climb off the bed) are identical, and "to climb off the bed..." relates to a situation where she already has a cloth in hand and simply does not wish to examine herself in bed. Thus, according to Rav Ashi, the length of time within which she becomes *teme'ah* is a bit longer than the length of time according to Rav Ḥisda.

Among *Rishonim*, Rashba rules in accordance with Rav Ashi that a woman must suspect *re'iyah meḥamat tashmish* if the blood was found within the time it takes "to climb off the bed" as well as within the time it takes "for her to reach under the

---

3. The cloth in question had to have been examined and found to be clean, so there is no doubt where the blood came from.
4. Rashi on *Niddah* 14a, s.v. "*nimtza dam al shelo*," states that when blood is found on the cloth that the husband used to wipe himself off, even after some time, it is certain that it came from the woman and not from anywhere else.
5. The Gemara (*Kereitot* 17b) mentions that if she finds blood after some time, they are obligated to bring a tenuous guilt-offering (*asham talui*) out of uncertainty, but not a sin-offering (*ḥatat*).
6. *Shulḥan Arukh, Yoreh De'ah* 190:20.
7. In rare cases, the source of blood can be the husband's semen, which would not render the couple prohibited to each other. An experienced *posek* is needed to rule on such a case. When there is a possibility that the source of the blood is the husband's semen, the *posek* is likely to rule that the husband must provide a semen sample to ascertain the source of the bleeding. See *Bet Shmuel, Even Ha-Ezer* 25:2, s.v. "*afilu im motzi zera*."
8. *Niddah* 14b.

pillow."[9] *Semag* and *Sefer Ha-Terumah* rule that blood found within the time it takes "to climb off the bed and rinse herself" is considered *re'iyah meḥamat tashmish* out of uncertainty;[10] *Tur* cites this as well.[11] *Shulḥan Arukh* writes "to reach her hand under the pillow,"[12] and Rema rules in accordance with Ra'avad[13] that we are not proficient at precisely measuring these lengths of time, so if she wiped soon after ("*samukh*") intercourse, there is concern for *re'iyah meḥamat tashmish*.[14]

Among *Aḥaronim*, there are various opinions about how to translate the lengths of time mentioned by the *Rishonim* and *Shulḥan Arukh* into precise units of time. *Mekor Ḥayim* writes that if the woman finds the blood within half an hour after intercourse, she is considered *ro'ah meḥamat tashmish*.[15] Against this, *Arukh Ha-Shulḥan* maintains that the status of *ro'ah meḥamat tashmish* applies only if the blood was found "a few moments" after intercourse.[16] What is the meaning of "a few moments" ("*rega'im sefurot*")? Maharsham says five minutes,[17] and *Shi'urei Shevet Ha-Levi* states that the relevant amount of time is up to 10 minutes after intercourse.[18] *Pri De'ah* in *Siftei Levi*[19] and R. Shlomo Kluger[20] adopt a far more limited measure: the time it takes to walk 22 *amot*, or no more than 15 seconds.[21]

R. Ovadiah Yosef cites all of these views and concludes that one should show concern for blood found no more than three minutes after intercourse.[22]

---

9. *Torat Ha-Bayit He-Arokh, bayit* 7, *sha'ar* 2, p. 6a.
10. *Semag*, negative commandment *siman* 111; *Sefer Ha-Terumah siman* 107.
11. *Yoreh De'ah siman* 187. It is not clear whether *Shulḥan Arukh* disagrees with *Tur* and maintains that there is a difference between the two lengths of time, or whether both rule in accordance with R. Ashi but use different terminology to describe the same amount of time.
12. *Yoreh De'ah* 187:1.
13. *Ba'alei Ha-Nefesh, Sha'ar Ha-Sefirah Ve-Habedikah*, p. 70.
14. *Shakh* (*Yoreh De'ah* 187:1) relates to a more common case where the woman found blood the next morning. In such a case, even according to Rema there is no concern about *re'iyah meḥamat tashmish*, and the blood is evaluated according to the laws of *ketamim*.
15. *Mekor Ḥayim, Yoreh De'ah* 187:12. This view is based on the amount of time that is considered "just before *minḥah*" with regard to the laws of prayer – namely, half an hour. *Responsa Divrei Ḥayim* (*Likutim siman* 18) states that this is an excessive amount of time, and one should not be concerned about *re'iyah meḥamat tashmish* for that long, but if she found blood within 15 minutes, further scrutiny is necessary.
16. *Arukh Ha-Shulḥan, Yoreh De'ah* 187:14.
17. *Responsa Maharsham* 2:219.
18. *Shi'urei Shevet Ha-Levi* 187:1:11, p. 68.
19. 187:7.
20. *Shiyarei Taharah siman* 187, responsum 10.
21. For an explanation of this calculation, see above, *Siman* 27: Blood on Toilet Paper.
22. *Taharat Ha-Bayit* 1:1:5, p. 203.

According to *Pri De'ah, re'iyah meḥamat tashmish* is a *deRabanan* concern, so to permit a couple to one another, one may adopt the more lenient view.[23] Since both R. Ḥisda and R. Ashi are only concerned about *re'iyah meḥamat tashmish* immediately after intercourse, according to R. Yaakov Warhaftig the ruling should be in accordance with *Pri De'ah* and R. Shlomo Kluger: There is concern for *ro'ah meḥamat tashmish* only if the blood is found within 15 seconds of the husband's withdrawal, as the alternative may result in intercourse being permanently prohibited to the couple. R. Yehuda Henkin concurs.[24]

In sum: If there is no lesion outside the uterus, in the cervix or vagina, causing the bleeding, the woman is *teme'ah*. If the blood was found within 15 seconds of the husband's withdrawal, the woman must perform a *bedikah* before and after the next intercourse,[25] and the husband must perform a *bedikah* after intercourse, to confirm that the bleeding was not caused by intercourse. However, blood found after more than 15 seconds is not considered *re'iyah meḥamat tashmish,* and it is judged according to the laws of *ketamim.*

M.R.

---

23. *Peri De'ah, Siftei Levi* 187:7: "Since *ro'ah meḥamat tashmish* is derivative of *vesatot,* which are *deRabanan,* and the amount of time after intercourse is certainly very short, we should adopt the smallest 'just after' in all the Talmud." *Badei Ha-Shulḥan* 187:26 also adopts the lenient view of 15 seconds in order to permit a couple to one another.
24. See *Badei Ha-Shulḥan* 187:26.
25. According to *Ḥavat Da'at* (186:2), if a woman has a *veset kavu'a,* she must perform this *bedikah* only once, when she and her husband next have marital relations; however, if she has no *veset kavu'a,* then she must perform *bedikot* the next three times they have relations, so that she can establish a *ḥazakah* that she is not *ro'ah meḥamat tashmish.* In the present case, the questioner is on the pill and is therefore considered to have a *veset kavu'a* (see above, *Siman* 39: Establishing a *Veset* with Hormonal Contraception). Therefore, it is sufficient for her to perform the *bedikah* on one occasion, when she and her husband next have relations.

Siman 44

Staining on a Panty Liner or Synthetic Clothing

Question

I'm on the pill, and I usually combine packs until I begin bleeding. Today I took the second pill from the second pack, and later on I saw several *ketamim* on an undergarment made of a synthetic material. Because of the *ketamim,* I put on a panty liner, and later I saw *ketamim* on it, too. Am I *niddah*?

Answer

As long as the light bleeding you experienced was not accompanied by a halakhically significant *hargashah,*[1] it is judged according to the laws of *ketamim*. Since neither a synthetic undergarment[2] nor a panty liner are deemed susceptible to *tum'ah,* the *ketamim* that you found on those surfaces do not make you a *teme'ah*.

The phenomenon you describe is well known. The risk of *ketamim* appearing at some point rises when you combine packs of pills. Should the spotting continue and you become *niddah,* since you are already on the second pack, it is recommended that you stop taking the pill and allow for withdrawal bleeding. It is very

---

1. On the definition of a halakhically significant *hargashah,* see above, *Siman* 25: The Law of *Hargashah* (Sensation of Menses).
2. In your question, you do not mention the color of the undergarment. If it is colored, you are certainly not *teme'ah* according to the laws of *ketamim* (Rema, *Yoreh De'ah* 190:10, based on *Niddah* 61b and *Mishneh Torah, Hilkhot Isurei Bi'ah* 9:7). See above, *Siman* 4: Spotting and Bleeding during Pregnancy.

likely that next time you will be able to extend the amount of time you can take the pill consecutively without spotting.

Halakhic Expansion

The Mishnah[3] states that a *ketem* on a surface that is not susceptible to *tum'ah* does not render a woman *teme'ah*: "[If] they [3 women] sat on a stone bench or on the seating-shelf [affixed to the wall] of a bathhouse – R. Neḥemiah deems them *tehorot,* as R. Neḥemiah would say: Anything that is not susceptible to *tum'ah* is not susceptible to *ketamim.*" This is the conclusion of the Gemara,[4] and this is the ruling of all *Rishonim, Tur,* and *Shulḥan Arukh.*[5]

Are synthetic clothes and panty liners susceptible to *tum'ah*?

The Status of Nylon or Synthetic Clothing

The Mishnah[6] states: "Everything from the sea is *tahor* except for the otter[7] who flees to dry land – says R. Akiva." R. Ovadiah of Bertinoro explains: "*Kelim* made from the skin of any marine creature are not susceptible to *tum'ah.* Likewise, anything that grew in water – in cisterns or in rivers – is not susceptible to *tum'ah,* and the same is true of anything whose growth is not from the earth." Rambam[8] rules accordingly that anything that originated in the sea is not susceptible to *tum'ah. Tiferet Yisrael*[9] writes that the same applies to something that grew in a river or sea. This seems to imply that nylon, which is made from petroleum, is akin to something whose growth is not from the earth and is therefore not susceptible to *tum'ah.*

The *Aḥaronim* disagree about whether nylon remains not susceptible to *tum'ah* even when made into a garment, or whether, like in the case of other types of garments, the manufacturing process renders them susceptible to *tum'ah.* Maharsham[10] takes this position with respect to rubber: Since it is used to make clothes and shoes, it need not be woven or spun to become susceptible to *tum'ah. Minḥat Yitzḥak*

---

3. *Niddah* 59a.
4. Ibid. 60b.
5. *Yoreh De'ah* 190:10.
6. *Kelim* 17:13.
7. The term *kelev mayim* in Mishneh *Kelim* is identified by Prof. Yehuda Felix as the otter. See *Ha-tzome'ah ve-ha'Ḥai ba-Mishnah,* p. 243.
8. *Mishneh Torah, Hilkhot Kelim* 1:3.
9. *Kelim* 17:103.
10. *Responsa Maharsham* 1:2. The responsum relates to using a sheet of rubber to plug a water pipe in a *mikveh.*

also states[11] that there can be no garment, of any material, that is not susceptible to *tum'ah*. This is also the view of *Badei Ha-Shulḥan*[12] and *Taharah Ke-Halakhah*.[13]

Others, however, maintain that nylon garments are not susceptible to *tum'ah*. *Ḥazon Ish* writes[14] that it seems that rubber is not susceptible to *tum'ah*. *Shi'urei Shevet Ha-Levi*[15] also writes that nylon is not susceptible to *tum'ah* at the level of *deOrayta*, and that one may therefore be lenient about *ketamim*. He also writes, regarding synthetic garments, that they are not susceptible to *tum'ah* as long as they are mostly made from a material that is not susceptible to *tum'ah*. However, one should take care to check how they are made, as their manufacture sometimes changes.

Igrot Moshe[16] states likewise that nylon, if made only from petroleum, is not susceptible to *tum'ah*, as it is considered as something that grew in the water, and not because it is not woven or spun, which is only a requirement with respect to *tzitzit*. This is implied by R. Elyashiv[17] as well. *Taharat Ha-Bayit* concludes that one may be lenient about a nylon garment when it comes to *ketamim*, which are *deRabanan*.[18]

It seems, therefore, that one should be lenient about *ketamim* on a synthetic garment, even though it is preferable, if possible, to wear a colored garment, which is not subject to as much of a dispute among the *poskim*. If the synthetic garment is colored, one may certainly be lenient.

The Status of a Panty Liner

Nowadays, there is a very wide range of materials that are used to make panty liners. Some are made of an outer layer of synthetic fiber or viscose; an acquisition layer made of wood fiber or polyester fiber whose task is to transport fluid to the center of the product; an absorbent core made of paper pulp, and a back sheet of polyethylene film to prevent leakage. Others are made partly of cotton,

---

11. *Responsa Minḥat Yitzḥak* 4:118.
12. 190:107.
13. 4:8:5 and in the notes *ad loc.*
14. *Hilkhot Mikva'ot* 126:7.
15. 190:3.
16. *Yoreh De'ah* 3:93.
17. Cited by R. Ovadiah Yosef, who heard this from him orally, in *Taharat Ha-Bayit* 1:6:2, p. 408.
18. Unless the nylon garment is sewn with linen or cotton thread, in which case it is considered susceptible to *tum'ah*, and one should be stringent with it. However, it is worth noting that this situation is actually very rare.

nylon or paper. We have already discussed nylon, and we will now discuss the status of paper.[19]

It emerges from the Mishnah in *Kelim* (10:4) that paper is not susceptible to *tum'ah*, and Rambam rules accordingly.[20] Throughout history, the material and methods used to make paper have changed,[21] and so we find *Aḥaronim* reopening the discussion of whether paper is susceptible to *tum'ah*. *Noda Bi-Yehudah*[22] rules that paper is susceptible to *tum'ah* whether it is made of grass or rags of clothing. However, many *poskim*[23] ruled in accordance with Rambam that paper is not susceptible to *tum'ah* since it is designated for writing and similar needs, not for use as a receptacle.

In light of this, one may be lenient about a *ketem* found on a panty liner, as it is made entirely of materials that are not susceptible to *tum'ah*.[24]

This would be sufficient to permit *ketamim* on a panty liner, but as mentioned above, on the market there are also panty liners made of a blend of materials or containing cloth or gauze. One cannot say that these panty liners are not susceptible to *tum'ah* based on the material that comprises them, but their status remains debatable for other reasons, as will be discussed below.[25]

19. One should stay up-to-date about the materials used in panty liners.
20. *Mishneh Torah, Hilkhot Kelim* 2:1.
21. In ancient times, paper was made of grasses. Later it was made from pulped rags, and nowadays it is made from tree bark. It is likely that even paper made from old clothing should not have the status of a garment, because it is altered completely during the manufacturing process and is now an entirely new object (per *Sidrei Taharah* 190:19). See *Taharat Ha-Bayit*, 1:8:10, p. 406.
22. *Yoreh De'ah* 2:105.
23. *Ḥatam Sofer* 6:81 (*Likutim*); *Ḥazon Ish* 89:2; *Arukh Ha-Shulḥan, Yoreh De'ah* 190:42; *Taharat Ha-Bayit*, 1:8:10, p. 406; and more.
24. This is the ruling of R. Ovadiah Yosef, *Taharat Ha-Bayit*, 1:8:10, pp. 405–6: "It seems that we should be lenient regarding the practice of many women to place thick, absorbent paper above the underwear, facing "that place" to absorb their discharges, [namely,] that if a *ketem* larger than a *gris* is found there absent a *hargashah*, the woman is *tehorah*. This is as we explain below, in par.10, that paper is not susceptible to *tum'ah*." R. Ovadiah Yosef does not distinguish here between a thick pad and a panty liner; it seems from his words that the halakhic determinant is only the material from which the pad is made.
25. Additionally, some women use reusable panty liners and dressings, which are made of cloth and can be washed and reused. These dressings have come back into use due to environmental considerations and the advent of recycling. Since these are cloth, they should be considered articles of clothing, and the rationale (discussed below) that it is not something that endures does not apply either.

It is designated for short-term use

Rambam[26] rules that a receptacle is susceptible to *tum'ah* even if it is made from a material that is not susceptible to *tum'ah,* like paper, if it is lasting. Rambam[27] defines receptacles that must be torn in order to remove their contents as *kelim* designated for short-term use, which are not susceptible to *tum'ah.* Similarly, *Igrot Moshe*[28] states about paper that since it cannot be laundered and reused, it is not susceptible to *tum'ah.* This determination would clearly be true of disposable panty liners and pads as well.[29]

It is smaller than the requisite size

Rambam[30] writes that a piece of a garment that is smaller than three *tefaḥim* by three *tefaḥim* (24 cm × 24 cm or 9.4 inches × 9.4 inches) is not susceptible to *tum'ah,* whereas a complete garment that was woven from the outset to be any size is susceptible to *tum'ah.* However, later[31] he defines "any size" ("*kol shehu*") being larger than three *etzba'ot* by three *etzba'ot* (6 cm × 6 cm or 2.4 inches × 2.4 inches).

Modern *poskim* disagree about the minimum size for susceptibility to *tum'ah*: *Sha'arei Orah* writes in the name of *Aḥaronim* that a panty liner of any size is susceptible to *tum'ah* because it was manufactured for this specific use.[32]

On the other hand, R. Ovadiah Yosef[33] discusses a *ketem* on a garment that is less than three *etzba'ot* by three *etzba'ot,* even if it was made that way especially, and concludes that anything that does not meet this minimum size is not susceptible to *tum'ah.* Moreover, the length and width are not combined, that is, a garment that is five *etzba'ot* by two *etzba'ot* is not susceptible to *tum'ah,* even though its surface area is larger than a garment that is three *etzba'ot* by three *etzba'ot.*[34]

---

26. *Mishneh Torah, Hilkhot Kelim* 2:1.
27. Ibid. 5:7; *Kessef Mishneh ad loc.* 7, s.v. "*ḥotal shel hutzin.*"
28. *Yoreh De'ah* 3:53.
29. See *Taharah Ke-Halakhah,* p. 83, n. 25 and p. 85, n. 37, which brings these reasons for leniency but remains inconclusive.
30. *Mishneh Torah, Hilkhot Kelim* 22:1.
31. Ibid. 22:21 and 23:3.
32. *Sha'arei Orah,* p. 89. It should be noted that according to R. Shlomo Levi (the author of *Sha'arei Orah*), this rationale can make even a single-use *kli* susceptible to *tum'ah.*
33. *Taharat Ha-Bayit* 1:8:9, pp. 400–2.
34. With regard to multi-use cloth underwear, it seems difficult to rely on the size in order to define them as being not susceptible to *tum'ah.* The length of the underwear is certainly more than 6 cm, and the width is very borderline.

A panty liner is not considered a receptacle

Any receptacle, no matter how small, is defined as a *kli* and is susceptible to *tum'ah*. Some write that since panty liners and dressings were made to absorb bodily discharges, they are considered receptacles, even though they do not have the concave form of a *kli*.[35] Other *poskim* reject this claim, asserting that the purpose of a panty liner is not to be a receptacle to hold the discharge, but to keep the other clothes from becoming soiled.[36]

We conclude by mentioning two more important details:

Color

The decree of *ketamim* was not applied to colored garments, so any colored panty liner, whether disposable or multi-use, would not render a woman *teme'ah*, according to all opinions.[37]

Something not susceptible to *tum'ah* on a surface that is susceptible to *tum'ah*

Sidrei Taharah[38] writes that if a *ketem* is found on something that is not susceptible to *tum'ah*, which is itself located on a surface that is susceptible to *tum'ah*, like the woman's hand, she is *teme'ah*.[39] *Shi'urei Shevet Ha-Levi* and *Taharah Ke-Halakhah*[40] state that most *Aḥaronim* hold that we don't follow this position, for otherwise there would be no discussion about wiping with toilet paper, as it is

35. This rationale is cited by *Sha'arei Orah*, p. 89, in the name of "some *Aḥaronim*."
36. See, for example, *Orot Ha-Taharah*, p. 135.
37. See *Niddah* 61a. *Shulḥan Arukh* and Rema rule accordingly, and most *Aḥaronim* and contemporary *poskim* rely on them. On the other hand, *Ḥatam Sofer* (*Responsa, Yoreh De'ah siman* 161) writes that the leniency of a colored garment does not apply when it is tight against the body. For more on this topic, see above, *Siman* 4: Spotting and Bleeding during Pregnancy. *Ketamim* found on a black or colored panty liner would be permitted even according to the stringent view, and it stands to reason that a black panty liner would also have psychological benefit to a woman who is anxious about *ketamim*. Nevertheless, they can be difficult to obtain and are usually more expensive, and it seems that a white panty liner can be used just the same. With regard to a multi-use cloth liner, as mentioned above, the color is the sole variable by which it can be defined as something not subject to the decree of *ketamim*.
38. *Yoreh De'ah* 190:93.
39. *Sha'arei Orah*, pp. 89–90, writes that we ought to rule stringently regarding stains larger than a *gris* found on a panty liner. He cites R. Elyashiv as saying that hygienic pads are placed to absorb uterine discharges, so the *ketamim* found on them are not subject to uncertainty as to their origin. This rationale is rejected by the many *Aḥaronim* who maintain that Ḥazal did not forbid a *ketem* even if it originated with certainty in the uterus. See *Taharat Ha-Bayit* 1:8:12–13, p. 409; *Taharah Ke-Halakhah*, p. 81; *Shi'urei Shevet Ha-Levi* 190:10:3.
40. *Shi'urei Shevet Ha-Levi* 190:10:2; *Taharah Ke-Halakhah*, p. 86.

always held in a hand. Therefore, there are no grounds to claim that the panty liner is susceptible to *tum'ah* because it is placed atop a cloth undergarment that is susceptible to *tum'ah*.

Summary

One may be lenient about *ketamim* found on most types of panty liners since they are made of materials that are not susceptible to *tum'ah*. Even a panty liner that contains materials that are susceptible to *tum'ah* (such as cotton) is designated for short-term use and is smaller than the requisite size for becoming susceptible to *tum'ah*.[41] The exception to this principle is a multi-use cloth liner, as discussed above.

N.L. and O.K.

41. This is the ruling of R. Warhaftig and R. Henkin regarding a woman who is *tehorah*. Regarding while one is counting the seven *neki'im*, see above, *Siman* 1: Panty Liners during the Seven *Neki'im* when Trying to Conceive.

Siman 45

A Suspected Lesion and Stain Location on a Bedikah Cloth

Question

I'm on the combined pill. I performed a *hefsek taharah* and began counting the seven *neki'im,* but with every *bedikah* I find a small red dot on the *bedikah* cloth, always in the same place, on the side. I suspect it is a *petza.* What should I do?[1]

Answer

Blood found on a *bedikah* cloth may be attributed to a lesion when there are grounds to assume that you have a bleeding *makkah* and that the blood on the *bedikah* cloth comes from the *makkah* and not the uterus. In some circumstances, it is possible to conclude that there is a bleeding *makkah* based on the location of the blood on the *bedikah* cloth, and on this basis to render the *bedikah* acceptable, but the mere presence of blood at the side of the *bedikah* cloth is not sufficient evidence of a vaginal *makkah.*

From your description, it is not sufficiently clear why you think that there is a lesion; perhaps further details will help contribute to a halakhic decision. If your supposition stems only from the location of the blood on the *bedikah* cloth, you can bring the cloth to someone proficient in assessing bloodstains ("*mar'ot*"), or alternatively, you may schedule a medical examination. If the examination

1. The question did not indicate on which day of the seven *neki'im* the questioner found the blood. Regarding the attribution of blood to a lesion during the first three of the seven *neki'im,* see above, *Siman* 21: Attributing Blood to a *Petza* during the Seven *Neki'im.*

clarifies that there is indeed a *makkah* that is likely to bleed, it will be possible to render the *bedikah* cloth *tahor*.

Halakhic Expansion

The source for permitting a bloodstain found on a *bedikah* cloth based on the location of the blood on the cloth is *Terumat Ha-Deshen,*[2] who discusses the case of a woman who finds a bloodstain that seems to come from "the sides."[3] The question of attribution to a *makkah* hinges on the dispute between Rashba and *Sefer Ha-Terumah*. According to *Sefer Ha-Terumah,*[4] as well as *Mordekhai,*[5] one may attribute blood to a *makkah* only if it is known for certain that this *makkah* bleeds. According to Rashba,[6] however, one may be lenient and attribute the bleeding to any *makkah*, even if it is not known for certain that the *makkah* bleeds.

Terumat Ha-Deshen permits attribution to a *makkah* in a case where the woman realizes that the blood is consistently found in a location that warrants the supposition that this blood is vaginal, not uterine. *Terumat Ha-Deshen* writes that this leniency applies only to a woman with a *veset*, and at a time when she is not anticipating menses. *Shulḥan Arukh*[7] rules that if every time a woman performs a *bedikah* the blood is found on the sides, she may attribute the blood to a *makkah*, and certainly if she experiences pain at the sides while performing the *bedikah*.[8]

In contrast to the position of *Terumat Ha-Deshen, Shulḥan Arukh* does not condition attribution to a *makkah* on having a *veset kavu'a,*[9] nor does he mention whether prior knowledge of the presence of a *makkah* is needed in order to rely on the location of the blood on the *bedikah* cloth.

The *Aḥaronim* disagree about how to understand *Shulḥan Arukh. Noda Bi-Yehudah*[10] writes that *Shulḥan Arukh*'s words refer to the earlier paragraphs of that *siman*,

---

2. *Pesakim U-Khetavim siman* 47.
3. *Bet Yosef* (*Yoreh De'ah siman* 187) says in the name of *Terumat Ha-Deshen* that the woman in question knows that she has a *makkah*. However, *Terumat Ha-Deshen* himself does not state this explicitly, even though it is implied by the fact that the questioner presumes that the blood is not uterine.
4. *Siman* 92.
5. 735:3.
6. *Torat Ha-Bayit, bayit* 7, *sha'ar* 4, p. 23.
7. *Yoreh De'ah* 187:7.
8. According to *Bi'ur Ha-Gra* 187:7, the addition of "certainly if she experiences pain there" brings us to the level of certainty required by *Mordechai* and *Sefer Ha-Terumah*, namely, that the woman must know that her *makkah* bleeds.
9. See *Taz* 187:10.
10. *Yoreh De'ah* 1:46, summarized in *Pitḥei Teshuvah* 187:37.

which discuss a woman who knows she has a *makkah*. Other *Aḥaronim*[11] write that *Shulḥan Arukh* should be understood in accordance with the plain meaning: Even where there is no other indication that the woman has a *makkah,* if she consistently finds blood on the site of the *bedikah* cloth, and the rest of it is clean, the woman can be deemed *tehorah* by attributing the blood to a *makkah.*

R. Ovadiah Yosef[12] cites the aforementioned *Aḥaronim* and rules in accordance with the lenient view, namely, that one may rely on the blood being found at the sides and attribute it to a *makkah* even if there is no known *makkah* and even when the woman does not have a *veset kavu'a.* In contrast, R. Shmuel Wosner[13] tends to rely on the lenient views only when the woman is *mesuleket damim* or post-menopausal.

In the present case, we must take into account that the questioner was under the influence of hormonal contraception.[14] A woman is considered *mesuleket damim* while she is on the pill.[15] However, if she tends to suffer from spotting that stems from uterine bleeding as a result of the pill, there is cause for concern that the bloodstain in the *bedikah* is not from a *makkah,* even if it appears only on the sides of the cloth, since uterine blood can reach the vaginal walls, or can result from the rotation of the cloth in the course of the bedikah.

In the present case, the woman's assessment is that there is a lesion. As stated above, *Shulḥan Arukh* mentions two yardsticks by which one may assume that the lesion is the source of bleeding: the location of the blood only on the sides of the *bedikah* cloth, and pain during the *bedikah.* Significant weight should be given to the woman's sensation and to the reasons she thinks there is a lesion. According to *Shulḥan Arukh,* when it is clear to the woman that the bleeding is not uterine, it should be treated as blood from a *makkah,* which would not make her *niddah.*[16]

It seems that even when there is no other indication that there is a lesion, if the woman is convinced, based on the appearance of the *bedikah* cloth and the location of the blood on it, that the blood is from a *makkah,* one should follow the

11. *Tiferet Le-Moshe* 32b; *Avnei Milu'im siman* 23; *Responsa Ḥakham Tzvi siman* 73; etc.
12. *Taharat Ha-Bayit* 1:5:9, p. 244.
13. *Shi'urei Shevet Ha-Levi* 187:7:1–3, p. 87.
14. The combined contraceptive pill contains both estrogen and progesterone. For some women, the hormonal effects of the pill cause vaginal dryness and, consequently, can lead to vaginal lesions and discomfort. This condition necessitates medical consultation and treatment.
15. While on the pill, a woman does not expect to menstruate. For a broader discussion, see above, *Siman* 39: Establishing a *Veset* with Hormonal Contraception.
16. *Shulḥan Arukh, Yoreh De'ah* 187:6.

lenient ruling of R. Ovadiah Yosef and attribute the blood to a lesion. On the other hand, if the woman is uncertain, she should be referred to a gynecologist or a nurse/*bodeket taharah*.[17] A medical examination that determines that the bleeding is not uterine counts as a *bedikah*.

Z.B.

17. A "*bodeket taharah*" is a nurse who has undergone halakhic training to identify vaginal and cervical lesions and diagnose whether the bleeding is uterine or not. A *bodeket* cannot answer halakhic questions or offer medical treatment. She can, however, help resolve questions that involve attribution to a *makkah*. A *bodeket* can also be asked to perform a *hefsek taharah* for a woman by avoiding the wounded area during a *bedikah*. It is, of course, a personal prerogative and not a halakhic obligation to turn to a *bodeket taharah* for assistance. Sometimes the examination entails some mild discomfort, much like a gynecological examination; but sometimes it can help a woman who suffers from lesions, especially when an immediate gynecological appointment is unavailable.

Siman 46

When a Contraceptive Pill Is Not Absorbed, Recommendations

Question

I'm on the pill. I recently had a virus that caused vomiting and diarrhea for several days. Since yesterday, I've been spotting. Am I *niddah*? And is it possible that because of the vomiting I'm not currently protected from becoming pregnant?

Answer

If the appearance of the *ketamim* was accompanied by a halakhic *hargashah,*[1] or the *ketem* was larger than a *gris* (between the size of a dime or penny) on a white garment or sheet or on your body, you are *niddah*. If so, the *halakhah* is to wait four or five days as per your custom, perform a *hefsek taharah,* count seven *neki'im,* and immerse in the *mikveh*. If you have become *teme'ah,* and you are nearing the end of the package of pills, it makes sense for you to stop taking this month's pills and get your period, in order to shorten the length of the separation. If you are not near the end of the package, we recommend consulting your doctor about whether to stop the pills mid-package.

If the *ketamim* you found were not accompanied by a *hargashah* that would make you *niddah,* and they were found on a panty liner or colored underwear, you are not *niddah*. However, we advise refraining from marital relations for 24 hours, to make certain that the spotting does not develop into menstrual bleeding.

---

1. See above, *Siman* 25: The Law of *Hargashah*.

In the event that you are not *niddah*, the answer to your second question depends on how far you have progressed in the current package of pills.

If you have been taking the pills for at least two weeks and are now nearing the end of the package, it is advisable to stop taking the pills now and get your period. After stopping for seven days, you can start a new pack, with the hope that the spotting does not recur. This will ensure the effectiveness of the contraceptive.

If you have only just started the package, it is recommended that you keep taking the pills, with the hope that the spotting will stop. Due to the vomiting and diarrhea, it is possible that the pills were not absorbed, and so there is a chance that you are not fully protected. Therefore, it makes sense for you to use a spermicide, such as a suppository or film,[2] which you can buy over the counter. Spermicides are not a very effective contraceptive on their own; but in this case, you are only using a spermicide as a backup. If you are very concerned about becoming pregnant, there is always the option of refraining from marital relations this month. Your risk of becoming pregnant depends on the timing and frequency of the vomiting and diarrhea, so you should consult a doctor.

Halakhic Expansion

According to Torah law, uterine blood causes *tum'ah* only if accompanied by a *hargashah*.[3] Any bleeding without *hargashah* is judged according to the laws of *ketamim* unless there is an actual flow of blood. *Mi-deRabanan, ketamim* cause *tum'ah* when they fulfill the following criteria: the *ketem* is larger than a *gris*;[4] it was found on a surface that is susceptible to *tum'ah*;[5] it is found on white fabric or on the body;[6] it is found where it could have emerged from the uterus;[7] it cannot be attributed to anything else;[8] and it is a color that causes *tum'ah*.[9] For sources on these laws, see above, *Siman* 17: Attributing Bleeding to Hemorrhoids, Postpartum; *Siman* 41: Extending the Cycle via Hormonal Contraception; *Siman* 44: Staining on a Panty Liner or Synthetic Clothing; *Siman* 54: Colors on *Bedikah* Cloths.

---

2. On this, see *Siman* 34: Spermicide Use.
3. *Shulḥan Arukh, Yoreh De'ah* 190:1.
4. Ibid. 5.
5. Ibid. 10.
6. Ibid. 8, 10.
7. Ibid. 11.
8. Ibid.
9. Ibid. 188:1. For further discussion of the definition of *ketamim* and on refraining from marital relations when experiencing spotting, see above, *Siman* 41: Extending the Cycle via Hormonal Contraception.

A woman who forgets to take the pill will likely experience spotting. This is true also in the present case where the pill was not absorbed properly. In such a case, the question of whether she should stop taking the pill and get her period or continue, with the hope that the spotting will stop, depends upon how far she has progressed in the current package of pills. It is important to remember that if a woman forgets to take the pill once or it is not absorbed properly, it impairs the effectiveness of the contraception for that cycle.

G.K.S.

Siman 47

Mikveh Immersion with a Hormonal Patch

Question

I use a contraceptive hormonal patch.[1] Last night, I forgot to remove it in the mikveh. Is the patch considered a *ḥatzitzah* (barrier) that requires me to immerse again?

Answer

Like a band-aid, a patch that is replaced every week constitutes a *ḥatzitzah,* and it must be removed before immersing. Any residual glue adhering to the skin also constitutes a *ḥatzitzah,* and must be removed.

There are differences of opinion among doctors regarding reuse of a patch that has already been removed from the body – whether it is still effective so long as the adhesive material remains, or whether it is preferable to use a new patch.[2] In either case, after immersing, the patch should be reaffixed, or a new patch should be affixed in order to maintain its effectiveness as a contraceptive.

---

1. The patch releases estrogen and progesterone, like the combined pill. The hormones are absorbed into the body through the skin. Over the course of three weeks, a patch is attached to the body for a week and replaced after a week. During the fourth week, the woman does not use a patch, at which point she should get her period. According to the manufacturer's instructions, the woman must check daily to make sure that the patch is firmly attached, and if it is not, she should remove it and affix a new patch. For further explanation, see below, Medical Appendix V: Contraception.
2. https://www.accessdata.fda.gov/drugsatfda_docs/label/2014/021180Orig1s046lbl.pdf.

If you forgot to remove the patch before immersing and are still at the *mikveh,* or if you returned home but have not yet had relations, you are required to immerse again, with a *berakhah.* If you discovered the patch only the next day, there is no need to immerse again.

Halakhic Expansion

From the verse, "And he shall bathe his flesh in water" (Vayikra 14:9), we learn that there can be no barrier between one's body and the water during immersion. The Gemara[3] explains that something that covers most of the body and which one takes care ("*makpid*") to remove constitutes a barrier (*ḥatzitzah*) on the *deOrayta* level, by virtue of a tradition handed to Moshe at Sinai, *halakhah l'Moshe mi-Sinai.* Additionally, Ḥazal established that anything regarding which a person is *makpid,* even if it covers less than half of the body, constitutes a *ḥatzitzah;* and something that covers most of the body, even if one is not particular about it, is likewise considered a *ḥatzitzah.*[4] *Shulḥan Arukh* rules accordingly.[5] Furthermore, Rema writes that, *lekhatḥilah,* a woman should take care that there is no barrier at all on her body, even something that only covers a small part of the body and regarding which she would not ordinarily be bothered.[6]

It would seem that for the purposes of *ḥatzitzah,* the feeling of the woman herself determines *hakpadah*: If she does not want something on her body and therefore wishes to remove it, it constitutes a *ḥatzitzah.*[7] However, even if she is not troubled by it – so long as most women would be troubled by it, it constitutes a *ḥatzitzah* for her too.[8] With regard to a medical dressing, the Mishnah states explicitly: "The following constitute a *ḥatzitzah* for humans… congealed pus upon a sore and a dressing on it."[9] *Shulḥan Arukh* rules accordingly.[10] This is despite the fact that the dressing covers only a small portion of the body; but we assume that its presence is troubling, and that the woman wishes it removed. Even if there is no intention of removing it at present, the

---

3. *Sukkah* 6a; *Eruvin* 4b.
4. Ibid.
5. *Yoreh De'ah* 198:1.
6. Ibid., citing *Hagahot Sha'arei Dura.*
7. *Mishneh Torah, Hilkhot Mikva'ot* 1:12.
8. *Yoreh De'ah* 198:1; *Bet Yosef,* s.v. "*u-mah she-katav ve-afilu kol shehu*"; *Baḥ,* based on Rashba.
9. *Mishnah Mikva'ot* 9:1–2.
10. *Yoreh De'ah* 198:10.

woman nevertheless wants it removed once the wound heals, so even now she is considered bothered.[11]

An adhesive bandage on a sore constitutes a *ḥatzitzah,* like a dressing. *Sidrei Taharah* writes that we are stringent about a dressing when it comes to immersion because the woman is *makpid,* whereas people are not *makpid* when it comes to *netilat yadayim* (handwashing).[12] However, a large group of *poskim* distinguished between a medical dressing and "medical *ḥatzitzot*" such as casts or temporary fillings that are intended to remain on the body for several weeks, and whose premature removal can entail pain or risk of limb.[13] Thus, the Sanzer Rav, in *Responsa Divrei Ḥayim,*[14] rejected the view of *Sidrei Taharah* and permitted a woman to immerse with a dressing that is always on the wound and whose removal entails the intense pain – and perhaps danger – of ripping off skin and hair. *Ketav Sofer*[15] likewise rejects the view of *Sidrei Taharah*[16] and considers ruling leniently in the case of a woman who has difficulty removing a bandage placed on her forehead and temples (apparently a treatment for migraines). He offers several reasons for the leniency: First, a woman is not considered *makpid* regarding something that is painful to remove, as she would rather leave the bandage in place than tear off skin. Moreover, a woman is not *makpid* regarding something needed for healing. A dressing is considered a *ḥatzitzah* only because one occasionally opens it to check the condition of the wound, unlike a bandage that is supposed to remain on the woman's head for several months. On the contrary, the woman takes care that the bandage remains on her body. Nevertheless, *Ketav Sofer* refrained from ruling leniently in practice, and even found written in *Responsa Teshuvah Me-Ahavah* that the law governing a dressing remains in force, and a bandage that remains in place for several months and cannot be removed without tearing the skin constitutes a *ḥatzitzah.*[17] *Tzitz Eliezer* permits a woman to immerse with a cast, citing the

---

11. *Responsa Tzemaḥ Tzedek (Lubavitch), Yoreh De'ah* 158:5. See also *Sidrei Taharah* 198:24, which notes that *Tur* rules stringently about a poultice when it comes to immersion but leniently when it comes to handwashing.
12. *Shi'urei Taharah, Yoreh De'ah* 198:24.
13. *Ḥokhmat Adam, Sha'ar Beit Ha-Nashim* 119:7; *Responsa Tzitz Eliezer* 4:9; *Responsa Har Tzvi, Yoreh De'ah* 169; *Responsa Yabi'a Omer, Yoreh De'ah* 3:12; *Taharat Ha-Bayit,* 3 *Dinei Ḥatzitzah* 12, p. 61.
14. *Yoreh De'ah* 2:65.
15. Ibid. 91.
16. *Shi'urei Taharah* 198:24.
17. *Responsa Ketav Sofer, Yoreh De'ah* 91.

aforementioned *Divrei Ḥayim.*[18] He further cites *Responsa Sho'el U-Meshiv,*[19] who allowed a woman to immerse with a temporary filling on the grounds that she wants the filling there and is therefore not *makpid.* R. Ovadiah Yosef wrote that, on the contrary, in such a case she is *makpid* that it remains in place; thus, it is permitted to immerse with a cast or a dressing that is supposed to remain in place for three or four months.[20]

At first glance, a hormonal patch would seem to be akin, in both its shape and its usage, to a band-aid. It is designed to remain on the body for a week, and that is what the woman wishes. However, after this amount of time, she is *makpid* to remove it and replace it. Some maintain that only something that remains on the body for a month or more is considered something that a woman is not *makpid* on,[21] whereas *Ḥelkat Yoav* states that even a week is considered permanent enough that a woman is not *makpid* on it – similar to the case of a permanent knot with respect to the laws of Shabbat.[22]

Nevertheless, it is difficult to include a hormonal patch in this leniency since its removal entails no danger or pain and it remains on the body for only a week, unlike the cases where some *poskim* ruled leniently. Moreover, removing the patch for a short while does not impair its effectiveness. On the other hand, a difference exists between a hormonal patch and a wound dressing in the other direction as well: A person suffers a wound against their will, and the removal of the dressing depends on whether it has healed, not on whether the person wants it there. In contrast, a woman wants the patch and wishes for it to remain in place; and even when she removes it, she immediately replaces it with another. It seems, therefore, that the entire notion of being *makpid* is questionable when it comes to a hormonal patch. Therefore, if the woman had relations with her husband, we do not rule stringently that she must immerse again, so as not to cast aspersions on the relations.[23]

---

18. *Tzitz Eliezer* 4:9; *Responsa Divrei Ḥayim, Yoreh De'ah* 2:65.
19. 2:3:108.
20. Ibid.
21. *Sha'arei Tevilah siman* 34, based on *Bet Yosef, Oraḥ Ḥayim siman* 317 regarding a knot that is considered permanent ("*shel kayama*") according to the Torah. *Badei Ha-Shulḥan* 198:179 rules accordingly. *Responsa Avnei Nezer, Yoreh De'ah* 253 and 262 maintains that something that is in place for half a year is considered nullified.
22. *Ḥelkat Yoav, Yoreh De'ah* 1:30.
23. See *Shakh, Yoreh De'ah* 188:25.

In a case where the woman discovered the patch prior to immersing on Shabbat or Yom Tov, it is not simple to permit its removal if it will pull out hairs. However, if the woman is anguished about not being able to become *tehorah* for her husband, there are grounds to rule leniently and permit its removal.[24]

Editors

24. See *Nishmat Avraham, Yoreh De'ah* 198:4:1, which cites a list of *Aḥaronim* who permit the removal of a bandage on Shabbat if it is causing pain, even if its removal will invariably pull out hairs. In a note in *Shemirat Shabbat Ke-Hilkhatah* (on 35:29), R. Neuwirth writes in the name of R. Shlomo Zalman Auerbach that one who is in pain because of a bandage may remove it on Shabbat, since this is an irregular (*ke-le'aḥar yad*) method of hair removal, it is destructive (*mekalkel*), and even though the hair removal is inevitable, it is unwanted (*pesik reisha de-lo niḥa lei*).

Siman 48

Bedikot with a Contraceptive Ring

Question

I use a vaginal contraceptive ring (NuvaRing). Do I need to remove it to perform a *hefsek taharah* and *bedikot*?

Answer

You must remove the contraceptive ring for the *hefsek taharah,* so that the examination is proper and thorough. During the seven *neki'im,* since the ring is not fixed within the body and can be pushed to the side in order to perform a thorough examination, you may perform *bedikot* without removing it. However, there are some *poskim* who maintain that the ring should be removed *lekhatḥilah* for one *bedikah* on the first day and one on the seventh.

Bedi'avad, if you forgot to remove the ring, or if it is difficult and you are concerned that you will cause a lesion, you may remove it for just one *bedikah* during the seven *neki'im*. You may even rely on the lenient opinions and perform all *bedikot* without removing the ring.

Halakhic Expansion

A NuvaRing is a hormonal contraceptive ring placed in the vagina.[1] As a result, halakhic questions about how to perform the *hefsek taharah* and *bedikot* during the seven *neki'im* are likely to arise.

Bet Yosef[2] stipulates two conditions for the effectiveness of a *bedikah* during the seven *neki'im*. The first is "*bedikat ḥorim u-sedakim*" – an internal self-examination that probes the recesses and folds, for a thorough examination of the entire length and breadth of the vaginal canal. The second condition is that the examination must probe to the depth of penetration, that is, as deep as possible, preferably to the cervix or near there.

These two conditions are based on the Gemara[3], which distinguishes between a *bedikah* and wiping. Accordingly, many *Rishonim* ruled that the *hefsek taharah* as well as the *bedikot* of the seven *neki'im* must be *bedikot ḥorim u-sedakim*;[4] any less thorough examination is considered merely wiping and is insufficient. *Shulḥan Arukh* rules accordingly.[5]

The second condition – that the *bedikah* be deep, "to the depth of penetration" – is cited by some *Rishonim*.[6] *Bet Yosef* addresses the physical difficulty of performing a *bedikah* to that depth and the concern about causing an abrasion; he therefore rules in *Shulḥan Arukh*[7] that it is sufficient to perform a *bedikat ḥorim u-sedakim* for the *hefsek taharah* and for the *bedikah* on the first of the seven *neki'im*. Rema[8] adds that even if she performed the deep *bedikah* on a different day, not the first

1. The ring contains estrogen and progesterone, like the pill. Its advantage over the pill is that it remains in place internally for three weeks running, so there is no concern of forgetting to take the pill. After three weeks, the woman removes the ring, and her period occurs within a few days. About a week after removing the ring, she inserts a new one. Thus, the *hefsek taharah* and the seven *neki'im* generally take place while the ring is in her body. The question of whether a ring constitutes a *ḥatzitzah* during immersion arises as well; see below, n. 16, and *Siman* 49: *Mikveh* Immersion with a Contraceptive Ring.
2. *Yoreh De'ah* 196:6.
3. *Niddah* 12a.
4. Rashba (*Torat Ha-Bayit, bayit* 7, *sha'ar* 5, p. 24b); Rosh (*Niddah* 10:5); and others. However, according to Ra'avad (*Ba'alei Ha-Nefesh, Sha'ar Ha-Sefirah Ve-HaBedikah,* p. 69), a more superficial vaginal examination suffices, even without a *bedikat ḥorim u-sedakim*. The phrase "*ḥorim u-sedakim*" comes from *Niddah* 5a: "Since she is excited about going home [to her husband], she does not insert [the *bedikah* cloth] into the recesses and folds."
5. *Yoreh De'ah* 196:6.
6. *Hagahot Maimoniyot* (*Hilkhot Isurei Bi'ah* 6:4); Rosh (*Niddah* 10:5); Rabbeinu Yeruḥam (*Toldot Adam Ve-Ḥavah, netiv* 26, part 2, p. 221d).
7. *Yoreh De'ah* 196:6.
8. Ibid.

day, the *bedikot* count. He then adds that, *bedi'avad*, "if she did not do so at all, but only performed a good *bedikah* in the *ḥorim* and *sedakim* as deeply as she can, even if it did not reach the depth "to where the attendant threshes," it suffices for her."

The deep *bedikah* can be performed even when a contraceptive ring is present, because the ring is not fixed in one place.[9] However, it is necessary to clarify whether it impairs the *bedikat ḥorim u-sedakim*; perhaps it impedes access to some parts of the vaginal canal.

The *Aḥaronim* address questions pertaining to the pessary,[10] a vaginal ring which is inserted to support the uterus in cases of uterine prolapse. Some *poskim* require its removal during *bedikot*, but many *poskim* rule leniently and write that one should remove it *lekhatḥilah*, but if this is difficult or impossible without medical assistance, a *bedikah*, including the insertion of a *mokh daḥuk* during the *hefsek taharah*, suffices.[11] *Arukh Ha-Shulḥan* rules accordingly,[12] adding that even though she cannot examine the location of the ring itself, there is no concern that the ring impedes the flow of blood, as the ring is smooth and leaves room for the discharge of blood.

Other *Aḥaronim* ruled even more leniently, stating that the ring does not impair the effectiveness of the *hefsek taharah* or *bedikot* at all, as it remains in the woman's body for more than a week and is thus considered part of the body.[13]

However, there are two differences between a contraceptive ring and the pessary discussed by the *Aḥaronim*: First, it can easily be removed by a woman herself, without medical assistance. Second, a pessary is inflexible and fixed in place, whereas the contraceptive ring is thin, flexible, and not fixed in place.

---

9. Another concern was raised by R. Udi Ratt on the Puah Institute website: Perhaps a drop of blood will remain on the ring and exit the woman's body only later, thus disqualifying the *neki'im* already counted. See https://puah.org.il/shut/בדיקות שבעה-נקיים-תוך-שימוש-בנוברינג/.
10. This refers not to a ring inserted into the uterus, but to a ring inserted into the vagina or the external os of the cervix to support the uterus from the outside. See above, *Siman* 20: *Bedikot* with Uterine Prolapse.
11. *Nishmat Avraham, Yoreh De'ah* 196:4, summarizes the views of the *Aḥaronim* on this subject. He cites *Responsa Zikhron Yosef* as stating that the *mokh daḥuk* should be left in place not only during the *hefsek taharah* but for an additional day as well. However, the language of the responsum indicates that this is not necessary; the matter requires further study.
12. *Yoreh De'ah* 196:29.
13. *Ḥeshev Ha-Efod* 2:118; R. Neuwirth and R. Shlomo Zalman Auerbach rule likewise according to *Nishmat Avraham* (loc. cit.).

In light of the first difference, and to enable good, thorough *bedikot,* some contemporary *poskim*[14] write that the contraceptive ring should be removed for the *hefsek taharah,* for one *bedikah* on the first of the seven *neki'im,* and for one *bedikah* on the seventh clean day.[15]

In contrast, in light of the contraceptive ring thinness and flexibility, and based on *Arukh Ha-Shulḥan,* Rav Nachum Rabinovitch[16] writes that there are better grounds for leniency in the case of a contraceptive ring than in the case of a pessary, and that it is not necessary to remove it at all – not for the *hefsek taharah* and not for the *bedikot* of the seven *neki'im* – because there is no concern that it blocks the flow of blood. On the contrary, if she would remove and re-insert it many times, she could injure herself and cause bleeding that would make it difficult for her to become *tehorah.*[17]

In sum, since a *hefsek taharah* requires a more thorough examination, it seems one should not be lenient, and the contraceptive ring should be removed before the *bedikah.* During the seven *neki'im,* one should *lekhatḥilah* remove the ring for one *bedikah* on the first day and one on the seventh. *Bedi'avad,* or if this causes the woman pain and difficulty, it is sufficient to remove it for one *bedikah* during the *neki'im,* or to rely on the lenient views and not remove it at all.

S.K.

---

14. R. Henkin in the Nishmat website: https://www.yoatzot.org/questions-and-answers/1072/; R. Udi Ratt on the Puah Institute website: https://puah.org.il/shut/בדיקות-שבעה-נקיים-תוך-שימוש-בנוברינג/.
15. During the *hefsek taharah,* it should be removed not only to enable a thorough *bedikah* but also to rinse blood off of it. It should therefore be rinsed before re-insertion into the body. According to the product instructions, the NuvaRing may be removed for up to three hours during the 21 days that it remains in the body, and one may rinse it without affecting its effectiveness. Therefore, removing it for a little while two to four times during the seven *neki'im* will not impair its effectiveness. Since the vagina is not sterile, there is no concern that its removal will cause infection, though it is, of course, advisable to keep one's hands clean and to put the ring down in a clean place.
16. *Responsa Si'aḥ Naḥum,* pp. 205–7.
17. He likewise writes that a NuvaRing does not constitute a *ḥatzitzah* to immersion. Other rabbis, including R. Henkin, ruled that *lekhatḥilah* one should remove it for immersion, though one may be lenient *bedi'avad.* According to R. Warhaftig, the NuvaRing is considered absorbed ("*balu'a*") into the body and does not constitute a *ḥatzitzah.*

Siman 49

Immersion with a Contraceptive Ring

Question

I use a NuvaRing. I forgot to remove it last night when I immersed in the *mikveh*. Must I immerse again?

Answer

A contraceptive ring is placed inside the vaginal canal, which is considered a "recessed place" ("*bet ha-setarim*"). Ideally you should remove any *ḥatzitzah* before immersing, even those in a *bet ha-setarim*, and there are even some *ḥatzitzot* in a *bet ha-setarim* that require re-immersion, even *bedi'avad*. However, if you did not remove the contraceptive ring before immersing, you need not immerse again, since the ring is not fixed in place and because it is located so deep within the vaginal canal that some *poskim* consider it to be absorbed as part of the body and not as a *bet ha-setarim*.

Halakhic Expansion

A NuvaRing is a ring that a woman places in the depth the vagina. It releases hormones for three consecutive weeks. It may be removed for up to three hours without adversely affecting its contraceptive effectiveness.[1] Since it has to be removed before immersing, it is advisable to remove it just before

1. See above, *Siman* 48: *Bedikot* with a Contraceptive Ring.

immersion and to re-insert it right after immersion, to ensure that it retains its effectiveness.[2]

Several aspects of the NuvaRing must be addressed: (1) its location within the body; (2) that it is not fixed in place; (3) whether one is *makpid* about it.

Location within the Body

The Mishnah states: "A recessed place (*bet ha-setarim*) or a folded place (*bet ha-kematim*) – it is not necessary for water to reach them."[3] The Gemara says: "'He shall bathe all of his flesh in water' – just as his flesh refers to the [body's] exterior, so too, anything on the [body's] exterior."[4] *Ḥakhamim* derive from here that only the exterior of the body requires immersion. Interior places like inside the mouth, the inside of the nose, and the inside of the vagina are considered recessed places and do not require immersion. The Gemara questions this assertion from an incident involving the maidservant of R. Yehudah Ha-Nasi, who immersed so that she could handle *tahor* food but then found a piece of bone stuck between her teeth: R. Yehudah Ha-Nasi required her to immerse again. The Gemara resolves this by saying that it is indeed not necessary for water to penetrate a *bet ha-setarim* in practice, but water must be able to penetrate.[5] This is derived from a teaching of R. Zeira: "For anything that can be blended, blending is not essential; for anything that cannot be blended, blending is essential."[6] Therefore, Rava says, "A person should always teach in his home that a woman should rinse her *bet ha-kematim* in water.... Granted, we do not require water to penetrate, but we require that the place be capable of penetration by water."[7]

---

2. There is no need to examine the ring when removing it, and one may rinse it in a stream of warm water without looking at it. However, if the woman looked and found a bloody discharge on the NuvaRing, it has the standing of an internal examination that confers *niddah* status. See below, *Siman* 59: A Spot on a Tampon, and *Siman* 60: Finding Blood on a Diaphragm.
3. Mishnah *Mikva'ot* 8:5.
4. *Kiddushin* 25a.
5. Ibid. 25a; *Niddah* 66b.
6. A meal offering (*korban minḥah*) requires a mixture of oil and flour. The Gemara (*Menaḥot* 18b) asks about a *minḥah* that has the right quantity for mixing ("*bilah*" – blending) but was not actually mixed. R. Zeira answers that any *korban minḥah* that can be properly blended is acceptable, *bedi'avad*, even if it was not blended. Rava applies this to the present case as well: Even though water need not penetrate the body's recessed places or folded places, these places must be capable of penetration by water, i.e., there can be no *ḥatzitzah* in them.
7. *Niddah* 66b.

Tosafot maintain that the requirement for a *bet ha-setarim* to be permeable by water is *deOrayta*,[8] whereas Ramban, Rashba, and Ritva maintain that the requirement is of rabbinic provenance.[9] R. Shlomo Levy[10] notes that the *poskim* relied on the more lenient view of Ritva if there was an added uncertainty. For example, Maharsham was asked about a woman who placed a linen *mokh* in the vagina canal and forgot to remove it before immersing.[11] Maharsham did not require her to immerse again, for two reasons: First, the water can penetrate the linen, so it is not a *ḥatzitzah*. Second, even if one were to claim that it is uncertain whether the water would penetrate, we can add the view of Ritva that a *ḥatzitzah* in a *bet ha-setarim* disqualifies immersion only at the rabbinic level.[12]

However, we must consider whether the location of the NuvaRing is even considered a *bet ha-setarim*;[13] alternatively, the location might be considered part of the body's interior ("*balu'a*"), where a *ḥatzitzah* does not disqualify an immersion. At first glance, the NuvaRing is comparable to a "pessary," a ring that prevents uterine prolapse,[14] which *Aḥaronim* discuss: *Noda Bi-Yehudah*, in context of a discussion of the pessary, writes that the laws of *ḥatzitzah* do not apply to internal areas of the body, and such areas need not even be capable of penetration by water.[15] An area is "*balu'a*" if it is so deep within the body

---

8. *Tosafot*, *Kiddushin* 25a, s.v. "*kol*."
9. *Ḥiddushim* of Ramban, Rashba, and Ritva, respectively, on *Kiddushin* 25a.
10. *Sha'arei Orah*, p. 165.
11. *Responsa Maharsham* 1:199; cited in *Sha'arei Orah*, p. 165.
12. Therefore, even though the woman's *niddah* status is established ("*itḥazek issura*"), "it is a double *deRabanan* concerning a small portion [of the body] about which one is *makpid*."
13. If the location of the NuvaRing is deemed a *bet ha-setarim*, then it seems that it would constitute a *ḥatzitzah* even *bedi'avad*. See *Yoreh De'ah* 198:24: "She must clean her teeth so that there is no *ḥatzitzah* in them, for if she immersed and found that something had adhered, her immersion did not count."
14. On one hand, the NuvaRing is not fixed in place like the pessary, but it is placed deep within the vaginal canal, which is how *Noda Bi-Yehudah* describes the location of the pessary. Additionally, a woman cannot remove a pessary by herself; it must be removed by a doctor.
15. *Responsa Noda Bi-Yehuda Kamma*, *Yoreh De'ah* 1:64, and 2:135. This is cited in *Pitḥei Teshuvah*, *Yoreh De'ah* 198:16. *Responsa Har Tzvi*, *Yoreh De'ah siman* 153 rules similarly. *Responsa Lev David siman* 41 challenges *Noda Bi-Yehudah*'s claim that the pessary's location is considered an internal part of the body, arguing that when a woman stands up while immersing, the pessary descends, so it cannot be considered absorbed inside the body, and thus constitutes a *ḥatzitzah*. He continues, however, and says that a woman is not *makpid* about a pessary, since she does not determine when it can be removed for cleaning. Rather, she is instructed by a doctor. However, in the case of the NuvaRing, a woman does not need the physician's assistance or directive, and so, according to *Lev David*, she would be considered *makpid*, and the NuvaRing therefore constitutes a *ḥatzitzah*.

that it is beyond the depth of penetration during coitus.[16] In contrast, *Elef Ha-Magen* cites R. Menaḥem Azariah ("Rema") of Fano as saying that any area that is sometimes exposed, such as during a *bedikat ḥorim u-sedakim*, is considered a *bet ha-setarim* and not *balu'a*,[17] and it therefore must be capable of penetration by water. *Arukh Ha-Shulḥan* writes that we accept the ruling of *Noda Bi-Yehudah* in the case of a ring that is hard, and even dangerous, to remove before immersing, and which is placed deep inside the vagina, beyond where the penis penetrates during marital relations. He concludes: "This is how we rule in practice."[18]

In light of this, *lekhatḥilah* the NuvaRing should be removed before immersing.[19] *Bedi'avad*, however, since the woman in question has already slept with her husband, she need not immerse again.

Loose within the Body

Another reason to be lenient in the case of a NuvaRing is that it is not fixed in place and sits loosely within the body.[20] This follows from *Zikhron Yosef*'s discussion of *ḥatzitzah* in a *bet ha-setarim*[21] and from *Responsa Si'aḥ Naḥum*, which states that the ring does not constitute a *ḥatzitzah* because it does not adhere to any specific place in the vaginal canal and is moistened by natural discharges from the area.[22]

16. Consequently, this ruling applies to an IUD, which has a string that dangles into the vaginal canal just beyond the cervix: The area is considered *balu'a*, and it need not be capable of penetration by water. The NuvaRing, however, is not as deep, and there are couples who report that they can feel the ring during marital relations – similar to what *Lev David* claims about a pessary.
17. *Responsa Elef Ha-Magen* 2:26. *Bet ha-kematim* is visible from the exterior, so it, too, must be capable of penetration by water. The author of *Elef Ha-Magen* maintains, like *Noda Bi-Yehudah*, that only until the area of "between the teeth" – that is, until the cervix or just outside it – is considered *bet ha-setarim*.
18. *Arukh Ha-Shulḥan, Yoreh De'ah* 198:55. R. Warhaftig rules accordingly, even *lekhatḥilah*. In a conversation with me, he added that since the NuvaRing is hidden from the eye, it is considered *balu'a* and does not constitute a *ḥatzitzah*.
19. Since, according to most contemporary views, the vaginal area is considered a *bet ha-setarim*. See *Darkhei Taharah*, p. 165; *Sha'arei Orah*, p. 165; *Taharat Ha-Bayit* 3, *Dinei Ḥatzitzah* 1, p. 10, 35, p. 144, 38, p. 156. R. Henkin also maintains that the area where the NuvaRing is placed should *lekhatḥilah* be considered a *bet ha-setarim*, as *balu'a* refers only to places that a person cannot reach.
20. Something that is loose does not constitute a *ḥatzitzah*. See *Shulḥan Arukh, Yoreh De'ah* 198:28.
21. *Responsa Zikhron Yosef, Yoreh De'ah* 10.
22. *Responsa Si'aḥ Naḥum siman* 61, p. 207. He adds that even one who is stringent and *lekhatḥilah* requires removal of the ring prior to immersion, if the woman forgot to remove it, the immersion still counts.

By the same token, *Darkhei Teshuvah* cites Rav Yoel Deutsch's ruling[23] that a woman who immersed without removing a *mokh* drenched with olive oil, which she had placed inside her vagina on a doctor's orders,[24] need not immerse again if she has already had relations with her husband. There are two reasons for this: (1) perhaps the *mokh* was inserted deeply enough that it is *balu'a,* in accordance with *Noda Bi-Yehudah;*[25] (2) perhaps the water can pass through the *mokh,* which is loose and not fixed in place.[26]

Being *Makpid*[27]

A third reason for leniency is that the NuvaRing is removed, according to medical instructions, only after three weeks, thus subjecting it to the dispute among *poskim* about something that covers a small part of the body and about which one is not *makpid.* Some maintain that one remains *makpid,* and the substance constitutes a *ḥatzitzah,* unless it will be on the body for more than thirty days.[28] Accordingly, the NuvaRing would be considered a *ḥatzitzah.* Others maintain that if it will be on the body for more than a week, one is no longer *makpid;* according to them, a NuvaRing would not be considered a *ḥatzitzah.*[29]

Summary

1. According to Ritva and other *Rishonim,* the law that a *bet ha-setarim* must be capable of penetration by water is *deRabanan.*

23. *Darkhei Teshuvah* 198:87.
24. *Responsa Yad Yosef siman* 89.
25. *Noda Bi-Yehudah,* loc. cit.
26. This is also implied by *Ḥazon Ish, Hilkhot Niddah siman* 94, regarding a cotton swab in the ear during immersion: Even though the water is not penetrating at present, it is called "capable" of being penetrated if it will seep through later.
27. For an extended discussion of this, see above, *Siman* 47: *Mikveh* Immersion with a Hormonal Patch.
28. *Sha'arei Tevilah siman* 34 (based on *Bet Yosef, Oraḥ Ḥayim* 317, which discusses a knot that is considered permanent ("*shel kayama*") according to the Torah. *Badei Ha-Shulḥan* 198:179 rules accordingly. However, *Badei Ha-Shulḥan* 198:385 writes that one should not be lenient about a *ḥatzitzah* in a *bet ha-setarim,* like a temporary filling, if it will be in place for less than 30 days.
29. *Ḥelkat Yoav, Yoreh De'ah* 1:30, compares the laws governing the prohibition of tying a knot on Shabbat with the status of a *ḥatzitzah* that will remain on the body for a long time: One violates the Torah prohibition only for tying a permanent knot ("*kesher shel kayama*"). *Mi-deRabanan,* a knot that will remain tied for a week is considered permanent. In light of this, *Ḥelkat Yoav* asserts that a person who intends to leave something that constitutes a *ḥatzitzah* at the rabbinic level on her body for more than a week is not considered *makpid,* and it therefore is not considered a *ḥatzitzah* that would disqualify her immersion.

2. The NuvaRing is inserted deeply enough that it might be considered *balu'a*.
3. It is not fixed in place, and it does not prevent water from passing it.
4. The NuvaRing can be considered part of the body given the amount of time that it remains in the body.

Therefore, in a case where a woman forgot to remove it, the immersion is still valid.

S.K.

Siman 50

Insertion of an IUD during the Seven Neki'im

Question

I am 43 years old and on the pill. I recently decided to switch to an IUD. Will inserting the IUD render me *niddah*? When is the best time to insert it, and what should I do if the doctor insists on inserting it during the seven *neki'im*?

Answer

The insertion of an IUD will not render you *niddah*, but it is common to experience bleeding after the insertion. If inserted during the seven *neki'im*, this can make becoming *tehorah* challenging for an extended period of time. Staining is common during the first months with a copper IUD, and even more so with a hormonal IUD. Sometimes the staining appears not immediately, but only a few days after the insertion of the hormonal IUD, as the body begins responding to the hormones. Therefore, halakhically, the best time to insert the IUD is when you are *tehorah*. However, doctors generally prefer to perform the procedure during the days immediately following menstruation, during the seven *neki'im*, because then it is certain that the woman is not pregnant, and because then the cervical os ("mouth") is more open and softer, making it easier to insert the device. If your physician agrees, we strongly advise asking her to insert the IUD immediately following *tevilah*, or alternately on the last of the seven *neki'im*, after the *bedikah* of the seventh day. If the procedure is nevertheless performed during the seven *neki'im*, it should be done after the *hefsek taharah* and the *bedikah* of the first day.

After insertion of the IUD, you are likely to experience bleeding for a day or two, as a result of the cervix having been held by forceps, and thus abraded, during the procedure. If you experience bleeding during the first 24 hours, and even if the bleeding lasts for two days, you may attribute it to the cervical abrasion, and this bleeding does not render you *niddah* even if it is found on a *bedikah* cloth. However, the cervical abrasion should heal after a day, so if you *begin* staining more than a day after the insertion of the IUD, or if the bleeding begins right after the insertion but lasts longer than two days, it can no longer be attributed to the cervical abrasion.

If the IUD was inserted during the seven *neki'im*, assuming that you performed the *hefsek taharah* and the *bedikah* of the first day, you may reduce the number of *bedikot* for the remainder of the seven days and wear either colored underwear or a panty liner. However, you must perform a *bedikah* at least on the seventh day so that you may immerse.

In the event that the IUD was inserted during the seven *neki'im*, any blood found during a *bedikah* after the aforementioned recovery time, unless there is solid evidence that it comes from the abrasion, will require you to perform a new *hefsek taharah* and count the seven *neki'im* from the beginning.

Halakhic Expansion

There are three parts to this question:

1. Does the insertion of the IUD render a woman *niddah*?
2. What is the status of bleeding that occurs following the procedure?
3. How should the woman conduct herself if the IUD was inserted during the seven *neki'im*?

The Insertion Procedure

An IUD is a small object made of copper or plastic that is inserted into the uterus and prevents pregnancy. We must consider whether the insertion procedure is considered "the opening of the uterus" ("*petiḥat ha-kever*"), and if so, whether it renders a woman *niddah* even if she does not experience bleeding.

The Gemara brings a disagreement about whether there can be *petiḥat ha-kever* without bleeding, that is, whether the cervical dilation renders a woman *niddah*, even if bleeding was not found.[1] According to Rambam,[2] there can

1. *Niddah* 21a-b.
2. *Mishneh Torah, Hilkhot Isurei Bi'ah* 5:13.

be *petiḥat ha-kever* without bleeding, but Ra'avad,[3] Ramban,[4] Rosh,[5] and Rashba[6] all rule that there cannot be *petiḥat ha-kever* without bleeding, and *Shulḥan Arukh* rules thus.[7] Following this dissension among *Rishonim*, the *Aḥaronim* differ as to whether the insertion of something into the uterus from the outside causes *petiḥat ha-kever*, or whether only something that emerges from inside the uterus can cause *petiḥat ha-kever*. *Noda Bi-Yehuda*[8] rules that a woman becomes *niddah* whether the uterus opens for something to be expelled or it opens by means of an insertion from the outside. *Igrot Moshe*[9] likewise rules that an insertion from the outside can cause *petiḥat ha-kever* and render a woman *niddah* even if there is no bleeding.

The *poskim* infer from the Gemara and *Shulḥan Arukh* that the law of *petiḥat ha-kever* applies only if the opening is wider than a "tube" ("*shefoferet*"). *Shakh*[10] defines this size as "the slightest of the slight." *Igrot Moshe*[11] states that the width in question is 19 mm (¾ of an inch).[12] To insert the IUD, an instrument with a diameter of no more than 4mm (0.16 of an inch) is used, and the IUD itself is

3. Glosses on *Mishneh Torah ad loc.*; *Ba'alei Ha-Nefesh, Sha'ar Ha-Perishah siman* 1.
4. *Hilkhot Niddah* 3:6.
5. *Niddah* 3:1.
6. *Torat Ha-Bayit He-Arokh, bayit* 7, *sha'ar* 6 (p. 26b).
7. *Yoreh De'ah* 188:3 and Rema, *Yoreh De'ah* 194:2.
8. *Yoreh De'ah* 2:120 at the end.
9. Ibid. 1:83; also *Responsa Har Tzvi, Yoreh De'ah siman* 152. For the lenient views regarding *petiḥat ha-kever* from the outside, such as from a doctor's examination, see *Responsa Tzitz Eliezer* 10:25:11; *Ḥazon Ish, Yoreh De'ah* 83:2. See also: *Taharat Ha-Bayit*, 2:11:7, p. 60, who understands this matter as a *sfek sfeika* (double uncertainty).
10. *Yoreh De'ah* 188:12.
11. Ibid. 1:89. R. Feinstein derives from the laws of *tum'ah* that the size of an opening that causes *tum'ah* is the size of the knob at the end of a knitting needle. According to him, this is less than the thickness of the little finger. In *Igrot Moshe, Oraḥ Ḥayim* 3:100, he defines this as ¾ of an inch (19 mm). In contrast to what he says about the minimum opening that can be considered *petiḥat ha-kever*, elsewhere (*Even Ha-Ezer* 3:21) he writes that a woman is rendered *niddah* by the insertion of an IUD. It seems that R. Feinstein was familiar with a reality in which the opening of the cervix caused by insertion of an IUD was greater than 19 mm.
12. There are other views about the minimum opening that can be considered *petiḥat ha-kever*. See *Responsa Teshuvah Me-Ahavah* 1:116, which states that the tube ("*shefoferet*") in question is a bit thicker than straw. He rules that if only a discharge or something very slight comes out, it is not considered *petiḥat ha-kever*. *Badei Ha-Shulḥan* (194:31) gives 15mm (0.6 of an inch) as the minimum size. In contrast, *Mekor Ḥayim Ve-Tiferet Tzvi* (188:9) defines the minimum size as the width of the thumb (approx. 25 mm /1 inch). R. Henkin and R. Warhaftig rule in accordance with *Igrot Moshe* that one need not be concerned about *petiḥat ha-kever* unless the opening is 19 mm (¾ of an inch) or more.

very slight, folded within the instrument. Therefore, according to the position that *petiḥat ha-kever* is only when there is an opening of 19 mm (¾ of an inch) or more, there is no presumption that the insertion causes *petiḥat ha-kever*. It should be noted that some *poskim* disagree and rule that inserting the IUD constitutes *petiḥat ha-kever*, and the procedure renders the woman *niddah*.[13]

Bleeding After the Procedure

As there is usually bleeding after the insertion of the IUD, we need to ascertain whether it is considered *dam niddah* or *dam makkah*. The possibility of attributing blood to a wound, *teliyah be-makkah* is discussed in the Gemara (*Niddah* 16a). Ramban[14] maintains that bleeding cannot be attributed to an abrasion unless we are proficient in distinguishing *niddah* blood from *dam makkah*. In contrast, Rambam,[15] Rosh,[16] and Rashba[17] write that one may attribute the bleeding to a known *makkah*.

Shulḥan Arukh[18] rules that we may attribute bleeding to a *makkah* if there is one in that place.[19] Rema[20] writes that a woman who does not have a *veset kavu'a* and finds blood at a time when she is not anticipating her *veset* must be certain that the *makkah* bleeds in order to attribute the bleeding to it. Regarding Rema's position, *Shakh*[21] maintains that one may attribute bleeding to a *makkah* only when the *makkah* is known to be bleeding, whereas *Taz*[22] maintains that as long as she knows that a *makkah* such as this can bleed, we may attribute the bleeding to it.[23]

13. This is the view of *Ḥut Ha-Shani* (*Niddah* 183:3:2, p. 28, and 188:10:4, p. 104). *Shi'urei Shevet Ha-Levi* (188:3:4, p. 100) rules stringently that any physical examination that probes inside the uterus itself makes the woman *teme'ah*.
14. *Hilkhot Niddah* 3:7; cited by Rashba in *Torat Ha-Bayit, bayit* 7, *sha'ar* 4, p. 23.
15. *Mishneh Torah, Hilkhot Isurei Bi'ah* 8:14 and 9:22.
16. *Niddah* 10:3, s.v. "*Gam ha-Ramban*."
17. *Torat Ha-Bayit, bayit* 7, *sha'ar* 4, p. 23.
18. *Yoreh De'ah* 187:5.
19. See *Shakh* 187:17, which cites *Baḥ*'s view that "that place" is the uterus itself. This is also the ruling in *Sidrei Taharah* 187:1.
20. *Yoreh De'ah* 187:5.
21. Ibid. 187:24.
22. Ibid. 187:10.
23. See also *Badei Ha-Shulḥan* 187:97, which states that it is enough to know that this type of *makkah* normally causes bleeding among other women. See also: *Responsa Noda Bi-Yehuda* (*Yoreh De'ah* 1:47), which states that according to *Taz*, the view of Rema applies only to a case of *ro'ah meḥamat tashmish* but not to all *makkot*.

Noda Bi-Yehudah[24] understands Rema as maintaining that one may rely on a double uncertainty (*sfek sfeika*): perhaps the bleeding is not uterine, and even if it is uterine, perhaps it is caused by a *makkah*. We may therefore be lenient and attribute bleeding to a *makkah* even during the *yemei libun*, and even when the bleeding is accompanied by a *hargashah*.[25]

Contemporary *poskim* disagree about attribution to a *makkah* when the bleeding is caused by an IUD. *Shi'urei Shevet Ha-Levi*[26] rules that "one should be stringent even if it is possible that the ring caused internal irritation; only when it is clear that she really has a bleeding *petza* internally can we be lenient provided she is not anticipating her *veset*, subject to a *she'elat ḥakham*." On the other hand, *Taharat Ha-Bayit*[27] states: "If a woman has a uterine contraceptive ring and finds blood on a *bedikah* cloth at a time when she is not anticipating her *veset*, and the physician says that the device caused the bleeding, it seems that there are grounds to be lenient, because when she is not anticipating her *veset* she is like a *mesuleket damim* ... so we attribute it to the *makkah*. ...".

According to R. Yaakov Warhaftig, we rule leniently for the first 24 hours following the insertion of the IUD, and likewise if the bleeding continues for an additional day, since according to doctors the procedure is likely to abrade the cervix and cause bleeding. However, if the bleeding continues beyond those additional 24 hours,[28] or if the bleeding begins only after 24 hours have elapsed following the procedure, the bleeding may not be attributed to abrasion of the cervix, as this abrasion should have already healed, and it is possible that the IUD itself causes some women to bleed hormonally. When the bleeding is uterine and we do not know whether it is caused

---

24. Responsa Noda Bi-Yehuda, *Yoreh De'ah* 1:41:5.
25. In contrast, *Ḥavat Da'at* (187:8) understands Rema as saying that one may rely on the *sfek sfeika* only if the bleeding renders a woman *niddah mi-deRabanan* – that is, it is not accompanied by a *hargashah*. However, bleeding that renders a woman *niddah mi-de'Orayta*, or during the *yemei libun*, when she does not have a presumption of *taharah*, we may not attribute the bleeding to a *makkah* unless the woman knows with certainty that the *makkah* bleeds.
26. 187:5 (at the end), p. 76.
27. *Taharat Ha-Bayit* 1:5:10, p. 253. R. Ovadiah Yosef does not specifically address bleeding that follows the insertion of an IUD; certainly, then, based on his ruling one may be lenient after the insertion. See also: *Ḥut Ha-Shani* 183:3, n. 2.
28. After consultation with gynecologists, we note that the wound usually heals within 24 hours. However, this is not a verified finding, and some are even more lenient, allowing the attribution of bleeding to an abrasion caused by the insertion of the IUD for an entire week; see R. Yehudah Paris, "Intrauterine Devices and Uterine Imaging," *Teḥumin* 15, p. 343 [Hebrew].

by hormonal activity or a *makkah* inside the uterus, it cannot be attributed to a *makkah* on the interior wall of the uterus.[29]

It is therefore recommended for a woman to wear colored underwear or a panty liner for several days.[30] It should be noted that staining due to the insertion of a Mirena IUD will sometimes begin several days after its insertion, as the body begins reacting to the progesterone it releases.

Inserting the IUD during the Seven *Neki'im*

When the IUD is inserted during the seven *neki'im*, bleeding can, as noted, be attributed to a *makkah* for 24 hours after the insertion procedure.[31] It is better to perform the insertion after the first three of the *neki'im*,[32] and at the very least, after a clean

29. The *poskim* disagree about when intrauterine bleeding can be considered a wound. See R. Eliezer Ben-Porat and Prof. Pesaḥ Kleiman, "The Definition of a *Makkah* for the Purposes of Attribution of Bleeding," *Assia* 83–84 (5768), pp. 141–49. R. Shlomo Zalman Auerbach (quoted in *Nishmat Avraham, siman* 187, p. 150) writes: "Even though the *makkah* discharges blood from the same vessels that rupture during menstruation, *dam niddah* is only blood that exits on its own, in the normal, natural way." R. Mordechai Halperin ("Bleeding due to an Intrauterine Device," *Assia* 63–64 [5759], pp. 138–43 [Hebrew]) concludes based on this that when bleeding occurs around the time when the onset of menstruation is expected, the woman must be deemed *niddah*, whereas bleeding that occurs when menstruation is not expected is not "in the normal, natural way," and it therefore can be attributed to a wound caused by the IUD. Ḥazon Ish (in a letter to *Ha-Pardes*, quoted in the aforementioned article, "The Definition of a *Makkah*") explains that there are three types of bleeding: (1) Residual blood that flows from the body, like waste blood that must be removed from the body lest it poison the lifeblood; this is the basic blood of menstruation; (2) blood that is discharged when menstruation is not expected due to some trauma, such as the pushing or striking of the uterus, which causes the flow of blood (similar to the bleeding that occurs during childbirth or miscarriage); (3) bleeding caused by an abrasion on the surface of the uterus, which is similar to the bleeding of a wound anywhere else on the body. The first two types of bleeding render a woman *niddah*, but the third is *tahor*. Based on the position of Ḥazon Ish, the aforementioned authors concluded that bleeding that occurs when inserting or removing an IUD is considered like bleeding due to injury and not like the natural bleeding of the uterine lining. In contrast, most *poskim* do not attribute bleeding to a *makkah* when it is not certain that there is a *makkah* inside the uterus. For a comprehensive discussion, see *Nishmat Avraham* 188:2.
30. See above, *Siman* 4: Spotting and Bleeding during Pregnancy.
31. As R. Ovadiah Yosef rules (*Taharat Ha-Bayit*, 1:5:7, p. 241) with regard to a *makkah* during the seven *neki'im*. See also the article "Bleeding due to an Intrauterine Device" (cited in n. 29 above).
32. According to Rema (*Yoreh De'ah* 196:10), the first three of the seven *neki'im* must be completely clean. Therefore, "we are not lenient to attribute bleeding to a *makkah* during the first three days, unless it is known that it discharges blood." See also *Pitḥei Teshuvah* (*ad loc.* 14) and *Igrot Moshe, Yoreh De'ah* 1:83.

bedikah on the first day.[33] R. Yehuda Henkin recommends, *lekhatḥilah,* inserting a Mirena IUD only after immersion, and not during the seven *neki'im.*

During the seven *neki'im,* the number of *bedikot* may be reduced, but the woman must still perform the *bedikot* of the first and seventh days. If the *ketamim* continue during the seven *neki'im,* and there is a serious concern that the *bedikah* of the seventh day may ruin the count and render the woman *niddah* for a prolonged period,[34] an eminent halakhic authority may consider exempting her from the *bedikah* of the seventh day in a situation of *she'at hadeḥak gadol,* very great need.[35] If the IUD was inserted on the sixth day of the seven *neki'im,* and there is bleeding on the next day, it can be attributed to the cervical abrasion, but the woman must then perform another *bedikah* so that she obtains a clean *bedikah* on the seventh day.[36] As stated, she may also wear colored underwear or a panty liner.

M.R.

---

33. Similarly, if the procedure takes place on a day that she is *tehorah,* it should not be performed on the thirtieth day or one of the other *onot ha-perishah,* in accordance with Rema's ruling (*Yoreh De'ah* 187:5): "At the expected time of her *veset,* or on the thirtieth day, she may not attribute [bleeding] to a *makkah,* for otherwise she would never become *teme'ah.*" See also: *Shi'urei Shevet Ha-Levi* 187:5:2. In a case where she must perform a *bedikah* on an *onat perishah* when she knows that she has *ketamim,* see below, *Siman* 55: *Bedikot* of *Onot Perishah* when Woman Experiences Spotting.
34. This concern is especially relevant to the Mirena IUD. The reaction to the Mirena is not uniform; some women experience no spotting at all, while others experience spotting as a result of insertion of the Mirena that lasts several months.
35. Relying on the view of *Arukh Ha-Shulḥan* 196:26 (though he addresses the case of a woman who cannot naturally become *tehorah,* whereas in the present case she can by removing the IUD). *Responsa Noda Bi-Yehuda, Yoreh De'ah* 2:129, writes that it is better to minimize the number of *bedikot* than to risk needing to attribute blood found during a *bedikah* to a *makkah* (even though he refers to the *bedikot* of the first and seventh days, whereas the present case is about relying on the *bedikah* of the first day only). See also above, *Siman* 4: Spotting and Bleeding during Pregnancy, and *Siman* 14: *Mokh Daḥuk* and *Bedikot* following Birth.
36. *Ḥavat Da'at* 196:3.

Siman 51

Does Removal of an IUD Render a Woman Niddah?

Question

I experienced bleeding after the removal of an IUD yesterday, and the bleeding has continued a bit today. Am I *niddah*?

Answer

Like the insertion of an IUD, the removal of an IUD does not render a woman *niddah*. After the removal, there will commonly be some mild bleeding for a day or two, resulting from cervical abrasion during removal. This bleeding is *dam makkah* (blood from a wound) and does not render you *niddah*. Prolonged, heavy bleeding reminiscent of menstrual bleeding is not expected after the removal of a copper IUD.

Upon removal of a hormonal IUD, there is often "withdrawal bleeding" because there is no longer an IUD releasing progesterone. This is hormonal bleeding, so if it reaches an intensity similar to menstrual bleeding, it renders one *niddah*. This bleeding will often begin two or more days after the removal of the IUD. Therefore, we can attribute to a *makkah* only the initial, mild bleeding that immediately follows the procedure, and only for a day or two.

We recommend removing the IUD while you are *tehorah*, especially in the case of the hormonal IUD. After the procedure, you should wear colored underwear or a panty liner and should not perform unnecessary *bedikot*.

Halakhic Expansion

The IUD is removed by the physician's pulling on a string that protrudes from the cervix. As a medical procedure that does not open the cervix more than 19 mm (¾ of an inch) is not considered *petiḥat ha-kever,* a woman is not rendered *niddah* from the removal of the IUD.[1] Even though the IUD is larger upon its removal than at the time of its insertion,[2] it is still not large enough for the action to be considered *petiḥat ha-kever.*[3]

If the woman experiences bleeding immediately following the procedure, we attribute it to the *makkah,* and it does not render the woman *niddah.* This bleeding can last for two days.[4] After two days, the bleeding may be hormonal, so we cannot attribute it to a *makkah.* We recommend that the woman wear colored underwear or a panty liner so as not to be rendered *niddah* by these *ketamim.*

In the case of a hormonal IUD, there is often "withdrawal bleeding" because there is no longer an IUD releasing progesterone. This is hormonal bleeding, so if it reaches an intensity similar to menstrual bleeding, it renders the woman *niddah.* This bleeding can begin two days or more after the removal of the IUD. Therefore, we may attribute only the initial, mild bleeding that immediately follows the procedure to a *makkah,* and only for a day or two.

If the IUD is removed during the seven *neki'im,* it is best to perform the procedure after the *hefsek taharah* and the *bedikah* of the first day. Afterwards, the number of *bedikot* may be reduced, and the woman may wear colored underwear or a panty liner. However, she must still perform the *bedikah* of the seventh day. In the case of a hormonal IUD, since hormonal bleeding is expected after its removal, it is very highly recommended to remove it while the woman is *tehorah.*[5]

M.R.

---

1. For more on this topic, see above, *Siman* 50: Insertion of an IUD during the Seven *Neki'im.*
2. The device's "arms" are closed during insertion (i.e., it is I-shaped), and they open in the uterus after insertion. The arms are "open" (T-shaped) when it is removed. However, even when it is open, the IUD is not wider than 19 mm (¾ of an inch).
3. Some disagree and maintain that a woman is rendered *niddah* by removal of the IUD. See *Nishmat Avraham, Yoreh De'ah* 194:5, which cites R. Shlomo Zalman Auerbach as saying that one must be concerned for *petiḥat ha-kever* upon removal of the device. For more on this, see above, *Siman* 50.
4. R. Henkin and R. Warhaftig rule that bleeding can be attributed to a *makkah* for up to two days after the removal of the IUD, as opposed to one day for its insertion, because the removal procedure usually scratches the uterine lining.
5. In order to avoid becoming *niddah* from hormonal stains as a result of having the IUD removed, we advise following the guidelines of dealing with staining, see *Siman* 41: Extending the Cycle via Hormonal Contraception.

Siman 52

Bleeding from an Abrasion Caused by an IUD

Question

I've had an IUD for the past year and a half. Recently, during the seven *neki'im*, a red spot began appearing on the *bedikah* cloth. My doctor's examination found that the string attached to the IUD is rubbing against the cervix and causing minor bleeding. Can I attribute the blood spot that appears on the *bedikah* cloth to this abrasion for as long as I have the IUD?

Answer

The rubbing of the string attached to the IUD can sometimes cause minor cervical bleeding. In such cases, it is best that your *bedikot* not be so deep as to reach the cervix. With a slightly more superficial internal *bedikah*, you can fulfill your obligation to perform a *bedikah* and also avoid moving or touching the string attached to the IUD.

Since your physician diagnosed a cervical abrasion, you may attribute blood spots to it in the near future. We recommend you ask the doctor how long this bleeding can reasonably be expected to last. At the same time, you must ascertain how to treat this problem. For guidance on how to perform the remaining *bedikot* under these conditions, see above, *Siman* 21.

Halakhic Expansion

When it is known for certain that the string attached to the IUD[1] comes into contact with the cervix and abrades it, the abrasion is deemed to be a *makkah* that is known to bleed,[2] and we may attribute to it even blood found on an internal *bedikah*.[3] The length of time that we can rely on a medical diagnosis and attribute blood stains to the *makkah* depends on the nature of the diagnosis and varies from case to case.

The woman should be instructed to ask her physician to verify and confirm the presence of an abrasion, and to give an opinion as to how long the bleeding can reasonably be expected to last and the conditions under which it is likely to bleed.[4] This assessment can help determine how long she will be able to attribute blood stains to the *makkah*.[5] Nevertheless, even when it is known that a *makkah* exists and bleeds, it is possible that the blood in question is not *dam makkah*, but uterine bleeding. This possibility always exists whenever we attribute bleeding to a *makkah*, especially when there is an IUD in the uterus. Therefore, we may not extend this situation over the long term[6] if it is at all avoidable.

The doctor may be able to shorten the string, to reduce the irritation.[7]

---

1. The IUD is inserted into the uterus, with a string that dangles from it into the vaginal canal. The string enables removal of the IUD when its use is no longer needed. See Medical Appendix V: Contraception.
2. See above, *Siman* 21: Attributing Blood to a *Petza* during the Seven *Neki'im*. See also: *Sefer Ha-Terumah siman* 92, s.v. "*ve-din*"; *Hagahot Maimoniyot, Hilkhot Isurei Bi'ah* 11 (cited in *Bet Yosef, Yoreh De'ah* 187:5); *Shi'urei Shevet Ha-Levi* 187:1, p. 75, s.v. "*ve-lakhen be-ishah*."
3. See above, *Siman* 21, for guidance on how to perform the *bedikot*.
4. A wound caused by abrasion usually heals quickly due to the mucous nature of the cervix and the vaginal lining. In contrast, it takes a long time for atrophy to heal, if it does heal.
5. Sometimes all the *bedikot* can be performed without touching the irritated area. See above, *Siman* 21, regarding a vaginal *makkah* that prevents the performance of *bedikot*.
6. The law of attributing to a *makkah* is learned in *Niddah* 66b, in the case of a *ro'ah meḥamat tashmish*. In such a case, the woman may be permanently forbidden from marital relations. Attributing the bleeding to a *makkah* saves her from becoming, in effect, an *agunah*. In less severe circumstances, where the woman will become *niddah* for a fixed amount of time, it is necessary to reach a higher degree of certainty about the abrasion in order to render the woman *tehorah*. See *Shakh, Yoreh De'ah* 187:24. According to *Shakh*, one may rely on *Mordekhai*, according to which a woman's general awareness that such a *makkah* normally bleeds is sufficient, even if she did not feel any actual bleeding in this case.
7. This solution is relevant when the abrasion is in the vagina or cervix. Shortening the string so that it does not descend into the cervix at all would make the IUD harder to remove when the time comes.

Even when attributing to a *makkah* caused by an abrasion or medical condition, it is proper to try to treat the problem and not rely in the long term on the permissibility of attributing to a *makkah.*[8]

When the blood stain is found during the *onat ha-veset,* when the woman expects the onset of her menses, she may not attribute the bleeding to a *makkah*[9] unless she feels the blood flowing from the *makkah.*[10]

Z.B.

8. This applies to wounds that are not medically problematic. If there is concern about a medical condition or another medical problem causing a lesion, it must, of course, be treated in accordance with the doctor's instructions. Cervical bleeding may indicate a problem that demands treatment – even urgent treatment.
9. Rema, *Yoreh De'ah* 187:5.
10. *Shakh ad loc.*

Siman 53

Premenstrual Staining

Question

I have a copper IUD, and I regularly experience spotting three or four days before the onset of my period. Sometimes the stains are red and sometimes brown. The staining intensifies progressively, so that by about the fourth day after the spotting began, the real blood flow begins and lasts for at least five days. As a result, I can't perform a *hefsek taharah* until the eighth or ninth day, and I can't go to the *mikveh* before the sixteenth day, in the best case. What should I do?

Answer

Many women who use an IUD experience spotting for several days before their periods. Sometimes there are isolated stains and sometimes more intense spotting, but in general there is a significant difference between what a woman experiences during these days and what she experiences during her regular menstrual flow.

During the days prior to your period, you can avoid becoming *niddah* by carefully following the laws of *ketamim*: Wear colored underwear or a panty liner, do not look at the toilet paper, and do not perform any unnecessary internal *bedikot*. If you wish to look at the toilet paper to determine whether you are spotting – if you are Ashkenazi, you should wait 15 seconds before wiping after you have finished urinating.[1]

---

1. On the difference between Ashkenazi and Sephardi halakhic rulings on this subject, see above, *Siman* 27: Blood on Toilet Paper.

As long as the menstrual flow has not begun, the *ketamim* are not considered menstruation and do not establish a *veset* or *onot perishah*, whether or not they render you *niddah*. This is on condition that the *ketem* is not accompanied by a halakhically significant *hargashah*. If, however, you are rendered *niddah*, you may count the days you must wait before performing a *hefsek taharah* (four or five days, depending on your custom) from when the *ketamim* began.

Even when the *ketamim* do not render you *niddah*, we recommend not engaging in marital relations during days of staining, so that grave questions about *ro'ah meḥamat tashmish*, bleeding as a result of intercourse, do not arise.

Halakhic Expansion[2]

Mi-de'Orayta, a woman becomes *niddah* when she experiences bleeding accompanied by a *hargashah*.[3] When the woman does not identify a *hargashah*, but there is a steady flow of menstrual blood (a blood flow heavy enough to require pads), some *Rishonim* maintain that she becomes *niddah* at the level of *deRabanan*,[4] while other *Rishonim* maintain that she is *niddah mi-de'Orayta* because of a *ḥazakah*, halakhic presumption, that menstrual bleeding is accompanied by *hargashah*,[5] or because this is the way a woman normally experiences menstrual bleeding.[6] It should be emphasized that there is no practical difference between becoming *teme'ah mi-de'Orayta* from a blood flow accompanied by *hargashah* and becoming *teme'ah mi-deRabanan* from a blood flow unaccompanied by *hargashah* (according to those who rule that such a flow confers the status of *niddah mi-deRabanan*).

Blood that is found without an accompanying *hargashah* is treated as a *ketem*, which renders a woman *niddah mi-deRabanan* except in those circumstances that Ḥazal described as not causing *tum'ah* (i.e., it was found on a surface not susceptible to *tum'ah* or on a colored garment, it was smaller than a *gris*, etc.).[7]

Several questions emerge from the situation described in the question:

---

2. For more on the status of *ketamim* on a panty liner, see above, *Siman* 1: Panty Liners during the Seven *Neki'im* when Trying to Conceive; and *Siman* 44: Staining on a Panty Liner or Synthetic Clothing.
3. See above, *Siman* 25: The Law of *Hargashah*.
4. See *Tosafot, Niddah* 58a, s.v. "*modeh*."
5. Rambam, *Mishneh Torah, Hilkhot Isurei Bi'ah* 9:1
6. Rashba on *Niddah* 57b, s.v. "*tartei sham'at minah*." Among contemporary *poskim*, see *Shi'urei Shevet Ha-Levi* 183:7, s.v. "*Shakh se'if katan 2*"; *Arukh Ha-Shulḥan* 183:47–48. See also above, *Siman* 42: When Staining Renders a Woman *Niddah* and *Siman* 25: The Law of *Hargashah*.
7. See the section on *ketamim* in *Siman* 41: Extending the Cycle via Hormonal Contraception.

1. Should *ketamim* that precede menstruation be considered menstrual bleeding if it is clear that this is how the questioner normally experiences menstruation?
2. How do we determine the first day of the cycle for the purposes of calculating the expected onset of the next cycle?
3. Are marital relations permitted during the days when spotting is occurring, prior to menstruation?

We will address each of these questions in turn.

Should These Days Be Considered a *Veset*?

Shulḥan Arukh, Yoreh De'ah 190:54 rules: "*Ketamim* are not considered [to establish] a *veset*. How so? If a woman found a *ketem* on the first of the month, even for three consecutive months, she has neither established nor uprooted a *veset*, unless the *ketamim* were on a clean *bedikah* cloth. Those cause *tum'ah* whatever the size, and are considered [menstrual] bleeding in every respect."

In several responsa, R. Moshe Feinstein relates to *ketamim* appearing before menstruation.[8] In his view it seems that, according to *Taz*,[9] the reason why *ketamim* do not create a *veset* is not due to lack of *hargashah* but because it is uncertain whether the blood in fact came from the woman's body. Thus, according to *Taz*, a *bedikah* cloth that was not pre-examined and has not been verified as clean would not establish a *veset*, even though insertion of the cloth presents a *safek hargashah* – because there is no certainty that the blood on the cloth actually issued from the woman's body. Accordingly, it stands to reason, if there was blood that definitely came from the body, even if there was no *hargashah*, such blood would establish a *veset*, despite the fact that the woman is still *tehorah mi-de'Orayta*. Therefore, in a case like ours, where the *ketamim* consistently precede menstruation, we cannot say that the blood originated elsewhere, as it makes no sense that blood from elsewhere or from a louse would consistently appear before the onset of menses. Therefore, a *veset* can be established even though the *ketamim* themselves do not render the woman *niddah*.[10]

---

8. *Igrot Moshe, Yoreh De'ah* 3:46 and 51.
9. *Yoreh De'ah* 190:41.
10. The *ḥiddush* in the words of R. Feinstein is that it is possible for a woman to establish a *veset* based on *ketamim* that did not make her *teme'ah*, even *mi-deRabanan*. See *Igrot Moshe, Yoreh De'ah* 3:46.

In another responsum,[11] R. Feinstein distinguishes between a situation wherein a blood flow accompanied by *hargashah* follows several days of spotting, and a situation where there is no *hargashah* even when the blood flow begins.[12] When the flow itself is not accompanied by a *hargashah*, the *veset* is determined according to the time when the *ketamim* were found. For women who experience a *hargashah* when the blood begins to flow, the *veset* is determined by when they experience bleeding with a *hargashah*. However, even for such women, if the blood flow accompanied by a *hargashah* was preceded by *ketamim* three times, the *veset* is determined by when the woman finds the *ketamim*, since it has become apparent that this is the nature of her *veset*; first she experiences drops of blood, and then the profuse blood flow begins. Consequently, the *veset* is expected to begin a month after she found the *ketamim*, and even though the *ketamim* were not accompanied by *hargashah*, the woman must observe the *onot ha-perishah* accordingly.

If there was an interval of at least 24 hours between when the *ketamim* were found and when the blood flow accompanied by a *hargashah* began, or if the woman performed a *bedikah* after finding the *ketem* and found herself *tehorah*, she need show concern only for the time when the blood flow accompanied by *hargashah* began. The *ketamim* would then have the status of *veset ha-guf*, which become established only after three occurrences.[13]

In contrast, R. Wosner[14] writes that a *veset* is not established via *ketamim*, even if they demonstrably came from the body, and even if these *ketamim* regularly

11. *Igrot Moshe, Yoreh De'ah* 3:51.
12. It should be noted that R. Feinstein treats the sensation of discharge flowing (*zivat davar laḥ*) as a *hargashah* that renders one *niddah*. See above, *Siman* 25: The Law of *Hargashah*. However, a woman can create a *ḥazakah* that the sensation of *zivat davar laḥ* does not make her *teme'ah* if she examines herself three consecutive times when she has this sensation and finds herself clean. This *ḥazakah* remains in force only during her *tahor* days, until the expected onset of menses. See *Igrot Moshe, Yoreh De'ah* 4:17:7–10.
13. *Responsa Divrei Yatziv, Yoreh De'ah* 86, cites *Levush* that *ketamim* and bleeding that certainly come from the body can establish a *veset* (similar to the aforementioned view of *Igrot Moshe*). On the other hand, *Shulḥan Arukh Ha-Rav* and other *poskim* state that even *ketamim* that certainly came from the body do not establish a *veset*, as *Shulḥan Arukh* rules. *Divrei Yatziv* offers a novel interpretation: Drops that appear before the *veset* have the status of *veset ha-guf*, which indicate the arrival of the *veset*. The *veset* itself is established on the day that the woman experiences a flow of blood accompanied by *hargashah*. If a *veset ha-guf* manifests as a *veset* comprised of a physical symptom at a particular time, we are concerned for it only when both elements appear together. If the physical symptom (in the present case, spotting) has not manifested, there is no need to observe an *onat perishah* on the day she found it.
14. *Responsa Shevet Ha-Levi* 3:118. In the second and third sections of this responsum, R. Wosner addresses the Gemara in *Niddah* 53b: "Our Sages taught: If a woman saw a *ketem*

precede menstruation. He proves this from the language of Ra'avad, which is the source for the ruling of *Tur* and *Shulḥan Arukh* that *ketamim* cannot establish a *veset*, since after Ra'avad[15] wrote that one need not be concerned about a *veset* for *ketamim*, he added, "and I further say that *ketamim* do not establish a *veset*." With this added sentence, he means to include a case where *ketamim* preceded menstruation on three consecutive occasions, where it is all but certain that the blood came from her body. The only exception to this rule is *ketamim* found on clean *bedikah* cloths; if she finds blood on the cloth three consecutive times, she establishes a *veset* for such bleeding.

Shulḥan Arukh Ha-Rav likewise rules that *ketamim* do not establish a *veset*.[16] In accordance with this ruling, *Taharah Ke-Halakhah*[17] states that we do not show concern for premenstrual *ketamim* with respect to *veset*; they are judged only according to the laws of *ketamim*. *Responsa Tzitz Eliezer* rules likewise.[18]

It therefore seems that we may be lenient in accordance with their ruling, especially since *vesatot* are *deRabanan*. The ruling of most contemporary *poskim* is that no *veset* is established on the days where there is spotting, only once the blood flow begins.

Defining the First Day of the *Veset* for the Purpose of Calculations

A woman who finds a *ketem* accompanied by a *hargashah* that renders her *niddah* establishes a *veset* for the day she sensed the *hargashah*. Other women define the beginning of the *veset* as the day where the blood flow – not mere spotting – begins.[19]

---

and then experienced bleeding, she attributes the *ketem* to the bleeding [if it was] within 24 hours. These are the words of Rabi [Yehudah ha-Nasi]...." Rashi understands that the woman counts the seven days of *niddah* from the day she found the *ketem* and immerses on the eighth night. This understanding seems to reinforce the view of *Igrot Moshe* that a *ketem* which appears before menstruation cannot be considered a *ketem* because it certainly comes from her body. To resolve the view of Rashi, R. Wosner cites *Tosafot Ha-Rosh*, who explains that in this case, she found the *ketem* at the time of her *veset*, on the day that she expects to experience bleeding. Only in such a case can we presume that the *ketem* was accompanied by a *hargashah*.

15. *Ba'alei Ha-Nefesh, Sha'ar Ha-Ketamim*, p. 65.
16. *Yoreh De'ah* 190:122.
17. *Hilkhot Vesatot siman* 594.
18. 6:21.
19. *Shulḥan Arukh Ha-Rav, Yoreh De'ah* 190:122 rules that even if there is actual bleeding, if there is no *hargashah*, a *veset* is not established, and the woman is *niddah* only *mi-deRabanan*. This seems to be the view of *Responsa Shevet Ha-Levi* 2:86, s.v. "*ve-khi teima*," which cites *Shulḥan Arukh Ha-Rav*. However, *Shi'urei Shevet Ha-Levi* 190:54:4 states that even according to *Shulḥan Arukh Ha-Rav*, one must be concerned about "bona fide bleeding" ("*re'iyah gemurah*"; menstrual

This is also the time when the woman is rendered *niddah* even if she was careful not to become *teme'ah* from a *ketem*.

Marital Relations on the Days When *Ketamim* Appear

We recommend refraining from marital relations when a woman experiences heavy staining. See above, *Siman* 42, for guidance on this subject.

O.K. and Editors

---

blood flow) and treat such as a *veset* even if a clear *hargashah* is absent, because it is presumed that most bleeding is accompanied by *hargashah*, unless the woman knows for certain that she did not experience a *hargashah*.

Siman 54

Colors on Bedikah Cloths

Question

I use an IUD (non-hormonal), and as a result, I occasionally find *ketamim*. My main problem is during the seven *neki'im*, when my *bedikot* have a dark brown color. When this happens, must I begin counting the seven *neki'im* from the beginning?

Answer

Technically, only a red or black appearance on a *bedikah* cloth invalidates the count. However, shades of brown can also be problematic if they contain a shade of black or red. A dark brown appearance is uncertain; it should be shown to a halakhic authority to determine its status.

Halakhic Expansion

The Mishnah in *Niddah* 19a lists five types and hues of blood that render a woman *teme'ah*. The Gemara expounds several verses to prove that only five types of blood cause *tum'ah*. In actuality, there are four types of blood; black blood was originally red but turned black due to disease or the passage of time. Over time, due to the difficulty in distinguishing between *tamei* and *tahor* shades of red, Ḥazal became reluctant to issue rulings based on the color of blood. The Talmud already mentions *Ḥakhamim* who "did not examine blood."[1]

1. *Niddah* 20a mentions R. Ashi, and 20b mentions R. Yoḥanan, R. Zeira, and R. Elazar.

Based on this, Rosh ruled: "We are not permitted to render *tahor* any blood that leans toward a reddish appearance."[2] That is, due to uncertainty, all shades of red are deemed *tamei,* and only a stain without any shade of red is deemed *tahor.* This is also the ruling of *Shulḥan Arukh,* who adds, based on the aforementioned Gemara, that black is considered *tamei* as well.[3]

The *Rishonim* mentioned white and yellowish green as *tahor* colors.[4] However, *Shelah* wrote that "one should not rush to be lenient" about a waxy, yellowish green.[5] Most *poskim* rejected this stringency,[6] but *Ḥokhmat Adam* wrote,[7] based on *Shelah,* that we should be stringent about a yellow appearance on a *hefsek taharah.* R. Wosner ruled likewise,[8] albeit with many reservations.[9] R. Ovadiah Yosef disagreed[10] and ruled leniently, in accordance with *Shulḥan Arukh.*

There are extensive discussions among the *Aḥaronim* about other colors,[11] especially regarding different shades of brown. *Sidrei Taharah*[12] mentions "brown" as a *tahor* color, describing it as "like the shell of a chestnut or like the drink coffee."[13] This ruling sparked a dispute among *poskim.* On one hand, some *poskim* view it as a *tamei* color (red that became flawed or black that faded).[14] On

---

2. *Niddah* 2:4.
3. *Yoreh De'ah* 188:1.
4. Rosh, *Niddah* 2:4, and *Shulḥan Arukh* in his wake. The "green" that they mention is closer to today's yellow.
5. *Shelah* (*Sha'ar Ha-Otiyot, ot kuf, Kedushat Ha-Zivug* 367, p. 100b), cited in *Pitḥei Teshuvah* 188:2.
6. See, for example, *Sidrei Taharah* 188:1:2, which cites *Shelah* and notes that most *Aḥaronim* omitted his words, indicating that they did not agree. He concludes: "A spiritually inclined person (*ba'al nefesh*) will conduct himself stringently, according to the circumstances."
7. 117:9.
8. *Shi'urei Shevet Ha-Levi* 188:1:9.
9. Only in the case of a woman for whom this is not a normal appearance, only on a *hefsek taharah,* not a *mokh daḥuk* or *bedikot,* and there are grounds for greater leniency if the couple has not yet fulfilled their obligation to procreate.
10. *Taharat Ha-Bayit,* 1:6:1, p. 292.
11. *Shi'urei Shevet Ha-Levi,* 188:1:1–14, pp. 390–91 (in the summary of the *halakhot*) quotes rulings about different shades of brown, gray, pink, and yellow. Likewise *Darkhei Taharah,* chap. 3, *Dinei Tzeva'im,* pp. 29–30.
12. *Sidrei Taharah* 188:1:1.
13. This description of "coffee" still includes many shades of brown, as there are many shades of coffee. Nevertheless, it is clear that this refers to a brown shade of coffee that contains no redness.
14. *Leḥem ve-Simlah* 188:1:2 states: "It is reasonable to say that it is red that became somewhat flawed." R. Wosner (*Shi'urei Shevet Ha-Levi,* 188:1, pp. 94–95) views it as black that faded. He is inclined to be stringent, though he distinguishes between different cases and situations,

the other hand, some *poskim* are lenient because these shades of brown have no red hue or because the concern that it is faded black is remote.[15]

Since these shades are very subtle and difficult to describe in writing, it is especially important to apprentice under *poskim* and learn the permitted and forbidden colors.[16] As *Badei Ha-Shulḥan* writes:[17]

> But know that it is difficult to be precise about these things in writing, because it is impossible to describe, in writing, the essence of how something appears, especially since red blood, when it dries on cloth, takes on an appearance very similar to brown. Therefore, a person should be very cautious about this and not rely on their own assessment. Rather, they should go to a *ḥakham* with expertise in the appearances of blood and ask for his ruling about any uncertainty that arises concerning the appearance of blood. The *ḥakham* should himself know that his eyesight is good enough to make subtle distinctions between colors. He should make it a point to amass a great deal of experience and test himself well before starting to issue rulings in this [specialization].

At the same time, it is important to encourage women to consult a rabbi or a Yoetzet Halacha[18] about brown hues; and not to assume that every hue causes *tum'ah*.

N. L.

---

ultimately concluding that one may be lenient for "women for whom it always has a brown appearance" (as in the present case).

15. *Arukh Ha-Shulḥan* 188:9; *Taharat Yisrael* 188:1:2; *Badei Ha-Shulḥan* 188:1:6. *Badei Ha-Shulḥan* cites this dispute and rules leniently in practice, "especially nowadays, when women have many ailments, and such appearances [on *bedikah* cloths] are common; and if we are stringent with them, they will not be able to become *tehorot* for their husbands."
16. See the article by R. Dr. Mordechai Halperin, "Can a *Posek* who Views *Ketamim* be Partially Color Blind?" *Assia* 77–78 (5766) (Hebrew). In chapter 9 of the article, he describes the disagreement about whether apprenticeship is necessary for viewing blood stains, or whether anyone can make a determination based on whether they perceive a red hue.
17. 188:1:6.
18. Many Yoatzot Halacha apprenticed extensively under rabbis with expertise in hues of blood and who answer such questions. The ability to ask a woman makes it easier for women to ask these types of questions.

Siman 55

Bedikot of Onot Perishah When a Woman Experiences Spotting

Question

I've had a copper IUD for the past two years. Last month, I got my period earlier than expected, on day 26. Today is my *onat ha-haflagah*. But today I began spotting on the panty liner. I occasionally experience spotting, generally three or four days before the real menstrual bleeding begins. I usually bleed for 6 or 7 days.

I presume that my period will begin in 2–3 days. I want to mention that my husband returns this evening from several days of army reserve duty. May I forego the *bedikah* of the *onat ha-haflagah*, which will probably make me *teme'ah* several days before menstruation and result in a prolonged separation of 17 or 18 days?

Answer

During her *onat ha-veset* – that is, the day a woman anticipates the onset of menses – the couple must abstain from relations and a *bedikah* must be performed. If the woman has a *veset kavu'a* (established *veset*), she must abstain on that day and perform a *bedikah* then. If she has no *veset kavu'a*, the couple abstains and the woman performs a *bedikah* on the three days for which the Sages presumed a high likelihood for the onset of menses: the *veset ha-ḥodesh*, the date of the Hebrew month corresponding to the date of the last onset of menses; the *veset ha-haflagah*, which is the interval between the onset of the last two periods; and the *onah beinonit*, which is the thirtieth day after the onset of the last menses, which is considered the interval experienced by most women.

The *veset ha-ḥodesh* and the *veset ha-haflagah* are not considered an established *ḥazakah* – that is, the degree of certainty that you will experience bleeding on one of those days is less than the degree of certainty of a *veset kavu'a* – so their status is not as strict. In the case of a *veset kavu'a*, if the day (*onah*) of the *veset* has passed and a *bedikah* was not performed, the couple must abstain from relations until the woman performs a *bedikah*. In this respect, the *onah beinonit* has the same status as a *veset kavu'a*. However, in the case of the *veset ha-ḥodesh* and the *veset ha-haflagah*, if the day passes and the woman neither experienced bleeding nor performed a *bedikah*, relations are permitted even without a *bedikah*.

In your case, the 26th day since the onset of your last period is your *onat ha-haflagah* this month. *Lekhatḥilah* a *bedikah* of the *onat ha-perishah* is to be performed. Likewise, *lekhatḥilah* you are required to perform a *bedikah* on the *onat ha-ḥodesh*. However, since the couple may resume marital relations if the *onat ha-haflagah* passed without bleeding, in your situation, you may simply abstain during the *onat ha-veset* without performing a *bedikah*. Thus, as long as the *ketamim* appear only on a surface that is not susceptible to *tum'ah*, and there is no *hargashah* that would render you *niddah*, you would not become *niddah* until the onset of menstruation or until you experience bleeding in a way that would render you *niddah*.

As long as you are not *niddah*, all forms of contact and intimacy are permitted to you and your husband. However, it is recommended that you abstain from relations on these days if the spotting continues, because there is a risk that you will bleed during intercourse. If the spotting stops for 24 hours, marital relations would then be permitted.

If you reach day 30, the *onah beinonit*, and still have not gotten your period, you would be required to perform a *bedikah* before resuming relations after the *onah*.

Halakhic Expansion

A side-effect of an IUD is prolonged menstrual bleeding and irregular bleeding. These types of bleeding differ from woman to woman and from time to time, and, as well, between the different types of IUDs. (See Appendix V). The on-going addition of days on which the couple must abstain from relations may cause or exacerbate tensions within the family.

We must clarify whether the status of a *veset she-eino kavu'a* is the same as that of a *veset kavu'a* and an *onah beinonit*, when marital relations are forbidden as long as the woman has not performed a *bedikah*. Likewise, we must clarify whether a *bedikah* is mandatory in all cases or only for the purpose of relations – and if the woman does not want to have relations, is she not obligated to perform a *bedikah*.

This has ramifications for women who experience spotting prior to the onset of menses but do not want other forms of intimacy and contact to be prohibited, even if marital relations are not permitted absent a *bedikah*.

According to all authorities, *lekhatḥilah* a woman who has a *veset kavu'a* must perform a *bedikah* at the time of her *veset*. In the Gemara, *Ḥakhamim* disagree regarding whether a *bedikah* is effective once the time of the *veset* has passed:

> It was stated: A woman who has a *veset*, and the time of her *veset* arrived and she did not perform a *bedikah*, and later she performed a *bedikah*.... R. Eliezer says she is *niddah*, and R. Yehoshua says she should perform a *bedikah*. And [the position of] these *Tanna'im* corresponded to [the positions of] other *Tanna'im* that we learned in a *baraita*: R. Meir says she is *teme'ah* as a *niddah*, and *Ḥakhamim* say: she should perform a *bedikah*. (*Niddah* 16a)

There are three opinions among the *Rishonim* regarding a woman with a *veset kavu'a* who has not performed a *bedikah*:

1. Even if she did not perform a *bedikah* at the time of the *veset*, if the woman performed a *bedikah* afterward, and it was *tehorah*, then she remains *tehorah*. This is because we rule that *vesatot* are *deRabanan*. Nevertheless, she may not have marital relations as long as she has not performed the *bedikah*. This is the view of Ra'avad,[1] *Tosafot*,[2] Ramban,[3] Rashba,[4] Rosh,[5] and other *Rishonim*.[6] *Shulḥan Arukh* rules that "there are those who say" ("*yesh omrim*") that this applies in the case of a *veset kavu'a* and *onah beinonit*; and this is the ruling of Rema.[7]
2. If the time of the *veset* passed without a *bedikah*, the woman need not perform one, and she and her husband have not become forbidden to one another. This is the ruling of Rif[8] and Rambam,[9] and Ran explains that there is no reason to perform a *bedikah* once the time of the *veset* has passed, for why

1. *Ba'alei Ha-Nefesh, Sha'ar Tikun Ha-Vesatot*, p. 31 (at the end).
2. *Niddah* 16a, s.v. "*Ve-Rav Naḥman*."
3. *Hilkhot Niddah* 5:10.
4. *Torat Ha-Bayit, bayit* 7, *sha'ar* 3, p. 15b.
5. Beginning of *Niddah*.
6. See *Taharat Ha-Bayit*, 1:3:2, p. 128.
7. *Yoreh De'ah* 189:4.
8. See Ran on *Shevu'ot*, p. 5 in the Rif pagination.
9. *Mishneh Torah, Hilkhot Isurei Bi'ah* 8:7.

should we expect her to find blood then? After all, every woman is considered *mesuleket damim* when it is not the time of her *veset.*[10] Therefore, since *vesatot* are *deRabanan,* she retains her presumption (*ḥazakah*) of *taharah* and is deemed *tehorah.* However, Ran writes that even though this explanation fits the words of Rif and Rambam, "it is an excessive leniency not to be concerned at all about neither the *veset* nor the *onah.*" *Hagahot Maimoniyot* writes: "Nevertheless, she should not have relations until she performs a *bedikah.*"[11] This is the unqualified (*stam*) view cited in *Shulḥan Arukh.*[12]

3. A *bedikah* is ineffective afterward, for we presume that the menses arrived at the expected time and the blood fell to the ground. Therefore, if she did not perform a *bedikah* immediately following her *veset,* there is no way to correct the situation, and she is *niddah.* This is the view cited by *Baḥ* in the name of *Sefer Yere'im, Sefer Ha-Terumah, Sha'arei Dura,* and *Semak.*[13]

All of this applies to a *veset kavu'a* or *onah beinonit.* However, with respect to a *veset she-eino kavu'a, Tur* cites Rashba as saying that if a woman with a *veset she-eino kavu'a* did not perform a *bedikah* during the *onat ha-perishah,* since she did not experience a *hargashah,* she is *tehorah* even absent the *bedikah.*[14] *Shulḥan Arukh* writes that she must abstain from relations and perform a *bedikah* at the time of her *veset* – that is, on the *onat ha-ḥodesh* and the *onat ha-haflagah* – but once the *onah* has passed, she and her husband may resume marital relations even without a *bedikah.*[15]

Bet Yosef writes in the name of Rashba that the prohibition of marital relations before a *bedikah* applies to a woman who has no *veset kavu'a* only on the 30th day (the *onah beinonit*), because, in his view, the 30th day is considered as a *veset kavu'a* for her. According to Rashba, if she had a *veset she-eino*

10. Ran on *Shevu'ot,* p. 5 in the Rif pagination.
11. *Hilkhot Isurei Bi'ah* 8:7.
12. *Yoreh De'ah* 184:9. *Taharat Ha-Bayit,* 1:3:3, p. 129 states that in *siman* 189, *Shulḥan Arukh* revised what he had written earlier in *siman* 184 as the "*yesh omrim*" position, and in *siman* 189:4 wrote as the "*stam*" position that in the case of a *veset kavu'a,* even though the *onah* has passed, the woman may not have relations until she performs a *bedikah* that is found to be *tahor,* and this is the *halakhah.* However, in the case of a *veset she-eino kavu'a,* once the *onah* has passed, she and her husband may resume relations even without a *bedikah.*
13. *Baḥ, Yoreh De'ah* 184. It has already been noted that since common practice nowadays is to wear form-fitting underwear, there is not much reason for concern that the blood fell to the ground.
14. *Torat Ha-Bayit, bayit* 7, *sha'ar* 3, at the end; *Tur, Yoreh De'ah siman* 184, at the end.
15. *Yoreh De'ah* 184:9 and 189:4.

kavu'a, no *bedikah* is required on the day of the *veset* (the *onat ha-haflagah*), even *lekhatḥilah*.[16]

This is somewhat implied by the language of Rashba himself:

> If she has a *veset she-eino kavu'a* and it is shorter than the *onah beinonit* – for example, she experienced bleeding on the 25th [day after the onset of the previous menses], or the like – even if she has not performed a *bedikah*, since she had no *hargashah* of bleeding, she is *tehorah* even without any *bedikah*.[17]

That is, because she experienced no *hargashah*, there was no reason to perform a *bedikah*. However, if, according to Rashba, she is required *lekhatḥilah* to perform a *bedikah*, he would not have had to explain that she did not perform a *bedikah* because she did not experience a *hargashah*. Rather, Rashba would have written that she forgot to perform a *bedikah*, or purposefully neglected to perform a *bedikah*, or the like.

Perishah,[18] however, does not read Rashba in this fashion. Rather, in his view, according to Rashba, only *bedi'avad*, if the *onah* passed without the woman's performing a *bedikah*, would she then no longer need to perform a *bedikah*. When Rashba writes, "she is *tehorah* even without any *bedikah*," he is referring, according to *Perishah*, only to a case wherein her husband returns from a trip; in that case, the husband need not ask his wife whether she is *tehorah*, for *Tur* cites his father as saying that a woman who has no *veset* may not have relations unless she performs a *bedikah* before and after relations, whenever she has relations. *Taz*[19] and *Sidrei Taharah*[20] already rejected the interpretation of *Perishah*; and *Sidrei Taharah* concluded: "Even intercourse is permitted."

Among contemporary *poskim*, *Badei Ha-Shulḥan* writes that a woman with a *veset she-eino kavu'a* need not perform a *bedikah*, even *lekhatḥilah*, but he concludes:

16. *Bet Yosef, Yoreh De'ah siman* 184, s.v. "*u-mah she-katav be-dibur ha-matḥil*," at the end of the paragraph.
17. *Torat Ha-Bayit, bayit* 7, *sha'ar* 3. Ramban in *Hilkhot Niddah* 6:18 writes with regard to a *veset she-eino kavu'a* merely: "If that *veset* arrives, and she has neither performed a *bedikah* nor experienced bleeding, since its *onah* has passed, she is permitted to her husband." He does not specify that she did not perform a *bedikah* because she did not experience a *hargashah*.
18. 184:18.
19. 184:13.
20. 184:13. He rejects *Perishah's* reasoning on several grounds, including that the question *Perisha* raises is upon the *Tur*, not Rashba.

"It is good to be stringent except under pressing circumstances."[21] R. Mordechai Willig inferred from the fact that she need not perform a *bedikah* if her husband is out of town, that even though she is required, *lekhatḥilah,* to perform a *bedikah* at the time of the *veset,* this applies only if she intends to have marital relations with her husband. Therefore, if she finds *ketamim* on colored garments and assumes that they will continue to appear until she becomes *niddah* – and therefore has no intention of having marital relations with her husband – she has no obligation to perform a *bedikah.* For if she performs a *bedikah* and finds blood, she and her husband would be bound by all of the *harḥakot,* whereas if she does not perform a *bedikah,* they may engage in other forms of contact and intimacy.[22]

In times of need, such as when the husband was in the army and just now managed to come home, or if a *bedikah* during the *onat ha-haflagah* will preclude them from having relations for a prolonged period, then as long as she has not established a *veset* and has not experienced a *hargashah,* we may consider, under the circumstances, relying on the view of Rashba and *Sidrei Taharah* that they have relations following the *onah* even without a *bedikah.* If they have no intention of having relations because they expect the spotting to continue until the onset of menses, then the woman may forego the *bedikah* of the *onat ha-haflagah* even *lekhatḥilah,* and even without extenuating circumstances. When *ketamim* are present, even if the *ketamim* do not cause *niddah* status, the couple should, nevertheless, abstain from relations, lest the woman find *ketamim* during intercourse.[23]

C.H. and Editors

---

21. 184:82.
22. *Kol Tzvi,* issue 10–11 (5768), p. 404. Even though there is a difference between the two situations – if her husband is out of town, there is no concern that other forms of intimacy will lead to relations – *Ḥakhamim* were not concerned about this and did not forbid other forms of intimacy during the *onat ha-veset* even of a woman who has a *veset kavu'a.*
23. The halakhic status of the *onah beinonit* is weightier than that of the *onat ha-haflagah* and is considered like a *veset kavu'a* because according to *Ḥakhamim,* thirty days is the interval experienced by most women. According to R. Warhaftig, given the prevailing reality nowadays, in which the chances of a woman getting her period during the *onah beinonit* are even lower than her chances of getting it on the *onat ha-haflagah* – under very pressing circumstances, there are grounds to be lenient and not require a *bedikah* even during the *onah beinonit.* The couple would thus be permitted to one another after the *onah beinonit* even without a *bedikah,* as in the case of the *onat ha-haflagah.* See his article, "*Onah Beinonit Be-Yameinu,*" *Teḥumin* 24, p. 235.

Siman 56

Minor Monthly Spotting

Question

I've had progesterone IUD for the past eight months. As a result, I don't menstruate, but I recently noticed that small *ketamim* appear each month on the dates that I would have gotten my period. Since I wear colored underwear, I have not become *niddah* yet, but I wonder whether these small *ketamim* constitute a *veset,* given their regularity.

Answer

The effect of the progesterone released by the IUD usually is a dramatic decrease in menstrual bleeding after a few months, and some women become amenorrheic. In this situation, it is possible that there will be a small amount of red discharges around the time you would be getting your period. As long as these discharges are not accompanied by a halakhically significant *hargashah* that would render you *niddah,* they are subject to the laws of *ketamim.* That is, if you find them on colored underwear or a panty liner, you are not *teme'ah.* If you expect *ketamim* on specific days of the month, we recommend you make sure to wear colored underwear on those days. Only if the spotting intensifies into a flow of blood like menstruation, or if the *ketamim* are found in a fashion that would make you *niddah* according to the laws of *ketamim* (for example, they are on white underwear, your hands or thighs, and are at least the size of a *gris*) would you become *niddah.*

On the days that you experience spotting, we recommend that you not engage in marital relations, for if you find blood immediately following relations, it may raise the possibility that you are *ro'ah meḥamat tashmish.* However, there is no need to calculate *onot perishah* because of *ketamim* because we do not establish or observe a *veset* based on *ketamim*.

Halakhic Expansion[1]

A woman becomes *niddah mi-de'Orayta* if she experiences bleeding accompanied by a *hargashah*[2] and *niddah mi-deRabanan* if she finds a *ketem* that meets the halakhic definition. During the course of the monthly cycle, one of these conditions will usually be met. There are three *hargashot* mentioned by the *poskim*: the opening of the uterus, bodily tremors, and the flow of fluid.[3] Many women sense the flow of fluid. However, many *poskim* differentiate between the flow from the uterus into the vagina, and the flow within the vagina or from there to outside the body: *Ḥavat Da'at*[4] writes that the sensation of *zivat davar laḥ* is considered a *hargashah* only when the woman senses the flow of blood from the uterus to the vagina; the sensation of a flow within the vagina only, would not be considered a *hargashah* halakhically.[5] However, according to *Noda Bi-Yehudah*,[6] the flow of discharge is considered a *hargashah* even if she senses the flow within the vagina itself. R. Moshe Feinstein writes[7] that since nowadays women do not distinguish between blood flow from the uterus and blood flow from the vagina, any sensation of blood flow out of the body is considered a *hargashah*.[8] R. Eliezer Waldenberg, in *Tzitz Eliezer*, was also stringent in his interpretation of the sensation of *zivat davar laḥ*, as detailed above in *Siman* 25. In the glosses of R. Barukh Frankel (author of *Barukh Ta'am*) on *Noda Bi-Yehudah*,[9] he writes that in reality it is impossible to sense

1. A hormonal IUD releases the hormone progesterone into the uterus. It works, in part, by suppressing the growth of the uterine lining and by thickening the cervical mucus, thus preventing implantation of an embryo. Bleeding between periods is common during the first 3–6 months of use, as the body adjusts to the device. After that, the bleeding generally diminishes, and in some cases even ceases altogether. Sometimes, instead of menstruation, there will be minor monthly spotting. See Medical Appendix V: Contraception.
2. For an extended discussion of *hargashot*, see above, *Siman* 25: The Law of *Hargashah*.
3. *Pitḥei Teshuvah, Yoreh De'ah* 183:1.
4. 190:1.
5. This is the ruling of R. Yosef Shalom Elyashiv with respect to the *hargashah* of *zivat davar laḥ*, as cited in R. Yeḥiel Mikhel Stern's *Sha'arei Taharah, siman* 3, p. 8, s.v. "*ve-hanilmad*." (R. Elyashiv's own view is that women who never experience a *hargashah* become *teme'ot mi-de'Orayta* even if they do not sense the flow of blood. See *Kovetz Teshuvot* 1:84.)
6. *Yoreh De'ah* 1:55.
7. *Igrot Moshe, Yoreh De'ah* 4:17:7.
8. However, the sensation of wetness outside the body is not considered *hargashah* see *Igrot Moshe* loc. cit.; *Shi'urei Shevet Ha-Levi* 190:2, p. 156.
9. *Yoreh De'ah* 1:55, s.v. "p. 4 line 1."

zivat davar laḥ within the body, and a woman cannot sense the flow of blood within the vagina, only the flow out of the body.[10] However, many *poskim* rule in accordance with *Ḥatam Sofer*[11] that *zivat davar laḥ* is not considered a *hargashah* that causes *niddah mi-de'Orayta*.[12] It is common for poskim to rely on this view to rule leniently on *ketamim*.[13]

When a woman sees a bloody discharge the size of a *gris* or larger on white underwear[14] or on her body,[15] she becomes *niddah mi-deRabanan* even without a *hargashah*. However, if she finds red discharge on a panty liner[16] or colored underwear,[17] and there is no *hargashah*, these discharges have the status of a *ketem* that does not cause *tum'ah*.

While using the the hormonal IUD, some women find *ketamim* at a regular frequency, usually once a month. According to R. Mordechai Willig's understanding of Rashba,[18] any bleeding that women regularly experience causes *tum'ah*. That is, what causes the prohibition *mi-de'Orayta* is not a *hargashah* or a quantity of blood, but the appearance of blood in a fixed cycle. According to R. Willig's reading of Rashba, *ketamim* that appear at a fixed frequency render a woman *niddah* if this is what she normally experiences. However, according to most *Rishonim*,[19] blood causes *tum'ah* only if it is accompanied by a *hargashah*. The *Aḥaronim* rule

10. In contrast to what R. Shimon Eider wrote in *The Laws of Niddah*, there is no disagreement between R. Frankel and R. Feinstein.
11. *Responsa Ḥatam Sofer, Yoreh De'ah siman* 145, s.v. "*akh*."
12. *Taharat Ha-Bayit*, 1:1:3, p. 6ff.
13. On the other hand, other poskim maintain that physical sensations that regularly accompany the onset of menstruation, like lower back pain, are halakhic *hargashot*. See *Responsa Maharam Schick, Yoreh De'ah* 184:1; *Pardes Rimonim, Pitḥei Niddah* 4:24, p. 33b; and *Tzitz Eliezer* 6:21 who writes that women nowadays sense the opening of the uterus and bodily tremors, but our terminology has changed, and today these are called premenstrual symptoms and cramps. See above, *Siman* 25. Some *poskim* maintain that these sensations constitute a *veset ha-guf*, not a *hargashah*. See the article by Yoatzot Halacha Dr. Deena Zimmerman and Dr. Tova Ganzel, "*Veset Ha-guf: Hebet Hilkhati U-Refu'i*," in *Teḥumin* 20, p. 363.
14. *Shulḥan Arukh, Yoreh De'ah* 190:5.
15. Ibid. 190:8. It should be added that, in addition to *ketamim* on a garment, several *ketamim* that are smaller than a *gris* can combine into a *ketem* that causes *tum'ah* if their total area is larger than a *gris*.
16. See above, *Siman* 44: Staining on a Panty Liner or Synthetic Clothing.
17. *Shulḥan Arukh, Yoreh De'ah* 190:10.
18. *Ḥiddushei Ha-Rashba* on *Niddah* 57b, s.v. "*tartei shamat minah*." R. Mordechai Willig explains the position of Rashba at length, see "*Hargashah Be-Zmaneinu*," *Beit Yitzchak* 39 (5767).
19. Rambam, *Mishneh Torah, Hilkhot Isurei Bi'ah* 9:1; Ramban, *Hilkhot Niddah* 4:1 and commentary on *Niddah* 52b; Rashi on *Niddah* 58a, s.v. "*mi-deRabanan*"; *Ḥiddushei Ha-Ran* on *Niddah* chapter 8, s.v. "*tartei shamat minah*." See also above, *Siman* 42: When Staining Renders a Woman *Niddah*.

accordingly. Therefore, if a woman experiences *ketamim* each month without a *hargashah,* she does not become *niddah* as long as the *ketem* itself is *tahor* according to the laws of *ketamim.*[20] Therefore, the monthly discharges related to IUD use should be assessed according to the laws of *ketamim* alone.[21]

There is no obligation to become *niddah* once a month. Therefore, to save herself from *ketamim* and avoid becoming *niddah* when experiencing such discharges, a woman may wear colored underwear or a panty liner.[22] On those days when she experiences spotting, we recommend refraining from marital relations for about 24 hours, lest the woman find blood right after intercourse.[23]

Even if a woman becomes *niddah* from such *ketamim* (for example, if she found them on her body), she need not calculate *onot perishah* for the next month on their account, because a *veset* is not established on the basis of *ketamim.*[24]

M.R.

---

20. For further discussion on the laws of *ketamim,* see *Siman* 41: Extending the Cycle via Hormonal Contraception.
21. R. Henkin and R. Warhaftig rule accordingly. The rabbis of Makhon Pu'ah quote R. Mordechai Eliyahu as saying the same. In contrast, as noted above, R. Mordechai Willig deems these monthly *ketamim* that result from the hormonal IUD to render the woman *niddah.*
22. *Shulḥan Arukh, Yoreh De'ah* 190:10.
23. This is the recommendation of R. Henkin and R. Warhaftig, *Shi'urei Shevet Ha-Levi* 188:1, "*He'arot le-dina be-inyan shinui mar'eh,*" subsection 2 (p. 93) recommends abstaining from marital relations in similar cases, when a woman has *ketamim* and does not know whether they will develop into menstrual bleeding.
24. *Shulḥan Arukh, Yoreh De'ah* 190:54.

Siman 57

Waiting before the Seven Neki'im

Question

I have a hormonal IUD (Mirena) and occasionally experience spotting. Yesterday I found a *ketem* that unfortunately made me *niddah,* about a week after I went to the *mikveh.* Must I wait five days before performing a *hefsek taharah,* or can I begin counting the seven *neki'im* now? If I wait, I will not be able to go to the *mikveh* before my next period.

Answer

There are different customs regarding this subject, and each woman should follow her family custom. One who observes Ashkenazi custom waits until after the fifth day since becoming *niddah* before starting to count seven *neki'im.* If one follows Sephardi custom based on the rulings of *Shulḥan Arukh,* then if marital relations did not take place for three days before finding the *ketem,* the woman need not wait at all before performing a *hefsek taharah* and counting the seven *neki'im.* If she has engaged in marital relations during the three days prior to becoming *teme'ah,* the woman may perform a vaginal douche to ensure that no semen remains in the vagina, after which she may perform a *hefsek taharah.* A woman who follows the rulings of *Ben Ish Ḥai* waits five days before starting to count seven *neki'im,* like the Ashkenazi custom.

Halakhic Expansion

For an expanded discussion of bleeding while using the hormonal IUD, see Medical Appendix V: Contraception.

As long as semen remains viable (for 72 hours after ejaculation), its expulsion from a woman's body cancels that day as one of the seven *neki'im*.[1] According to the Sages, this viability lasts for six 12-hour periods, or three days, which extend across four calendar dates. Therefore, one may not begin counting the seven *neki'im* until at least four days have elapsed since engaging in intercourse.[2]

For most women, menstrual bleeding lasts at least five days, so in general the end of menstruation corresponds to when the counting of seven *neki'im* may begin. However, even if bleeding was for a very brief period, the count of seven *neki'im* can begin only after viable semen has been expelled.[3]

Terumat Ha-Deshen[4] adds two stringencies to this law. First, it is decreed that all women must wait, even if they did not engage in relations during the days before the bleeding, so as not to differentiate between different cases.[5] Thus, according to *Terumat Ha-Deshen*, the four-day waiting period begins with the beginning of bleeding, not from the last intercourse. The second stringency of *Terumat Ha-Deshen* is that another day is added to the waiting period in order to prevent errors in the counting of days. For example, if the couple has relations at *sh'kiah*, they may mistakenly think it was still daytime and count it as the first day. According to this stringency, one may begin counting the seven *neki'im* only once five days have elapsed since the onset of bleeding.

Shulḥan Arukh[6] does not accept the stringency of *Terumat Ha-Deshen*, writing that a woman does not begin counting the seven *neki'im* until the fifth day[7] after

---

1. The 72 hours (six 12-hour periods) is based on the view of *Ḥakhamim* in *Shabbat* 86a. According to Rambam, it is sufficient to wait three 12-hour periods. See *Mishneh Torah, Hilkhot She'ar Avot HaTum'ah* 5:15.
2. This is the ruling of most *Rishonim*: *Semag*, negative commandment *siman* 111, p. 37c; *Semak siman* 293, p. 321; *Sefer Ha-Terumah siman* 95; *Hagahot Maimoniyot, Hilkhot Isurei Bi'ah* 6:2; Rashba, *Torat Ha-Bayit He-Arokh, bayit* 7, *sha'ar* 5, p. 26a. It is also the conclusion of Rosh, *Niddah* 4:1, and *Bet Yosef* (*Yoreh De'ah siman* 196) writes that Rosh inferred this from the words of Rabbeinu Yonah as well. Ra'avad, on the other hand, explains the passage in the Gemara as dealing only with *taharot*.
3. If possible, a woman may perform a *hefsek taharah* before the fifth day. However, she may not begin counting seven *neki'im* until the halakhically mandated waiting period has elapsed.
4. *Siman* 145.
5. "We do not differentiate (*lo plug*)... and we decree regarding one who has not had intercourse because of one who has had intercourse."
6. *Yoreh De'ah* 196:11.
7. I.e., after six 12-hour period have elapsed, since the seven *neki'im* must be counted on days when there is no possibility of expelling semen – which would negate the counting of that day. To ensure that there are six full 12-hour periods or day or night, it is not sufficient to wait 6 *onot*, but rather, 8 *onot*.

she last had relations – that is, after waiting for four days. Rema[8] rules in accordance with *Terumat Ha-Deshen*, and this is the Ashkenazi custom.

In addition, *Shulḥan Arukh* permits a woman who wishes to begin counting on the day after she experiences bleeding to perform a thorough vaginal douche and then perform a *hefsek taharah*. According to Rema, on the other hand, one may not do so, because we are not proficient in the proper methods of cleansing. Rema further writes that we should not make distinctions when it comes to the customs of counting, and that, "One who breaches a fence will be bitten by a snake" (*Kohelet* 10:8).[9]

Consequently, if the questioner is Ashkenazi, she must wait for five days after becoming *niddah*, despite the difficulty this causes.[10] R. Ovadiah Yosef[11] writes that one should follow the unreserved view of *Shulḥan Arukh* and wait four days since last having relations or douche thoroughly, so that no residual semen remains, and then perform a *hefsek taharah* immediately.[12] Those who follow *Ben Ish Ḥai* accept the Ashkenazi custom on this matter, and this is the ruling of R. Mordechai Eliyahu.[13]

Z.B.

8. *Yoreh De'ah* 196:11, 13.
9. Why are *poskim* so stringent about this, imposing stringency after stringency? Perhaps because usually, when a woman becomes *niddah* from menstruation, it is uncommon that she can perform a *hefsek taharah* before the mandated waiting period has elapsed. *Bet Yosef* (*Yoreh De'ah* 196:11) mentions this to explain why Rif and the *Ge'onim* omitted this law, writing that the omission does not necessarily mean that they did not rule accordingly, only that in most cases there are no practical ramifications.
10. In extreme cases, one may take into consideration that there are those who rule leniently about this law.
11. *Taharat Ha-Bayit* 2:13:11, p.392.
12. One should first ascertain if she had intercourse in the past four days. If she has, she is instructed to clean out her vagina so that no semen remains before beginning to count the seven *neki'im*.
13. *Darkhei Taharah*, p. 137. He qualifies this when it comes to a woman who is trying to conceive and there is concern that she will miss her ovulation. In such a case, he rules leniently, following *Shulḥan Arukh*. Some have a custom of waiting even more than five days – for example, part of the Djerban community. See R. Raḥamim Ḥai Ḥawita HaKohen, *Yalkut Kehunah, Yoreh De'ah*, p. 259. Many have written in opposition to these stringencies and the problems they may cause.

Siman 58

Douching before Internal Bedikot

Question

Since the insertion of a hormonal IUD two months ago, I have experienced a great deal of staining. I went to the *mikveh* last week after five weeks of separation, and now I am once again *teme'ah*. How can I count seven *neki'im* with incessant spotting?

Answer

During the first months after the insertion of a hormonal IUD, there is likely to be a lot of spotting. The situation usually improves after 3–6 months, whereupon the bleeding generally decreases in volume and duration, and in some cases even ceases altogether. Sometimes, instead of menstruation, there will be minor monthly spotting. If the spotting does not cease after several months, it is advisable to consider a different solution together with your physician.

We recommend that you confirm that the *ketamim* you are finding indeed confer upon you *niddah* status according to the laws of *ketamim*.[1] If they indeed make you *niddah*, it is worthwhile, during the first months after the insertion of the IUD, to conduct yourself as follows:

With regard to *bedikot* of the seven *neki'im*, you may perform the minimum number of *bedikot* necessary to become *tehorah*: that is, the *bedikah* of the *hefsek*

1. Detailed guidance appears above in *Siman* 20: *Bedikot* with Uterine Prolapse.

taharah, one *bedikah* on the first day, and one *bedikah* on the seventh day. During the seven *neki'im*, we recommend that you wear colored underwear and/or use a disposable panty liner, which is not susceptible to *tum'ah*.

If you are concerned that even with these measures you will not manage to obtain clean *bedikot* and become *tehorah*, you may douche prior to the *bedikah* of the first day and then wait several minutes before performing the *bedikah*.[2] If you think that even on the seventh day you will not be able to obtain a clean *bedikah*, you may contact a halakhic authority to determine whether there are grounds for further leniency. After immersing in the *mikveh*, make sure that you continue wearing colored underwear and observe the instructions pertaining to *ketamim*.

Halakhic Expansion

Reactions to the hormonal IUD differ from woman to woman. According to current medical data, 40–70% of users are likely to experience frequent staining during the first 3–6 months of use, while the rest experience no staining at all.[3] Some women will manage to avoid becoming *niddot* as a result of *ketamim* during this period while others may become *niddot* and then find it difficult to become *tehorot* for a long time thereafter.

Regarding the possibility of minimizing the number of *bedikot* during the seven *neki'im* or foregoing the *bedikah* of the seventh day, see above, *Siman* 24: Reducing *Bedikot* following a Miscarriage, n. 18.

With regard to douching, in *Responsa Ḥelkat Yaakov*,[4] R. Mordekhai Yaakov Breisch was asked about a woman who constantly finds green and brown *ketamim* and cannot manage to become *tehorah*: May she douche before performing a *bedikah* on the first and seventh days, or is douching akin to turning a blind eye to a prohibition? R. Breisch inquires into the purpose of *bedikot* during the seven *neki'im*. Are they to prove that there was no bleeding between one *bedikah* and the next, or are they to establish a *ḥazakah* of *taharah* and thus only examine the woman's status at

2. Douching, or vaginal irrigation, entails introducing a stream of water directly into the vagina to remove any discharges. Douching kits are sold in pharmacies, and one can prepare douching fluid at home. For the most part, douching is not recommended because it alters the natural balance of vaginal bacteria and can cause vaginal irritation. Therefore, it should not be done regularly except when recommended by a medical authority. However, if one douches only irregularly, as in the present case, it is generally not a problem.
3. See Medical Appendix V: Contraception.
4. *Yoreh De'ah siman* 4 (2:87 in the old printing).

the moment of the *bedikah*? He cites the view of *Ḥavat Da'at*[5] regarding a woman who experienced menstrual bleeding and then developed a bleeding *makkah* that makes it impossible for her to perform a *bedikah* without finding blood. In such a case, according to *Ḥavat Da'at*, it is sufficient to obtain one clean *bedikah* in addition to a *hefsek taharah* to establish a presumption of *taharah*.[6] Based on this, R. Breisch concludes that *Ḥavat Da'at* maintains that the purpose of a *bedikah* is not to prove that she did not experience bleeding in the intervening days, but to establish a *ḥazakah* of *taharah*. Based on this reasoning, douching prior to performing a *bedikah* is permitted.

A similar debate about the purpose of *bedikot* is evident from a dispute among the *Rishonim* about the required number of *bedikot* during the seven *neki'im*. Rosh[7] and Rashba[8] maintain that the *bedikot* are necessary to establish a *ḥazakah* of *taharah*, and one *bedikah* over the course of seven days is sufficient to establish this presumption. The requirement to perform a *bedikah* on each of the seven *neki'im* is for a different reason, namely, that each day must be "counted before us," that is, that each day must be "counted" independently and have its own established *ḥazakah* of *taharah*. This is the reasoning behind the view of R. Yehoshua and R. Akiva in the Mishnah.[9] However, *bedi'avad*, one *bedikah* during the entire seven days suffices. Rosh quotes Ra'avad regarding the status of a *bedikah* that was performed in the middle of the seven days – a case that does not appear in the Gemara. In his view – and Rashba concurs[10] – a *bedikah* in the middle of the seven days is preferable to a *bedikah* on just the seventh day, because it establishes a *ḥazakah* for all subsequent days. This seems to be the rationale of other *Rishonim* who rule that one *bedikah* per day is sufficient.[11] In contrast, it seems that the reasoning of the *Rishonim* who require two *bedikot* per day[12] is to confirm that she did not experience bleeding since the last *bedikah*.[13]

---

5. 196:3.
6. *Responsa Har Tzvi, Yoreh De'ah siman* 146, writes that a woman with a lesion requires a *hefsek taharah* and *bedikot* on the first and seventh of the *neki'im*. However, he writes that he was pleased to see his view corroborated in *Responsa Maharash Engel* 3:83, but that responsum states that a *hefsek taharah* plus one *bedikah* is sufficient.
7. *Niddah* 10:5.
8. *Torat Ha-Bayit, bayit* 7, *sha'ar* 5.
9. *Niddah* 68b.
10. *Torat Ha-Bayit, bayit* 7, *sha'ar* 5 and *Mishmeret Ha-Bayit ad loc*, s.v. "*amar ha-kotev*."
11. Ramban, Rashba, Rosh, and *Hagahot Maimoniyot*, cited in *Bet Yosef, Yoreh De'ah* 196:4.
12. *Semag, Semak, Sefer Ha-Terumah, Mordekhai*, cited in *Bet Yosef, Yoreh De'ah* 196:4.
13. This understanding of the two views appears in *Igrot Moshe, Yoreh De'ah* 1:94.

R. Breisch also raises the question of turning a blind eye to a prohibition. In this regard, he cites Maharsham,[14] who discusses wearing colored undergarments during the seven *neki'im*, concluding that in a case of *igun*, where the couple would be prohibited to each other for an indefinite period of time, we do not show concern about turning a blind eye, and it is permitted. Thus, according to *Ḥelkat Yaakov*, one may permit douching prior to the *bedikah* of the first day, since the woman performed a *hefsek taharah* the day before and found it to be clean. The *bedikah* is to establish the *ḥazakah* of subsequent days, so she may certainly douche beforehand. Regarding the *bedikah* of the seventh day, *Ḥelkat Yaakov* cites Rashi[15]: "'And here it teaches [that a *bedikah*] at the end [of the seven clean days is sufficient] even though there was no [*bedikah*] at the beginning [of the seven clean days]' – for by virtue of the *bedikah* of the seventh [day], we presume the *taharah* of all six previous days." It seems, according to Rashi, that the *bedikah* of the seventh day demonstrates that there was no bleeding throughout the seven days, for if there was bleeding, it would be found during the *bedikah*. If so, douching undermines the purpose of the *bedikah*, because it will prevent us from assessing the previous days.

Later, R. Breisch brings a different understanding of Rashi's interpretation: A clean *bedikah* inherently produces a presumption of *taharah*, making any demonstration or assessment of her status on previous days unnecessary.[16]

In conclusion, R. Breisch rules that the woman may douche before the *bedikah* of the first day. This is because its purpose is to establish a *ḥazakah* for subsequent days, and there is not yet a situation of double leniency (the leniency of douching and the leniency of reducing the *bedikot* of the remaining days, as she has not yet been lenient about these other *bedikot*). However, regarding the *bedikah* of the seventh day, whose purpose, according to the straightforward meaning of Rashi's words, is to establish the *ḥazakah* of the previous days, by demonstrating and assessing by means of *bedikah* that there was no residual blood, and after

14. *Responsa Maharsham* 1:81 and 82.
15. *Niddah* 69a.
16. *Responsa Ḥelkat Yaakov, Yoreh De'ah siman* 100: "If so, we can understand the meaning of Rashi's aforementioned comment in this way as well. 'For by virtue of the *bedikah* of the seventh [day], we presume the *taharah* of all six previous days because she stopped bleeding [and performed a *hefsek taharah*] on the third day [after the onset of bleeding]' – not because of a demonstration or assessment that if she had experienced bleeding on the previous days it would be apparent now as well, as we reasoned earlier, but because we see on the seventh day that she is *tehorah*, so we establish her presumption of *taharah* for all the previous days, which are now deemed to have been examined and counted."

she has already been lenient about *bedikot* during the five intervening days, it is impossible to add another leniency and permit douching.

Taharat Ha-Bayit[17] permits douching for reasons of health during the seven *neki'im*: "It seems that it is fine to do so, and we are not concerned that perhaps blood was rinsed away by the stream of water, for we do not presume a problem once the *bedikah* of the *hefsek taharah* established her *ḥezkat taharah*." However, he does not address a case where the woman knows that she has *ketamim*, which, it would seem, weakens her *ḥazakah*.

R. Moshe Feinstein,[18] after discussing the reasoning behind the views of the *Rishonim*, addresses the reasoning of *Shulḥan Arukh*, which rules that *lekhatḥilah* a woman must perform *bedikot* twice a day, and then cites Rosh that, *bedi'avad*, one *bedikah* per day is sufficient. *Shulḥan Arukh* further adds that, *bedi'avad*, one *bedikah* on the first and one of the seventh of the *neki'im* suffices. *Sidrei Taharah* proves that with regard to the purpose of a *bedikah*, *Shulḥan Arukh* agrees with Rosh but nevertheless required *bedikot* at the beginning and end (i.e., on the first and seventh days) since there is concern about violating a transgression whose punishment is *karet*, and it is not clear with whom the *halakhah* accords. Therefore, it is proper to be stringent.

On the other hand, R. Feinstein continues, one can argue that perhaps *Shulḥan Arukh* agrees with *Semag*, who maintains – like Rosh – that the purpose of the *bedikot* is to establish the *ḥezkat taharah* that the day is clean; but that it is impossible to establish such a *ḥazakah* without performing two *bedikot* in one day, thus demonstrating that there was no bleeding for an entire day or night – as is required for *taharot*. According to this understanding, *Shulḥan Arukh* only differs from *Semag* with respect to a *bedi'avad* case or under pressing circumstances: *Shulḥan Arukh* rules that one *bedikah* suffices in such cases because "part of the day is equivalent to its entirety" ("*miktzat ha-yom ke-kulo*"). For this reason, one should take care to perform the morning *bedikot*.

Since the reasoning of *Shulḥan Arukh* is not entirely clear, R. Feinstein writes that there are grounds to permit douching only after the *bedikah* of the first day and after the *bedikah* of the seventh day. Only under truly pressing circumstances may one rely on the reasoning of *Sidrei Taharah* and permit douching between the *hefsek taharah* and the *bedikah* of the morning of the first clean day.

---

17. Part 2, pp. 315–21.
18. *Igrot Moshe, Yoreh De'ah* 1:94.

R. Feinstein's responsum addresses douching that is necessary for medical reasons, in cases where there is no reason to suspect that there is any bleeding. This situation is different from the one in the question, in which a woman asks whether she may douche if she knows she has *ketamim*. R. Feinstein addresses this question elsewhere:[19]

> Regarding whether she may wash herself thoroughly in that place [i.e., douche] before *bedikot*: For a typical woman, there is no drawback to this, as there is already a *ḥazakah* that she stopped bleeding. However, she should wait a little while – about a quarter of an hour – and then perform the *bedikah*. However, regarding this woman, who for several months has regularly found brown stains, if there is any uncertainty about the status of the stain, she should not douche, for if she does not find [stains] as she normally does in recent months, perhaps it is because of the douching.

Thus, according to *Igrot Moshe,* one should not douche when there are known to be *ketamim* of uncertain status. However, in this responsum,[20] R. Feinstein is addressing the case of a woman who regularly finds a *ketem* on the first of the seven *neki'im* – and on that day only. Therefore, there is no risk of *igun* here – that is, there is no concern that the couple will be forbidden to one another for a long time.

It therefore seems, in conclusion, that in more complicated cases, we may rely on *Ḥelkat Yaakov* and douche before the *bedikah* of the first day. And if it seems, on the seventh day, that it will be impossible to obtain a clean *bedikah*, we may rely on those who rule "[a *bedikah*] at the beginning [of the seven clean days is sufficient] even though there was no [*bedikah*] at the end [of the seven clean days]" and forego the *bedikah* of the seventh day.

However, in the present case, R. Yehuda Henkin disagrees and maintains that we may not rely on the ruling of *Ḥelkat Yaakov* in this case. *Ḥelkat Yaakov* is addressing a case of real *igun,* whereas in the present case, the questioner can remove the IUD, and the *ketamim* will stop. Moreover, in the present case, the woman managed to become *tehorah,* so who says she will not manage again in

19. *Igrot Moshe, Yoreh De'ah* 2:71. See also *Ḥazon Ish, Niddah siman* 81 at the beginning, which implies that if she douched and performed a *bedikah* a while later, the *bedikah* counts, but in principle it is better not to douche.

20. *Igrot Moshe, Yoreh De'ah* 2:71: "Regarding your wife, who for many months obtains a clean *hefsek taharah* and *mokh daḥuk* throughout *bein ha-shemashot,* but on the morrow, the first of the seven *neki'im,* in the morning *bedikah,* finds a brown [stain]...."

the future? Therefore, in the present case, where there is a merely theoretical uncertainty about whether there will be *igun,* we should not rush to be lenient. On the other hand, there is concern that the husband or the couple will stumble and transgress; this is what R. Breisch meant when he wrote that the contemporary generation is weak. Ultimately, the *posek* can only go by what he sees, based on his familiarity with the couple.

O.K.

Siman 59

A Spot on a Tampon

Question

I have been using the hormonal IUD for a year. Since its insertion, I have continued getting my monthly period, but sometimes it is very light – not more than a few spots. This time, I thought I was about to get my period, and so I inserted a tampon. Ultimately, I did not get my period, but when I removed the tampon, I found a brown spot on it. Am I still considered *niddah* because I thought that I was getting my period?

Answer

If a woman thinks she became *niddah* but later ascertains that she was mistaken, she is not *niddah*. Therefore, you are not *niddah* on account of mistakenly thinking that your period began.

Regarding the brown spot: Had the spot been found on a panty liner or undergarment, unaccompanied by a halakhically significant *hargashah*, the spot would have been judged according to the rules of *ketamim*, and it would not render you *niddah*. However, blood found on a tampon has the status of blood found through an internal examination. Therefore, if the spot is of a hue that renders one *teme'ah*, then you are *niddah*, regardless of the size of the spot.

In the future, when you think you are about to get your period, we recommend that you use a panty liner or pad and not use a tampon until you are certain that the bleeding has already begun.

Halakhic Expansion

The Mirena[1] is a hormonal IUD that releases progesterone. After an adjustment period of several months, women often experience brief or light menstrual bleeding, or no bleeding at all.

Blood found on a tampon[2] has the same status as blood found during a *bedikah,* for there is concern that the woman may have experienced a *hargashah* but did not notice it.[3] Therefore, any reddish hue found on it renders the woman *teme'ah,* no matter the size of the spot.[4]

It should be noted that if a woman used a tampon to perform a *bedikah* or as a *mokh daḥuk,* following the *bedikah* she must open the tampon and inspect it thoroughly.[5] A superficial inspection is insufficient, because the tampon, due to its absorbency, may appear clean on the outside, but once it is opened and its folds are inspected, a drop of blood that it absorbed is likely to be discovered.

On the other hand, in the present case, where the woman was not required to perform a *bedikah,* she could have *lekhatḥilah* discarded the tampon without inspecting it.[6] However, once she has seen the spot on the tampon, she is required to ascertain its status.

We must also clarify whether the sensations that led the woman to insert a tampon constitute a *veset ha-guf,* in which case she would need to separate

1. Hormonal IUDs are marketed as Mirena and under other brand names. See Medical Appendix V: Contraception.
2. If a woman suspects that the chafing of the tampon or a vaginal lesion caused the blood stain, see above, *Siman* 52: Bleeding from an Abrasion caused by an IUD.
3. *Shulḥan Arukh, Yoreh De'ah* 190:33. R. Henkin raises the possibility that, according to the position that a halakhically recognized *hargashah* is almost not found nowadays, there is today no longer any reason to be concerned about it expressly when inserting a tampon or performing a *bedikah*. Therefore, under very pressing circumstances, perhaps blood found on a *bedikah* cloth or a tampon can be judged according to the laws of *ketamim*. R. Zvi Sobolofsky, in *Taharat Ha-Kodesh: The Laws and Concepts of Niddah* (p. 313), makes a similar suggestion in the name of R. Mordechai Willig, namely, that in cases of great need, one may be lenient even with respect to blood found during an internal examination.
4. For further discussion of this, see below, *Siman* 60: Finding Blood on a Diaphragm.
5. R. Yaakov Ariel permits, *bedi'avad,* the use of a tampon to perform a *hefsek taharah* as long as the woman cleaned and examined herself well before inserting the tampon, and as long as the tampon completely seals the place, such that not even a drop of blood could slip out. See the Torah VeHa'aretz website: https://bit.ly/HefsekTaharahRAriel. Under pressing circumstances, it seems that one may offer such guidance as long as she is careful to open the tampon for close examination following the *hefsek taharah* or *bedikah*.
6. This is the ruling of R. Warhaftig.

in anticipation of her *veset*. If they are clearly symptoms of the onset of menstruation, for example, if the woman feels a particular type of back pain that she only experiences at the onset of menstruation, it is considered a *veset ha-guf*.[7] However, if the sensations are more general and do not clearly indicate the onset of menstruation – for instance, she has a stomach ache that she may also experience from an upset stomach, or the like – there is no need to treat them as a *veset ha-guf* that precedes the onset of menses.[8] Even if the woman feels, based on these sensations, that the onset of menses has indeed arrived, as long as she cannot identify a specific sensation that clearly indicates the onset of menses, she need not observe it.[9] In the present case, it is recommended that you not insert a tampon so that you do not become *niddah* before the onset of menstruation.[10]

In addition, we must consider the question from the perspective of "*shavyeih a-nafsheih ḥatikhah de-issura*" (lit., "He has rendered this thing forbidden to himself").[11] In the present case, has the woman rendered herself *niddah* – even though she has not experienced any bleeding – by virtue of her words[12] or actions,[13] based on the laws of *nedarim*, vows, or due to the credibility that a person has with regard to themselves?[14] The Gemara explains that such a

7. *Shulḥan Arukh, Yoreh De'ah* 189:19. In other words, in such a situation, the next month she must observe the *onot ha-perishah* of the *veset ha-guf*.
8. See *Responsa Shevet Ha-Levi* 3:117, which states that sensations not specific to menstruation are not considered *veset ha-guf* that must be observed, even if they occur around the onset of menstruation.
9. On the physiological sensations that render one *teme'ah* under the laws of *hargashah*, see above, *Siman* 25.
10. For a broader discussion of monthly spotting due to the hormonal IUD, see above, *Siman* 56: Minor Monthly Spotting.
11. The principle that a person can render something forbidden to himself is learned in *Kiddushin* 65a. The case there relates to a man who claims that he betrothed a woman. Even though she denies it, he is forbidden to marry any of her relatives.
12. *Shulḥan Arukh, Yoreh De'ah* 185:3: "If she said to her husband, 'I am *teme'ah*,' and then said, 'I am *tehorah*,' she is not believed."
13. *Shulḥan Arukh, Yoreh De'ah* 185:2: "If she is presumed to be *niddah* on account of her neighbors, who saw her wearing the clothing she reserves for *niddah*, she is considered *teme'ah* with certainty."
14. *Responsa Mahari ben Lev* 1:19 states that the rule of "*shavyeih a-nafsheih*" is akin to accepting a prohibition as a vow. In contrast, *Noda Bi-Yehudah, Even Ha-Ezer* 2:23 states that the prohibition is based upon the laws of *nedarim*, on the premise that a person has credibility with respect to himself. A practical ramification of the difference between the two approaches would be in a case where a woman has a pretext for her actions. In such a case, she has not undermined her general credibility; rather, she has provided an alternative explanation for her conduct. However,

woman can be rendered *tehorah* if she has a pretext ("*amatla*") that explains her conduct.[15] It is therefore important that as long as the woman is not *teme'ah* for certain – for example, if she experienced spotting – she should not tell her husband that she is *niddah* even if she thinks that the spotting indicates the onset of menstruation. Nevertheless, if it becomes clear that she has mistakenly considered herself *teme'ah,* she and her husband are not forbidden to one another. Even if she told her husband that she will certainly get her period very soon, and ultimately she did not get her period, her declaration does not render her *niddah,* because she merely said that she would soon be *teme'ah.* Insertion of a tampon, on its own, is not considered an action that attests that a woman is *niddah,* because it is not a public action.[16] Moreover, the action only indicates that she is preparing for the onset of menses, not that the bleeding itself has begun.[17]

M.R.

---

according to the laws of vows and oaths, if she vowed that she is *niddah,* the vow remains valid even if she provides an excuse for her motives.

15. *Ketubot* 22a. If a woman has a reasonable excuse for why she said she is *niddah,* she is believed and is not *teme'ah.* The Gemara recounts that Shmuel did not accept his wife's pretext, but as an act of piety, not because *halakhah* requires it.

16. The commentators on *Shulḥan Arukh, Yoreh De'ah* 185:2 discuss whether an *amatla* works even in a case where the woman's actions attest that she is *niddah,* and she does not simply say that she is *niddah.* See *Taz* 185:2 and *Torat Ha-Shelamim* 185:6. According to them, an *amatla* cannot cancel a public action like wearing the clothes of *niddah* in the presence of friends. In contrast, *Shakh* 185:5 rules that if she can explain why she acted how she did, the *amatla* works, and she is not *teme'ah.* In the present case, her actions are private and hidden. For a discussion of the differences between words and deeds and between private and public acts in this regard, see *Bet Yosef, Yoreh De'ah siman* 185.

17. *Shi'urei Shevet Ha-Levi* 185:3:2 addresses the question of whether an *amatla* has validity against an action like wearing the clothes of *niddah* at the time when she anticipates the onset of menstruation. According to R. Wosner, the *amatla* neutralizes even action, and even when she anticipates her *veset,* because at the time of her *veset* there is no presumption *mi-de'Orayta* that she will experience bleeding, only that she must be concerned for it and perform a *bedikah* to confirm that she has not.

Siman 60

Finding Blood on a Diaphragm

Question

I use a diaphragm for contraception. Yesterday, when I removed the diaphragm, I found a spot of blood on the side that faces inward. Am I *niddah*?

Answer

Finding blood on a diaphragm renders a woman *niddah* just as finding blood on a *bedikah* cloth does. If the stain you found is one of the prohibited colors, you are *niddah* and must wait four or five days, depending upon your custom, perform a *hefsek taharah*, and count seven *neki'im*.

If you think that you may have scratched yourself while removing the diaphragm, and that this is what caused the bleeding, we recommend that you consult a gynecologist to ascertain whether there is indeed a cut that can bleed. If there is, you are not *niddah*. It is important to add that you are not obligated to inspect the diaphragm when you remove it. We recommend that in the future you rinse the diaphragm without looking at it and thus avoid uncertainty.

Halakhic Expansion

For an expanded discussion of the diaphragm as a contraceptive, see Medical Appendix V: Contraception. A diaphragm is used as follows: The woman folds it, inserts it deep inside the vagina, and leaves it there for at least six hours after intercourse. Since it is deep inside the vagina,[1] a place deemed free of lice, blood found in the inner side of the diaphragm (i.e., the side facing the cervix) has the status of blood found on a *bedikah* cloth,[2] which renders the woman *niddah*. Therefore, as long as the blood is of a color that would cause *tum'ah*, the woman is *niddah*, regardless of the size of the stain.[3]

The Gemara (*Niddah* 57b) determines, based on the verse, "If a woman has a discharge, blood discharging from her flesh" (Vayikra 15:19), that a woman becomes *teme'ah* as a *niddah* only when she feels the sensation of the discharge of blood from her body. According to Rambam,[4] who maintains that any blood from the uterus can be presumed to have been accompanied by a sensation (*hargashah*), there are grounds to say that blood found on a *bedikah* cloth or diaphragm renders one *teme'ah mi-de'Orayta*, since it certainly came from the uterus.[5] Even those who disagree with Rambam about the presumption that there was a *hargashah*, blood found on a diaphragm nevertheless renders the woman *niddah* in light of the Gemara's statements about situations where the woman might not have noticed a *hargashah* accompanying the discharge of blood.[6]

In three situations, the Sages[7] presume that a woman may have experienced a *hargashah* without being aware of it during the discharge of blood: while urinating, while performing a *bedikah*, and during intercourse. There is concern that, while performing a *bedikah*, a woman will mistakenly attribute the sensation of the

1. R. Nachum Rabinovitch (*Responsa Si'aḥ Naḥum siman* 56, p. 191) maintains that blood found on a diaphragm should be viewed as blood discharged from a woman's body through a tube, which does not make her *teme'ah* since it never touched her skin. R. Tzvi Pesaḥ Frank (*Responsa Har Tzvi, Yoreh De'ah* 148) brings a similar rationale from a rabbi who proposed ruling leniently about blood found on a diaphragm. However, R. Frank rejects this on the grounds that the diaphragm is not actually attached to the cervix and does not cause the discharge of blood, but merely covers the external os of the cervix and catches blood that is discharged.
2. *Shulḥan Arukh, Yoreh De'ah* 190:33.
3. *Igrot Moshe, Yoreh De'ah* 4:17:16. For further discussion of blood found on a *bedikah* cloth, see above, *Siman* 59: A Spot on a Tampon.
4. *Mishneh Torah, Hilkhot Isurei Bi'ah* 9:1.
5. *Arukh Ha-Shulḥan, Yoreh De'ah* 183:54–56 rules that a woman is *teme'ah mi-de'Orayta*, with certainty, if she finds blood on a *bedikah* cloth. He bases this ruling on *Mishneh Torah, Hilkhot Isurei Bi'ah* 5:5: "Blood found in the *prozdor* (vaginal canal) – from the *lul* (external os) inward is *tamei*, because it presumably came from the uterus." Therefore, when she finds blood during a *bedikah*, it is certain that it was discharged from the uterus; even if she did not experience any *hargashah* now, the discharge was certainly accompanied by a *hargashah*.
6. For an extended discussion of *hargashot*, see above, *Siman* 25: The Law of *Hargashah*.
7. *Niddah* 57b.

discharge of blood to the sensation of the *bedikah* cloth; therefore, the bloodstain on the cloth is treated as an experience of bleeding accompanied by a *hargashah*.[8]

There is an authority who rules that as long as a woman states with certainty that she had no sensation of a discharge of blood, we may rely on her words even in the instance of a *bedikah* cloth, and there is no concern that she was mistaken about a *hargashah*.[9] According to this position, blood found on the *bedikah* cloth should be judged according to the laws of *ketamim*.[10] However, in *Shi'urei Shevet Ha-Levi*,[11] R. Wosner writes that this is a *ḥiddush* that does not seem to be supported by the wording of *Shulḥan Arukh*. It therefore seems correct that blood found on a *bedikah* cloth makes a woman *niddah*, as this is an uncertainty about a *deOrayta* prohibition, even if the woman claims with complete confidence that she did not experience a *hargashah*.[12] Certainly, then, blood found on a diaphragm renders her *niddah*, since it is placed deep inside the vagina for several hours, including during intercourse; and presumably, a woman could not say for certain that she experienced no *hargashah* of blood being discharged for all those hours. Moreover, we do not know whether the bleeding occurred when she inserted the diaphragm, or during intercourse, or when she removed the diaphragm – moments when she could have experienced *hargashah* without noticing.

It should be noted that there is a chance that a woman may scratch herself with a fingernail when removing the diaphragm, thus causing mild vaginal bleeding. Therefore, if she senses an abrasion, she may consult a doctor or a *bodeket*

---

8. Rashi on *Niddah* 57b, s.v. "*de-argishah*," offers the inverse explanation: Perhaps the woman thought she sensed the discharge of blood but really sensed the *bedikah* cloth. For an expanded discussion, see above, *Siman* 27: Blood on Toilet Paper.
9. *Responsa Neta Sha'ashu'im siman* 21.
10. Other *poskim* consider the concern that a *hargashah* was masked by the sensation of a *bedikah* cloth to be at the *deRabanan* level. Accordingly, blood found on a *bedikah* cloth is treated as a *ketem* and not as stringently as bona fide menstrual bleeding. See *Responsa Shav Yaakov siman* 36; *Responsa Maharash Engel* 2:61. R. Ovadiah Yosef, in *Taharat Ha-Bayit*, 1:1:5, p. 17, says that the ruling hinges on the depth of the *bedikah*: If she did not insert the *bedikah* cloth "to the depth of the uterus" (i.e., into the depth of the vaginal canal), the blood is judged according to the laws of *ketamim*. A diaphragm covers the external os of the cervix and so, it seems, is similar to a *bedikah* "to the depth of the uterus."
11. *Shi'urei Shevet Ha-Levi* 190:54:7, p. 216.
12. On the other hand, R. Henkin questions this: Considering the widespread acceptance of the lenient view that women nowadays do not generally experience a halakhic *hargashah* accompanying the discharge of blood, it is unclear why we would hold that a woman who is presumed never to experience a *hargashah* in general might experience one precisely when performing a *bedikah*. Therefore, under pressing circumstances, we may be lenient, and this requires further study.

taharah to ascertain whether there is indeed a bleeding abrasion to which the blood can be attributed.[13]

Since when a woman is not *niddah,* she has a *ḥazakah* of *taharah,* she therefore is not required to inspect the diaphragm when she removes it. It is therefore recommended to refrain from doing so, in order to avoid unnecessary questions.[14]

It should be noted that even if the woman becomes *niddah* due to blood she found on a diaphragm, she need not observe the time she found the blood as a *veset.* This is similar to the case of a woman who found blood on a *bedikah* cloth, who does not observe the *onot perishah* unless she became *teme'ah* by finding blood on the cloth for three consecutive cycles.[15]

M.R.

13. A "*bodeket taharah*" is a nurse who has undergone halakhic training to identify vaginal and cervical lesions and diagnose whether the bleeding is uterine or not. A *bodeket* cannot answer halakhic questions or offer medical treatment. She can, however, help resolve questions that involve attribution to a *makkah.* A *bodeket* can also be asked to perform a *hefsek taharah* for a woman by avoiding the wounded area during a *bedikah.* It is, of course, a personal prerogative and not a halakhic obligation to turn to a *bodeket taharah* for assitance. Sometimes the examination entails some mild discomfort, much like a gynecological examination; but sometimes it can help a woman who suffers from lesions, especially when an immediate gynecological appointment is unavailable.
   See also above, *Siman* 21: Attributing Blood to a *Petza* during the Seven *Neki'im.*
14. Similarly, *Aḥaronim* instruct women not to look at toilet paper, so as not to cause the proliferation of questions. (See *Shi'urei Shevet Ha-Levi* 191:20, p. 222; *Sha'arei Orah,* p. 89; *Taharah Ke-Halakhah* 2:16) Thus, there is no need to inspect the diaphragm when removing it.
15. *Shulḥan Arukh, Yoreh De'ah* 190:54. This is also the ruling of *Shi'urei Shevet Ha-Levi* 190:54:7, p. 216.

Siman 61

Onot Perishah with Fertility Awareness Method (FAM)

Question

For the past six months, I have been using the Fertility Awareness Method to prevent conception. Based on my ovulation date, I know for certain when I will get my period, and this has happened more than three times. Can I consider this a *veset kavu'a*? This can potentially save us from two days of separation.

Answer

Based on your description, you have established a *veset ha-guf* through your experience of bleeding at a fixed interval after ovulation. As with any *veset kavu'a*, you must perform a *bedikah* on the day that you anticipate getting your period. You need not observe the other *onot perishah*.

Halakhic Expansion

The Fertility Awareness Method (FAM)[1] tracks the hormonal changes expressed in body temperature, the viscosity of cervical mucus, and changes in the position of

1. For a detailed explanation of FAM, see Toni Weschler, *Taking Charge of Your Fertility* (New York: HarperCollins, 2015), With FAM, a woman takes a training course to detect when she ovulates based on the physical changes brought about by ovulation. Thus, a couple knows when to refrain from relations in order to avoid conception, or, alternatively – if active contraception is permitted for them – when to use barrier methods of contraception, such as a diaphragm or spermicide suppositories. Without the addition of these methods, FAM limits the number of days when an observant couple may have relations.

the cervix itself in order to detect the right time to conceive or, alternatively, to avoid intercourse so as to prevent conception. It also makes it possible to predict the onset of menses.[2] As in the case of a *veset ha-guf*, a woman must be attentive to physical changes in order to track her hormonal cycle and predict the expected onset of menses.

A *veset ha-guf* is a bodily phenomenon that manifests before the onset of menses and indicates its arrival.[3] The Mishnah states[4]: "If she yawns, or sneezes, or she feels pain in the navel or her lower abdomen, or she experiences discharge, or she is gripped by chills, or the like – if she establishes [a pattern of experiencing such a bodily phenomenon prior to the onset of menses] three times, it is a *veset*." The Gemara[5] elaborates that "or the like" includes "a woman whose head aches, or her limbs ache, or she trembles or belches."

Do the symptoms mentioned in the Mishnah and Gemara constitute an exhaustive list of what establishes a *veset ha-guf*? Most *Rishonim* copy the wording of the Mishnah and Gemara alone, and some conclude, based on their lack of elaboration, that their intent is to exclude other symptoms.[6] However, Rambam concludes his list with, "or the like,"[7] and in his commentary on the Mishnah,[8] he includes symptoms such as depression, drowsiness, and headaches.[9] Rosh[10] writes that "any sensation of bodily change, once it has become established as a pattern, indicates that the body is preparing to expel blood," and *Tur* writes this as well.[11]

---

2. A woman using FAM monitors her body temperature on the days immediately before, during, and immediately after ovulation. The body temperature usually rises after ovulation. A woman who detects this rise in body temperature three times in a row establishes a *veset ha-guf*. Based on the sign (the rise in body temperature) and the fixed interval between it and the onset of menses, she calculates the *onat ha-perishah*, when the couple must abstain from relations.
3. It is also possible for specific volitional actions, such as jumping, to precipitate bleeding, in which case the *veset* is triggered by the action (*veset ha-kefitzot*). The present question concerns a *veset ha-guf* precipitated by an involuntary action, like a yawn (*veset ha-pihuk*). In such cases, the physical symptom *indicates* the arrival of menses but does not *cause* or trigger the arrival of menses. See below.
4. *Mishnah Niddah* 8:9.
5. *Niddah* 63b.
6. *Responsa Divrei Yatziv, Likutim Ve-Hashmatot siman* 80 and *Yoreh De'ah siman* 80, though he did not mention Rambam's wording, which is puzzling.
7. *Mishneh Torah, Hilkhot Isurei Bi'ah* 8:2; *Hilkhot Metamei Mishkav U-Moshav* 3:6.
8. *Niddah* 9:8.
9. See the comprehensive article by Yoatzot Halacha Dr. Deena Zimmerman and Dr. Tova Ganzel, "*Veset Ha-guf: Hebet Hilkhati U-Refu'i*," in *Teḥumin* 20, p. 363ff.
10. *Niddah* 9:1[b].
11. *Yoreh De'ah siman* 189. *Igrot Moshe* (*Yoreh De'ah* 1:84) includes "chest pain" as well; perhaps this refers to breast tenderness. See also *Orot Ha-Taharah* 8:24. Dr. Deena Zimmerman and Dr. Tova Ganzel infer from R. Zeraḥiah Ha-Levi's glosses on *Ba'alei Ha-Nefesh* that eating sharp

Yet we still must clarify: Is there a maximum time interval that can elapse between the appearance of the symptom and the onset of menstrual bleeding for the symptom to qualify as a *veset ha-guf*? The Gemara[12] discusses whether jumping can precipitate the onset of bleeding the next day:

> Rav Ashi says: For example, if she jumped on Sunday and saw [bleeding], again jumped on Sunday and saw [bleeding], [then jumped on Shabbat and did not see bleeding], but then saw [bleeding] on Sunday without jumping. Lest you say that the matter is revealed retroactively that it was the day that triggered [the bleeding] and not the jumping, [the *baraita* therefore] teaches us that yesterday's jumping can also trigger it, and the reason she did not see [bleeding] is because the time when jumping [can trigger bleeding] has not yet arrived.

Based on this passage in the Gemara, *Shulḥan Arukh*[13] rules that if a day elapses between jumping and the onset of bleeding, it cannot be considered a *veset*, as the jumping cannot be linked to the next day's bleeding. However, *Shakh*[14] cites the view of several authorities that yesterday's jumping can indeed trigger today's bleeding. *Noda Bi-Yehudah*[15] infers from *Shakh* that the two events can be linked even when separated by a day. *Shevet Ha-Levi* states that unlike the act of jumping, that is an action that *triggers* the onset of bleeding, a yawn – which is a physical *reaction* to or *indicator* of the onset of menses – can be linked to bleeding that begins after even an interval of two days or longer.[16]

The interval between the end of the premenstrual symptoms and the onset of bleeding determines when the *onat ha-perishah* must be observed. Thus, *Shulḥan Arukh*[17] rules that if a woman regularly experiences bleeding after the cessation of a symptom, the *onat ha-perishah* does not begin until the symptom ceases. *Igrot Moshe*[18] addresses the case of a woman who has no

---

foods should be included as a *veset ha-guf* because it is the premenstrual bodily changes that increase the appetite for sharp foods. See their aforementioned article, pp. 365–66.

12. *Niddah* 11a.
13. *Yoreh De'ah* 189:17.
14. Ibid. 189:49.
15. Ibid. 2:93.
16. *Shi'urei Shevet Ha-Levi* 189:19:10 and *Responsa Shevet Ha-Levi* 3:124, s.v. "*ve'al pi hana"l.*" However, he adds: "But if the interval is excessive, it requires further study, because the uterus does not fill with menstrual blood many days beforehand." See also *siman* 117.
17. *Yoreh De'ah* 189:24.
18. Ibid. 1:84.

veset based on days but always experiences chest pain a week before the onset of menses; the pain subsides, and only then does the bleeding commence. R. Feinstein rules that the *onat ha-perishah* must be observed only once the pain subsides. In *Responsa Shevet Ha-Levi*,[19] R. Wosner rules that a woman who experiences bleeding three days after a yawning fit need not observe *onot perishah* on the first and second days. And in *Shi'urei Shevet Ha-Levi* he writes about longer intervals, namely, that when the physical symptoms appear ten or twelve days before the onset of menses, she does not observe the symptoms as a *veset ha-guf*. He concludes: "A woman must know how many days there are between the appearance of the symptoms and the onset of menses ... and she must observe [*onot perishah*] at the conclusion of the smallest number of days after which she regularly experiences bleeding."[20] Even if we do not accept his physiological descriptions, we learn from here that a *veset ha-guf* can precede the onset of bleeding even by many days.

Symptoms of ovulation generally precede menstruation by twelve to sixteen days, a range that varies from woman to woman and possibly even from month to month. *Gufei Halakhot*[21] writes to rule leniently in the case of women who identify their time of ovulation by taking their temperature with a basal thermometer, that they need not observe *onot perishah* that coincide with days when they will certainly not experience bleeding. He cites *Responsa Riva* as saying that even if a woman experiences premenstrual physical symptoms that cease several days before the onset of bleeding, it still constitutes a *veset ha-guf*.[22] He further writes that symptoms of ovulation are considered a bona fide *veset ha-guf* even if the onset of menses does not occur at a fixed interval of fourteen days after ovulation. Nevertheless, he leaves this inconclusive ("*tzarikh iyun*") because ovulation does not produce a body temperature that is consistent for all ovulations; rather, the curve of body temperature over the month is what indicates ovulation. Moreover, ovulation is not linked conclusively enough to menstruation, as occasionally there can be menstruation without ovulation or ovulation without menstruation.[23]

However, with FAM, a woman detects ovulation on the basis of three symptoms, not just one: body temperature, the position of the cervix, and the texture of the

19. *Responsa Shevet Ha-Levi* 3:117.
20. *Shi'urei Shevet Ha-Levi* 189:19:10, s.v. "*u-vazeh nafka minah.*"
21. *Niddah siman* 189, *Mishnat Sofrim* 12.
22. Ibid. 16.
23. *Gufei Halakhot* (vol. 1), *Niddah siman* 189, *Mishnat Sofrim* 12.

cervical mucus. Therefore, if all three symptoms were identified, it seems that these physical changes can be considered an absolute *veset ha-guf*, which predicts the onset of menses in twelve to sixteen days, at a fixed interval that corresponds with the woman's past experience. Regarding this, R. Yaakov Warhaftig and Yehuda Henkin concur.

Ramban writes that a woman with an established *veset ha-guf* must still observe the *onah beinonit.*[24] However, *Shulḥan Arukh*[25] rules in accordance with Rashba that a woman who has established a *veset kavu'a* does not observe the *onah beinonit.*[26] This can be inferred from *Taz*[27] as well. Therefore, once a woman has established a *veset ha-guf* based on indicators of fertility, she must observe only the *onot* based on her established *veset* and no other *onot*, not even the *onah beinonit.*[28]

S.K. and Editors

24. *Hilkhot Niddah* 5:6: "For it is impossible that she will never again experience [bleeding]."
25. *Yoreh De'ah* 189:1.
26. *Torat Ha-Bayit, bayit* 7, *sha'ar* 2, the laws of *perishah.*
27. *Taz, Yoreh De'ah* 189:1.
28. For a broader discussion, see the article by R. Yaakov Warhaftig, "The *Onah Beinonit* Nowadays," *Teḥumin* 24 [5764], pp. 235–42 (Hebrew).

Siman 62

Checking for Secretions with Fertility Awareness Method (FAM)

Question

I use the Fertility Awareness Method, a natural method for ascertaining the precise time of ovulation and the days when a woman is fertile each month and to prevent conception. The method is based on internal vaginal examinations, through which the woman monitors changes to cervical secretions. When I looked at the secretions on my fingers at the time of ovulation, I saw a bit of blood. Does this render me *niddah*? Is there a way for me to conduct these examinations without becoming *niddah* under similar circumstances in the future?

Answer

The insertion of your fingers into the vagina has the same status as a *bedikah*. Therefore, if the blood is of a hue that causes *tum'ah*, you are considered *niddah*, regardless of the quantity of blood. You must wait four or five days, depending on your custom, and then count seven *neki'im*.

In the future, we recommend that you conduct external examinations only, using toilet paper. You should perform the examination before urinating, so the urine does not rinse off the secretions.[1]

1. To use this method, formal training and diligence are vital. In this way, each woman learns the optimal way to examine her secretions during ovulation.

If an external examination such as this does not allow you to detect subtle changes in the viscosity of the secretions, and you therefore must examine with your fingers, you can examine the secretions around the vulva without inserting your fingers into the vaginal canal itself.

Halakhic Expansion

Fertility Awareness Method (FAM) enables a woman to ascertain precisely when she ovulates. Thus, she can know on which days each month she can become pregnant or, alternatively, when to avoid relations so as to prevent conception.[2] The method is based on the detection of physiological symptoms that accompany ovulation and that a woman can recognize on her own. One of the clearest indicators of ovulation is the change in the natural cervical secretions. Before ovulation, the cervical mucus is relatively dry, viscous, and acidic. Around the time of ovulation, the secretions become more watery, clearer, and can be stretched between the fingers. This change in cervical mucus creates an environment that helps sperm travel through the cervix, uterus, and fallopian tubes to the ovum. After ovulation, the secretions once again become cloudy and drier, and they cease being slippery.

The generally accepted guideline for women using this method is to insert two fingers into the vagina to sample the secretions and check whether they are viscous or slippery. For about 5% of women, ovulation is accompanied by mild bleeding, a result of lower estrogen levels. Sometimes the bleeding is so miniscule that the woman is not even aware of it, and sometimes it is heavier.

Halakhically, a woman is not obligated to check for bleeding during her days of *taharah* or during ovulation. Therefore, if she makes sure to wear colored underwear or a panty liner[3] and does not look at the toilet paper after urinating, she can generally avoid becoming *niddah* from the staining described. However, if she conducts internal examinations during ovulation, there is a good chance that if she indeed experiences some bleeding, she will discover the blood and become *niddah*.

With regard to an examination wherein a woman inserts her fingers deep inside the vagina, it has the status of an internal *bedikah*, and there is concern that she may have experienced a *hargashah* when the blood was discharged from the uterus, but did not notice it because she attributed the sensation to the contact of her fingers. Therefore, in such a case, as with a *bedikah* cloth, the

2. For an expanded discussion of FAM, see Medical Appendix V: Contraception.
3. See *Shulḥan Arukh, Yoreh De'ah* 190:10.

blood she finds on her fingers renders her *niddah*, as there is uncertainty at the *deOrayta* level. She therefore must presume that any drop of blood she finds on her fingers, regardless of the size of the bloodstain or quantity of blood, renders her *niddah*.[4]

If the examination was not conducted inside the vagina, but only outside of it, even if she touched the area around the vulva,[5] blood found on the fingers has the status of a *ketem* found on the body. Rambam[6] rules that a *ketem* on the body causes *tum'ah* even if it is less than the size of a *gris*, but Ra'avad[7] and Rashba[8] disagree; they maintain that even a *ketem* found on the body causes *tum'ah* only if it is the size of a *gris*. *Shulḥan Arukh*[9] rules in accordance with Ra'avad and brings Rambam's view as "some say" ("*yesh omrim*"). *Shakh*[10] rules in accordance with Rambam.

If several blood stains were found on the body, each smaller than a *gris*, even if the spots do not touch one another, they combine to become one *ketem*; if their combined area is larger than a *gris*, the woman is rendered *niddah*.[11] However, if she examines herself externally with synthetic (polyethylene, vinyl, and the like) gloves, the glove is considered an article of clothing, which is not susceptible to *tum'ah*. In such a case, each *ketem* is measured separately, and they do not combine to become a *ketem* the size of a *gris* as long as the individual spots do not touch one another.[12]

---

4. Ibid. 34. See *Taz, ad loc.* 20, who explains that since the blood is found in a place deemed free of lice, there is a disagreement about whether it can be attributed to lice, and therefore the laws of *ketamim* do not apply to such blood.
5. See *Igrot Moshe, Yoreh De'ah* 4:17:16.
6. *Mishneh Torah, Hilkhot Isurei Bi'ah* 9:4.
7. *Ad loc.*
8. Rashba, *Torat Ha-Bayit HaArokh, bayit* 7, *sha'ar* 4 (p. 15b).
9. *Yoreh De'ah* 190:6.
10. Ibid. 190:6:10.
11. This accords with the "*yesh omrim*" cited in *Shulḥan Arukh, Yoreh De'ah* 190:8. Most *poskim* rule in accordance with this position. For an expanded discussion of this, see above, *Siman* 41: Extending the Cycle via Hormonal Contraception. See also *Baḥ*, s.v. "*ve-im ein be-ketem be-makom eḥad*," for a discussion of the source of the ruling about combining stains of blood found on the body into one *ketem*.
12. *Shulḥan Arukh, Yoreh De'ah* 190:8. It should be noted that using rubber gloves can impair the proper examination of the viscosity of the cervical secretions.

It is therefore recommended for a woman concerned that she may find blood during ovulation to conduct the FAM examinations before urinating[13] by wiping the vaginal area externally only, without inserting the toilet paper into the vagina.[14] Since toilet paper is not susceptible to *tum'ah,* even if she finds blood on it before urinating, it will not render her *niddah.*[15]

If examination via toilet paper does not allow the woman to detect subtle changes in the thickness of the secretions, and she therefore must examine with her fingers, she can also examine the secretions around the vulva without inserting her fingers into the vagina.

M.R.

---

13. She may examine after urinating as well, if she waits for 15 seconds after urinating before examining her secretions. (See above, *Siman* 27: Blood on Toilet Paper.) However, as mentioned above, this can impair the possibility of accurately detecting the nature of the secretion.
14. It is also possible to examine the secretions found on the underwear. Alternatively, the woman may conduct an internal examination with the fingers without looking at the secretion, determining its character based on texture alone. Likewise, it is possible to track the sensation of the secretions at the vulva throughout the day.
15. See above, *Siman* 27: Blood on Toilet Paper.

Siman 63

The Mitzvah of Onah on Mikveh Night with Fertility Awareness Method (FAM)

Question

Lately I have been using Fertility Awareness Method to prevent conception. According to this method, the couple abstains from relations at the time of ovulation, when the woman is fertile.[1] The fertile days generally include *mikveh* night and several subsequent days. Is there an obligation to have relations on *mikveh* night? If there is such an obligation, is it better to postpone going to the *mikveh* until after the fertile days have passed?

Answer

The obligation to have relations on the night of immersion in the *mikveh* is part of the mitzvah of *onah*, a mitzvah *deOrayta* under which a husband has conjugal duties toward his wife at specific times, including the night she goes to the *mikveh*. A wife must likewise be with her husband, as part of her duties toward him.[2] Additionally, it is likely that after two weeks of distance, both husband and wife desire physical intimacy, which is a fundamental element of their shared life. Moreover, a

1. FAM is based on the woman gaining intimate familiarity with her body and learning to identify the days when she is fertile. Then, she will either avoid marital relations on those days or use a barrier method of contraception, such as a diaphragm.
2. The scope and parameters of the mutual duties are discussed extensively by others and falls beyond the purview of the present work.

woman's libido is generally at its peak around *mikveh* night. Therefore, when using Fertility Awareness Method (FAM), assuming it is permitted for you to practice contraception, it is worth considering the use of barrier contraceptive methods during the days you are fertile, instead of abstaining from marital relations.[3]

However, as long as there is mutual consent, a couple may abstain from marital relations on *mikveh* night. It is important that this consent be achieved through open and honest communication between husband and wife, and that the decision is made jointly. In principle, if you go to the *mikveh* on time and have decided to postpone marital relations, you may engage in other forms of physical intimacy, such as kissing and hugging. However, in practice it is not always easy for a couple to stand firm in their decision to postpone relations after almost two weeks of separation. This situation can be especially difficult for your husband and raise concerns that he will violate the prohibition of "*hotza'at zera le-vatalah*." Therefore, it is worthwhile for the two of you to consider that perhaps it is better to postpone *mikveh* night or, alternatively, to delay counting the seven *neki'im*, so that *mikveh* night will not coincide with ovulation. On the other hand, it is possible that you will find out retroactively that it was unnecessary to delay counting the seven *neki'im* because ovulation occurred early that month.

Choosing among the three options mentioned – postponing immersion in the *mikveh* after counting seven *neki'im*, delaying the count of seven *neki'im*, and immersing on time but refraining from marital relations on *mikveh* night – depends on your needs and a pragmatic assessment of your ability to stand firm in your decision. As noted, if it is permitted for you to use contraceptives, we recommend that you consider using a diaphragm during the fertile days instead of unnecessarily adding days when you must be apart.

Halakhic Expansion

The night of immersion in the *mikveh* is a time favored for the fulfillment of the mitzvah of *onah*.[4] In addition, marital relations at that time are especially

---

3. There are temporary contraceptive methods like spermicide suppositories, but their effectiveness is low. See Medical Appendix V: Contraception for the efficacy of each method. It is also possible to use a diaphragm on the fertile days. On the permissibility of using a diaphragm, see above, *Siman* 35: Diaphragm Use. Women who use FAM generally use this method, because they do not want to use the pill, which can have side effects. See *Responsa Si'aḥ Naḥum siman* 94.
4. Rashi on *Berakhot* 24a, s.v. "*yom tevilah havah*"; *Shulḥan Arukh, Oraḥ Ḥayim* 240:1. In contrast, *Sidrei Taharah* (184:14, s.v. "*ha-rotzeh latzeit la-derekh*") notes that marital relations on *mikveh* night are in no way preferable to any other time for fulfilling the mitzvah of *onah*, when his wife desires him.

important for the fulfillment of the mitzvah of procreation ("*piryah u-riviyah*") as, according to the Gemara, a women conceives around the time of her immersion in the *mikveh*.[5] Even if the husband already fulfilled the mitzvah of procreation, continuing to have children fulfills the mitzvah of *la-erev*, "in the evening (*la-erev*), do not withhold your hand." In a case where contraception is permitted and the couple chooses to refrain from marital relations during the woman's fertile days, a question arises: Is it better to refrain from marital relations on *mikveh* night, or to postpone the immersion itself?

Ḥazal disagree about whether it is a mitzvah for a woman to immerse on time.[6] According to R. Yose, immersion on time is a mitzvah, whereas according to R. Yose ben Yehudah, it is not. Rabbeinu Ḥananel rules in accordance with R. Yose that immersion on time is a mitzvah,[7] whereas Rabbeinu Tam maintains that immersion on time is not a mitzvah.[8] Nowadays, however, women count seven *neki'im* before immersing, and there is a question whether immersion at the end of the seven *neki'im* is even considered "on time." *Bet Yosef*[9] cites a dispute among the *Rishonim* about this matter: Some say that since this is the established time for immersion that the Sages ordained, immersion at this time is considered "on time,"[10] whereas others maintain that immersion after the seven *neki'im* is not considered "on time." *Shulḥan Arukh*[11] rules that there is no mitzvah to immerse on time except to fulfill the mitzvah of *onah* or procreation.[12] Therefore, on a night when it is forbidden to fulfill these *mitzvot*, such as Yom Kippur or Tisha Be-Av,[13] or when one of the couple is not home, the woman is not required to immerse.

---

5. *Ḥakhamim* disagree (*Niddah* 31b) whether a woman becomes pregnant around the time she immerses or just before the onset of menstruation. The view that she becomes pregnant around the time of immersion matches what we know medically today. See Medical Appendix I: The Female Reproductive System.
6. *Shabbat* 121a; *Niddah* 30a; et al.
7. *Tosafot* to *Niddah* 30a, s.v. "*u-shema minah*."
8. *Tosafot* to *Yoma* 8a, s.v. "*de-khulei alma*."
9. *Yoreh De'ah* 197:2.
10. *Semag*, negative commandment *siman* 111; *Hagahot Maimoniyot, Hilkhot Isurei Bi'ah* 4:4; *Mordekhai, Hilkhot Mikva'ot (Shevu'ot) siman* 752.
11. *Yoreh De'ah* 197:2; *Taz, Yoreh De'ah* 197:3.
12. See *Bet Yosef, Oraḥ Ḥayim siman* 240, s.v. "*aval im ro'eh*," which states that the mitzvah of *onah* is independent of the mitzvah of procreation and applies even when the wife is pregnant or nursing.
13. *Shulḥan Arukh, Oraḥ Ḥayim* 544:8; see also *Mishnah Berurah ad loc.* 17.

In light of this, the question is whether a woman may forego her rights under the mitzvah of *onah* and whether a couple for whom contraception is permitted may postpone immersion, by mutual consent, and thus delay fulfillment of the mitzvah of *onah*.

Rambam clarifies that a woman may forego her conjugal rights under the mitzvah of *onah*,[14] and the *Aḥaronim* rule accordingly, provided that the mitzvah of procreation has already been fulfilled.[15] Thus, in the present case, the wife may forego the mitzvah of *onah* of the night she immerses. *Responsa Mateh Levi*[16] wrote regarding a woman who had received a *heter* to use contraception, and for whom using absorbent material will not provide sufficient contraceptive protection, it is preferable to postpone immersion and refrain from relations until her fertile days have passed. Similarly, *Responsa Ḥedvat Yaakov* suggests that the wife immerse at the proper time but conceal her immersion from her husband for several days.[17]

However, *Responsa Ḥatam Sofer*[18] wrote that it is necessary to distinguish between the mitzvah of the pleasure of *onah*, which is the wife's right and which she may therefore forego, and the wife's obligation to be responsive to her husband when possible – an obligation that stems, *inter alia*, from her duty to ensure that he does not sin. From this standpoint, *Ḥatam Sofer* writes, she has a mitzvah not to postpone her immersion unnecessarily. Therefore, the couple's decision about whether to postpone relations should take into consideration the impact of the postponement on the husband.[19]

---

14. *Mishneh Torah, Hilkhot Ishut* 15:1 (cited by *Mishneh Berurah* 240:2). *Leḥem Mishneh* (*ad loc.*) explains that this is acceptable only if she wholeheartedly forgoes her conjugal rights.
15. R. Moshe Feinstein (*Igrot Moshe, Even Ha-Ezer* 1:102) wrote accordingly in the case of a couple that already fulfilled the mitzvah of procreation and abstains from marital relations during ovulation to prevent pregnancy.
16. 2:31, s.v. "*ve-hilkakh*."
17. *Responsa Ḥedvat Yaakov* 2:37, s.v. "*ve-hineh le-ishah zo*." In this case, it is dangerous for the woman to become pregnant, and she is concerned that using an absorbent material will not provide sufficient protection. It is therefore preferable for her to refrain from intercourse during the days when she can become pregnant.
18. *Yoreh De'ah* 2:162. He wrote as follows concerning a woman who sought to travel to a distant place for the purpose of a mitzvah just before *mikveh* night: "She would do a great mitzvah... by protecting her husband from transgression," so out of concern for her husband, she should not cancel her *onah* or immersion.
19. *Responsa Shevet Ha-Levi* 8:271 states, in a note at the end of the responsum, that if the husband is concerned that it will be too difficult for him if his wife immerses but they cannot have marital relations, it is better that she not immerse during those days, so that the husband does not have to withstand the trial presented by physical contact.

In addition to the implications of postponing immersion for the couple's relationship, we need to clarify whether there is any independent value in the wife being *tehorah* even in the absence of marital relations. The Yerushalmi[20] states: "R. Ḥaninah said: This means that it is forbidden for a woman to remain in her *tum'ah*." The Vilna Gaon[21] explains that this applies only when the immersion takes place at the time prescribed by the Torah. Therefore, nowadays, a woman has no obligation to rush to remove her *tum'ah*.[22] However, R. Menashe Klein[23] understands that even if there is no immersion "on time" nowadays, it is nevertheless proper for a woman to hurry to become *tehorah*. Similarly, R. Wosner writes that a woman should try to be *tehorah* for her husband irrespective of physical intimacy.[24] For these reasons, there are grounds to prefer that the wife immerse on time, even if they will not have marital relations for several days.[25]

On the other hand, perhaps it is preferable to postpone counting the seven *neki'im* so that the wife is not put in a position where she can immerse but does not. The *Aḥaronim* write that the obligation to immerse on time applies only once she has counted the *neki'im*.[26] As long as she has not counted the seven *neki'im*, her duty to expedite her immersion has not taken effect, and with her husband's consent, she may postpone the beginning of the count.

Nevertheless, there is a good reason why it is not advisable to delay counting the *neki'im*: The menstrual cycle is not always regular, and it is possible that there will be no ovulation one month, or that the ovulation will occur during the seven *neki'im*. In such a case, delaying the count of seven *neki'im* serves no purpose. Additionally, the delay can cause the count to end near the onset of the next menses, when some women have a greater likelihood of spotting.

Therefore, for numerous reasons, it is best to immerse on time, so that physical intimacy are permitted even if they refrain from relations; for the intimacy of

20. *Niddah* 2:4.
21. *Bi'ur Ha-Gra, Yoreh De'ah* 197:3.
22. In the past, the custom was that a woman would not immerse if her husband was out of town, as it was considered dangerous. Nowadays, however, most *poskim* have no such concern. See *Responsa Bnei Banim* 2:33.
23. *Responsa Mishneh Halakhot* 9:179, s.v. "*ve-hanir'eh pashut*."
24. *Shi'urei Shevet Ha-Levi* 196:11, on *Taz* 196:6 (p. 297). He cites a derivation from the verse, "everyone of your household who is *tahor* may eat it" (Bamidbar 18:11), from which it can be inferred that "everyone of your household" refers to a man's wife.
25. Some favor immersing before Rosh Ha-Shanah and Yom Kippur as part of repentance, but this has no connection to immersion at all other times. See *Responsa Bnei Banim* 3:5.
26. *Responsa Bet She'arim, Yoreh De'ah siman* 281.

hugging and kissing, even without relations, constitutes a fulfillment of the mitzvah of *onah*.[27] However, this alternative can place strain on the couple's relationship during these days and can lead to concern about *hotza'at zera*.[28]

In conclusion, all three alternatives are permitted, but each has its drawbacks as well.

M.R. and O.K.

27. *Responsa Maharam Lublin siman* 53, cited by *Shakh, Yoreh De'ah* 197:3. This is also the view cited in *Badei Ha-Shulḥan siman* 197, *bi'urim*, s.v. "*mitzvah litbol be-zmanah*."
28. However, *Ḥut Ha-Shani* (197:3, p. 266) writes that where there is concern about *hotza'at zera le-vatalah*, it is better to postpone immersion. Since husband and wife have different needs and different reactions to the stimulation of physical intimacy, it is quite likely that their attitudes and reactions to the possibility of immersion for the sake of limited physical intimacy, after two weeks without physical contact, will differ. It is possible that this option will be more acceptable to the wife than to the husband.

Medical Appendices

Yoetzet Halacha Rabbanit Dr. Deena Zimmerman

Medical Appendix I

The Female Reproductive System

The parts of the female reproductive system located in the pelvic area include the uterus, the ovaries, and the vagina.

The **uterus** is a hollow, muscular organ that is shaped like an inverted pear. Its muscular walls are lined with a mucus membrane called the endometrium. This membrane alternately thickens and sheds monthly, based on cyclical hormonal changes.

The lower, narrower part of the uterus is called the **cervix**. It is connected to the upper part of the vagina and protrudes somewhat into it. The cervix is elongated and has two openings, one at each end; the opening into the uterus is called the "internal os" and the opening into the vagina is called the "external os". Menstrual blood is discharged from the uterus into the vaginal canal through these openings.

The two **Fallopian tubes** branch out from the upper, wider part of the uterus, one from each side and lead to the ovaries.

The **ovaries** are two small glands located on either side of the uterus; but not connected to it. They are responsible for producing some of the hormones (primarily estrogen and progesterone) that play a role in the menstrual cycle. The woman's ova (egg cells) are also stored in the ovaries. Each cycle, a number of ova begin to mature within the ovary, with one dominant one being released during ovulation. The released ovum is collected into the Fallopian tube by movements of the fimbriated ends of the tube and then it makes its way to the uterine cavity.

The **vagina** is a canal with an average length of about 8 centimeters (3 inches). It is very elastic and can expand enough to allow a baby to pass through it during childbirth. Most girls are born with a thin membrane, called the **hymen**, covering part of the outer opening of the vagina. The hymen has a small opening that allows the discharge of menstrual blood.[1] The hymen is stretched and torn during the woman's first sexual relations, and it generally disappears after a few instances of sexual relations.

The external female sex organs are called the **vulva**. The vulva contains two sets of labia ("lips"): The outer ones are called the labia majora, and the inner ones are called the labia minora. Just below the upper junction ("hood") of the labia minora is the clitoris. During sexual relations, stimulation of the clitoris increases the woman's physical pleasure and builds up to orgasm.

Located just in front of the vaginal opening in a standing woman (and above it if a woman is lying on her back) is the opening of the urethra, through which urine exits the body.

Behind the vagina (or below when lying down on one's back) is the anus, through which feces exit the body.

The area between the vaginal opening and the anus is called the perineum.

For the anatomy of the female reproductive system, see https://www.yoatzot.org/health-and-halacha/653/.

The Menstrual Cycle

The professional literature commonly describes the menstrual cycle as a 28-day process that begins on the day of the onset of menstrual bleeding and ends on the last day before the onset of the next cycle. This is a convenient representative model, as it is easily divisible into four weeks. In actuality, any menstrual cycle whose length is between 21 and 35 days[2] in duration is considered normal.

The Follicular Phase

Several hormones play a role in the process of ovulation and menstrual bleeding. The process begins when the pituitary gland secretes follicle-stimulating hormone (FSH), which stimulates the maturation of approximately 15–20 ova and their surrounding cells within the ovary (an ovum and its surrounding cells are called a

1. The size and shape of the hymen can vary from woman to woman.
2. Some extend this to 42 days.

"follicle"). These follicles "compete," and the largest emerges as the "dominant follicle," from which the ovum is released during ovulation. The remaining follicles are absorbed and disappear.

Ovulation

During the follicular phase, the level of estrogen secreted by the ovaries increases. When estrogen levels reach a certain threshold, the pituitary gland releases a surge of another hormone, called "luteinizing hormone" ("LH") which causes the expulsion of the ovum through the wall of the ovary; this is ovulation.

Around the time of ovulation, the consistency of the mucus secreted by the cervix changes; it goes from being thick and sticky to being thin and watery. This is one of the signs of impending ovulation. Other signs are changes in basal body temperature (body temperature as measured right after waking up, before getting out of bed) and the location and position of the cervix. At this time, there is a concomitant decrease in estrogen levels. For approximately 5% of women, this decrease can cause spotting, known as ovulation spotting.[3]

After the ovum is expelled from the ovary into the abdominal cavity, it is collected by the "fingers" (fimbriae) at the end of the Fallopian tube, and it makes its way through the tube toward the uterus. If the ovum encounters sperm cells along the way, it can be fertilized, resulting in pregnancy. If fertilization does not occur within approximately 24 hours, the ovum loses its viability and breaks down.

The Luteal Phase

The cells that had surrounded the ovum remain in the ovary after ovulation and form the corpus luteum (Latin for "yellow body"). It draws its name from the color of its appearance under a microscope. The corpus luteum secretes a hormone called progesterone. Progesterone strengthens and thickens the endometrium. If fertilization does not occur, the corpus luteum stops functioning after approximately 12-16 days, and production of progesterone stops. The decrease in the body's progesterone levels leads to the breakdown of the endometrium and the resultant bleeding that marks the beginning of the next cycle.

---

3. S.S. Dasharathy, S.L. Mumford, A.Z Pollack, et al. "Menstrual Bleeding Patterns among Regularly Menstruating Women." *American Journal of Epidemiology* 175, no. 6 (2012): 536–45.

Regular and Irregular Bleeding

The natural breakdown of the endometrium, which occurs regularly and predictably at intervals of 21 to 35 days, is called "menstrual bleeding" or "the period."[4] Bleeding that occurs sooner than expected is called "intermenstrual bleeding."

The duration of menstrual bleeding varies from woman to woman and can even change for the same woman over time. Bleeding that lasts 2–7 days is considered normal. A woman who regularly experiences bleeding for longer than this should consult with a medical professional.

Menstrual blood is generally a shade of red, but at the beginning and the end of menstruation its appearance can be a shade of brown.

Symptoms of Hormonal Changes

In the beginning of the cycle, many women may experience vaginal dryness. At this point, the body's estrogen levels are low, which causes a sensation of dryness. As estrogen levels build up before ovulation, there is increased dampness and vaginal discharge.

For many women, hormonal changes during the course of the menstrual cycle can also cause emotional swings. If these emotions impact on her daily functioning, a woman should turn to her health care provider as they are often modifiable. Steps such as assuring proper rest, nutrition and exercise have been shown to decrease this phenomenon. If these fluctuations impact a woman's marriage in a significant way she may desire to seek help from a Sexual Health Professional or Psychologist.

Many women experience specific sensations around the time of menstruation, such as stomach aches, backaches, and sensitive breasts. When physical and emotional sensations manifest just prior to menstruation, they are called "premenstrual syndrome" or "PMS."

If the symptoms are severe or have a detrimental effect on a woman's quality of life, she can consult with a medical professional for advice about how to ease the symptoms or to intervene with medication.

Particularly strong menstrual cramps are called "dysmenorrhea." Medical intervention can ameliorate the pain, so it is advisable for those who suffer such pain to consult a medical professional.

---

4. It should be emphasized that menstrual bleeding is not a mechanism for ridding the body of toxins, but the rather the breakdown of the endometrium in the absence of the hormonal levels sufficient to sustain it.

From a halakhic perspective, the follicular phase generally overlaps with the period when the woman is *teme'ah* – during menstrual bleeding and part of the seven clean days. Ovulation generally occurs around the time of immersion in the *mikveh*, or slightly afterward. The luteal phase generally overlaps with the time when a woman is *tehorah*. It should be noted that there is a great deal of variation from woman to woman, and even from cycle to cycle for the same woman. A doctor can diagnose whether a woman is in the follicular or luteal phase, and whether ovulation has already transpired (for example, when there is concern that ovulation prior to immersion in the *mikveh* leads to an inability to conceive).

Medical Appendix II

Pregnancy

Pregnancy is a multi-stage process that requires medical attention even before it begins.

Pre-Pregnancy

The state of a woman's health prior to and during pregnancy can affect the health of the fetus. It is therefore important that the woman be in touch with a doctor even before becoming pregnant. So despite the practical and emotional pressure the couple is under in the lead up to the wedding and the feeling that pregnancy is not impending, it is nonetheless best to establish a relationship with a gynecologist even before marriage.

Besides carefully maintaining healthy living habits,[1] there are additional steps one can take to improve the baseline for pregnancy. For example, taking folic acid from 3 months prior to conception until childbirth has proven effective for decreasing certain types of congenital defects.[2] If the couple did not undergo genetic testing before marrying, it is still possible – and important – to do so at

1. R.L. Floyd, B.W. Jack, R. Cefalo, et al. "The Clinical Content of Preconception Care: Alcohol, Tobacco, and Illicit Drug Exposures," *American Journal of Obstetrics and Gynecology* 199, no.6, suppl. a (2008): S333–S339.
2. P.M. Gardiner, L. Nelson, C.S. Shellhaas, et al. "The Clinical Content of Preconception Care: Nutrition and Dietary Supplements," *American Journal of Obstetrics and Gynecology* 199, no.6, suppl. a (2008): S345–S356.

the beginning of the marriage. See below.[3] In addition, new screening tests become available regularly, so one should see a Genetics Nurse prior to every pregnancy to ensure she is up-to-date.

The Beginning of Pregnancy

Pregnancy begins with the fertilization of the ovum by a sperm cell. It takes place within one of the Fallopian tubes. (See Medical Appendix I: The Female Reproductive System.) The fertilized egg develops by cell division into a mass of cells called a blastocyst This mass makes its way down the Fallopian tube and implants itself in the uterine wall.

The first sign of pregnancy is usually the delay of menstruation. At this stage, pregnancy can be confirmed by means of a blood or urine test. The test detects the hormone beta-hCG, which is secreted by the developing placenta.

The urine test detects the presence of the hormone and confirms the pregnancy, whereas the quantitative blood test provides information on the level and concentration of the hormone in the blood. The blood test is more sensitive and can detect pregnancy 3–4 weeks after the woman last menstruated, even before the delay of the next cycle. In contrast, the results obtained from the urine-based home pregnancy test is considered reliable 7–10 days after the next menstrual cycle should have begun (subject to the instructions attached to the test kit).

If the results are negative but the expected onset still has not arrived, it is worth taking another test a few days later. Early in the pregnancy, beta-hCG levels can be too low for detection by a home pregnancy test, but the levels should build up with time, so a second test a few days later may detect the hormone and produce a different result.

The blood test, of course, requires a referral from a doctor (not necessarily a gynecologist), whereas the urine test can be bought at a pharmacy without a prescription.

Even though fertilization actually occurs about two weeks after menstruation, the gestational age is commonly calculated from the beginning of the last menstrual

3. Zimmerman DR. *Genetics and Genetic Diseases: Jewish Legal and Ethical Perspectives*. Jersey City: Ktav, 2013. In the event that testing shows risk that their child will be born with certain congenital defects, in some cases a preimplantation genetic diagnosis can be performed, and using IVF, a fetus that is not diseased is returned to the mother's body. Even if she is already pregnant, parents can prepare themselves to treat the child, so that optimal results are obtained.

period. According to this calculation, a woman is already "pregnant" two weeks before fertilization.

Pregnancy

During pregnancy, the fetus is nourished through the placenta. The placenta is a structure that develops at the beginning of pregnancy, alongside the fetus. It contains numerous blood vessels. In general, the placenta implants on one of the uterine walls, but sometimes it is located in the lower part of the uterus and partially or fully covers the cervix. This condition is called "placenta previa." Usually, the placenta slides upward as pregnancy develops, but if the placenta remains low in the uterus as the due date approaches, vaginal delivery poses the threat of severe bleeding, and a c-section will be performed. Vaginal bleeding throughout pregnancy can indicate placenta previa, though sometimes there will be no external indications of its presence, and it can be discovered only through ultrasound examination.

The normal duration of pregnancy is 38 to 42 weeks. A baby born before the 37th week is considered premature,[4] and a pregnancy that lasts more than 42 weeks is deemed a "post-term pregnancy." Each of these situations carries risks that demand the attention of medical caregivers, so it is important to know the gestational age. The Last Menstrual Period (LMP) is accurate for a woman with a 28 day cycle based on her ovulation on day 14, but given the fact that many women ovulate at different times, the LMP may not be entirely accurate. The results of an ultrasound performed before week 12 are accurate within 5 days in either direction, and therefore the calculated date of the last menstrual period is changed if there is a larger than 5 day difference in size of the fetus as seen on the ultrasound compared to the expected size based on her last period.

Pregnancy is commonly divided into three "trimesters." The first trimester lasts until week 12; the second covers weeks 13 through 28, and the third extends from week 29 until childbirth.[5]

Monitoring Pregnancy

Nowadays it is common for pregnancy monitoring to include monitoring the mother's health, monitoring the health of the fetus, and detecting congenital defects. It is important to encourage women to be meticulous about monitoring their pregnancy.

---

4. According to the definition of the World Health Organization.
5. www.womenshealth.gov.

Maternal Health

Monitoring pregnancy begins with the clarification and documentation of the mother's personal and familial medical history. For the duration of the pregnancy, the mother's weight, urine and blood pressure will be routinely checked. Monitoring her weight ensures that the fetus is growing properly and that the mother is gaining the healthy amount of weight. Meticulousness about healthy, balanced nutrition[6] and suitable physical activity[7] help maintain the health of the mother and fetus.[8]

Routine tests are performed to determine the possible need for intervention that can help improve the health of the mother and fetus. For example, tests are administered to detect gestational diabetes, which can have serious ramifications for the fetus, including severe congenital defects and even stillbirth. This is something that can be controlled with the right medical advice and monitoring.

Monitoring pregnancy is crucial not only during the first pregnancy, as people commonly think. A woman's health and medical condition can change from one pregnancy to the next, and her advancing age can also require a change in approach. With each pregnancy, the mother's child-bearing history must be reexamined, and suitable tests must be conducted accordingly. The personal and familial histories and the history of past pregnancies are also very important. Sometimes, complications and difficulties from earlier pregnancies can recur during subsequent pregnancies if they are not treated. In addition, medical caregivers can at times improve a woman's experience of pregnancy if they are apprised of her experiences during past pregnancies.

Occasionally, women who already had several children are insufficiently aware of the importance of consistent prenatal care. The preoccupations of daily life and taking care of the home and the children can cause women to forego some of the needed tests. It is important to raise awareness of this issue among women and to encourage them to adhere to all recommendations.

Fetal Health

The health of the fetus is directly affected by the condition and conduct of the mother, and certain maternal actions can place the fetus at risk. Therefore, care

---

6. https://www.choosemyplate.gov/nutritional-needs-during-pregnancy.
7. https://www.acog.org/clinical/clinical-guidance/committee-opinion/articles/2020/04/physical-activity-and-exercise-during-pregnancy-and-thepostpartum-period.
8. https://www.choosemyplate.gov/moms-breastfeeding-nutritional-needs.

for the fetus begins by directing the mother to avoid behaviors such as drinking alcohol, smoking, and consuming certain foods.

In Israel, regular ultrasounds are performed throughout the pregnancy to confirm gestational age and monitor growth and wellbeing of the fetus. In this examination, a transducer that sends out sounds waves is inserted into the vagina or placed on the lower abdomen. Usually, during the early stages of pregnancy, the exam is vaginal, and during subsequent stages it is abdominal. The ultrasound does not give off radiation and is not harmful to the fetus.

Prenatal Tests

Nowadays it is common to refer pregnant women for numerous tests that detect birth defects.[9] Sometimes, women turn to rabbis for advice on whether to conduct these tests. It is therefore necessary for rabbis who offer such halakhic guidance to become intimately familiar with the various tests conducted during pregnancy and to understand the quality and reliability of their results.

Prenatal tests can help in a variety of situations. Foreknowledge of the presence of certain defects allow parents and medical professionals to prepare properly for the birth, and proper preparation by an obstetric team can raise the fetus's chance of survival. Sometimes it may even be possible to perform fetal surgery during the pregnancy to repair certain defects. It should be mentioned that the professional committees that exist in Israel to approve abortions, may do so in situations that *halakhah* forbids. On the other hand there are circumstances where even Halakhic Authorities will advise terminating a pregnancy.

There are four types of prenatal tests to detect fetal defects:

1. Genetic tests

Ideally, couples will have undergone genetic testing prior to marriage. There are many tests to identify genetic diseases; the specific combination of tests administered to the couple is determined by the genetic counseling that proceeds them, taking into consideration the ethnic origin and family history of each person. These tests can be done through testing via the health care system, or through organizations like Dor Yesharim, which work to prevent marriages between carriers of the same hereditary disease. A couple that was not tested before marriage can be tested after the wedding and even at the beginning of pregnancy. Many of the tests recommended after obtaining genetic counseling are covered

---

9. In a future volume, we will discuss the various kinds of tests at length, including prenatal tests.

by medical insurance – this should be checked on a case by case, and country by country, basis.

2. Testing for chromosomal abnormalities

The best-known chromosomal abnormality for which there is prenatal screening is Trisomy 21 (Down Syndrome). Currently, screening for this chromosomal abnormality includes sampling fetal DNA from maternal blood during pregnancy (NIPT),[10] first-trimester screening at 11 to 13 weeks ("nuchal translucency scan" and "biochemical markers") and another screening blood test at 16 to 20 weeks (the "quadruple test"). These tests provide a more accurate assessment of the risk of genetic defects in the fetus, beyond the risks that result from the mother's age.

Unlike chorionic villi sampling ("CVS") or amniocentesis (described below), these tests are screening tools that do not provide conclusive results. Thus, if they produce abnormal results, further clarification, by means of invasive tests, will be recommended.[11]

3. Invasive tests

If the screening tests indicate elevated risk of genetic defects in the fetus, these suspicions can be confirmed or rejected by taking a sample of the fetus's own genetic material. There are two types of invasive tests for this purpose:

Amniocentesis

Amniocentesis is done from week 15 of the pregnancy. In this test, a needle (guided by ultrasound) is inserted into the amniotic sac through the abdominal wall and a small sample of amniotic fluid is taken. The fetal DNA contained in the fluid is tested in a laboratory. These tests give a clear picture of the fetus's condition and provide conclusive information about genetic defects affecting the fetus. Since the needle is inserted through the abdomen and not the vagina, the procedure should not cause vaginal bleeding. Nevertheless, given that it is an invasive procedure, there is a small chance (less than 0.5%) that it will lead to termination of the pregnancy.

10. J. Gekas, S. Langlois, V. Ravitsky, et al. "Identification of Trisomy 18, Trisomy 13, and Down Syndrome from Maternal Plasma," *The Application of Clinical Genetics* 7 (2014): 127–31.
11. E.R. Norwitz, B. Levy. "Noninvasive Prenatal Testing: The Future Is Now," *Reviews in Obstetrics and Gynecology* 6, no. 2 (2013): 48–62.

Chorionic villi sampling (CVS)

In the CVS test, a tissue sample is taken from the placenta for genetic testing. In the past, this test was conducted very early in the pregnancy, around week 6. This milestone is of the utmost importance for halakhically observant couples, since the test results were obtained within 40 days of immersion, when the fetus is still considered "mere water." (See above, *Siman* 32). However, performing an invasive test at the beginning of the pregnancy (before week 10) entails higher risk of harming the development of the fetus's organs. Therefore, nowadays it is common to perform CVS tests during weeks 10–12, when the halakhic advantage no longer applies. This test entails greater risk than amniocentesis, which can affect halakhic considerations about whether to conduct the test.

4. Tests to detect congenital defects

The quadruple test described above can also identify other conditions unrelated to genetic syndromes. For example, twin pregnancy or neural tube defects – such as anencephaly (absence of significant parts of the skull) or spina bifida (malformation of the spinal cord). If suspected, these conditions are confirmed with additional testing such as ultrasound.

Many other defects can be identified by ultrasound throughout the pregnancy. The ultrasound examination conducted mid-pregnancy around week 20–24 (also called the "structural scan" or the "morphology scan") can give a good picture of the fetus's condition. Its purpose is to confirm that the fetus is growing as expected and that limbs, organs, and vital systems are developing normally.[12] Many couples opt to have an early morphology scan (week 14–17) in addition, in order to become aware sooner of any potential defects in order to enable early intervention. However the early morphology scan does not replace the 20–24 week ultrasound exam.

Symptoms during Pregnancy

Nausea

Many women report various physical symptoms during pregnancy, including exhaustion and nausea. These symptoms often improve at the end of the first trimester, but some women continue to feel unwell throughout pregnancy. In contrast, some women flourish during pregnancy and feel better than ever.

---

12. ISUOG. "Practice Guidelines for Performance of the Routine Mid-Trimester Fetal Ultrasound Scan," *Ultrasound Obstetrics and Gynecology* 41 (2010): 102–113. Available at https://www.isuog.org/uploads/assets/uploaded/fdae60c8-4825-46d3-924df9b8d39d5582.pdf.

Bleeding during pregnancy

About 25% of women experience vaginal bleeding during pregnancy. In some cases, this is normal – for example, in the case of minor bleeding during the implantation of the fetus. In other cases, the bleeding indicates a problem like abnormal placement of the placenta or the death of the fetus. A woman who experiences bleeding during pregnancy must consult her primary doctor immediately, especially if the bleeding is accompanied by abdominal pain. The doctor's examination will generally include an internal speculum examination as well as an ultrasound. Women should be trained to ask the doctor about the source of the bleeding (i.e., whether it is uterine, placental, vaginal, etc.), so that it will be possible to distinguish between bleeding that makes her *teme'ah* and bleeding that does not.

Medical Appendix III

Labor and Childbirth

Indicators of Impending Labor

The "due date" is only an estimate; there is no way to know for certain when childbirth will occur. However, there are various signs that indicate that labor is about to begin:

Release of the mucus plug

The mucus plug is a sticky mucous secretion that seals the cervical canal during pregnancy and protects against infection. The "plug" is usually discharged before the onset of labor, though sometimes it is discharged during labor itself. The mucus plug will generally be found on undergarments. The discharge can appear in a variety of colors and is often blood-tinged.

Water breaking

During pregnancy, the fetus is inside the amniotic sac, suspended in amniotic fluid. At a certain stage, the sac ruptures and the fluid drips or leaks out. This is when the "water breaks." Labor generally begins soon after the water breaks, if not before.

Contractions

Toward the end of pregnancy, irregular pangs may manifest as the uterus begins to contract. As labor begins, the contractions become regular.

When one of these symptoms manifests, the woman should consult a medical caregiver about when to go to the delivery room.

Contractions cause the widening ("dilation") of the cervical canal and the shortening ("effacement") of the cervix itself. During labor, the medical team tracks the progression of these two processes. Dilation is measured in centimeters, and 10 cm is considered "complete dilation." When the cervix is completely dilated, contractions help push the baby down the birth canal and out into the world.

Childbirth generally begins spontaneously and progresses naturally. However, some situations necessitate medical intervention to induce or accelerate labor.

Induction of Labor

"Induction" is the generic term for any medical intervention with the purpose of causing labor to begin. It is chosen when continuing pregnancy may put the mother or the fetus at risk. Induction can be performed in a few ways, depending on many factors. For example, by administering prostaglandins with the goal of "softening" the cervix and facilitating its dilation. The prostaglandins are usually applied to the cervix in the form of a topical gel or inserted into the vagina in the form of a suppository. Alternatively a balloon catheter may dilate the cervix through mechanical pressure. Once the cervix is "ripened" Pitocin is usually administered to cause uterine contractions and labor pains. The pangs caused by Pitocin may be experienced as more intense than pangs that develop naturally. Sometimes the membranes are artificially ruptured to accelerate the pace of labor.

A similar procedure, called acceleration or augmentation of labor, is done when labor begins spontaneously but does not progress. In such situations, Pitocin is administered or the membranes are ruptured.

Other actions are also accepted as helpful to the progression of labor. These actions have a medical basis, but they have not been studied systematically.

Nipple stimulation

Stimulating the nipples increases the production of oxytocin, the natural hormone on which Pitocin is based. This may cause labor to progress if conditions are ripe.

Stripping the membranes

In this procedure the doctor uses a finger to separate the membranes of the amniotic sac from the walls of the uterus. In certain cases, this stimulation of the cervix helps labor begin.[1]

1. E.M. Finucane, D.J. Murphy, L.M. Biesty, G.M. Gyte, A.M. Cotter, E.M. Ryan, M. Boulvain, D. Devane. "Membrane Sweeping for Induction of Labour," *The Cochrane Database* 2 no. 2 (February 27, 2020): CD000451.

Childbirth

Contractions and the effort of pushing the baby out are usually accompanied by intense pain. There are several ways to reduce the pain; nowadays, the primary method is epidural anesthesia. An anesthetic is injected through a thin needle inserted between the vertebrae into the space between two layers of the dura, a membrane covering the spinal cord. The epidural anesthesia numbs the pain and decreases the mobility of any part of the body below the point of injection along the spinal column. Therefore, once someone has received an epidural, she can no longer walk and will need help changing positions on the bed. There is also spinal anesthesia, in which the needle is inserted closer to the spinal cord, but it is not as desirable for vaginal birth and is therefore less commonly used. In the case of an emergency c-section, an epidural or spinal anesthetic can be used, and sometimes general anesthesia will be necessary.

Another form of pharmaceutical intervention that is occasionally used is the intramuscular or intravenous injection of sedatives like pethidine (Demerol). However, such injections can cause the babies to be born drowsy, so many women may choose to avoid these. Non-pharmaceutical methods of pain relief, like meditation, breathing exercises, acupuncture or a warm shower, can decrease the need for pharmaceutical intervention. Assuaging the fears of the woman in labor and making sure she always has someone there to support her can also reduce the need to administer drugs.

If labor is not progressing despite interventions, there is concern for the welfare of the fetus or when there are medical reasons that prevent vaginal birth, it is necessary to perform surgery – called a Caesarean section (or "c-section" for short) – to extract the baby. When the decision is made in the labor ward to perform an emergency caesarean, sometimes there is not enough time to linger before making the decision. In contrast, when the doctor recommends a planned (elective) c-section, it is important to study the subject, become familiar with the possible scenarios, and ask any questions that arise. Once a woman has undergone a c-section, there is a greater chance that future births will also be Caesarean, but it is far from certain that this will need to be the case.

The Postpartum Period

Breastfeeding is the natural and preferred continuation of childbirth, and it has many advantages for the health of both mother and baby. The medical recommendation is to allow breastfeeding immediately (and no longer than one hour) after birth. Ideally, this would happen when the baby is placed directly on the mother's body ("skin to skin") immediately after delivery. It has been proven that this practice increases the chances of successful nursing and promotes the contraction of the uterus, thus preventing postpartum bleeding. "Rooming-in" – keeping the baby next to the mother – should be encouraged, and the baby should have unlimited opportunities for breastfeeding.

Although breastfeeding is natural, some women experience pain and difficulties when they try to nurse. It is important to realize that breastfeeding is not supposed to hurt, and if it does, one should consult a professional as soon as possible. Individual guidance to assure proper latch on at the breast and appropriate frequency of feeding is a major contributor to successful breastfeeding.

After birth, recovery and recuperation begin. The cervix closes, returning to its normal state within about two weeks. Once the cervix is closed, the risk of infection is significantly lower, and it is no longer necessary to be concerned about sitting in a bath or immersing in a *mikveh*. It is likely that the time it takes for the cervix to close will depend on the circumstances of the childbirth. Therefore, it is recommended that the new mother consult a doctor or midwife about this and obtain detailed instructions regarding bathing before leaving the hospital. There is generally no medical reason to refrain from immersing in a *mikveh* when it is halakhically possible.

There is no consensus among doctors regarding how long one must wait after childbirth before resuming marital relations, though waiting 6 weeks is often advised. It is recommended to raise the issue with the medical caregivers at the hospital before discharge from the maternity ward.

The first six weeks after birth are called the "postpartum period." During this period, the mother is still under the influence of hormones that cause weakening of the pelvic cartilage, so she must beware of heavy lifting and abrupt movements. After about six weeks, the uterus returns to its normal size and pre-pregnancy condition. This is the generally accepted time to have a postpartum medical examination. An appointment can be scheduled even before this period is over if there is a specific need or if a question arises, for instance, about contraception.

A woman who underwent a c-section requires a longer recovery period, as she must recuperate from surgery in addition to childbirth. Pain in the area of the incision can continue for a prolonged period and fatigue can last many weeks.

Recovery from childbirth, getting accustomed to the new situation, and caring for a newborn demand a lot of energy from a mother. Any woman who recently gave birth needs help at home during those first weeks, and the need is even more acute in the case of a Caesarean birth. After the ordeal of childbirth, mood swings and mild feelings of "being blue" are normal during those first days. They are the direct result of the extreme hormonal changes that a woman undergoes postpartum. If these phenomena persist beyond two weeks after childbirth or significantly impact on function, it is important to confirm that they do not indicate postpartum depression. If these symptoms do not moderate and moods do not improve after a few days during which the mother was able to relax and get a good amount of sleep, she should be encouraged to consult her doctor. Postpartum depression can be treated and cured, but deferring treatment can have severe ramifications for both mother and baby.

For many women, even if they do not suffer from postpartum depression, it may be a while before they show interest in marital intimacy. Underlying this is hormonal changes, lack of sleep, and emotional factors: The mother is focused on the newborn baby, whose needs demand her complete devotion. If she continues to feel completely sexually disinterested for a prolonged period, consulting a doctor is recommended.

Postpartum bleeding lasts, on average, about 4 weeks; for some, the bleeding lasts longer, and for others, shorter. It occurs as well in women who gave birth by c-section or women whose pregnancies did not result in live birth; they all experience bloody discharges for varying amounts of time. Postpartum bleeding differs in character from the familiar menstrual bleeding; it can come and go in waves, disappearing completely and then returning. When a woman feels that the bleeding has stopped and that she is ready to begin the process of becoming *tehorah,* there is nothing that prevents it, but it is important to realize that the bleeding may return and negate the count of the "clean days."

If the mother reaches the routine examination six weeks after birth and has not yet stopped bleeding, she should discuss with the doctor at what point the matter requires further clarification. Women whose postpartum bleeding lasts shorter than average can complete the *taharah* process and immerse in the *mikveh* even before the 6-week visit to the doctor.

The return of regular menstruation after childbirth hinges on several factors, and there are many differences among women in this regard. For women who are not nursing, menstruation will usually resume about two months after childbirth. Nursing mothers can go several months without any menstrual bleeding, a condition called "lactational amenorrhea." This is the body's natural mechanism for putting space between childbirth and the beginning of the next pregnancy so that the mother can recuperate.

Medical Appendix IV

Miscarriage

Sadly, some pregnancies do not develop normally and do not result in a live birth. The older the woman, the greater the chances that her pregnancy will result in miscarriage.

A miscarriage occurs when a pregnancy spontaneously terminates (or as a result of injury to the mother or fetus). The most common indicator of a miscarriage is bleeding; however, it is important to know that not all bleeding indicates miscarriage. Many women have at least one miscarriage in their lifetime. Sometimes a miscarriage occurs in the earliest phases of pregnancy, before the mother even knows she is pregnant; the bleeding will seem like a late period, and she will remain unaware that she miscarried. In some cases, the mother experiences no bleeding at all, but an ultrasound shows that the fetus has no heartbeat. This is called a "missed abortion," and in such cases it may be suggested that the pregnancy be terminated artificially, by medical means. In other cases, the fetus develops normally until later stages of pregnancy, but dies in utero. In this case, the mother will go through the entire process of childbirth even though the fetus is no longer alive. This is called "stillbirth."

Most miscarriages occur at the beginning of the pregnancy and result from genetic defects in the fetus. This minimizes the chances of delivering babies with genetic defects. Sometimes the fetus does not develop within the amniotic sac, and so the empty sac is delivered. Miscarriages at later stages of pregnancy generally stem from problems with the uterus or placenta.

A miscarriage at an early stage of pregnancy does not always require medical intervention; the body can often complete the process on its own. In other cases, especially at later stages of pregnancy, the doctor is likely to recommend terminating the pregnancy with medication or by performing D&C (dilation & curettage). The woman can ask the doctor whether medical intervention is necessary or whether the natural process can be allowed to run its course.

In principle, one or two early miscarriages do not mandate a comprehensive medical investigation, despite the emotional difficulty of miscarrying. In contrast, the phenomenon of repeated miscarriages (usually three or more) should be investigated. The doctor will refer the woman for a series of tests to try to clarify the cause of the miscarriages and consider treatment methods.

Miscarriage is an emotionally difficult and painful experience. The expectation and anticipation of pregnancy is replaced by grief over loss, which is often accompanied by weighty decisions and medical conditions. In general, when miscarriage occurs during the early stages of pregnancy, the couple will grieve alone, and those around them will not even know about their pregnancy and their loss. If word of the pregnancy had already spread through their social circles, the couple might have to cope with the need to tell of their loss when answering questions and when people express interest in their expected pregnancy and childbirth.

Miscarriage is a common occurrence, and there is nothing shameful or blameworthy about it. This must be emphasized to the couple, who will likely need support and help in dealing with their loss. Each spouse will likely process and mourn the loss differently. It is important to be aware of this and to grant each of them the space to react in their own way. Despite the great pain and difficulty, innumerable couples have been through it and have handled the challenge, and we can hope that couples who face this painful challenge in the future will do likewise.

It is difficult to predict when a woman will be able to immerse in the *mikveh* and become *tehorah* after a miscarriage or stillbirth. The duration of bleeding after such occurrences differs from woman to woman, varying from the equivalent of a longer, heavier period to several weeks of continuous bleeding, like after childbirth.

Medical Appendix V

Contraceptives

Already in ancient times, various methods were employed to prevent conception. Some methods were behavioral (abstaining from sexual relations; coitus interruptus), some were based on natural medicines ("infertility potions"), and some blocked the passage of sperm or impaired its potency ("*mokh*"). Starting in the mid-20th century, various contraceptive methods were developed on the basis of medical research and knowledge. This field is constantly in a process of intensive research and development. Every method has its advantages and disadvantages, both medical and halakhic. Most contraceptives are meant for women to use, but a few are for men. Different methods are marketed in different countries, and methods available may change with time.

There are two main groups of contraceptives: hormone-based and others. Non-hormonal methods are further divided into various types: barrier methods, which block the passage of sperm cells; methods that impair the function of the sperm cells; and methods based on the timing of sexual relations.

HORMONAL METHODS

The two main hormones that take part in the menstrual cycle are estrogen and progesterone. Pharmaceutical contraceptives contain synthetic hormones that are similar to these hormones, in different dosages. To work, they must be taken in accordance with the instructions, even when the woman is not *tehorah*.

1. Progestogen-Only

Taking synthetic substitutes for progesterone (called "progestogen" or "progestin") regularly, each day, affects the body's hormonal balance in a way that often indirectly prevents the occurrence of ovulation. Progesterone also affects the mucus produced by the cervix, the endometrium, and the Fallopian tubes, making conception very unlikely.

How it is used

There are several hormonal contraceptive preparations based on progestogen only. The most common of them is the pill, although there are also preparations that are injected and subdermal implants. There is also an IUD that releases progestogen, which will be discussed below.

Progestogen-only pills (POPs) are known as "mini-pills" or "breastfeeding pills" since they are meant primarily for nursing mothers, as estrogen can adversely affect milk production. Thus, at least for the first few months of breastfeeding, doctors try to avoid prescribing estrogen-containing pills for nursing mothers. Such pills do not harm the baby and are therefore not forbidden for nursing mothers, but, as mentioned, they can adversely affect the milk production of some women.

POPs are taken every day, consecutively, without interruption. Taking the pill precisely on time can have the effect of minimizing the possibility of bleeding during use.

There are several types of POPs on the market, and they contain one of four synthetic progestogens: norethisterone, levonorgestrel, desogestrel, and ethynodiol acetate. These synthetic progestogens are not identical, so if a woman experiences unpleasant side-effects during use, she can try a different one.

Progestogen-only contraceptives can also be administered by injection (Depo-Provera). With this method, progestogen is injected into the arm, and from there it is released into the body. In the past, the injection was intramuscular, but a new development allows subcutaneous injection. The active ingredient is released over the course of three months, whereupon another injection is administered, which likewise lasts for three months.

Contraceptive progestogen is also available as a subdermal implant. The implant is inserted under the skin of the inner part of the upper arm. The procedure is simple and can be performed in a clinic. The version available today is called Implanon. The implant releases progestogen into the body for three years.

Effectiveness

Given perfectly proper use of progestogen preparations, 3 pregnancies were documented in one year out of 100 women using the pill; in other words, it is 97% effective. In practice, however, the effectiveness of POPs is only 91% (9 pregnancies per year per 100 users).[1] Efficacy of a progestogen injection or implant is higher (less than 1% failure rate) because the chances of forgetting an injection that is administered four times a year is small. The implant is even more effective (with less than 1% becoming pregnant per year),[2] as it is implanted in the body, remains there for three years, and it is less affected by the woman's behavior.

Side-effects

Intermenstrual bleeding is expected during the initial period of use of any progestogen-only preparation. It is estimated that 40–70% of women experience bleeding during the first three months of use.[3] For most women, spotting is expected to diminish after a few months, and for some women, bleeding will decrease to the point that it stops altogether (amenorrhea).

When it comes to spotting, the long-term contraceptive methods are more problematic. A woman who experiences bleeding while using POPs can stop taking them whenever she wants and choose a different method. However, a woman who received an injection will have to wait about half a year before the body completely flushes out the active ingredient, and a woman with an implant will have to undergo a surgical procedure to remove it and to stop its effects.

Mood changes (especially depression) and weight gain are also considered common side-effects of progestogen-based contraceptives (even though weight gain is unproven for long-term use). New studies indicate that there is no link between progestogen-based contraceptives and breast cancer, so using them does not affect a woman's risk of developing it.

2. Combined Hormonal

Other hormonal contraceptives are not based on progestogen only, but contain a combination of estrogen and a synthetic progestogen.

1. https://www.cdc.gov/reproductivehealth/unintendedpregnancy/pdf/contraceptive_methods_508.pdf.
2. https://www.accessdata.fda.gov/drugsatfda_docs/label/2012/021529s006lbl.pdf.
3. https://www.ncbi.nlm.nih.gov/pmc/articles/PMC5683158/.

How it works
Combined hormonal contraceptives generate a consistently high level of estrogen in the blood – one that does not rise and fall cyclically, as happens in the body over the course of the month. High levels of estrogen suppress the secretion of pituitary hormones that would otherwise stimulate ovulation. As a result, ovulation does not occur, rendering conception and pregnancy impossible.

How it is used
There are various kinds of combined hormonal contraceptives: pills, patches, injections, and vaginal rings.

Pills
There are very many types of combined estrogen-progestogen pills, and their availability varies from country to country. It is common to divide pills into three classes, based on the quantity of hormone it contains: The lowest dosage manufactured today contains 15 micrograms of estrogen; low-dosage pills contain 20 mcg; and medium-dosage pills contain 30 mcg of estrogen. In the past, there were pills with higher dosage, but they are no longer in use.

Most pills on the market today are designed for cyclical use of four weeks: the woman takes the pill for three weeks, and on the fourth week, she does not take pills, or takes a placebo with no active ingredient. This structure imitates the "classic" natural cycle of 28 days. While the woman is taking the active pills, there should be no bleeding. (Bleeding that began earlier will not cease immediately when one begins taking pills.) When she stops taking pills, the hormone levels in the body decrease, and within 2–4 days after stopping, she can expect to experience "withdrawal bleeding."

There are also pills that are meant to be taken for three months consecutively, interrupted with a placebo or a lower dose of estrogen. In this case, withdrawal bleeding is supposed to occur every three months. With a doctor's recommendation, one can produce a similar situation by combining packs of pills meant for a month's use. That is, one skips the week-long break between active pills.

There is another type of combined pill that is taken without interruption and is supposed to cause a state of general amenorrhea. With this type of usage, there will be no monthly bleeding; rather it will be less frequent, depending on the cycle established by the pill. This can make things easier for halakhically observant couples. On the other hand, taking hormonal pills consecutively, with no break, increases the risk of unexpected bleeding.

To minimize the possibility of such bleeding, and to prevent the frustration it entails, it is recommended to start using hormones based on the standard instructions (three weeks of pills with the active ingredient, followed by a week of nothing or a placebo). Later, one can gradually extend the period of taking active pills, until it lasts for several months.

Unexpected bleeding is common during the first cycle or two of use, and the chances that such bleeding will occur is inversely proportional to the dosage; the lower the dosage of the pill, the greater the changes of bleeding or spotting. It is estimated that intermenstrual bleeding will occur among 30–50% of women upon starting combination hormonal contraception Intermenstrual bleeding is even more common with lower dosages; 40–70% of women who take a lower dosage can experience it.[4] For most of them, this bleeding will stop within the three months of starting. At this stage, it is not advisable to change the type of pill because of bleeding, and the generally accepted course of action is to continue taking the same type, since in most cases the bleeding stops after an adjustment period. Only if the problems continue beyond 2–3 months is there room to consider switching to another pill, bearing in mind that the initial period of usage of the new type of pill might entail similar or different side effects.

Patches

Hormonal contraceptives based on a combination of estrogen and progestogen are also available as a patch that is affixed to the body for a week. The hormones, which are in the glue of the patch, are absorbed into the body through the skin throughout the time that the patch is affixed to the body. As with the pills, the basic guideline is to use the patches in a four-week cycle: three weeks using three patches (one week per patch), followed by a fourth, patch-free week. Withdrawal bleeding is expected during the fourth week because of the decrease in the body's hormone levels. With patches, too, it is possible to extend the time from withdrawal to withdrawal by using patches for more than three consecutive weeks.

Vaginal ring

The vaginal ring is a flexible plastic ring laced with hormones. The ring is inserted into the vagina, and the hormones are absorbed into the body through the vaginal lining. The ring is inserted by squeezing it on both sides so that it is oblong and can be inserted like a tampon. When one stops squeezing, it reverts to a shape that allows it to remain in the vagina and prevents it from falling out. The ring

4. Unscheduled bleeding and contraceptive choice: increasing satisfaction and continuation rates https://pubmed.ncbi.nlm.nih.gov/29386936/.

is supposed to remain in the vagina for three weeks. During the fourth week, the ring is removed, and she will therefore bleed during the course of that week. Similar to the extended use of combination pills, the next ring can be inserted into the vagina without a break in order to prolong the amenorrheic time frame.

Injections

Although it is impossible to obtain this contraceptive in Israel or the USA today, there are places around the world where injections containing estrogen and progestogen are available. These injections are administered monthly (with an interval of no more than 33 days between injections).[5]

Effectiveness

Combined hormonal contraceptives are 99% effective with perfectly proper use. In actuality, the effectiveness is only 92%, generally because of improper usage on the part of the woman – like forgetting to take the pill. Such misuses are more typical of the pill and affects other hormonal methods less.

Side-effects

As mentioned above, intermenstrual bleeding is common at the beginning of use, but the situation generally improves with time.

The estrogen component increases the risk of blood clots, which can reach the lungs (pulmonary embolism), the heart (myocardial infarction), or the brain (stroke). Even if this is a relatively low risk (10–20 instances per 10,000 women), it is still higher than the risk in the general population (5–10 instances per 10,000 women). Nevertheless, it is worth recalling that even this elevated risk is still lower than the risk of blood clots during pregnancy (60–120 instances per 10,000 women).

Various genetic risk factors, and especially a family propensity for excessive clotting, can increase risk for some women. The same applies to smokers and to women with a significant history of migraines.

The link between estrogen- and progestogen-containing hormonal contraceptives and breast cancer is a matter of disagreement.[6] There is a connection with

---

5. An injection of this type called Lunelle was approved for use in the US in 2000, but it was removed from use two years later. In other countries, other formulations of the injection are available.
6. https://www.endotext.org/chapter/contraception/.

cervical cancer.[7] Combination oral contraception has proven to reduce the risk of endometrial, ovarian and colorectal cancer[8]. Therefore, the decision of which contraception to use should take into consideration the risk profile for the individual woman.

About one-third of women who use hormonal contraceptives report changes of mood, and they can also adversely affect sexual desire.

Use of hormonal contraceptives is only with a prescription issued by a licensed professional after examining the patient's personal and family history. If there are side-effects from one type of pill, it is reasonable to try another type.

INTRA-UTERINE DEVICES (IUDS)

There are two contraceptive methods that involve placing a device inside the uterus: the copper IUD, which is non-hormonal, and the hormonal IUD (IUS or LNG IUD).

1. The Non-Hormonal IUD

How it works

The copper IUD is engineered to stay within the uterine cavity. It releases copper ions into the uterine cavity, creating an environment that impairs the viability of the sperm cells. At the same time, the presence of a foreign body within the uterus alters the composition of the endometrium, so that even if fertilization takes place, it will be difficult for the fertilized egg to undergo implantation.

How it is used

The IUD is inserted by a gynecologist in a simple clinical procedure. The vagina is widened with a speculum, bringing the external os of the cervical canal into view. The cervix is held in place by a medical device, enabling the precise insertion of the IUD. The IUD is inserted, in its closed position, into the uterus through an applicator tube. The applicator is very thin, generally less than 10mm (0.4 of an inch) in

---

7. International Collaboration of Epidemiological Studies of Cervical Cancer. Cervical cancer and hormonal contraceptives: collaborative reanalysis of individual data for 16,573 women with cervical cancer and 35,509 women without cervical cancer from 24 epidemiological studies. *The Lancet*. 2007; 370:1609–21.
8. J.M. Gierisch, R.R. Coeytaux, R.P. Urrutia, L.J. Havrilesky, P.G. Moorman, W.J. Lowery, M. Dinan, A.J. McBroom, V. Hasselblad, G.D. Sanders, E.R. Myers. "Oral Contraceptive Use and Risk of Breast, Cervical, Colorectal, and Endometrial Cancers: A Systematic Review," *Cancer Epidemiol Biomarkand Prevention* 11 (November 22, 2013): 1931–43. doi: 10.1158/1055-9965.EPI-13-0298. Epub September 6, 2013. PMID: 24014598.

diameter. When the applicator is removed, the IUD is released and opens up into a shape that allows it to remain in place within the uterine cavity. There is another type of IUD, called Gynefix, whose insertion is slightly more complicated, and which partially fastens to the uterine wall. In general, a thread is attached to the outer end of the device, which dangles out of the cervix. If one inserts a finger deep into the vagina, the thread can be felt, thus confirming that the device is in place. The doctor uses the thread to remove the IUD when the woman no longer desires its continuation or the time has arrived for replacement.

An IUD can be emplaced immediately after birth and at any point of the menstrual cycle. It remains in the uterus and effectively prevents pregnancy for 5–10 years, depending on the type of device.

Effectiveness

The IUD is a very effective contraceptive method. Its failure rate is 0.6%. Its use is not affected by the woman's behavior, so its practical effectiveness is almost identical, or 0.8%.

Side effects

The main side effect of the IUD is irregular bleeding. This side effect is expected during the first few months of use. Additionally, menstrual bleeding may endure a bit longer or be heavier than usual.

The IUD does not increase the chances of an ectopic pregnancy, but it is less effective in the prevention of such pregnancies, as it has a local effect on what happens inside the uterus but does not interfere with the endocrine system as a whole.

In contrast to what was previously thought, the IUD does not harm the uterus or increase the likelihood of uterine infection.

2. The Hormonal IUD (IUS)

How it works

The hormonal IUD is similar in shape to some of the normal copper IUDs, but it includes a cylinder containing progestin. The progestin is regularly released into the uterus over the course of years, and it causes the endometrium to be very thin, thus making the implantation of a fertilized egg impossible. The progestin released by the IUD also disrupts ovulation and thickens the cervical secretions. The combination of all these effects prevents the possibility that a pregnancy will occur or become implanted.

How it is used

Like the regular copper IUD, the hormonal IUD is inserted into the uterus in a simple clinical procedure. The hormonal IUD effectively prevents pregnancy for 3–5 years depending on the hormonal dose

Effectiveness

The IUD is considered the most effective contraceptive method, with a theoretical and actual failure rate of 0.1%.

Side effects

Irregular spotting and intermenstrual bleeding are very common side effects for the first 3–6 months of use, but with time, there is generally a gradual reduction.

BARRIER METHODS

Barrier methods use physical obstacles to prevent sperm from reaching the uterus and fertilizing the ovum. Such methods include: spermicides, condoms, sponges, cervical caps, and diaphragms.

1. Spermicides

How they work

Many spermicides contain the chemical nonoxynol-9, which impairs function of sperm cells. Other spermicides are based on lactic acid buffering.

How they are used

There is a range of preparations that contain spermicide: gels, films, vaginal suppositories, and creams. Their availability varies from place to place. Vaginal contraceptive films and spermicide suppositories must be inserted at least 15 minutes before intercourse in order to dissolve and disperse. If more than 3 hours have elapsed before intercourse, another film must be inserted. Spermicidal foams and gels are effective immediately. A repeat application is required prior to each additional act of intercourse. They can be used as a sole contraceptive method or can accompany the use of a different contraceptive, as will be described.

Effectiveness

With perfect use of nonoxynol 9 as a sole contraceptive, (using the standard dosage of 100 mg), there will be an 18% pregnancy rate. In actuality, the failure rate of spermicide is 29%.

2. Diaphragm

How it works

A diaphragm is a latex or silicone dome designed to cover the opening of the cervix (external os), thus blocking the path of the sperm and preventing them from entering the uterus. To impair the function of sperm, which can overcome the obstacle, a spermicide is added.

How it is used

The diaphragm is inserted into the vagina before sexual intercourse (no more than an hour beforehand) and must be left there for six hours afterward. According to the instructions, diaphragm use should be accompanied by a spermicide, and a second dose of spermicide should be added if there will be a second sexual encounter soon after the first. The diaphragm should not be removed for the next 6–8 hours. After removing the diaphragm, it should be cleaned with water and can be reused. Diaphragms come in several sizes, and it is necessary for a woman to be fitted for the exact size before acquiring it. In the event of significant fluctuations in body weight (5kg or more), or after pregnancy, another fitting should be done to confirm the size is still right for this woman. Recently, a "one size fits all" diaphragm has appeared on the market.

Effectiveness

Given perfectly proper use, the diaphragm has a 6% failure rate. In actuality, the failure rate of is 16%. The one size diaphragm is somewhat less effective in ideal use.

3. Cervical Cap

How it works

A cervical cap is like a small silicone bowl precisely fitted to cover the opening of the cervix (external os). It blocks the opening and prevents the sperm from entering the uterus. Use of a cervical cap is likewise in tandem with spermicide, which impairs the function of sperm that reach it.

How it is used

The cervical cap is inserted into the vagina before sexual intercourse and should be left there for six hours. It can remain there for up to 48 hours. In contrast to the diaphragm, during use, it is not necessary to add spermicide in the event of a second sexual encounter. A cervical cap can be purchased with a prescription, and it is available in three sizes, corresponding to the woman's childbirth history. One must leave it in for 8 hours after intercourse.

Effectiveness
The failure rate of the cervical cap available today is 16% among women who never gave birth, and 32% among women who have given birth vaginally at least once.

4. Sponge

How it works
A contraceptive sponge is a small, round sponge that contains one gram of the spermicide nonoxynol-9. The sponge itself forms a physical barrier that blocks sperm cells from entering the cervix, and the spermicide is released during use, impairing the function of sperm cells.

How it is used
The sponge is inserted into the vagina before sexual intercourse. It must remain in place for at least 6 hours after intercourse. They can be purchased in pharmacies without a prescription.

Effectiveness
In normal use, the failure rate of the sponge is 16–32%.

5. Condom

How it works
A condom is a physical barrier that prevents the passage of sperm cells into the vagina. Using a condom in tandem with a spermicide achieves impairment of the function of sperm cells as well, thus increasing the overall contraceptive effectiveness.

How it is used
There are two types of condom: one designed for use by men, and one designed for use by women. A man's condom is fitted over the erect penis before vaginal penetration. A woman's condom is in the shape of a soft, thin tube with a flexible ring at either end. The inner ring, at the closed end of the condom, is used to insert the condom inside the vagina and hold it in place. The outer ring, at the open end, remains outside the vulva.

Effectiveness
In normal use, the failure rate is 18% for a male's condom, and 27% for a females's condom.

EMERGENCY CONTRACEPTIVE METHODS

In contradistinction to standard contraceptives, which are applied before sexual intercourse, there are contraceptive methods designed for cases where it is necessary to prevent pregnancy after sexual relations. These emergency contraceptives delay ovulation and prevent fertilization or implantation in cases of unprotected sexual relations. Combined hormonal pills, progestogen pills, antiprogestogen preparations, and even IUDs can be used effectively for these purposes.

1. Combined pills

According to this method (called the "Yuzpe Method"), two large doses of the combined hormonal contraceptive pill are taken 12 hours apart. This can prevent conception even after sexual relations.

2. Progestogen pills

It has been proven that taking levonorgestrel (the progestogen found in the hormonal IUD) in a dose of 150mg (or two doses of 75mg with a separation of 12 hours) within 72 hours is an effective way to prevent pregnancy after unprotected sexual relations. This preparation does not entail the side-effect of nausea as much as the combined pill does but can result in irregular bleeding.

3. Antiprogestogens

Mifepristone is a pill used to perform first-trimester abortions, and it can be used for a similar purpose as an emergency contraceptive. Since the original purpose of this pill was to cause the termination of a pregnancy, it requires a prescription and is not easily obtained. A similar pill (ulipristal acetate) has been approved for use as an emergency contraceptive in Europe and the US. It is marketed under the brand name "Ella."

4. IUDs

The insertion of a copper, non-hormonal IUD within 5 days of sexual relations has proven effective as an emergency contraceptive. An advantage of this method is that the IUD can remain in the uterus and continue to function as a contraceptive.

Effectiveness

The general failure rate is up to 3% for all methods. The combined hormonal pill is considered the least effective. Progestogen or antiprogestogen is more effective. The most effective method for this purpose is the insertion of an IUD; the failure rate of this method is 0.1%.

Side effects

Taking large doses of combined pills can cause nausea and vomiting. Progestogen can cause early onset of menstruation. Antiprogestogen (like mifepristone) can delay the onset of menstruation.

NATURAL CONTRACEPTIVE METHODS

1. The Fertility Awareness Method (FAM)

This contraceptive method is based on abstaining from sexual relations on the days when the woman is fertile. These methods can be combined with various barrier methods to increase the safety and effectiveness of this method.

How it works

This method is based on the fact that the lifespan of an ovum is short; it remains viable for only 24–36 hours from the moment it is released from the ovary to the Fallopian tube during ovulation. Fertilization can occur only if sperm reach it within this window of time. It must be taken into consideration that the lifespan of sperm is longer, and during the fertile days, it can remain viable within the woman's bodily secretions for up to five days. Refraining from sexual relations during this time frame significantly reduces the possibility of conception.

How it is used

The most efficient implementation of this method relies on identifying the "window of fertility" by tracking three symptoms: basal body temperature, the nature of the cervical secretions, and the position of the cervix. This contraceptive method demands study and skill. The woman learns to meticulously record her body temperature at the moment she wakes up in the morning, recognize her vaginal secretions, and examine the position of her cervix. The combination of these three parameters can indicate the time of ovulation, and the couple then abstains from sexual relations (or uses a barrier method of contraception) during the fertile period around the time of ovulation. Outside of this time frame, the couple can have sexual relations without using other contraceptives.

Effectiveness

Skilled use of this method has a 2–3% failure rate. However, with typical use it is only 75% effective. Effectiveness also depends on the couple's motivation to observe all that this method demands.

2. Contraception Based on Lactational Amenorrhea

How it works

This method is based on the fact that while a woman is amenorrhoeic because she is breastfeeding exclusively, the chances of her getting pregnant are naturally low.

How it is used

According to this method, a woman up to six months postnatal, who breastfeeds exclusively, and whose menstrual cycle (for these purposes, this is defined as any bleeding that began on or after day 56 after childbirth) has not returned is considered very unlikely to become pregnant. In such cases, a couple can choose to have sexual relations without using any other contraceptive, on the assumption that the woman is not fertile at that time.

Effectiveness

When all three conditions are met, the chances of getting pregnant are 2%.[9]

9. https://www.endotext.org/chapter/contraception/

Medical Bibliography

S.S. Dasharathy, S.L. Mumford, A.Z Pollack, et al. "Menstrual Bleeding Patterns Among Regularly Menstruating Women." *American Journal of Epidemiology* 175, no. 6 (2012): 536–45.

E.M. Finucane, D.J. Murphy, L.M. Biesty, G.M. Gyte, A.M. Cotter, E.M. Ryan, M. Boulvain, D. Devane. "Membrane Sweeping for Induction of Labour," *The Cochrane Database* 2 no. 2 (February 27, 2020): CD000451.

R.L. Floyd, B.W. Jack, R. Cefalo et al. "The Clinical Content of Preconception Care: Alcohol, Tobacco, And Illicit Drug Exposures." *American Journal of Obstetrics and Gynecology* 199, no.6, suppl. a (2008): S333–S339.

P.M. Gardiner, L. Nelson, C.S. Shellhaas et al. "The Clinical Content of Preconception Care: Nutrition and Dietary Supplements." *American Journal of Obstetrics and Gynecology* 199, no.6, suppl. a (2008): S345–S356.

J. Gekas, S. Langlois, V. Ravitsky, et al. "Identification of Trisomy 18, Trisomy 13, and Down Syndrome from Maternal Plasma." *The Application of Clinical Genetics* 7 (2014): 127–31.

J.M. Gierisch, R.R. Coeytaux, R.P. Urrutia, L.J. Havrilesky, P.G. Moorman, W.J. Lowery, M. Dinan, A.J. McBroom, V. Hasselblad, G.D. Sanders, E.R. Myers. "Oral Contraceptive Use and Risk of Breast, Cervical, Colorectal, and Endometrial Cancers: A Systematic Review," *Cancer Epidemiol Biomarkand Prevention* 11 (November 22, 2013): 1931–43. doi: 10.1158/1055-9965. EPI-13-0298. Epub 2013 Sep 6. PMID: 24014598.

International Collaboration of Epidemiological Studies of Cervical Cancer. "Cervical Cancer and Hormonal Contraceptives: Collaborative Reanalysis of Individual Data for 16,573 women with Cervical Cancer and 35,509 Women without Cervical Cancer from 24 Epidemiological Studies," *The Lancet*. 2007; 370: 1609–21.

E.R. Norwitz, B. Levy. "Noninvasive Prenatal Testing: The Future is now." *Reviews in Obstetrics and Gynecology* 6, no. 2 (2013): 48–62.

D.R. Zimmerman. *Genetics and Genetic Diseases: Jewish Legal and Ethical Perspectives*. Jersey City: Ktav, 2013.

FURTHER REFERENCE ON MEDICAL ISSUES

G.R. Bergys, S.R. Pallone. "Fertility Awareness-Based Methods: Another Option for Family Planning." *American Board Family Medicine* 22 (2009): 147–57.

L. Cheng, Y. Che, A.M. Gülmezoglu. "Interventions for Emergency Contraception." *The Cochrane Database of Systematic Reviews* 8 (August 15, 2012): CD001324.

L.A. Cook, K. Nanda, D.A. Grimes, L.M. Lopez. "Diaphragm versus Diaphragm with Spermicides for Contraception." *The Cochrane Database of Systematic Reviews* 1 (2003): Art No.: CD002031 DOI: 10.1002/14651858. CD002031.

M.F. Gallo, D.A. Grimes, K.F. Schulz, L.M. Lopez. "Cervical Cap versus Diaphragm for Contraception." *The Cochrane Database of Systematic Reviews* 4 (2002): Art. No.: CD003551. DOI: 10.1002/14651858.CD003551.

D.A. Grimes, L.M. Lopez, E.G. Raymond, V. Halpern, K. Nanda, K.F. Schulz. "Spermicide Used Alone for Contraception." *The Cochrane Database of Systematic Reviews* 5, no. 12 (December 5, 2013): CD005218.

M.A. Kuyoh, C. Toroitich-Ruto, D.A. Grimes, K.F. Schulz, M.F. Gallo, L.M. Lopez. "Sponge versus Diaphragm for Contraception." *The Cochrane Database of Systematic Reviews* 3 (2002): Art. No.: CD003172. DOI: 10.1002/14651858. CD003172.

J. Trussell. "Contraceptive Efficacy." In *Contraceptive Technology: Twentieth Revised Edition,* edited by RA Hatcher, J Trussell, AL Nelson, W Cates, D Kowal, M Policar. New York: Ardent Media (2011).

C. Van der Wijden, C. Manion. "Lactational Amenorrhea Method for Family Planning." *The Cochrane Database of Systematic Reviews* 10 (2015): Art. No.: CD001329.

Halakhic References, Aḥaronim and Contemporary Poskim

SIFREI HALAKHAH

Arukh Ha-Shulḥan, R. Yeḥiel Mikhel Epstein (1829–1908), Novardok, Belarus.

Arukh La-Ner, R. Yaakov Ettlinger (1798–1871), Altona, Germany.

Badei Ha-Shulḥan, R. Shraga Feivel Cohen (Contemporary), New York, USA.

Bet Shmuel, R. Shmuel ben Uri Shraga Feivish (late 17th century), Furth, Germany and Shydlow, Poland.

Barukh Ta'am, R. Barukh Frankel-Teomim (1760–1828), Wisnicz, Poland and Leipnik, Moravia.

Birkei Yosef, R. Ḥaim Yosef David Azulai (*Ḥida*), (1724–1806), Jerusalem, Israel.

Darkhei Taharah, R. Mordekhai Eliahu (1929–2010), Jerusalem, Israel.

Darkhei Teshuvah, R. Tzvi Hirsch Shapira (1850–1913), Munkatch, Hungary.

Devar Shemu'el, R. Shmuel Abuhav (1610–1694), Venice, Italy.

Ein Yitzḥak, R. Yitzḥak Yosef (b. 1952), Jerusalem, Israel.

Gufei Halakhot, R. Yehoshua Wolhendler (1953–2011), New York, USA.

Ha'amek She'elah, R. Naftali Tzvi Yehudah Berlin (1817–1893), Volozhin, Belarus.

Ḥavat Da'at, R. Yaakov Lorberbaum (1760–1832), Lissa, Poland.

Ḥazon Ish, R. Avraham Yeshayah Karelitz (1878–1953), Bnei Brak, Israel.

Ḥelkat Meḥokek, R. Moshe Lima (c.1615–1670), Vilna and Brisk, Lithuania.

Ḥokhmat Adam, R. Avraham Danzig (1748–1820), Vilna, Lithuania.

Ḥut Ha-Shani, R. Nissim Karelitz (1926–2019), Bnei Brak, Israel.

Ish ve'Isha, R. Elyashiv Knohl (1948–2018), Kfar Etzion, Israel.

Kovetz Bet Yitzḥak, R. Mordekhai Willig (b. 1947), New York, USA.

Kovetz Teshuvot, R. Yosef Shalom Eliashiv (1910–2012), Jerusalem, Israel.

Leḥem Ve-Simlah, R. Shlomo Ganzfried (1804–1886), Ungvar, Hungary.

Mar'eh Kohen, R. Yitzḥak Mordekhai Rubin (b. 1961), Jerusalem, Israel.

Mekor Ḥayim Ve-Tiferet Tzvi, R. Shneur Ziskind Gundersheim (c.1790), Frankfurt, Germany.

Mishmeret Ha-Taharah, R. Moshe Mordekhai Karp (Contemporary), Kiryat Sefer, Israel.

Naḥalat Shiv'ah, R. Shmuel ben David Halevi (1624–1681), Bamberg, Germany.

Neta Sha'ashu'im, R. Tzvi Hirsch Kara (1740–1814), Buchach, Poland.

Nidrei Zerizin, R. Shlomo Kluger (1785–1869), Brody, Galicia.

Nishmat Avraham, R. Dr. Avraham Avraham (b.1935), Jerusalem, Israel.

Nit'ei Gavriel, R. Gavriel Zinner (Contemporary), New York, USA.

Orḥot Taharah, R. Yitzḥak Isaac Kahane (Contemporary), Jerusalem, Israel.

Orot Taharah, R. Zekharia Ben Shlomo (Contemporary), Sha'alvim, Israel.

Pardes Rimonim, R. Moshe Yitzḥak Avigdor (1801–1865), Kovna, Lithuania.

Pitḥei Teshuvah, R. Avraham Tzvi Hirsh Eisenstadt (1812–1868), Bialystok, Poland.

Pri De'ah, R. Azriel Dov Halevi (c. 1860), Karsan, Galicia.

Sha'arei Orah, R. Shlomo Levi (b. 1952), Gush Etzion, Israel.

Sha'arei Taharah, R. Yeḥiel Mikhel Stern (b. 1949), Jerusalem, Israel.

Shem Yosef, R. Yisrael Ḥaim Yosef Elyakim (d. 1791), Sofia, Bulgaria.

Shemirat Shabbat Ke-Hilkhatah, R. Yehoshua Neuwirth (1927–2013), Jerusalem, Israel.

Shevivei Taharah, R. Shmuel Eliezer Stern (b. 1948), Bnei Brak, Israel.

Shirat Ha-Yam, R. Mordekhai Yehuda Kraus (Contemporary), Yeruḥam, Israel.

Shi'urei Shevet Ha-Levi, R. Shmuel Halevi Wosner, (1913–2015), Bnei Brak, Israel.

Shiyurei Berakhah, R. Ḥaim Yosef Dovid Azulai. *Ḥida.* (1724–1806), Jerusalem, Israel.

Shulḥan Arukh Ha-Rav, R. Shneur Zalman of Liadi (1754–1812), Vitebsk, Russia.

Sidrei Taharah, R. Elḥanan Ashkenazi (1713–1780), Danzig, Poland.

Taharat Ha-Bayit, R. Ovadia Yosef (1920–2013), Jerusalem, Israel.

Taharah Ke-Halakhah, R. Yekutiel Farkash (Contemporary), Jerusalem, Israel.

Taharat Ha-Kodesh, R. Zvi Sobolofsky (Contemporary), New York, USA.

Taharat Yisrael, R. Yisrael Yitzḥak Yanovsky (c. 1900), Warsaw, Poland.

Torat Ha-Shelamim, R. Yaakov Reischer (1661–1733), Metz, France.

Va-Ya'an Yosef, R. Yosef Greenwald (1903–1984), New York, USA.

Yalkut Kehunah, R. Raḥamim Ḥai Ḥawita HaKohen (1901–1959), Djerba, Tunisia.

Yam Shel Shlomo, R. Shlomo Luria (1510–1573), Lublin, Poland.

Zikhron Yosef, R. Yosef Steinhart (1720–1776), Furth, Germany.

RESPONSA

Responsa Aḥiezer, R. Ḥaim Ozer Grodzinski (1863–1940), Vilna, Lithuania.

Responsa Avodat Ha-Gershuni, R. Gershon Ben Yitzḥak Ashkenazi (1618–1693), Vienna, Austria.

Responsa Ayalah Sheluḥah, R. Naftali Hertz Klotzkin (1822–1893), Warsaw, Poland.

Responsa Binyan Tzion, R. Yaakov Ettlinger (1798–1871), Altona, Germany.

Responsa Bnei Banim, R. Yehuda Herzl Henkin (1945–2020), Jerusalem, Israel.

Responsa Divrei Ḥayim, R. Ḥaim Halberstam (1793–1876), Sanz, Poland.

Responsa Divrei Yatziv, R. Yekutiel Yehudah Halberstam (1905–1994), Kiryat Sanz, Israel.

Responsa Dovev Mesharim, R. Dov Ber Weidenfeld (1879–1966), Jerusalem, Israel.

Responsa Elef Ha-Magen, R. Moshe Natan Rubinstein (b. 1852), Lvov, Ukraine.

Responsa Har Tzvi, R. Tzvi Pesaḥ Frank (1874–1960), Jerusalem, Israel.

Responsa Ḥatam Sofer, R. Moshe Sofer (1763–1839), Pressburg, Hungary.

Responsa Ḥedvat Yaakov, R. Tzvi Aryeh Yehuda Yaakov Meislish (1851–1933), Lask, Poland.

Responsa Ḥelkat Yoav, R. Yoav Yehoshua Weingarten (1845–1922), Kinsk, Poland.

Responsa Ḥemdat Shlomo, R. Shlomo Zalman Lipszyc (1765–1839), Warsaw, Poland.

Responsa Ḥeshev Ha-Efod, R. Ḥanokh Dov Padwa (1908– 2000), London, England.

Responsa Igrot Moshe, R. Moshe Feinstein (1895–1986), New York, USA.

Responsa Kenei Bosem, R. Meir Brandsdorfer (1934–2009), Jerusalem, Israel.

Responsa Kinyan Torah, R. Avraham Dov Horowitz (1911–2004), Strasbourg, France.

Responsa Lev David, R. David Feldman (1884–1955), Manchester, England.

Responsa Maharam Lublin, R. Meir ben Gedaliah (1558–1616), Lublin, Poland.

Responsa Maharam Padua, R. Meir Katzenelenbogen (1482–1565), Padua, Italy.

Responsa Maharam Schick, R. Moshe Schick (1807–1879), Ḥust, Hungary.

Responsa Maharash Engel, R. Shmuel Engel (1853–1935), Radamisle, Poland.

Responsa Maharif, R. Yaakov al-Faraji, (c. 1650–1730), Alexandria, Egypt.

Responsa Maharshal, R. Shlomo Luria (1510–1573), Lublin, Poland.

Responsa Maharsham, R. Shalom Mordekhai Schwadron (1835–1911), Brezan, Galicia.

Responsa Mateh Levi, R. Mordekhai Halevi Horowitz (1844–1910), Frankfurt, Germany.

Responsa Melamed Le-Ho'il, R. David Tzvi Hoffmann (1843–1921), Berlin, Germany.

Responsa Me'il Tzedakah, R. Yonah Landsofer (1678–1713), Prague, Bohemia.

Responsa Minḥat Asher, R. Asher Weiss (b. 1953), Jerusalem, Israel.

Responsa Minḥat Shlomo, R. Shlomo Zalman Auerbach (1910–1995), Jerusalem, Israel.

Responsa Minḥat Yitzḥak, R. Yitzḥak Yaakov Weiss (1902–1989), Jerusalem, Israel.

Responsa Mishneh Halakhot, R. Menashe Klein (1924–2011), New York, USA.

Responsa Mishpetei Uziel, R. Ben-Zion Meir Hai Uziel (1880–1953), Jerusalem, Israel.

Responsa Nezer Kohen, R. Zamir Cohen (b. 1965), Beitar Illit, Israel.

Responsa Noda Bi-Yehudah, R. Yeḥezkel Landua (1713–1793), Prague, Bohemia.

Responsa Rav Pe'alim, R. Yosef Ḥaim (Ben Ish Ḥai) (1835–1909), Baghdad, Iraq.

Responsa Seridei Esh, R. Yeḥiel Yaakov Weinberg (1884–1966), Montreux, Switzerland.

Responsa Shav Yaakov, R. Yaakov Poppers (d. 1742), Frankfurt, Germany.

Responsa Shevut Yaakov, R. Yaakov Reischer (1661–1733), Rzeszów, Poland.

Responsa Sho'el U-Meshiv, R. Yosef Shaul Nathanson (1810–1875), Lvov, Poland.

Responsa Sho'el Ve-Nish'al, R. Moshe Ha-Cohen Kalphon (1874–1950), Djerba, Tunisia.

Responsa Si'aḥ Naḥum, R. Naḥum Eliezer Rabinovitch (1928–2020), Ma'ale Adumim, Israel.

Responsa Teshurat Shai, R. Shlomo Yehudah Tabbak (1832–1907), Sighet, Hungary.

Responsa Teshuvah Me-Ahavah, R. Eliezer Fleckeles (1754–1826), Prague, Bohemia.

Responsa Teshuvot Ve-hanhagot, R. Moshe Sternbukh (b. 1926), Jerusalem, Israel.

Responsa Tiferet Adam, R. Moshe David Ostreikher (1883–1953), New York, USA.

Responsa Tzitz Eliezer, R. Eliezer Yehudah Waldenberg (1915–2006), Jerusalem, Israel.

Responsa Vayashev Moshe, R. Moshe Zev Zargar (Contemporary), Jerusalem, Israel.

Responsa Yabi'a Omer, R. Ovadiah Yosef (1920–2013), Jerusalem, Israel.

Responsa Yad Yosef, R. Yosef Yozefa Stern (1739–1826), Zhovkva, Ukraine.

Responsa Yehudah Ya'aleh, R. Yehudah Assad (1794–1866), Semnitz, Hungary.

Glossary[1]

Aḥaronim – Later (Early Modern, and Modern) halakhic authorities.

Amah (pl. Amot) – Cubit, measurement of approximately 48 cm.

Amatla – Pretext.

Amora (pl. Amora'im) – A sage during the period of the Gemara.

B'sha'ah tovah – "May it be at a good time," a blessing expressed to a pregnant woman.

Ba'al nefesh – A spiritually conscientious person.

Ba'alei teshuvah – Jews from a non-Orthodox background who have begun to practice Orthodox Judaism.

Balu'a – Internal area of the body.

Baraita – A statement of Oral law contemporary with the Mishnah, but not included in it.

Barukh Hashem – "Blessed be God," an expression of thanksgiving.

Bedi'avad – After the fact.

1. Glossary by Yoetzet Halacha Ilana Sober Elzufon.

Bedikah ***(pl. Bedikot)*** – An internal self-examination to check for bleeding. A *bedikah* is performed by inserting a clean, soft white cloth into the vaginal canal and rotating it to check inside recesses and folds.

Bedikat emtza – A *bedikah* performed on one of the intermediate days of the seven *neki'im*.

Bedikat ḥorim u-sedakim – A *bedikah* (internal self-examination) of the recesses and folds of the vaginal canal.

Berakhah – Blessing (e.g., the blessing recited by a woman upon immersing in the *mikveh*).

Bet ha-setarim – Recessed area of the body (e.g., the inside of the mouth). The water of the *mikveh* does not need enter the *bet ha-setarim*, but such areas should be free of barriers that could theoretically impede contact with the water.

Bi'ah she-lo ke-darkah – Anal intercourse.

Brit, Brit milah – Ritual circumcision.

Dam makkah, Dam petza – Blood from a wound, lesion, sore, cut, or abrasion. Such blood does not render a woman *niddah*.

Dam tohar – Bleeding during days 8–40 after giving birth to a boy, or days 15–80 after giving birth to a girl. Historically, this bleeding did not render a woman *teme'ah*. Today, it is treated like any other uterine bleeding.

DeOrayta – A matter of Torah law.

DeRabanan – A matter of rabbinic law.

Etzba ***(pl. Etzba'ot)*** – Thumbsbreadth, measurement of approximately 2 cm. (¾ of an inch)

Ge'onim – Early post-Talmudic halakhic authorities.

Gemara – A central text of Jewish law, consisting of Rabbinic discussion of and elaboration on the Mishnah.

Gezeirat ha-Katuv – A decree of the Torah.

Gris – A broad bean (*ful*), or a circle with a diameter of 19mm (¾ of an inch), equivalent to the size of such a bean. Halakhically relevant for the laws of stains (*ketamim*).

Ḥafifah – Preparation for *mikveh* immersion, including washing and combing the hair, bathing, and removing any barriers to immersion.

Ḥakham – A halakhic authority.

Ḥakhamim – The Sages (used in the Mishnah to refer to the opinion of the majority of sages).

Hakpadah – Being particular or meticulous.

Halakhah l'Moshe mi-Sinai – A tradition handed to Moshe at Sinai, i.e., a *deOrayta* level *halakhah* that is not explicitly stated in the Torah.

Halakhah (pl. Halakhot) – Jewish Law, or any particular Jewish law.

Halakhic – Pertaining to Jewish Law (*Halakhah*).

Hargashah – A halakhically significant physical sensation accompanying the onset of uterine bleeding.

Hargashat ha-ed – The sensation of performing a *bedikah*, which can be mistaken for a halakhically relevant *hargashah* (see *safek hargashah*).

Harḥakot – Restrictions observed by a married couple during *niddah*, beyond the prohibition on marital relations. These include a prohibition on all physical contact, as well as adaptations to sleeping arrangements, shared meals, and other areas of interaction.

Hashḥatat zera – Destroying sperm.

Ḥatzitzah (pl. Ḥatzitzot) – A barrier or obstruction between a person immersing and the water of the *mikveh*. Depending on the circumstances, a *ḥatzitzah* can invalidate immersion.

Ḥazakah – Halakhic presumption.

Ḥazal – Acronym for *Ḥakhamim zikhronam li'vrakhah,* refers to the Sages of the Mishnah and Gemara.

Hefsek taharah – A *bedikah* that a woman performs to confirm that all uterine bleeding has ceased and initiate the process of becoming *tehorah.*

Ḥerem De-Rabbenu Gershom – A rabbinic decree enacted about 1,000 years ago, binding on Ashkenazic Jewry, prohibiting polygamy.

Heter – Halakhic permission.

Ḥezkat taharah – Halakhic presumption that a woman is not experiencing uterine bleeding.

Ḥiddush – New insight.

Ḥoleh she'yesh bo sakanah/Ḥolah she'yesh bah sakanah – A person with a life-threatening illness.

Ḥoleh she-ein bo sakanah/Ḥola she-ein bah sakanah – A person who is ill with a non-life-threatening illness.

Hotza'at zera le-vatalah – Wasting sperm.

Ḥumra – A stringency.

Igun – A situation in which it is very difficult for the wife to become *tehorah,* so that the couple will be prohibited to each other indefinitely.

K'derekh kol ha'aretz – In a normal manner (refers to conduct of marital relations).

Ke-gris – A circle with a diameter of 19mm (¾ of an inch), the size of a broad bean (*ful*). Halakhically relevant for the laws of stains (*ketamim*).

Ketem (pl. Ketamim) – A bloodstain found on a woman's body, her clothing, or another external surface. A *ketem* renders a woman *niddah* if it meets certain specific criteria.

Ketubah – Marriage contract, which guarantees the wife a sum of money if she is divorced or widowed.

Kiddushin – Marriage.

Kli (*pl.* ***Kelim***) – Vessel or implement.

Kvatter – At a *brit milah,* the couple who pass the baby from the mother to the father are called the *kvatter* and *kvatterin.*

L'ḥumra – Stringently.

L'kula – Leniently.

Lekhatḥilah – Ideally, properly.

Lo plug – So as not to draw distinctions, so as not to introduce fine distinctions.

Ma'akholet – A body louse.

Ma'aseh Er v-Onan – Intercourse where ejaculation deliberately takes place outside the vagina to avoid pregnancy (see *Bereishit* 38).

Ma'ayan patuaḥ – "Open spring," a case where it is assumed that uterine bleeding, once it has begun, is likely to continue.

Makkah – Wound, lesion, sore, cut, or abrasion. Blood from a *makkah* does not render a woman *niddah.* (Also called *Petza.*)

Makpid – Particular or meticulous.

Meineket – Nursing mother. Halakhically, this refers to a woman within 24 months postpartum, whether or not she is actively breastfeeding.

Mesuleket damim (*pl.* ***Mesulakot damim***) – Amenorrheic. A woman who is halakhically not expected to menstruate, generally due to age or because she is pregnant or breastfeeding.

Midat ḥasidut – An expression of piety.

Mi-divrei Sofrim – A matter of rabbinic law.

Midrash – Rabbinic explications of Biblical texts.

Mikveh – A pool (or natural body of water) that is halakhically suitable for ritual immersion. A woman immerses in the *mikveh* to exit the *niddah* status.

Mil – 2,000 *amot,* distance of approximately 960 m.

Mishnah – Authoritative written compilation of halakhic statements of the Oral law, or a statement from this compilation.

Mokh daḥuk/Mokh **(1)** – A *bedikah* cloth inserted into the vaginal canal after the *hefsek taharah,* from sunset until nightfall, to detect any traces of renewed uterine bleeding as a woman enters the seven *neki'im.*

Mokh **(2)** – Absorbent wadding placed within the vaginal canal for contraceptive purposes.

Moredet – Rebellious wife, a wife who refuses marital intimacy on principle.

Niddah, Niddut – The halakhic status of a woman who experiences uterine bleeding not due to trauma. While the most common cause of *niddah* is menstruation, *niddah* and menstruation are not synonymous. During *niddah,* physical contact between husband and wife is prohibited. A woman while she is in this status is referred to as a *niddah.*

Onah **(1)** – A time period. In the context of *vesatot,* it refers to one day (sunrise to sunset) or one night (sunset to sunrise).

Onah **(2)** – Marital sexuality, a man's conjugal duties toward his wife.

Onah beinonit – The "average interval," an *onat perishah* that falls on the thirtieth day from the onset of a woman's previous menses.

Onat ha-ḥodesh – An *onat perishah* that falls on the same date of the Hebrew month as the date of the onset of menses the previous month. (Also called *Veset ha-ḥodesh.*)

Onat perishah, Onat ha-veset – A day on which a woman is halakhically required to anticipate the onset of menses. During this *onah,* the couple refrain from relations and the woman performs a *bedikah.*

Pesikah – Halakhic ruling.

Petiḥat ha-kever – Opening of the uterus. Under certain circumstances, significant dilation of the cervix can render a woman *niddah* even without bleeding.

Petiḥat hamakor – Sensation of uterine opening, one form of *hargashah.*

Petza – Wound, lesion, sore, cut, or abrasion. Blood from a *petza* does not render a woman *niddah.* (Also called *Makkah.*)

Piryah u-riviyah – The mitzvah of procreation.

Poskim – Halakhic decisors.

Re'iyah meḥamat tashmish – Uterine bleeding experienced as a result of marital relations.

Rishonim – Early (medieval) halakhic authorities.

Ro'ah meḥamat tashmish – A woman who experiences uterine bleeding as a result of marital relations.

Safek (pl. Sefekot) – Uncertainty.

Safek hargashah – A situation in which *halakhah* is stringent due to a concern that a woman may have had a *hargashah* (sensation) that she did not notice.

Samukh – Adjacent, in time or space.

Seven neki'im – After establishing that uterine bleeding has ceased, a woman counts seven days during which she confirms that it has not resumed. During the seven *neki'im* (lit., clean days), she performs daily *bedikot* and wears white undergarments.

Sfek sfeika – Double uncertainty.

Shalom bayit – Marital harmony.

She'at hadeḥak gadol – Very great need.

She'elat ḥakham – Consulting a halakhic authority.

Shikhvat zera l'vatalah – Wasting sperm.

Shinui – Performing an act in an unusual fashion.

Siluk damim – Amenorrhea. (See *Mesuleket damim.*)

Stam – A halakhic statement made without attribution or qualification.

Taharah – Ritual purity, the state of being *tahor/tehorah*. In this book, the term *taharah* generally refers to that halakhic status of a woman who is not a *niddah* or *yoledet.*

Taharat ha-mishpaḥah – Family purity, the laws of *niddah* and *mikveh.*

Taharot – Items that needed be kept ritually pure during the historical period when the laws of ritual purity were practiced.

Tahor/Tehorah – Ritually pure. In this book, the term *tehorah* describes a woman who is not a *niddah* or *yoledet.* When a woman is *tehorah,* physical contact between husband and wife is permitted.

Takanah – A rabbinic enactment.

Talmud – A central text of Jewish law, consisting of the Mishnah and the Gemara.

Tamei / Teme'ah – Ritually impure. In this book, the term may refer to a woman who is a *niddah* or *yoledet,* or to other forms of ritual impurity relevant to the laws of stains. When a woman is *teme'ah,* physical contact between husband and wife is prohibited.

Tanna (pl. Tanna'im) – A sage during the Mishnaic period.

Tanna kamma – In a *mishnah* or *baraita,* the first opinion stated.

***Tefaḥ** (pl. **Tefaḥim**)* – Handsbreadth, measurement of approximately 8 cm (3 inches).

Teliyah – Attribution. In the context of the laws of *niddah*, the term refers to attributing bleeding or staining to a source that will not render a woman *niddah*.

Teliyah be-makkah – Attributing bleeding to a wound, lesion, sore, cut, or abrasion.

Tevilah – Ritual immersion in the *mikveh*. A woman immerses to exit the *niddah* status.

Tum'at leidah, Tum'at yoledet – The halakhic status of a *yoledet* (a woman in the process of, or immediately after, giving birth), similar to the *niddah* status.

Tum'ah – Ritual impurity. While most laws of ritual purity are not currently practiced, some aspects of these laws remain relevant today. In particular, the laws of stains distinguish between objects and surfaces that are "susceptible to *tum'ah*" (can become *tamei*, or ritually impure) and those that are not.

Tzitzit – Ritual fringes attached to a four-cornered garment.

***Veset** (pl. **Vesatot**)* – A menstrual pattern, according to which a woman halakhically anticipates her menses on certain days.

Veset ha-glulot – A menstrual pattern based on hormonal contraceptives.

Veset ha-guf – A menstrual pattern based on a physical symptom that consistently precedes menses, or on a physical activity that consistently induces menses.

Veset ha-haflagah – An *onat perishah* that falls when an interval (*haflagah*) has elapsed which is the same as that which separated a woman's previous two periods.

Veset ha-ḥodesh – An *onat perishah* that falls on the same date of the Hebrew month as the date of the onset of menses the previous month. (Also called *Onat ha-ḥodesh.*)

Veset ha-kefitzot – A menstrual pattern based on a physical activity like skipping or jumping that consistently induces menses.

Veset kavu'a – A regular menstrual cycle, established when a woman's menses follow a consistent and predictable pattern over at least three consecutive cycles. A woman who has established a *veset kavu'a* anticipates her menses only on the date of her *veset kavu'a.*

Veset she-eino kavu'a – An irregular menstrual cycle (i.e., one that does not meet the halakhic criteria for a *veset kavu'a*). A woman with a *veset she-eino kavu'a* anticipates her menses on *onah beinonit, onat ha-ḥodesh,* and *onat ha-haflagah.*

Yemei ha-mevukhah – A limited, fixed range of days within which a woman regularly experiences the onset of menses, and which can be considered her *veset* (lit., "days of uncertainty").

Yemei libun – Another term for the seven *neki'im,* based on the *halakhah* that a woman wears white undergarments while counting.

Yesh omrim – "Some say" – used in halakhic texts to indicate one out of two or more halakhic opinions.

Yishuv ha-da'at – Assuaging or settling the mind.

Yoledet (pl. Yoldot) – A woman in the process of, or immediately after, giving birth. The halakhic status of a *yoledet* is similar to that of a *niddah.*

Yoledet be-zov – A woman who was a *zavah* prior to giving birth. Nowadays, every woman is considered *yoledet be-zov.*

Za'azu'a haguf – Bodily tremors.

Zav – A man who experiences a certain type of abnormal genital discharge.

Zavah – A woman who experiences certain patterns of non-menstrual uterine bleeding. In practice, we no longer distinguish between the status of *zavah* and that of *niddah.*

Zivah – The status of a woman experiencing certain patterns of non-menstrual uterine bleeding (*zavah*), halakhically similar to the status of *niddah.*

Zivat davar lakh – The sensation of fluid flowing within the vaginal canal.

Index